Resilient Storage Networking

Digital Press Storage Technology Series

Consulting Editors: Jerry Cochran and Howard Goldstein

The Storage Technology Series from Digital Press provides computer professionals with the latest information on this topic. Our editorial board includes storage and networking experts Jerry Cochran of Microsoft Corporation and Howard Goldstein, President of Howard Goldstein Associates, Inc. (HGAI), a storage networking education services company based in Colorado.

Jerry is currently Group Program Manager for Technology Integration Planning at Microsoft OTG, with responsibility for Information Worker, Messaging, and Management technology programs. Previously, he served as Microsoft technologies liaison within Compaq–HP Global Services. He frequently writes for *Windows & .NET* magazine; his first book, *Mission-Critical Microsoft Exchange 2000*, was published by Digital Press in 2001.

Howard has over thirty years in the information systems industry specializing in storage networking, data communications, and telecommunications networking. He has a diverse background in technology, management, and education. He has practical experience in all aspects of network technologies including architecture, design, planning, management, implementation, network systems programming and administration, operations, and problem determination and resolution. His technical focus has been with various network architectures and products including TCP/IP, SNA, and Storage Networking technologies such as Fibre Channel, IP Storage, and SCSI. Howard holds a Bachelor of Science in Computer Science from the University of Massachusetts at Amherst and a Master of Science in Telecommunications from Pace University in White Plains, New York.

Howard Goldstein is also the lead technical reviewer for "Resilient Storage Networks."

The first title in this series, Jerry Cochran's *Mission-Critical Microsoft Exchange 2003: Designing and Building Reliable Exchange Servers* (ISBN 1-55558-294-X), was published in 2003.

Forthcoming titles include *Efficient Storage for Microsoft Exchange Server 2003* by Pierre Bijaoui (ISBN 1-55558-308-3).

Resilient Storage Networking

Designing Flexible Scalable Data Infrastructures

Greg Schulz

ELSEVIER
DIGITAL
PRESS

AMSTERDAM • BOSTON • HEIDELBERG • LONDON
NEW YORK • OXFORD PARIS • SAN DIEGO
SAN FRANCISCO • SINGAPORE • SYDNEY • TOKYO

Digital Press is an imprint of Elsevier
200 Wheeler Road, Burlington, MA 01803, USA
Linacre House, Jordan Hill, Oxford OX2 8DP, UK

∞ Recognizing the importance of preserving what has been written, Elsevier prints its books on acid-free paper whenever possible.

Library of Congress Cataloging-in-Publication Data
A catalog record of this book is available from the Library of Congress

ISBN: 1-55558-311-3

British Library Cataloguing-in-Publication Data
A catalogue record for this book is available from the British Library.

For information on all Digital Press publications
visit our website at www.digitalpress.com and www.bh.com/digitalpress

Transferred to digital printing in 2009.

Illustrations by Greg Schulz

This book is dedicated to the friends and families of individuals involved with storage and storage networking throughout the world. Friends and families are the unseen sources of support and understanding for those involved with designing, developing, testing, promoting, implementing, and managing the storage infrastructure that enables our always-on (resilient), 24 hours a day, 365 days a year world.

Contents

Part IV [illegible] It All Together

Foreword

Why build resilient storage networks?

This book is about building a storage environment where data is always available for the needs of the business. A resilient storage network is a major part of that overall picture, and this book will put into perspective all the factors that need to be considered. While you already may have some knowledge about storage networking, the overall understanding provided here should be very valuable to everyone concerned about storage and storage networking. The importance of storage networking is worth a cursory look just to reaffirm the reason for this undertaking. While relatively new in the overall scheme of storing and retrieving data, putting servers, storage, and special-purpose components in a network has been a logical evolution of information technology. The storage industry has rarely been static; great changes have occurred in technology and the application of technology to solve business problems. We've seen very large, expensive rotating disks with less than a megabyte of capacity evolve to palm-sized devices with hundreds of gigabytes for pennies per megabyte. The transitions of disk storage have been incredible and that has happened in the relatively short time of the last 40 years, with magnetic tape being about 10 years older. Storage of digital data as we think of it today is relatively young, when compared with the earliest recordings by man on ancient stone tablets.

The demand for storing more data, driven by business needs such as expanding business, regulatory requirements to retain more data, and data for Internet applications, has led to the development of more efficient devices and software to manage storage, as well as the need to provide an infrastructure to connect the elements to provide not only access to the data but a reliable way to make the data always available.

Building a storage network is a business issue. It is justified in the economics of the cost of administration, usage of resources, and the ability to accommodate the changing business needs. The storage network needs to be a part of an overall strategy of data management that a company has to meet the business requirements.

A resilient storage network

A resilient storage network is what you wanted and expected in the first place. This is one of the promises of putting in a storage network. The storage network has to be architected to be resilient. There will be hardware problems where a path to a device is blocked. There will be a device failure of some type. There will be excessive workloads that skew the access for other operations.

Another function that must be integrated into the storage network design is the ability to provide business continuation in the event that a significant disruption occurs. This includes protecting data and data-recovery capabilities. The need for data protection has influence on the elements and functionalities of storage networks. The protection needed includes not only integrity concerns of the data being transmitted and stored on a storage system, but also an audit trail of access to the data, protection of the data as it is transmitted, and protection from unauthorized or inadvertent access.

It is necessary to have a base knowledge of the business factors at work and the technologies available to be able to begin a design of a resilient storage network. Practical product knowledge is required for the software and hardware that will be used to build the infrastructure and exploit its capabilities. This book will educate you on the considerations for all this technology, as well as how to make informed choices based on the business needs. It will provide a foundation of knowledge that will be very useful in understanding a resilient storage network for both designing and improving as technology continues to evolve. More importantly, it is a vendor- and technology-neutral examination of the principles and best practices needed for a practical implementation of a resilient storage network.

If you are involved in storing and retrieving information in any facet of information technology, you should be armed with this book and the education it provides. It represents a compendium of useful information based on long-term experience and research. It will serve as a guide and a reference as demands continue to evolve and expansion of the storage network is required. In short, it will be useful for everyone involved with storage.

Randy Kerns,
Senior Partner,
Evaluator Group, Inc.
(www.evaluatorgroup.com)

Preface

Organization of this book

This book is organized into four parts—Part I: Why Build Resilient Networks? Part II: Networking with Your Storage, Part III: Resilient Storage Networks, and Part IV: Putting It All Together. Each chapter starts with a brief overview and ends with a summary.

Part I starts with Chapter 1 (Importance of Information) and looks at why storage networks are needed to support the growth of information. Chapter 2 (Data Storage Fundamentals) looks at how data is organized and accessed, as well as various classifications of data, part of what is referred to as data and information life-cycle management (ILM).

Part II starts with Chapter 3 (Networking with Your Storage), covering various data access methods, including block; Network Attached Storage (NAS), also known as file based; and content addressable storage (CAS), also known as object based. Chapter 4 (Storage and I/O Networks) looks at various storage networking interfaces and protocols, while Chapter 5 (Fiber-Optic Essentials) takes a closer look at fiber-optic cabling and connectors. In Chapter 6 (Metropolitan and Wide Area Storage Networks) distance-based storage networking is covered, including Fibre Channel over IP, SONET/SDH, and Dense Wave Division Multiplexing (DWDM). Various storage networking devices are discussed in Chapter 7 (Storage Networking Devices), including servers, adapters, switches, routers, and other devices.

Part III begins with Chapter 8 (Storage Network Design), looking at topics related to designing storage networks with the various topologies covered in Chapter 9 (Storage Networking Topologies). Storage networking capacity planning and performance are discussed in Chapter 10 (Performance and Capacity Planning for Storage Networks) with storage networking management and software tools being covered in Chapter 11 (Storage Management). Data protection schemes, including backup, recovery, RAID, and local and remote mirroring are discussed in Chapter 12 (Protecting Data), with storage networking security being addressed in Chapter 13 (Securing Storage and Storage Networks).

Part IV contains various storage networking examples, with Chapter 14 covering small storage networking environments, including small–medium businesses (SMBs). Chapter 15 looks at consolidation and intermix examples. Chapter 16 looks at metropolitan and wide area storage networking examples. Chapter 17 covers large and high-performance storage networks with Chapter 18 as a wrap-up and summary chapter. At the end of the book, Appendix A contains some useful storage and storage networking URLs and Web sites, Appendix B contains a list of items to consider for resilient storage networks, and Appendix C is a brief glossary.

Throughout the book you will find various notes, recommendations, cautionary notes, and best practices along with some references to useful Web sites. Since technology is constantly changing, and this is especially true with storage networking, this book takes a vendor- and technology-neutral approach. Consequently, you will not see plugs for various products or vendors (with a couple of exceptions to help clarify a topic). Summary storage and storage networking comparison matrices can also be found at www.evaluatorgroup.com/charts. You can find additional information about storage networking–related technology, manufacturers, and providers on the "Resilient Storage Networking" Web site (www.storageio.com), along with other useful links. As mentioned earlier, storage networking is an evolving topic, so your comments, feedback, and questions are important; you can provide these via the Web site (www.storageio.com), where you can also find information about various storage networking events and other published material by the author.

Who should read this book

This book is for anyone who needs to understand storage and storage networking. This book covers storage networking with regard to high availability, business continuance, disaster recovery, and resilient environments. It looks at implementing resilient storage networks for small business, workgroups, and departmental and enterprise environments. Various technologies are discussed; this book is unique in that it provides a technology-independent view and approach to storage networks. It covers procedures, policies, and practices for designing, implementing, and managing local, metropolitan, and wide area storage networks. This book takes a horizontal approach to storage networking to look at and utilize different technologies to support various business functions and applications. The essence of this book is to provide an understanding of the technologies associated with storage networking and how to use them. If it is still not clear who should read this book, perhaps the following will help:

- Engineers, designers, and architects who need knowledge of storage networking
- Database, systems, network, and storage administrators and specialists
- Performance and capacity planning analysts and disaster-recovery personnel
- Networking administrators and telecommunications people
- Sales and marketing professionals involved with storage and storage networking
- Open Systems, Linux, UNIX, Windows, and S/390 (zSeries) audiences
- Anyone needing to have a better understanding of storage and networking

Conventions used in this book

The following are some conventions, notations, and symbols that are used throughout this book to help illustrate and explain specific items.

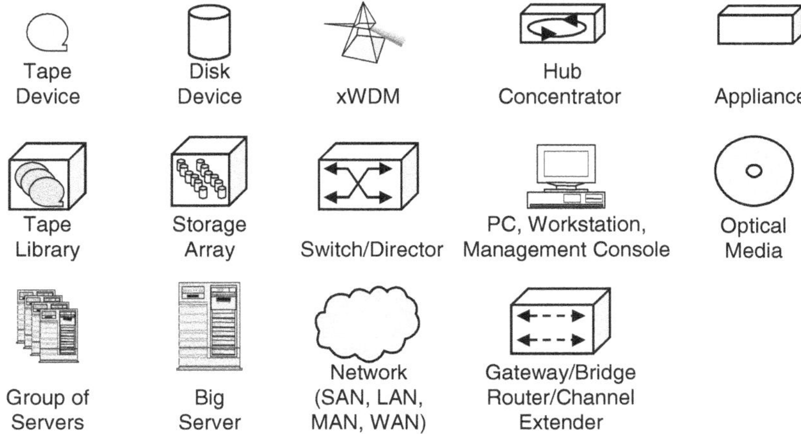

Conventions used in this book

Acknowledgments

Writing a book involves many behind-the-scenes activities and people to make a concept a reality. I would like to thank fellow authors Tom Clark, Marc Farley, Mark Friedman, Evan Marcus, Paul Massiglia, and David Schwaderer for their suggestions and feedback. Thanks to all the reviewers, subject matter experts, and fellow "storage junkies" from around the world, including Wayne Adams, Tony Almeida, Tom Becchetti, Greg Brunton, Damien Clark, John Clarke, CRB, John Dean, Dave Deming, Ray Dickensheets, Peter Doob, Jim Dyer, Jim Ellingson, Jim Gerrity, Katherine Karter, Kevin Liebl, Steve Muskovin, Amy Novotny, Cliff Oberholtzer, Mike Olsen, Phil Ruff, Bill Peldzus, Bruce Ravid, Rich Ramos, Dave Signori, Dave Simpson, Marc Staimer, Louise Stich, John Webster, Sherrie Woodring, SW, SNIA tutorial committee members, and any others not mentioned.

Thanks to Bill Bolton, Patty Barkley, Jim Morin, Dan Cockett, Kevin Eamigh, Eric Flavin, Brian Larsen, Mike Naylor, Mike Pecora, Dan Raup, Christine Schmidt, JW, and everyone else at CNT, and the former INRANGE. Thanks to everyone at the Evaluator Group.

Writing a book requires finding a publisher that is as interested in working with you as you are with them. Thanks to Alan Rose, Georgina Edwards, George Morrison, Theron Shreve, and the others in the Digital Press, Multiscience Press, and Elsevier organizations. Having an awesome editor, who is enthusiastic, provides on-going support, encouragement, and flexibility is also a must—that would be Pam Chester of Digital Press!

Special thanks to Damaris Larson, my proofreading magician and babysitter of the "kids"; Howie Goldstein for his technical review of this book; Randy Kerns for his feedback and for writing the Foreword; friends and family for their support while I was busy writing during evenings, weekends, and holidays. And a very special thanks to my wife Karen and the kids, Babe and Leo, for their love and support. They all deserve special heartfelt thanks—Atta Boy and Atta Girl!

Why Build Resilient Networks?

What This Chapter Will Do For You

This chapter points out various threats that can impact the availability of data and the subsequent need for resilient, flexible, and scalable storage access infrastructures for enterprise and Small Medium Business (SMB) environments. Some of the items you will learn about in this chapter include:

- Critical understanding of threats that impact data availability
- Important applications that are contributing to the growth of storage
- Information life cycle management can help reduce storage management costs
- Distance and flexibility are critical to maintain data accessibility and resiliency

1

Importance of Information

1.1 Overview

The following sayings might be familiar regarding how you handle data stored in computers, Personal Digital Assistants (PDAs), and other technologies:

This is important so I better keep it in case I need it.

I know I put it somewhere; I just cannot seem to find where I put it.

I just got rid of that last week; I knew I should have kept it.

It takes too much time to perform spring cleaning; I will simply buy more storage.

These sayings also apply to how you handle traditional information documents, files, folders, and items of importance at home. This chapter looks at the importance of information today and why it needs to be kept available and accessible. There is no doubt the amount of information being created and stored continues to grow at increasing rates each year. This is a trend that is not expected to change in the foreseeable future and applies equally to small and medium businesses (SMB) and to the world's largest organizations. The importance of information and its uninterrupted accessibility is one of the reasons for implementing resilient storage networks.

1.2 Importance and reliability of information

Data and information protection and accessibility applies equally to organizations of all types. The size or business function alone does not dictate the importance of protecting a data center or storage networking environment. Ultimately it's the importance of the data and information resources being used that characterize what is important and critical. Over the years I have seen many mega data centers that were critical as well as many small sites of equal importance and value to the business. In fact, recent events have shown us that some systems and functions, including e-mail, that have been perceived as noncritical have become essential to the operation of organizations. A common theme is ensuring access to information resources when needed. This theme of "access when needed" and "information resources" has two points and includes the fact that a protection scheme is only as good as its ability to make transparently available access to information when the user or consumer needs to get at it. If a file or data set is backed up and can be made available on-line at a recovery site or primary site, what good is it if the program or application to use and display it is not available? In Figure 1.1 various examples of how information is utilized from a variety of access devices are shown, with information processing and resilient storage networks at the core to process, store, and protect data.

Similarly, what good is the application and its supporting cast of operating systems, filesystems, databases, utilities, tools, and data when there is no access via a network to actually use it? This would lead to the existence of an information island, where the contents and ability to support the business are there; they just cannot be used or accessed. We saw some examples of this with the tragedies of September 11, 2001, where businesses were protected,

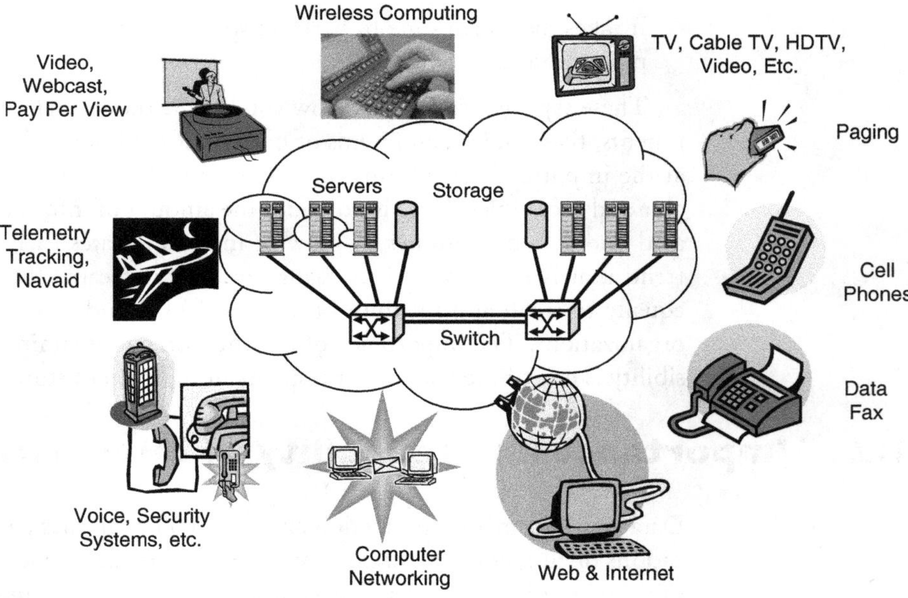

Figure 1.1 *The relationship of information access and underlying data storage networks.*

and data was backed up and mirrored off-site, yet either people could not get to these sites to manage them or the telecommunications and network infrastructure was not available or stable enough to support normal processing. Scaling data centers and storage networks is more than just physical size; it also must address scaling functionality, scaling management, scaling support tools, and features to secure, protect, and maintain accessibility.

There has been an increase in the amount of Terabytes (Tbytes) of storage shipped per year of 80 times that of what was shipped per year just ten years ago. The majority of the increase has occurred in the open systems (Windows, UNIX, and Linux) environments, with legacy environments for the most part flat, with some increasing and some decreasing but overall remaining flat. For example, the average page of text in this book, double-spaced, contains about 250 to 300 words, or about 1,700 to 1,900 characters (not including graphics). Each character represents 1 byte (8 bits) with 1,024 bytes being a Kilobyte (Kbyte) and a Megabyte (Mbyte) being 1,000 Kbytes (1,000 × 1,024). Consequently, a Terabyte (1,000 × 1,000,000) is 1,000 Mbytes.

Some factors contributing to this growth in storage include:

- More copies of data are being made for accessibility at more locations.
- Data is being kept longer for regulatory compliance and protection.
- The value of information is realized and heightened by world events.
- Legacy information is being migrated to digital formats.
- Increases in available storage capacity enable more data to be stored.
- More data is being "born digitally" (created by digital devices).

1.3 Types of information and data

There are many different types of information, with data having various characteristics. Some data is fairly static and seldom accessed; other data is frequently used. Data can be structured (e.g., database information) and nonstructured (e.g., a video stream for a movie). Some data is text based, while other data is multimedia with various combinations. Multimedia data refers to video, audio, digital photo images, and related material. Some of the characteristics that pertain to information include:

- How long does it need to be retained (days, weeks, months, years)?
- How often does it need to be accessed (continuously, hourly, daily, monthly, yearly)?

- Can the data be reproduced from another source (from a CD, tape, or another system)?
- How often does the data change (frequently, seldom, never)?

Just as there are many different characteristics to data, data is also accessed and utilized by many different types of applications. Some applications include workgroup and office functions, e-mail, and financial and insurance services. Additional applications include manufacturing, retail, travel, and entertainment. Some other applications are Customer Relations Management (CRM), Enterprise Resource Planning (ERP), On-Line Transaction Processing (OLTP), data warehouse and data mining applications, telemetry and surveillance, geophysics for energy and mineral exploration, pharmaceuticals, life sciences research, medical and health services, Computer-Assisted Design (CAD), and Computer-Assisted Manufacturing (CAM).

Data is generally referred to as transactional or reference depending on its intended usage and purpose. Transaction data is data that changes regularly, including OLTP, databases, Web-based shopping, and others that are not static. Reference data is information that has value and needs to be retained over long durations in unmodified forms that can include e-mail and attachments; presentations and proposals; legal documents; CAD/CAM design documents and schematics; source code for software; Web content; digitized images of checks, tickets, and other instruments of trade; medical images; geophysical and seismic; video and surveillance; this book; transaction and telephone call detail logs; video; and even audio. As more data becomes available, the demand on the infrastructure is increased to support more requests as well as growth.

1.4 Information, data, and storage life-cycle management (xLM)

Data, information, and storage life-cycle management, or what I refer to as xLM (x is whatever term you choose to use), is part of a process that looks at how information is created, stored, accessed, and retained. Information has a life cycle from the time it is created until the time it is retired and discarded. The business and technology reason for understanding and doing this is to properly align information with the best approach for managing and storing data.

All information is not equal; some information has more value, some has longer life, some has shorter life, and some needs faster access and retrieval. This is similar to the fact that all applications are not the same and thus may need different types of hardware resources (e.g., CPU, memory, I/O, storage space, network access). While information has different values today, for the most part all information is stored and protected in the same manner. One of the challenges today with information management, which collectively includes data and storage management, is that more data is being generated; however, while much of it has become dormant, it is not being removed. The approach of treating all data equally is expensive; however, one size fits all may be easy, but it leads to work. This results in more information that has to be protected, requiring more storage to save it on and to protect and manage it. Put bluntly, we are addicted to storage and keeping data.

One approach to reducing storage and storage management costs is to classify storage and its usage patterns. Armed with information about usage patterns, different classes of data can be moved to different tiers of storage. For example, data that is infrequently accessed could be moved to slower, more cost effective storage devices. This data would be protected via a backup or remote copy and would not have to be backed up every day. More frequently accessed data would be placed on higher-performance storage for improved utilization. This data classification and movement could be done manually, which is sometimes done today, or it can be automated. New technology is emerging to help address data classification, analysis, movement, and storage. These are sometimes referred to as hierarchical storage management (HSM), system managed storage (SMS), and, more recently, ILM.

In order to support the resilient enterprise or SMB, a storage network needs to be stable and scalable without adding complexity of management. Storage networking in its most basic description is the plumbing and utilities enabling seamless and transparent access to information resources. In a house there are networks of pipes, wires, cables, networks, and other conveyance systems that bring services (e.g., water, heating, cooling, ventilation, electricity, telephone, TV, and the Internet) to where they are needed. The major differences between a typical home or small office environment and an office building or data center are additional communications facilities and larger scale and perhaps redundant power, cooling, and heating. These infrastructure items are important to resilient storage networking to provide electricity to operate the hardware and networks, cooling to keep equipment safe and within operating limits, communications for networking and dial-up support and diagnostics, and water and sanitary services for the people to maintain the environment. A lesson learned from the September 11, 2001, tragedy was that equipment and data were safe in many cases, but people could not get to them to enact business continuance plans, and telecommunications services were severely disrupted. There have been other incidents not so tragic, ranging from communications lines being accidentally severed, electrical and utilities being cut off due to flooding, and support personnel not being able to gain access to equipment and facilities for reasons such as labor strife, air quality problems, hurricanes, and snowstorms.

Usually, these infrastructure items are transparent other than for some occasional maintenance and so they are taken for granted. This is similar to the role that storage networking should perform to provide the infrastructure to support applications and servers to access and safely store information. In a nutshell the storage network has to be ready and able to support data movement, including data recovery when needed. A resilient storage network provides stable and predictable access to information to support a resilient and virtual enterprise.

Similar to how networking enabled multiple computers to talk to each other over Local Area Networks (LANs) and Wide Area Networks (WANs), storage networks today are enabling multiple computers to access and share storage and data. Networks are used to access information available on different computing resources or platforms. Storage networks enable computing resources or platforms to access data on various storage devices or media. For now, they are separate networks, but this could and probably will change and in fact already has to some degree. For example, storage is accessed today via networks when performing file and data sharing over a LAN/WAN interface. However, that is not quite the same as leveraging a standard network for accessing large amounts of data as is done using storage and input/output (I/O) channels. In theory it should be possible; however, 10 to 15 years ago the theory of an easy-to-use Internet, or LAN, was regarded as simple, but in reality it took several years and work is still continuing.

1.5 Threats and requirements for data protection

The importance of information requires various levels of protection to maintain accessibility and availability when it is needed. Information needs to be protected to ensure availability in case of:

- Regulatory and contractual requirements
- Acts of nature

- Acts of man (intentional and accidental)
- Technology failure
- Event chains and fault containment

1.5.1 Regulatory and contractual requirements

Regulatory and contractual requirements for protecting data have taken on new importance and focus over the past couple of years. Some of the regulatory and contractual requirements for protecting data include the Health Insurance Portability and Accountability Act (HIPAA). HIPAA is a law that places stricter data management and accountability requirements on health-care (life-sciences) organizations involving data protection, retention, security, and so forth. Patient records need to be secured over different lengths of time—for example, adults at least 7 years and minors up to 21 years or more.

Medical- and life-science-related regulations include HIPAA and the retention of patent records for their lifetime plus two years for postanalysis. CAT scans may be held for longer periods, resulting in very large files or folders for customers/patients. In addition to patient records and profiles, there is also financial, insurance, and other information that must be kept. There are also requirements regarding how rapidly various patient records need to be retrieved and made available.

Other U.S. government regulations and rules include the Sarbanes-Oxley (Sarbox) Act of 2002 and those of the Securities Exchange Commission (SEC). SEC Rule 17a-3 and 4, part of the SEC Act of 1934, revised in 1998 and then again in September 2002, states that brokers, dealers, and transfer agents must preserve electronic data generated from the time of the 1998 revision on Write Once Read Many (WORM) storage media for a period of not less than six years, along with logs of when the data is accessed and modified. These must show the data, including e-mail and instant messages, with quick retrieval per transaction for two years.

1.5.2 Acts of nature

Some acts of nature that can threaten the availability and accessibility of data include earthquakes, volcanoes, fires, and floods. Other natural threats include wind, hail, snow, ice storms, lightning and tornados, hurricanes, and typhoons. Epidemics and health hazards typically do not directly pose a threat to information resources and IT technology, but there are side effects. For example, during the Severe Acute Respiratory Syndrome (SARS) break-out in 2003 some organizations in the impacted areas isolated their personnel. The precautions were taken to prevent and protect against any potential infection spreading across the organization. This scenario, while rare, takes business continuance to a higher level beyond simply having redundant data centers and copies of data. By having separate staffs isolated, should one group become afflicted, the other should remain safe to support the business and its technology resources. Note that some of these events may be predictable or seasonal, while others may not. For example, a tornado can strike unexpectedly in some areas other than in an annual tornado season. Floods can occur randomly from storms and other events, including flash thaws and, lately, unusual weather patterns.

1.5.3 Acts of man (intentional and accidental)

Various threats to data availability and accessibility by man include acts of war, terror, and accidents. The tragic September 11, 2001, attacks in New York City, and Washington, DC, along with subsequent anthrax scares, are some examples. Acts of sabotage and espionage by foreign governments, businesses, or individuals are other examples. Accidents and human error, such as during the "Big Dig" in Boston to relocate the freeway, which was located above ground, to underground tunnels, caused some equipment to fall and cut some fiber-optic cables. This accident severed four (Optical Carrier) OC-48 network communication circuits, rendering some data hosting (co-location) sites without network access up and down the East Coast. Proper configuration, or perhaps avoiding cost cuts, could have averted this situation and the subsequent finger pointing.

1.5.4 Technology failure

Technology failure is another cause for concern to protect data and accessibility utilizing redundant components and good design practices. Some examples of technology failures include bugs in software and silicon (memory leaks and errors, processor glitches, crashes), component failure and lack of redundancy, environmental failure (loss of power, cooling), and inadequate testing.

1.5.5 Event chains and fault containment

Event chains describe how something simple, yet important, can cause a whole chain of events to occur that leads up to or results in something significant and perhaps catastrophic. While events may not be eliminated, preventive measures and proactive activities can reduce the impact of chains addressing fault containment. The premise of fault containment is to design, implement, and manage to contain faults from spreading into event chains. Managing the process is important as well because of how things are done and how they will be done. For example, change control and processes can have an impact on availability by deploying the wrong version of software or configuration files. A change control process that address fallback and contingency plans can help to isolate problematic changes. Event chains can be a combination of human error, technology failures, acts of nature, and others. A chain of events can be triggered by something relatively simple, which, if not contained, spreads, causing a snowball or avalanche effect on other systems.

The August 2003 electrical power grid blackout in the northeast United States is an example of a chain of events. The blackout appears to have been caused by a transmission line component somewhere in Ohio, part of the electrical network becoming overloaded. Alarms that would have alerted operators appeared not to have worked, were ignored, or masked by other events, triggering a chain of events. Many electrical generators did not fail over, leaving people without power. As power transmission lines became overloaded, they were taken out of service to protect the electrical grid, which placed more loads on the surviving systems. This snowball effect cascaded, gaining momentum and overloading additional systems until a portion of the electrical grid (www.nerc.com) was shut down. Early IP networks saw similar chains of events occur when different adapters and transceivers were attached to an Ethernet cable. Back in the late 1980s and early 1990s, while adhering to existing standards, not all components played well with others, resulting in network broadcast and fire storms. The late 1990s and early years of the new millennium have seen similar occurrences with storage networking components as they to mature.

1.6 Maintaining information accessibility

Access to information depends on the systems and subsystems storing and processing the data being available and accessible. There are many different factors that can impact the availability and accessibility of information, ranging from technology failures to human error to acts of nature. The amount of data protection needed will vary with your availability and accessibility requirements. Another factor to determine how much availability protection you need is what are you protecting against. For example, are you looking to protect data and accessibility from:

- Component and technology failure
- Data corruption and accidental deletion
- Localized and regional acts of nature
- Electrical and other infrastructure utility failure
- Acts of terror and war

Depending on your environment and business service requirements you may need:

- Localized protection in the same equipment room, building, campus, or city
- Metropolitan and regional protection to isolate against regional events and disruptions
- Global protection to protect against events impacting countries and parts of the world

In Figure 1.2 the vertical scale shows the cost and complexity involved with maintaining availability, while the horizontal scale shows the amount of recovery time, or amount of disruption and lack of access to information.

Figure 1.2 shows that, moving from the left to right, at one extreme you could do nothing. This may not be practical; however, moving to the right, if you and your business can tolerate days of downtime and disruption, tape

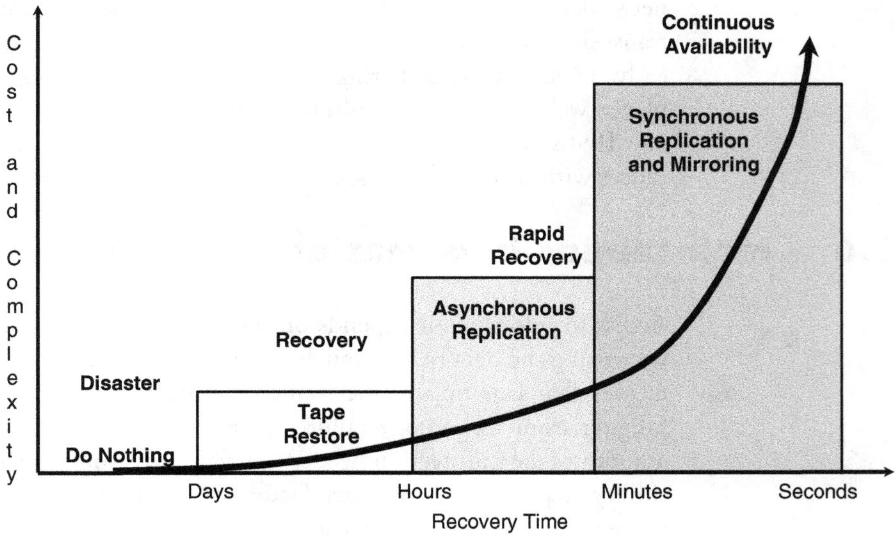

Figure 1.2 *Cost and complexity of availability.*

or other off-line backup media can be used to perform recovery and restoration. For more cost, reducing downtime to hours, a combination of backup and restore along with asynchronous (time delayed) mirroring and replication can be used. For more availability, with downtime and disruption measured in minutes, and for more cost, clustering, failover, high availability, and synchronous mirroring (no delay) can be implemented. At the far end of the scale, on the right, is continuous availability and accessibility; however, the costs to implement this approach can also be expensive.

An important note about the examples for availability is that you may decide that certain applications and data have different value and importance. Consequently, you may implement different levels of protection and availability to balance costs with accessibility and service requirements. How much accessibility and in what time frame will be a function of your specific business needs and requirements. Applications and information that in the past were not considered to be high availability—for example, e-mail—in some organizations are now being thought of as more strategic.

So what is right for your environment or application may vary greatly depending on different factors, including Quality of Service (QoS), Service-Level Agreements (SLAs), business drivers, and so on. There is a trade-off in terms of cost and survivability that is addressed in terms of recovery point

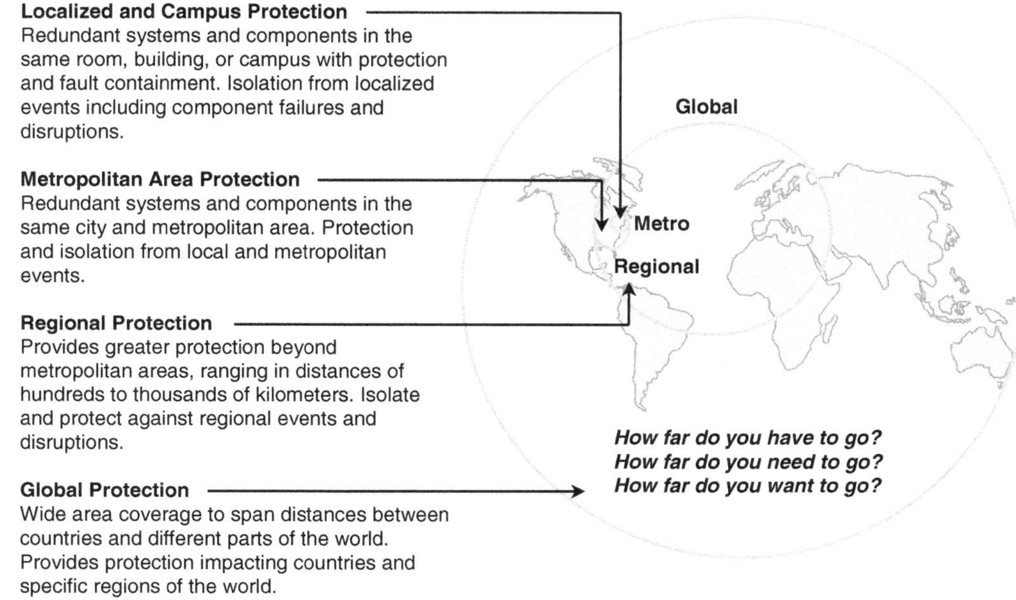

Localized and Campus Protection
Redundant systems and components in the same room, building, or campus with protection and fault containment. Isolation from localized events including component failures and disruptions.
Metropolitan Area Protection
Redundant systems and components in the same city and metropolitan area. Protection and isolation from local and metropolitan events.
Regional Protection
Provides greater protection beyond metropolitan areas, ranging in distances of hundreds to thousands of kilometers. Isolate and protect against regional events and disruptions.
Global Protection
Wide area coverage to span distances between countries and different parts of the world. Provides protection impacting countries and specific regions of the world.
Global
Metro
Regional
How far do you have to go?
How far do you need to go?
How far do you want to go?

Figure 1.3 *How much distance do you need for information protection?*

objectives and levels of recoverability. You might be able to broadly categorize your environment or specific applications and functions. You might have different categories for your applications that dictate the level of protection and resiliency that is needed by each of them.

In Figure 1.3, different levels of protection are shown with respect toward distance and geographical threats and events. The various rings show local, metropolitan, regional, and global protection. The amount of distance and protection needed for your environment will vary based on your business objectives and susceptibility to different events.

1.7 Chapter summary

So what does all of this have to do with storage networks and, in particular, resilient storage networks? Simply put, information is growing; information is becoming more valuable in terms of its content and the need to keep systems running. Information and data are the lifeblood to keep information systems running. Resilient infrastructures are needed to keep the systems running, and resilient storage networks enable businesses to move, protect, and access critical information on a small as well as a large scale both locally and remotely.

What This Chapter Will Do For You

This chapter explains how data is organized and stored along with classification of data and storage access. Some of the items you will learn about in this chapter include:

- Understanding how data is stored as the foundation for subsequent chapters
- Data has different value yet it is being managed uniformly, adding to expense
- How to leverage various storage techniques to reduce storage management costs

2

Data Storage Fundamentals

2.1 Overview

There are two primary components for storage networking: storage and networking. This chapter looks at how information and data are organized and stored in order to be accessed via storage I/O interfaces, the networks in storage networking. For those already familiar with storage fundamentals, you may choose to skip over this chapter; however, you may want to review the material on storage and access classification.

2.2 How data is accessed and organized

Storage is often taken for granted and is to some perhaps a mystery, yet it is an essential component to supporting information processing. Data can exist in a computer's random access memory (RAM) or saved to some type of recordable storage medium. Storage is an extension of memory, and cache is a convergence of memory and external recordable storage media. Digital data at a low level is stored as 1s and 0s (binary) bits that are implemented using different physical techniques depending on the physical storage medium (disk, tape, optical, solid-state memory—RAM). The data bits are generally grouped into bytes (8 bits) and subsequently organized into larger groups of bytes, words, and other data structures for different purposes. Data is defined into a usable format (data structures) understood by the application and written to and read from files or database objects. In a traditional paper environment you write on, type, or in some other manner transfer data to paper in some organized way (structured data). You might then group related documents and material into a file and store them in a file cabinet. An example of this is shown in Figure 2.1, using a file cabinet example on the right with disk storage shown on the left. In the middle of

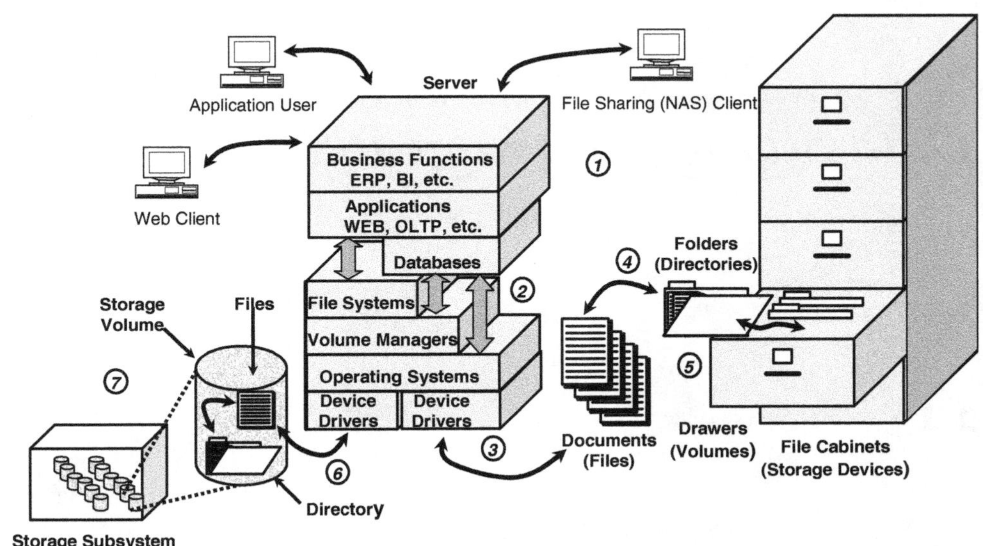

Figure 2.1 *How data is stored and accessed.*

Figure 2.1 are the various software layers associated with performing I/O, storing, and processing data.

Using a traditional storage management paradigm on the left in Figure 2.1 shows how data is processed through a server with the various layers of software (1). For example, a Web browser accesses a Web site, which might be a combination of HTML web pages, Java applications, XML data, and rich media such as JPEG and MPEG videos. The Web site being supported by a Web server might make I/O requests to a database server to respond to information, update profiles, process credit cards if you are buying something online, and other things. The Web server also reads and writes files that are stored on disk locally or perhaps via a Network Attached Storage (NAS) device for data and file sharing. The database server performs I/O to its database structures that are on disk using either a filesystem or raw I/O (direct to disk) to bypass the filesystem for performance considerations.

Data moves to and from applications (ERP, CRM, CAD/CAM, BIA, office functions) using various software application tools. These software application tools include Web servers, transaction processing facilities, e-mail, and others. These tools access databases or filesystems that maintain data organization and synchronize access to data records and objects. Some databases bypass filesystems (see [2] in Figure 2.1) and volume managers to communicate directly with operating system I/O facilities and storage device driver software. In other instances, databases and applications access and organize data via filesystems and, optionally, volume managers, providing a layer of abstraction, also known as a form of storage virtualization. A volume manager is storage software that is used to organize, group, and manage storage devices. The data flows (3) from the server over a storage interface in a storage format as blocks of data that represent files organized into directories (4) and stored in storage device volumes (5).

In Figure 2.1 the storage volumes represented as a file cabinet would be a storage volume accessible by the server. The folder contains the files and represents a directory structure to keep track of the files and their metadata information. Metadata is the information that describes the file, including location, size, creation and modification dates, security and access control policies, and other information that describes the file. The file contains data being stored, which could be text, graphics, video, audio, or a combination in a format known to the application. On the left in Figure 2.1 a companion view using a storage volume (6) is shown with a folder to represent a directory and files. The storage volume could be an individual disk device or part of a larger storage subsystem accessed via a storage interface.

In Figure 2.2 a typical computer server processor and I/O subsystem architecture is shown. In this example, a processor accesses RAM where data is stored and staged for processing. If data is not in the memory or no longer needed in memory, then an I/O (read or write) is performed to an external storage device. Data is moved in and out of memory or from I/O devices and includes application programs and data to be processed. Data that has been processed is then moved back to memory, moved to a storage device, or displayed using a graphics or video display adapter. The I/O bridge interface is used to move data via I/O data paths called busses, which in turn support devices such as RS-232 serial ports, parallel printer ports,

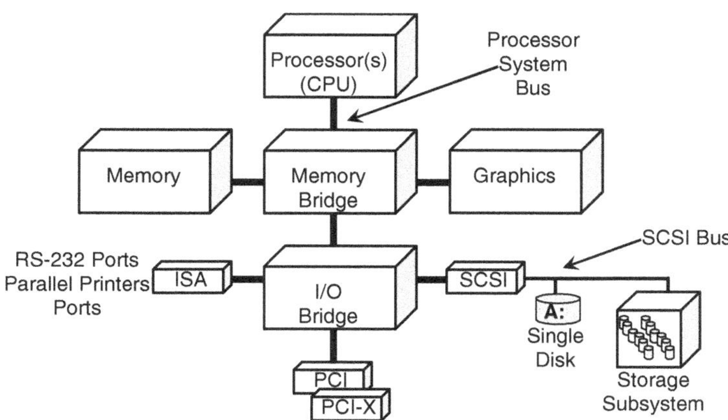

Figure 2.2 *CPU, memory, and storage model.*

network interfaces, and storage ports. One of the important things to note about this generic model is that memory is part of the I/O process and I/O is part of the memory subsystem.

2.2.1 Data organization (from bits to bytes)

Data is organized into various data structures that describe data for different purposes, with the smallest unit being a bit. A bit represents a binary value in that it is either set (on) or clear (off), which is represented as a one or a zero. Groups of bits organized into bytes, words, and other data structures are used to store and represent data. Since bits are either on (1) or off (0), multiple bits grouped together as a byte (8 bits) are used to describe characters. For example, 8 bits grouped together as a byte with individual values of 0 0 1 1 0 0 0 1 would represent the character 1 (hexadecimal—base 16, or decimal 49—base 10). This example uses little endian notation, which indicates the order that the sequence of bytes is stored in a computer's memory. IBM mainframes use big endian, while most computer systems utilize little endian (as in the previous example). Character sets include ASCII, which is used by most computer systems today, and EBCDIC for IBM mainframe environments. A Web search on the words ASCII and EBCDIC produces numerous Internet Web sites with various character tables and data conversion utilities.

Another example is the word "byte", which would require 4 bytes (6 including quotes), and the phrase "bits and bytes", which would require 14 bytes without quotes. Assuming no formatting characters (including line breaks), a file with "bits and bytes" would only have 14 bytes of data. However, the smallest unit of storage is typically a block or page, which is at least 512 bytes or larger. Consequently, there would be a lot of wasted space if you were to create hundreds of files each with only the phrase "bits and bytes." This is an oversimplified example of a real problem today, which is that there is a lot of storage that is being allocated but not fully utilized. Many database systems pre-allocate storage to optimize future use. So, while a database may not be full, it still utilizes physical space on a storage volume. Files and data with large amounts of empty or blank space are referred to as being sparse; these files and data can also be compressed to utilize less space—for example, during backups. Typically a file will be made up of many blocks of data, with larger files being made up of hundreds if not thousands of blocks of data or more. Thin provisioning is a new technique that can address traditional storage over provisioning. Thin provisioning enables applications to think they have storage pre-allocated and only require storage capacity for what is actually used.

Table 2.1 *Data Units of Measures*

Unit of Measure	Acronym	Size
Byte	Byte	8 Bits
Block or Page	Blk	512 Bytes
Kilobyte	KB	1,024 Bytes
Megabyte	MB	1 Million Bytes
Gigabyte	GB	1,000 MB
Terabyte	TB	1,000 GB
Petabyte	PB	1,000 TB
Exabyte	EB	1 Million TB
Zetabyte	ZB	1,000 EB

Table 2.1 shows some data units of measures, ranging from a single bit to a byte on up to some storage capacities that may seem unimaginably large. Keep in mind that ten years ago a 1Gbyte disk drive spinning at 5,400 revolutions per minute (RPM) was considered big and fast. Today disk drives are in the 140 to 200Gbyte and larger range spinning at up to 15,000 RPM. So while a petabyte, exabyte, or even zetabyte may seem big today, wait a while and watch how data continues to grow and how your storage gets used.

A closer look at data storage and formats is shown in Figure 2.3, where a file is read or written (1) to a storage device volume (2) as an I/O stream of bits and bytes. The file is stored on disk at a location determined by the filesystem as blocks of data that are usually 512 bytes or a multiple of 512 bytes. The file format is determined by the application that created the file, and it could contain text data, graphics, video, or audio. To the storage subsystem, the file is simply a collection of bits and bytes grouped together as blocks of data by the filesystem and application that created the file.

Also shown in Figure 2.3 is a representation of a spinning disk storage medium (3) with platters attached to a spindle powered by a motor to rotate the platters. The physical platters are logically divided and allocated into cylinders, tracks, and sectors as part of the disk subsystem's formatting. Each sector contains one or more blocks of data depending on the blocking factor that is used to format the disk. For example, a block size of 512 bytes would map one to one a 512-byte sector to a 512-byte block of data, which

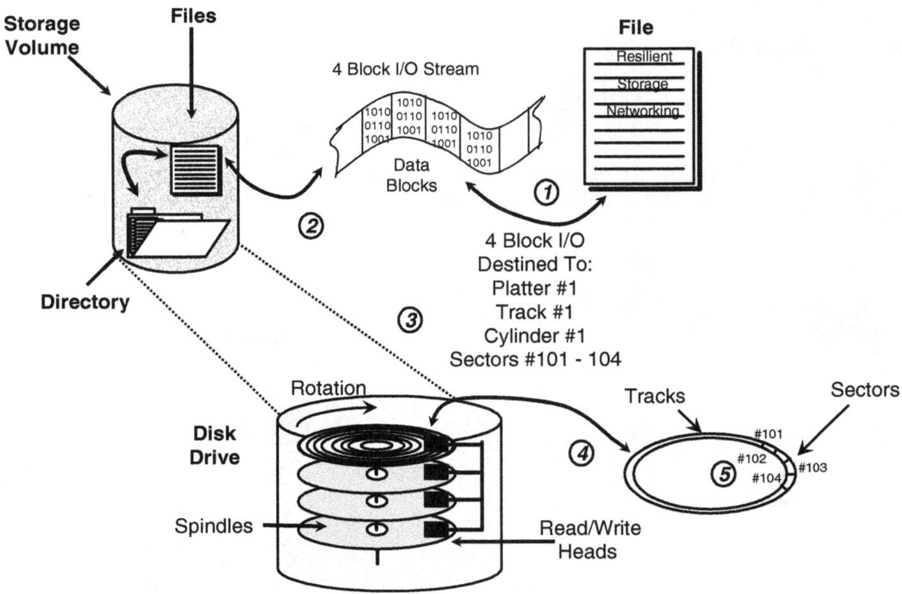

Figure 2.3 *Data storage format and organization.*

in turn maps to a 512-byte page of memory. The blocking factor could be a higher value—for example, 1,024, 2,048, 8,096, or higher for larger volumes (also known as the disk's cluster size). The cluster size is not to be confused with high-availability clustering of servers; rather, the cluster size of the disk determines how many blocks of data will be grouped together. For larger capacity storage devices, a larger disk cluster size is needed to keep track of all the data blocks. Data is accessed on the disk by a physical and logical address, sometimes known as Physical Block Number (PBN) or Logical Block Number (LBN). The filesystem or an application performing direct (raw) I/O keeps track of what storage is mapped to which logical blocks on which storage volumes. Within the storage controller and disk drive, a mapping table is maintained to associate logical blocks with physical block locations on the disk or other media—for example, tape.

Some operating systems also use different block sizes, while others use variable block sizes—for example, IBM mainframes, Count Key Data (CKD), and Extended Count Key Data (ECKD). These environments are referred to as variable-block architectures. Environments that have fixed block sizes are referred to as fixed-block architectures, which would apply to open systems and Windows platforms. For fixed-block architecture, the typical block size is 512 bytes; however, this can vary depending on the operating system and other influences, including the size of the device. For example, a storage device might be formatted for 528-byte blocks (sectors) at a low level yet present as 512 bytes, with the extra bytes being used for parity protection and other things.

2.2.2 Storage access and classes of storage

Not all data is equal in value and importance, yet generally all information is treated equally in the way it is stored and managed. While the cost of storage is decreasing, more can be done to leverage the costs. In Chapter 1, life-cycle management and data classification were covered briefly, so let's expand on these a bit to help better understand where and how to store data. It is important to understand which is the best or applicable interface and access method to use. In Chapter 3, various access methods are discussed, including Network Attached Storage (NAS), also known as file sharing; block, also known as Storage Area Network (SAN); and Direct Attached Storage (DAS). Also covered in Chapter 3, is object-based storage, known as content addressable storage (CAS). Traditional storage has been accessed via an address, which can be a real or virtual address as to where the data is actually stored.

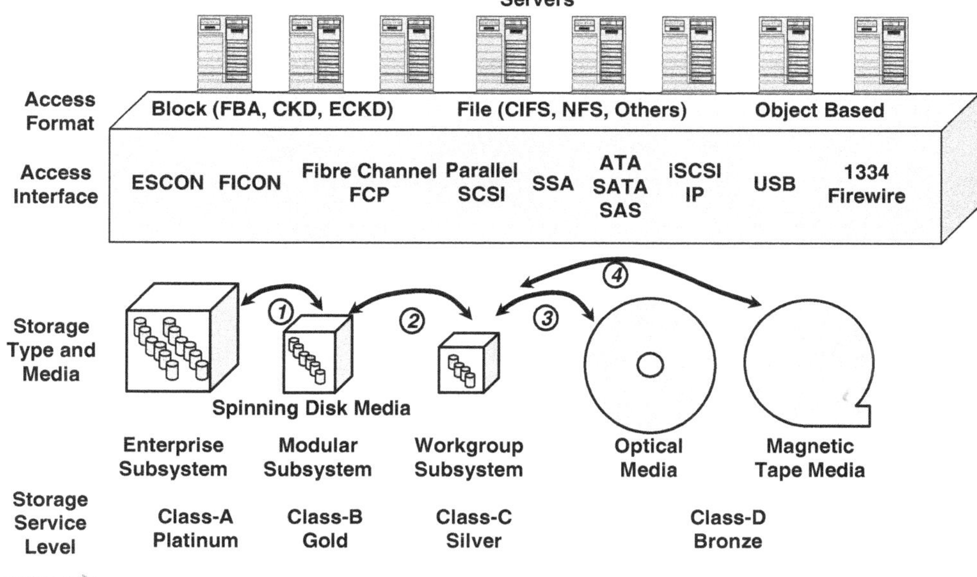

Figure 2.4 *Types of storage and access classes.*

The example shown in Figure 2.4 represents servers with different applications and operating systems, including open systems and legacy platforms. These servers access storage resources via access methods (block, file, or object) using different access interfaces. Various storage networking interfaces are covered in more detail in Chapter 4. The servers access various classes of storage resources implemented with different storage media types. For example, Class-A in this example represents high-performance, enterprise-class storage. Less frequently accessed data may be migrated (1) to modular storage (Class-B), which may incorporate lower-cost ATA/SATA storage devices. To facilitate backup smaller storage subsystems (2) could be used to support disk to disk to tape (D2D2T) backup to reduce backup windows and expedite recovery times. Less frequently accessed data, along with backup data, could then be migrated (3) to magnetic tape or optical media for long-term retention. This process could be done via manual intervention, in-house developed scripts and software, or vendor-supplied backup and life-cycle management tools.

In Table 2.2 various storage attributes are shown, along with some common classification terminology, including tier, class, and level. Also shown are some general characteristics, along with features and functions for each type of storage and some representative applications. Another way to view the information is by using a pyramid with memory and cache at the top, then Solid-State Disk (SSD), followed by the various tiers (1–4) in decreasing order of performance and cost.

Table 2.2 *Some Storage Classifications and Characteristics*

Tier/Class	Level	Characteristics	Features and Functions
1/A	Platinum	On-line storage	Cache centric (read and write cache)
		High performance	Remote mirroring and replication
		High availability	Many ports for server attachment
		Advanced functionality	Monolithic or modular design
		Multiple interconnects	Redundant components and software
		Enterprise storage	SCSI, SSA, and Fibre Channel disk
		Storage sharing	Snapshots and point-in-time copies
		Traditionally higher cost	Some levels of RAID
			Volume management features
			Supports enterprise, including open systems and S/390 mainframe

Table 2.2 *Some Storage Classifications and Characteristics (continued)*

Tier/Class	Level	Characteristics	Features and Functions
2/B	Gold	On-line	Active/Active for redundancy
		High performance	Active/Passive for failover
		Some advanced features	Read cache, write back cache
		Open interconnect interfaces	Fewer number of interconnect ports
		Potentially lower cost	Modular design and packaging
		General application usage	Open interconnect ports and protocols (Fibre Channel [FCP], SCSI, iSCSI/GbE)
			Point-in-time (PIT) copies and snapshots
			Remote mirroring and replication
			Redundant components
			SCSI, Fibre Channel, ATA, and SATA storage devices (back-end)
			Some levels of RAID
			Volume management features
			Supports open systems
3/C	Silver	On-line and near-line storage	ATA/SATA disk drives
		Alternative to tape media	Block-based interface
		General applications for workgroup, SMB, and departmental environments	Possible tape (virtual tape) interface
		Useful for long-term data retention and storage of reference data	Can also include WORM technology
			Optical media and tape media
			Fewer number of interconnect ports
			Good to adequate performance
			Open systems interface ports
			Block and File (NAS) access
			Possible RAID support
			Random access characteristics
			Small to large storage capacity
			Some redundancy capabilities
			Some volume management features
4/D	Bronze	Off-line and near-line data	Random capabilities
		Removable media	Random access for optical media
		Interchangeable media	Semisequential access for tape
		Lowest cost of storage	Tape can be in standalone device
		Lower performance	Automated tape and media handling
		Ideal for backup and archive	

Table 2.3 *Some Storage Interface and Access Classification Characteristics*

Tier/ Class	Level	Characteristics	Features and Functions
1/A	Platinum	High availability High performance Redundant paths Clustering and failover	Fibre Channel (FCP) and FICON as well as ESCON and SCSI for legacy storage interfaces Full bandwidth for performance Nonblocking and high-speed LAN, Metropolitan Area Network (MAN), WAN, SAN Higher costs
2/A	Gold	Good performance Good availability Single paths (attachment)	Block access NAS file access SCSI, Fibre Channel, iSCSI iSCSI adapters with TCP/IP Offload Engines (TOEs) to enhance performance Moderate-speed long-distance interfaces, including SONET/SDH and IP
3/C	Silver	Moderate performance Lowest cost SMB and workgroup Slower wide area interfaces	iSCSI with Gb Ethernet using standard adapters (NICs) SATA interfaces for disk storage Leverage Ethernet infrastructure
4/D	Bronze	Robotic or possibly manual handling of storage media Slower network interfaces Slowest wide area interfaces	Various interfaces and media types Various media and handling characteristics

Table 2.3 shows various characteristics and classifications for storage access interfaces for local, metropolitan, and wide area situations. Storage interfaces are covered in more detail in the following chapters, along with access methods.

2.3 Chapter summary

Not all data and information are the same in terms of frequency of access and retention, yet typically all data is treated the same. While the cost per unit of storage is decreasing, the amount of storage that can be managed per person is not increasing at a proportional rate, resulting in a storage management efficiency gap. Information data can be stored in different formats on various types of media and use various interfaces to access it. In Chapter 3, we will take a closer look at how data is accessed using block, file, and object access methods. Storage I/O and networking access interfaces will be covered in subsequent chapters.

Networking with Your Storage

What This Chapter Will Do For You

Data can be accessed from storage using different methods for various needs and applications. Some of the items you will learn about in this chapter include:

- All data is not the same, use the appropriate access method for the specific need
- How to protect data over distance for continual access and recovery
- Cost-effective techniques for sharing storage and data across servers

3

Networking with Your Storage

3.1 Overview

There are similarities and differences between traditional I/O interfaces and enterprise messaging networks, including LANs, MANs, and WANs. Traditional storage and I/O interfaces have been constrained in support over long distances compared with LANs, MANs, and WANs. This chapter takes a look at logical storage access, including techniques for accessing data and storage such as direct attached, network attached, block, storage network (SAN) attached, file, and object. Also covered in this chapter are different uses for storage networks, including server to storage, storage to storage, server to server, and SAN to SAN for multisegment storage networks. Physical networking, storage interfaces, and logical protocols are covered in Chapter 4.

3.2 Networks and I/O channels

Often taken for granted with computer systems of all sizes today is the I/O subsystem, which encompasses many things, including keyboards, monitors, disk, tape, networking interfaces, and even memory. Consequently, there is an association between networking and data storage that often gets blurred by various extensions and operational focus. While networks and storage I/O interfaces support different aspects of computing, they both support moving information between processors, I/O interfaces, and peripheral devices. Over time, storage I/O interfaces have become specialized to support the needs and characteristics of storage I/O moving data between servers and storage as well as between storage devices.

Networks, on the other hand, have been optimized for the general movement of data over varying distances between computers. As applications needed access to more data faster, larger and higher-performance devices and networks were needed. For resiliency, storage needs to be backed up and protected with off-site copies at other locations. With growth in computing, more processors and servers appeared and to simplify the management of a growing storage environment, more sharing of resources to improve utilization was needed.

Enterprise messaging networks and I/O channels are similar to roads and freeways in a city; there are the large expressways with many lanes (large amounts of bandwidth) to support large numbers of vehicles (communications, data transfers). These freeways (in network terms, backbones or trunks) are accessed by on-ramps or access roads that are smaller and, in turn, flow into tributary roads. Networks are similar in that there is a large amount of fast bandwidth available around the world. Figure 3.1 shows a global network linking multiple cities and regions together. Conceptually this is a basic diagram that could be scaled down to a smaller geographical area. This example can also be applied to a campus or metro area environment. On a larger scale, this example could be a worldwide resilient network as part of a resilient enterprise infrastructure to support storage networks. With all of the bandwidth available the challenge can be gaining access to it and affording it. Bandwidth and other metropolitan and wide area storage networking topics are covered in more detail in subsequent chapters.

Storage has traditionally been accessed using I/O and storage interfaces (sometimes called busses and channels). Some examples include bus & tag, ESCON channels for IBM S/390 mainframes, parallel SCSI and its derivatives, and SCSI Fibre Channel Protocol (FCP) for open systems (Windows, Linux, UNIX) and other platforms, IDE/ATA and Universal Serial Bus (USB). There are some similarities between general-purpose enterprise

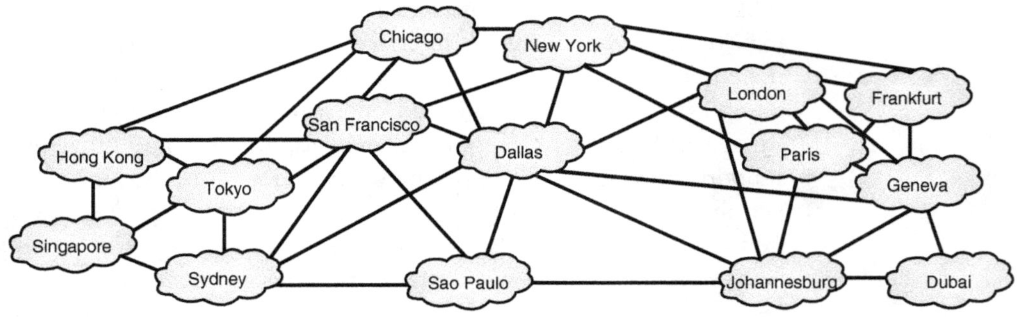

Figure 3.1 *Multicity global network.*

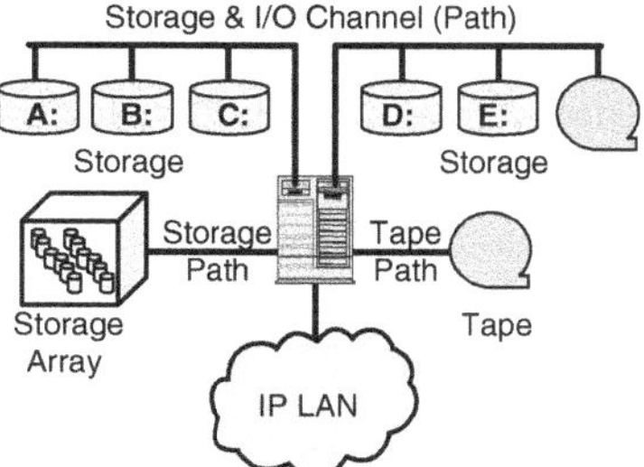

Figure 3.2
Servers, storage, and I/O channels.

messaging networks and storage I/O interfaces, their evolution, and functions. These include:

- Both move data and information and thus serve as I/O interfaces.
- Storage interfaces are optimized for high performance over relatively short distances.
- Storage interfaces are optimized for deterministic behavior.
- Networks are optimized for distance and ease of use.

However, simply comparing storage I/O interfaces and networks in an apples to apples manner is not as meaningful, since they are optimized for different functions and yet are complementary for creating storage networks.

Figure 3.2 shows a typical storage configuration with I/O paths for attaching storage devices, including disks, tapes, CDs, printers, and other peripherals. These storage I/O paths could be ESCON and FICON on an IBM mainframe, parallel SCSI and Fibre Channel on a larger open systems server, or IDE, Serial ATA (SATA), USB, or some other interface on a workstation or PC. Also shown in Figure 3.2 is a connection to a Local Area Network (LAN) enterprise messaging network using Ethernet as an interface to support a TCP/IP (IP) network.

3.3 Relationships between enterprise communications and the data center

A challenge facing IT managers today is how to provide continuous access to corporate information and IT applications. With the growth of e-commerce, Enterprise Resource Planning (ERP), Business Intelligence Analysis (BIA), Customer Resource Management (CRM), and other applications, not to mention the push for regulatory compliance, the need and dependence on data and IT systems being available 24 hours a day, 365 days a year has become an important topic. Corporations need to move data between global locations for business continuance and disaster preparedness as well as regulatory compliance for access from anywhere in the world. The focus on regulatory compliance is placing new demands on IT infrastructures and consequently storage networks to support on-demand access to stored information regardless of its location.

Analogous to using the right tool to do the right job, networking technology that works well for one application may not be best for others. Sometimes the best method is not always possible, particularly with new technology, and thus you use what is available and practical. Unlike first-generation networks that were tied to specific technology (physical interfaces and logical protocols), with the maturity and evolution of networking a LAN or MAN can be built using the appropriate interface for a particular application. TCP/IP (IP) has become the common denominator as an enterprise messaging protocol. IP-based networks can be built using different types of physical interfaces, including Ethernet and ATM, which are covered in more depth in Chapter 4.

3.4 Enterprise messaging network usage

The enterprise messaging network (more commonly referred to as LANs and WANs) has become essential in supporting data functions, video, and even voice over common networks. Many applications are served by TCP/IP (NAS, FTP, HTTP, storage mirroring), and others (backup, database, video) are better suited to traditional I/O and storage interfaces using block data access. Some common characteristics of LANs and WANs are that they move data to support I/O devices, and they are more general purpose compared with a storage interface with longer-distance and lower-cost interfaces. A common mistake, however, is to make comparisons of general-purpose networking and storage networking technology—for example, adapter cards. This is an apples to oranges comparison in that there are 1Gb Fibre Channel and 1Gb Ethernet cards, so simply comparing speed alone does not take into account the different functions that each addresses. This sort of a comparison is simply focused on the speeds/feeds and wire versus the networking interfaces, protocols, application support, and tools. While a 1Gb Ethernet card may be less expensive than a 1Gb or even 2Gb Fibre Channel card, the Fibre Channel card has processing to offload the host server of CPU cycles in order to perform I/O functions. This capability is being added to newer Ethernet cards and is called TCP Offload Engines

(TOEs). There are additional differences, including general-purpose networks that are designed for flexibility and lowest common denominator capability including performance and data integrity. Storage I/O networks are designed around deterministic performance behavior, and data integrity. Thus, it comes down to using the right combination of tools for the job or application at hand. This is where the convergence of storage I/O interfaces and networking technology is enabling storage networking.

Some applications and uses for LANs and WANs today include:

- Heartbeat and synchronization information between systems
- Data movement, staging, sharing, and distribution
- Lock management for databases, clusters, and filesystems
- Web and other client access, including PDAs, terminals
- Backup, restore, and other maintenance activities
- Replication, mirroring, archiving, and data retention
- Voice and video applications, including Voice over IP (VoIP)

Some of these applications, including backup, mirroring, replication, data copy and movement, and file sharing, are storage-related applications and consequently part of a storage network. Storage networks, contrary to popular myths, are not tied to any given physical interface or logical protocol; rather, they have the common characteristic of supporting storage applications. When it comes to building a resilient enterprise, distance is critical for survivability. Distance is important, since the further active and recovery data are separated, the more resilient the infrastructure. There are various degrees of distance providing different levels of protection and business continuance; however, there are also different burdens, including cost, performance, and capability. A resilient storage network to support a resilient infrastructure may require multiple levels of distance support and a combination of synchronous and asynchronous protection. So why are storage networks and local area networks needed? This is a good question, and the solution lies more with the function as compared with the implementation. Too often the comparison is made more on the physical and logical interfaces and connections, such as IP versus Fibre Channel, as opposed to what function that network and, more specifically, I/O interface and protocol is supporting. While storage I/O and general-purpose networking can utilize common technology, and in some cases common cabling and networks, they are targeted at different applications. A general-purpose network supports data movement between computer systems and user devices while storage networks move data between storage and computer devices. They are both I/O interfaces, and they both move data; however, they function with different service requirements and operational focus.

The attack on the World Trade Center (WTC) in New York City on September 11, 2001, brought to light the importance of distance and disaster recovery. Previous attacks and events helped some enterprises to have business continuance plans and capabilities in place. Many of these plans involved having mirrored copies of data and facilities across one of the rivers on both sides of New York City. These plans protected against site failures; however, due to the widespread impact to the greater New York area and disruption to telecommunications recovery, using the protected systems was delayed in some cases. Another aspect to distance recovery was the relative proximity of the recovery centers to the disaster when the New York metropolitan area infrastructure was disrupted. Businesses with recovery and standby sites farther away from Ground Zero in New York city were able to regroup their systems and staff with greater ease. This is an example that illustrates that the farther the standby backup data center is from the primary location, the less impact there should be. Consequently, as shown in Figure 3.3, multitier recovery and continuance solutions are needed to protect against site, campus, metropolitan, and regional disruptions.

September 11, 2001, also pointed out a flaw in many disaster recovery (DR) plans that relied upon transportation (local or remote) to move people and information. Another aspect is performance and speed of recovery, which has resulted in some firms now setting up secondary sites and tertiary sites even farther away. For example, in the New York City area many firms in the immediate vicinity of the World Trade Center disaster had redundant

Figure 3.3 *Distance is critical for business continuance.*

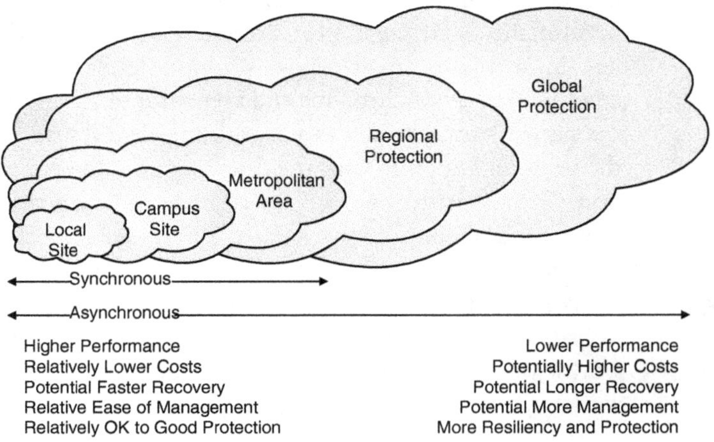

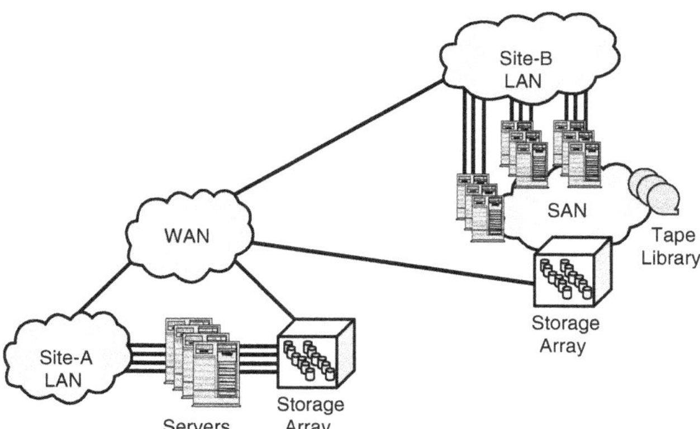

Figure 3.4 *Wide area enterprise messaging and storage networks.*

sites located across the Hudson River in New Jersey. While these resilient infrastructures enabled firms to stay in business, these events demonstrated the importance of a third copy even farther away.

Figure 3.4 shows more detail, including LANs, in different locations that connect to each other via a backbone network. Storage is accessed by servers at each location using a storage network with enterprise storage devices being mirrored to each other using a WAN interface. The WAN interface enables the storage devices to be located physically farther apart instead of using dedicated I/O interfaces such as Fibre Channel, FICON, and ESCON to support business continuance over hundreds to thousands of miles. The storage network at each location could be a simple point-to-point connection using Fibre Channel, FICON, or even parallel SCSI or a switched environment with some small Fibre Channel switches or larger Fibre Channel/FICON switching directors. Some other possibilities for the storage network include using iSCSI for distributed SMB and open systems platforms and InfiniBand for high-performance clustering environments. This could also be a campus or metro area environment, where a mix of Fibre Channel, Gigabit Ethernet, Dense Wave Division Multiplexing (DWDM), and other technologies are used to span distances over 100km.

With the development of storage over IP, specifically iSCSI and NAS, in theory you could eliminate Fibre Channel and build your entire storage network over an IP-based network. For some environments, including smaller SMB and workgroups, this may well be the case; however, as with networking, over time the SCSI I/O protocol for moving block data will become an enabler similar to IP for networking. The SCSI block I/O protocol runs on Fibre Channel (FCP) and over IP (iSCSI) so that the right physical interface can be used for the applicable environment or application.

There is overlap of the underlying physical interfaces for storage networking and enterprise messaging networks. This overlap of interfaces will help make storage networking and enterprise messaging networks more complementary as they converge closer to each other and enable the resilient infrastructure and enterprise.

3.5 Deterministic behavior

Deterministic behavior refers to the predefined or expected behavior of how something will be accomplished. What this means for storage and networking is that a deterministic behavior has been expected and predetermined results have been compared with nondeterministic behavior. Nondeterministic behavior would result in unpredictable behavior. For example, traditional storage interfaces are said to be deterministic in that when an I/O is issued, they are expected to either complete gracefully in an expected manner in an expected amount of time, or they will fail gracefully. This means that the interface has a higher assumed quality of service and capability with deterministic behavior so that packets will not be dropped, collisions will be avoided, and so on.

In Figure 3.5 the WAN network in the middle could be based on an OC-96 (Optical Carrier 4.9Gbps) Synchronous Optical Network (SONET) and Synchronous Digital Hierarchy (SDH) network interface with the local locations using an OC-48 (2.5Gbps) and remote access at under 1Mbps (dial-up, broadband, ISDN, Frame Relay, WiFi, and WiMax). In this scenario performance may not approach the full network bandwidth capability due to other traffic on the same network (shared

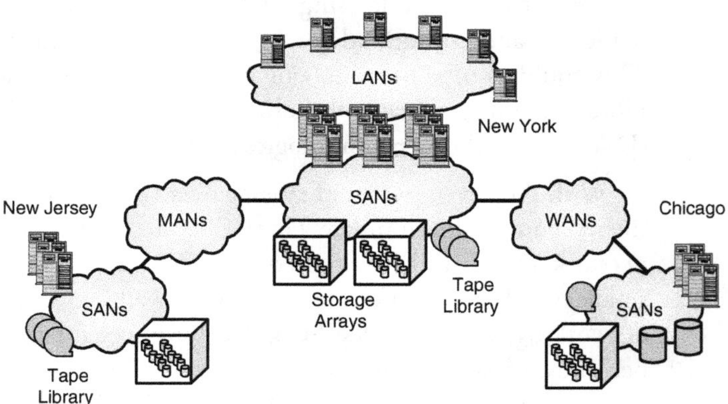

Figure 3.5
SANs, MANs, WANs, and LANs.

bandwidth), which type of traffic is going over the network, and other factors that can potentially impact performance. For example, if you were trying to back up a computer in Hong Kong to a site in New York, your performance would be affected by the speed of the interface between the computer and the backbone network in Hong Kong. Some other factors to consider are propagation delay (also known as latency) to make the long trip from New York to Hong Kong and the type of data that is being backed up. Another example (Figure 3.5) is a network between New York and New Jersey, which can be referred to as a Metro Area Network (MAN). The available bandwidth or performance on the MAN can be much higher to enable data centers to span up to 100km in distance with minimal to no loss in performance.

Disaster tolerance, extended distances, and worldwide availability have placed an emphasis on storage being scalable, highly available, fast, and cost effective. As host servers continue to become faster, support more memory, and have larger I/O capacity, storage interfaces also are changing to support longer distance and more performance. Thus, it is important to understand how storage networking can be implemented to address business and technology issues to support the resilient enterprise. (See Table 3.1)

Table 3.1 *Various Networking Interfaces*

Interface	Speed	Distance	Protocols	Characteristic	Usage
Fibre Channel	1–2Gbps Emerging 4–10Gb	10–80km+	FCP, FICON, IP, VI	Deterministic Channel	Local, Metro
Ethernet (10/100)	10–100Mbps	Variable	IP, VI, iSCSI, iFCP	Network LAN	Local, Metro
Gigabit Ethernet	1Gb 10Gb	150km 40km+	IP, FCIP, iSCSI, iFCP	Network LAN	Local, Metro
MetroIP	Variable	Variable	IP, FCIP, iSCSI	Network	Metro, WAN
ATM	OC1–OC192	Variable	IP, VI, FCBB	Network	Local, Metro, WAN
SONET/ SDH	OC1–OC192	Variable	ATM, IP, FCBB	Network Backbone	Metro, WAN
DWDM	Over 100Tb	100–200km+	All	Multiple Networks	Local, Metro

Delving deeper into wide area communication for the resilient storage networks reveals physical networks and interfaces, along with multiple protocols, including:

- SAN/LAN—Fibre Channel and Gigabit Ethernet beyond 10km and even 100km
- MAN—Metro Area and Optical Networking using Dense Wave Division Multiplexing (DWDM), Time Division Multiplexing (TDM), and SONET/SDH over fiber optics
- WAN—ATM, IP, and other public networks, including SONET/SDH

Similar to a LAN supporting IP or a storage network SAN supporting SCSI (FCP) or FICON, different physical interfaces are used to build a wide area communications network. Many networks still utilize copper wiring (ISDN, dial-up, and broadband). Fiber optics are more commonly used to build networks (SONET/SDH, ATM, MetroIP, Gigabit Ethernet, Fibre Channel SANs) locally and over long distances. For local, campus, and metro environments, where dark fiber (dedicated physical fiber) is available, DWDM can be used to build a fiber optic–based backbone. The fiber optic–based backbone can support ATM, Fibre Channel, Ethernet, and other network interfaces over longer distances, with more capacity and performance. By using wireless communications, including WiFi and IP, a storage network to support iSCSI, NAS, and Fibre Channel over IP can also be built. The current downside with wireless-based storage networks is performance and distance limitations; however, as with other networking technologies, this is improving.

Copper wiring (electrical) interfaces have been the traditional medium for communications and networking. Electrical-based interfaces are used in LAN, WAN, MAN, first-generation storage networks, telecommunications, and entertainment (cable TV). Some examples of electrical-based networks include ISDN, dial-up modems, cable modems, DSL, and Ethernet. Wireless technology, including WiFi and WiMax, capable of supporting broadband or high-speed bandwidth for wide area data class applications is emerging, particularly for remote access use. While not yet as robust as it needs to be, wireless technology holds potential to support wide area communications. Technical issues that need to be addressed include performance, standards, reliability, distance, and security. Long-distance, high-performance networking is in a state of evolution. It is important for an enterprise implementing resilient information services to understand the actual capabilities of the different long-distance storage networking technologies available today.

3.6 I/O busses and paths

To initiate and receive information, whether it is being moved over a storage I/O interface or general-purpose LAN interfaces, involves a server, storage device, or both at either end. For now, let's look at the server side of things; later we will look at server host bus adapters and storage devices in more detail. In Figure 3.6 a server is shown with memory and processors (CPU) connected by various system busses. Also connected is an I/O bus to support various peripheral interconnect interfaces to attach peripherals (disk, tape, CDs, scanners, printers, cameras, memory sticks, networks, and other I/O devices). Figure 3.6 shows support for the Peripheral Computer Interface (PCI) I/O bus that various adapters could be attached to.

PCI (www.pcisig.com) is the most commonly used I/O bus that supports both adapters in PCI expansion slots as well as devices via internal embedded interfaces. For example, on a laptop computer you might have various I/O interfaces, including SCSI, IDE, USB, and Ethernet, that interface via an onboard PCI controller chip. If you have a desktop tower or workstation, you may have expansion slots for adding additional graphics and I/O cards that attach to the PCI bus. PCI has been around since 1992, when it was introduced by Intel and other industry leaders to create a

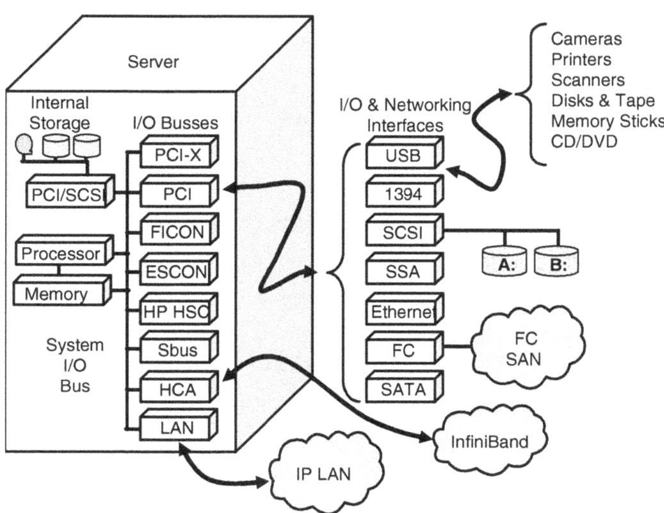

Figure 3.6
Servers and I/O interfaces.

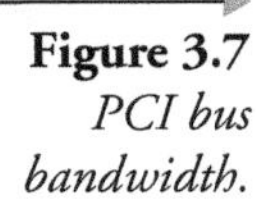

Figure 3.7 *PCI bus bandwidth.*

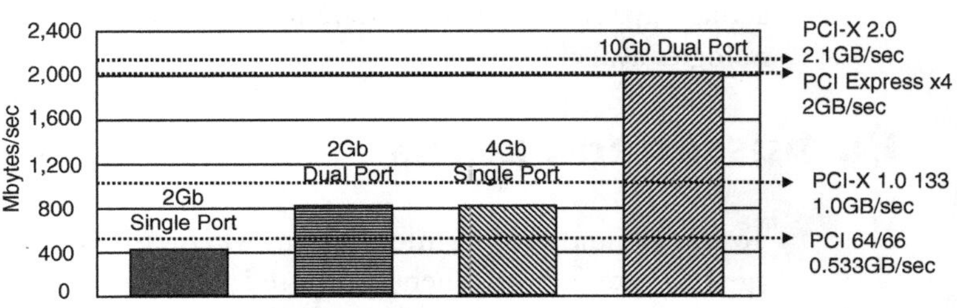

common I/O interface. PCI continues to be enhanced with PCI-X to increase bandwidth to support new interfaces, including 4Gb and 10Gb. Some other I/O buss interfaces, shown in Figure 3.6 and found on systems of all sizes, include Sbus for Sun Solaris systems, HP-UX HSC and HP-PB for older legacy systems, and ESCON and FICON for IBM mainframes.

Figure 3.7 shows full-duplex (full) bandwidth of PCI and PCI-X along with the corresponding bandwidth needs of 2Gb, 4Gb, and 10Gb Fibre Channel technology. Full-duplex communication enables both transmit and send data paths to be used concurrently for better performance. Many devices support PCI 32 bit/33MHz, which operates at a slower speed providing about 1.5Gbytes/second of bandwidth. This is adequate for 1Gb devices; however, to fully support 2Gb and beyond, faster PCI implementations are needed. Looking from left to right, we see the bandwidth needed for a single-port, 2Gb Fibre Channel adapter operating at full speed (400Mbytes/second), which is just inside the bandwidth of a PCI 64-bit/66MHz (533Mbyte/second) interface. The figure shows that the PCI 64-bit/66MHz bus has a maximum bandwidth to support 2Gb but not two 2Gb or 4Gb let alone a 10Gb interface. Using PCI-X adds bandwidth and headroom to support 2Gb and 4Gb adapters, and with PCI-X 2.0 there will be room for 10Gb.

3.7 Data access infrastructures

A sound foundation provides a stable infrastructure on which to build. Whether it is a sound design for your applications, your business, or your home, the infrastructure seldom supports the entire environment. Storage networks (also known as SANs) provide such an infrastructure for the resilient enterprise on a local, campus, metro, and wide area basis.

First-generation and early storage networks have been predominately Fibre Channel SANs built around hubs and switches, similar to how first-generation LANs came into being. As with first-generation LANs, these early SANs had interoperability issues and tended to be constrained to vendor-specific technology. For example, a characteristic of early and even current storage networks has been vendor-specific SANs, which has resulted in SAN islands. This has been done, in part, because of interoperability issues, including isolating various vendor host bus adapters (HBAs) from each other and limiting the number and type of storage devices on a common SAN. While some interoperability issues still exist between various vendors and technology, today it is possible for multiple storage devices from different vendors to coexist in the same zone; different host operating systems and HBAs; and switch-to-switch, switch-to-director, and director-to-director interoperability using FC-SW-2 Fabric Shortest Path First (FSPF) routing, World Wide Nodename (WWN) zones, and expansion ports (E_Port) for interoperability. On the interoperability front, the Fibre Channel Industry Association (FCIA) SANmark program exists as a means to test interoperability of fabric components. From a more applied and disaster recovery–specific standpoint, the Storage Networking Industry Association (SNIA) has launched the Supported Solutions Forum (SSF) for interoperability and support across different vendor hardware and software products.

Heterogeneous storage networks can contain different servers with different operating systems, different storage devices from different vendors, different switches and directors from different vendors, different HBAs and other components, and different management tools—in other words, a real-world storage network to meet your needs as opposed to what a vendor will support or wants you to map your environment to. Several things enable a heterogeneous open storage network to exist, including standards, interoperability, testing, vendors working together on supported solutions such as those in the SSFs initiatives, experience, and education.

Some might argue that it's the type of network that distinguishes between a SAN, NAS, and storage network. Others will say it's the software. A storage network is the combination of hardware, software, networks and procedures, politics, service requirements, operating and management paradigms, and principles to deliver the storage services to meet the application needs.

A storage network can be as simple as a point-to-point connection between one or more servers attached to and sharing one or more storage devices, including disk and tape. A storage network can also be as complex as multiple subnets (segments or regions) spanning local, metropolitan, and global sites using multiple topologies and technologies. Similar to a network, a storage network can be one logical network with different segments isolated from each other with firewalls, security, virtual LANs,

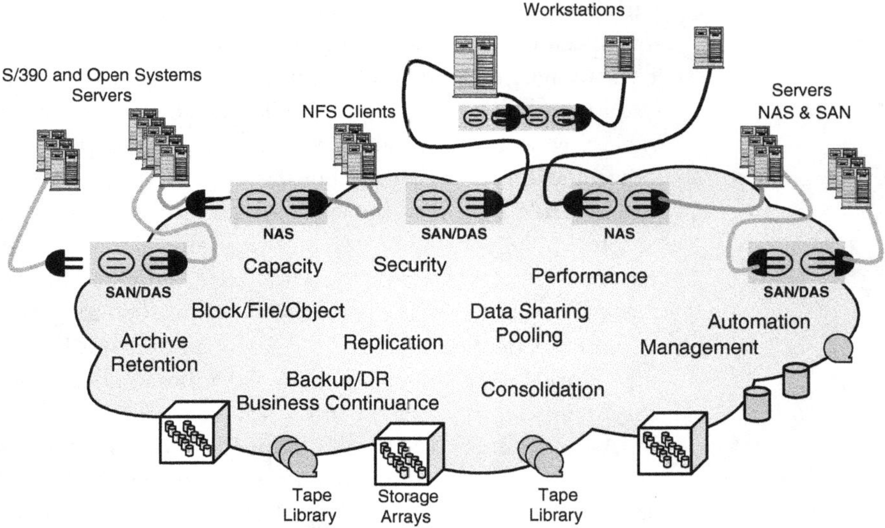

Figure 3.8 *Sample storage network.*

and different physical network types all under a common management framework or domain. So a storage network could share the same physical network interfaces as a messaging network or LAN; the storage network is defined by the software, applications, and principles of operations. Similarly, a LAN can use common network interfaces of a storage environment such as IP over Fibre Channel, IP on CTC (channel to channel) for S/390 mainframes, or a common carrier network shared with voice, data, and video. (See Figure 3.8.)

3.8 Accessing storage networks

Storage is accessed via some form of interface, also known as an I/O channel. Traditional I/O interfaces and channels were proprietary and by today's standards slow and limited in distance and capacity in terms of number of devices supported. Storage interfaces and I/O channels were typically deployed as point to point or bus topology with a processor (also known as a CPU or server) attached to one end of an I/O bus and a storage controller on the other. The processor would have some form of I/O adapter that interfaced the storage bus to the internal data bus to move and access data. The storage controller would attach to the storage interface, similar to the processor, to allow access to disk, tape, printers, or other devices.

3.9 Network storage interfaces

While parallel SCSI (pSCSI) performance has increased and costs have been driven down, these are not adequate to support the increased performance, distance, and capacity demands of existing and new applications. To support the resilient enterprise storage networks we must provide the flexibility of networks with the reliability and robustness of storage I/O channels to share and access storage resources. Some storage networking benefits include:

- Physically removing storage from servers
- Improved server resiliency and clusters
- Diskless servers using shared resources
- Storage resource and data sharing and consolidation
- Improved backup and recovery, shared tape, LAN-free backup
- Improved distance, capacity, and performance
- Simplified management and lower total cost of ownership (TCO)

Storage networking combines traditional storage interfaces and access methods with the flexibility of networking. Storage networking is not a new concept, having been implemented with proprietary interfaces on S/390 systems (ESCON) and OpenVMS clusters (CI and FDDI). While distance and performance were constrained, pSCSI has been used to build small storage networks for clusters in the past.

Storage networking has evolved from proprietary interfaces for different server and operating systems to open Fibre Channel Storage Area Networks (SANs) and Network Attached Storage (NAS). New emerging technologies are enabling wide area storage networks for distributed storage and backups to support the resilient infrastructure and enterprise. InfiniBand will enable access of storage at rates beyond 2Gbyte/second and serve as an open CTC interface, also known as computer-to-computer interconnects for low-latency messaging to support clusters, distributed file systems, and lock management.

Fibre Channel is the most commonly used interface for building block-based storage networks today, supporting FICON for mainframes and FCP for open systems. NAS, using Ethernet and IP as interfaces and transport protocols supporting Network File System (NFS), and Common Internet File System (CIFS) for Windows are the most common interfaces for file-based access. iSCSI is beginning to gain some momentum after some early false starts as an alternative interface to support SCSI block movements over IP-based networks.

The SNIA looks at storage networking from a broader view than simply Fibre Channel, interfaces, devices, and management tools. SNIA membership is made up of storage networking vendors and end users. SNIA SSFs bring a level of comfort to customers, proving that multivendor storage networks can be installed and supported. For resilient infrastructure and enterprise there are SNIA SSFs, combining mixed storage; tape, volume, and path management; and backup software on a common, large-scale, resilient fabric. More information about SNIA can be found at www.snia.org.

A benefit of a SAN is that storage I/O can be isolated to a separate network, so that traditional network traffic is not impacted by storage I/O traffic such as backups and restores. To help add some perspective, the SNIA has an architectural model, called the SNIA shared storage model, which is shown in Figure 3.9. This model shows how and where the physical interfaces and protocols such as Fibre Channel, FICON, iSCSI, and others coexist along with aggregation or virtualization tools. Also shown in the SNIA model are some storage networking services, including management, security, and discovery, regardless of which physical interfaces are used. In addition to the SNIA, there are many other storage networking–related organizations, including the InfiniBand Trade Association, SCSI Trade

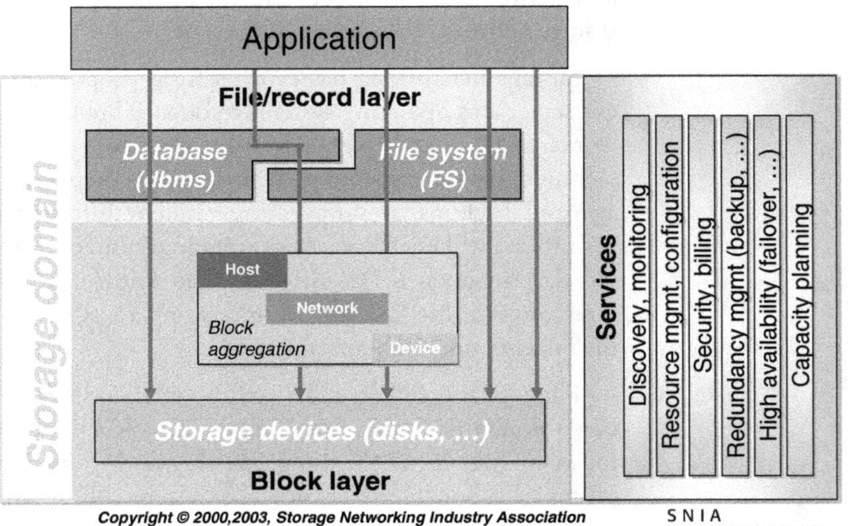

Figure 3.9 *SNIA shared storage model—courteous SNIA.*

Association, ANSI T11, IETF, CMG, SPC, PCISIG, 10GEA, and iSCSI forums to name a few.

Storage networking as seen in the SNIA model does not make a distinction between interconnect types used. SANs are being built with Fibre Channel, and, consequently, the term *SAN* has lost its original protocol independent–meaning; however, this is changing with new interfaces and protocols maturing.

3.10 Networks for storage

First-generation "proprietary" storage networks include shared interfaces such as S/390 Mainframe ESCON, IBM SSA, HP (formerly DEC) Open VMS CI, and, later, FDDI and DSSI. While not popular from a multi-server standpoint, parallel SCSI from a shared storage bus standpoint (multi-initiator SCSI) has also been deployed for small clusters. First-generation LAN networks were deployed in vendor-specific proprietary topologies, media, and protocols that later gave way to open and standard Ethernet and IP as a networking combo. Similarly, storage networks are evolving toward open- and standards-based—away from proprietary—interfaces and protocols. With the advent of IP and the Network File Systems (NFS) as a common shared file access system, file sharing, more commonly called NAS today, was born. This capability enabled storage on different servers to be served via the network to various clients.

Some storage networking applications include:

- Global clustering and data sharing
- Storage and server consolidation
- Remote backup and electronic vaulting
- Remote mirroring and replication
- Data retention or archiving

An important storage networking application is maintaining copies of data at multiple locations using mirroring and backup techniques. Even with mirroring and replication, data still needs to be backed up (disk or tape) and kept (on-line or off-line) for retention and recovery. In addition to keeping data for recovery purposes, these copies are useful should data be deleted, corrupted, or otherwise unavailable. Another use is for retention to meet government or other regulatory purposes. For example, after some sort of event (disaster or technology failure), archived information

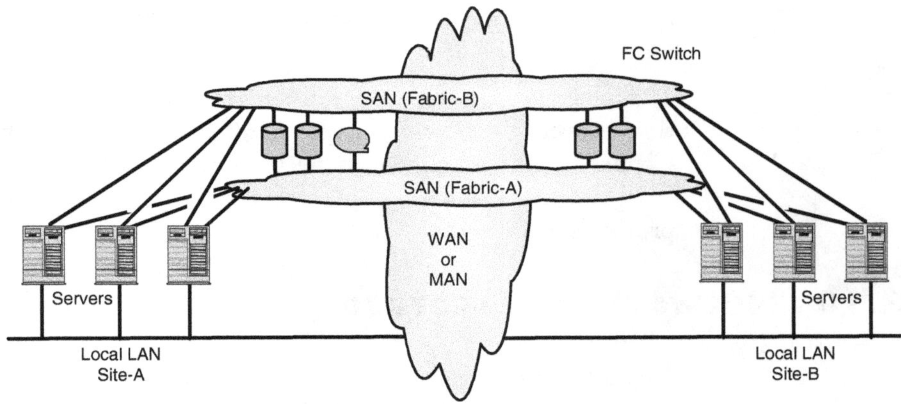

Figure 3.10 *Wide area clusters and storage networks (SANs).*

may help with investigative activities and thus needs to be restored in a timely manner.

There are as many variations on how and where to implement a storage network as there are permutations of hardware, software, networks, people, and business. What is right for your environment is best described as what is applicable, what supports the business, and what makes practical sense. For SMB environments, file and data sharing with integrated backup might be applicable. Another variation of these could be to introduce iSCSI to enable the Linux and Windows NT/2000 systems to access block storage resources, including disk and tape for backup and shared storage. (See Figure 3.10.)

There are three principal methods, as shown in Table 3.2, for accessing data: block-based addressing (commonly associated with SAN), file-based addressing (commonly known as NAS), and, more recently, object-based addressing, known as Content Addressable Storage (CAS). Traditional applications, regardless of the platform, access data via block mode, where the host server performs an I/O to a storage subsystem.

3.10.1 Block access—SAN, FAS, DAS

In Chapter 2, how data is organized, stored, and accessed using different formats was discussed. Storage Area Network (SAN), Fabric Attached Storage (FAS), and Direct Attached Storage (DAS) refer to how storage is attached to a server. Block-based data access today is the lowest level of access, whether it be via a filesystem, database, or some other mechanism. Ultimately the data is read and written from the disk in blocks. A typical

Table 3.2 *Various Storage Access Methods*

Access Method	Commonly Known As	Applications	Description and Characteristics
Object	CAS	Reference data and retention of data for preservation for compliance and regulatory purposes	Content-addressable storage (location independent). Applications access data via a unique identifier that is derived from the contents of the data being stored. Once the identifier is known, then the data is retrieved by ultimately issuing physical block I/Os.
File	NAS	File sharing and data sharing	Filename that maps via a directory structure to a fileserver that issues block I/O on its behalf.
Block	Block, SAN, DAS, DASD	Block-oriented access. OLTP and transactional processing. More common form of I/O access.	Data is accessed by logical or physical location with a starting location, ending location, or number of blocks and what size to move.

block, also known as a page of memory for open systems, will usually be a multiple of 512 bytes. Open systems environments are known as Fixed-Block Architectures (FBA) in that their block sizes are fixed when the disk and filesystem are formatted. While there can be multiple blocks and even larger blocks, they are still based upon 512 bytes of data, which is also what the disk drives are formatted on. For IBM mainframe environments, a variable format referred to as CKD and ECKD is used.

With block-based data access, an application can perform the I/O to the storage device via a filesystem. An application can also make a request to a Database Management System (DBMS), which, in turn, issues the I/O request (either directly using raw access or via a filesystem). Block I/O relies on a storage device being told where and how much data to be returned using logical and physical addressing—for example, a starting Logical Block Number (LBN) and how many blocks to read or write; these are then mapped to the physical cylinder and sector on a disk device.

3.10.2 File access—NAS and file/data sharing

File-based NAS access is another method of data access that is common with distributed and Internet applications that share common data from a server. A NAS fileserver (filer) can use Fibre Channel to access shared storage on the same storage device as the database server, which simplifies storage management. The NAS filer uses a storage interface (IDE, SCSI, SSA, or Fibre Channel) to serve data within the data center to other servers using IP over Fibre Channel and IP over Ethernet to communicate with other servers on the LAN. In this scenario the filer and the database servers share the Fibre Channel attached tape library for backup. Using library sharing software backups can safely be performed over the shared interfaces to offload IP-based networks.

The clients make requests to the filer to process I/O requests on a file basis. Some examples of distributed filesystems include Network File System (NFS), Windows Sharing (CIFS), and AFS. NAS file sharing relies on storage being attached to a host server that utilizes a standard storage interface such as SCSI or Fibre Channel. Sometimes the fileserver is simply called an appliance or filer. The filer presents (serves) data from the storage device to other host servers via the network using a file-sharing protocol such as NFS. An example of this is Windows shared volumes from a fileserver in an office or over a network. In this scenario, Fibre Channel is used to move block data between database servers and the shared storage device with redundant paths.

File-based access relies on additional software to serve storage and data (files) to other servers and clients. One of the most common examples of this is with a Windows file share that utilizes Common Internet Filesystem (CIFS) for sharing. The server has the physical storage attached and performs block-level I/O in response to file requests. The fileserver is making file access available to other servers while it maps file requests into logical block I/Os. File-based access is most commonly referred to as Network Attached Storage (NAS) and in addition to CIFS it utilizes the Network File System (NFS) common on UNIX and other systems.

3.10.3 Object access—CAS/object

Content Accessible Storage (CAS), also known as object-based storage, is a new way of accessing storage that builds on block and file access. With CAS an application stores and retrieves information using unique key identifiers that are derived from the contents of the data being stored. Should the data being stored change so too would the identifier, which in some ways functions similar to a checksum of the data. Files also have identifiers; however, these are a function of the location where the storage is saved as well as a directory structure. While there are variations in how CAS can be implemented, the common approach is to add a level of abstraction as well as to preserve data uniqueness for compliance and other retention applications. An early example of CAS-based solution is the EMC Centera.

3.11 Storage and data sharing

SAN and NAS are both part of storage networking. SAN is associated with Fibre Channel and iSCSI block-based access and NAS with LAN NFS or CIFS file-based access. Each has its place to address different business needs. For a resilient NAS environment, along with simplified storage management, shared SAN storage can be used. A SAN can also provide high-speed backup of NAS filers using Fibre Channel or iSCSI to access shared tape devices. Similar to the benefits of host servers, NAS filers also benefit from storage and backup sharing for resiliency.

In Figure 3.11, examples of directly attached dedicated storage (DAS) are shown along with network attached shared storage (NAS). This example shows how a server on the left can access a locally attached disk as well as access a network attached served disk. The served disk (volume D:) is physically attached to the NAS server on the right. The NAS server using file access sharing software (NFS, CIFS, DAFS) makes the contents of the storage available to the other servers as a shared volume for reads and writes. If you have ever used a Microsoft Windows shared volume, this is an example of NAS file sharing using Windows CIFS. In Figure 3.11, there is also an example of shared storage in the middle, where the servers all attach via a storage networking interface to a shared storage device. The storage device is partitioned into three different device logical unit numbers (LUNs) and volumes (A:, B:, and C:), with each server accessing only its specified volume. This differs from data sharing in that volume D: is being served by the NAS filer, other servers can also read and write to the same volume. This sharing of data is accomplished by using the file- and data-sharing software that helps make a NAS environment. Hence, there is a difference between

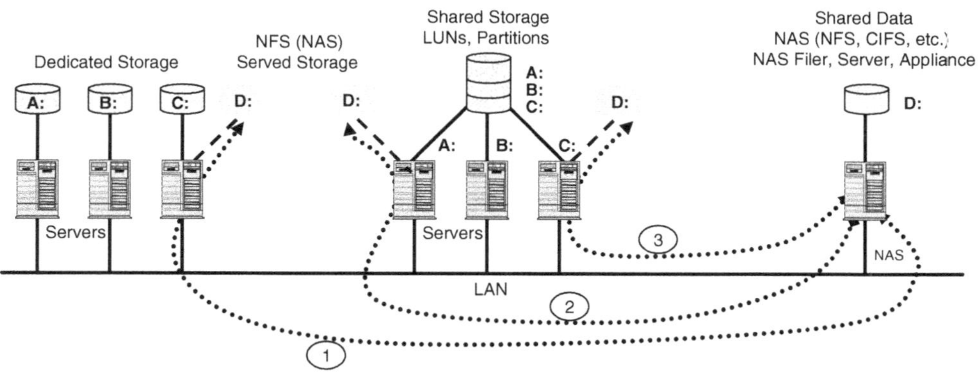

Figure 3.11 *Storage and data sharing.*

storage sharing, as seen in the middle example, and data sharing using NAS. With storage sharing, each server is allocated a different portion of a storage device for its use. Data sharing enables all authorized servers to share data and storage.

3.12 Storage networking access models

Storage and storage networks can be deployed to support various functions, including server to storage, server to server, storage to storage, and network to network (also known as SAN to SAN), as seen in Table 3.3.

The most common access method or model is server to storage, where a host server or processor accesses a device (disk, tape, printer, etc.) either locally or remotely. Device to device has become more common, providing remote mirroring and data replication on a local and remote basis. Server to server has traditionally been accomplished using standard LAN networking technology with TCP/IP and Ethernet, proprietary interfaces including S/390 mainframe CTC over ESCON and FICON, or other high-speed, low latency interfaces and protocols. The fourth access model is SAN to SAN, which is also a general catchall category generically used to describe and enable all of the above.

Distance limitations have been a limiting factors plaguing access and availability to data in terms of performance, latency, and cost. Applications and business environments are taxing and outgrowing the ability of first-generation 1Gb Fibre Channel to extend data beyond 10km. Current Fibre Channel supports speeds of 2Gb with 4Gb and 10Gb with distances of well beyond 10km. User requirements are forcing IT administrators to examine the use of SANs, storage over IP, and optical networking to create global

Table 3.3 *Storage Networking Access Applications*

Access Model	Description	Examples
SAN to SAN	Interfabric	Site to Site, Local to Remote
Device to Device	Remote Mirroring	EMC SRDF and MirrorView, HDS True Copy, IBM PPRC and Volume Copy, HP Business Copy, STK PPRC, LSI Remote Volume Manager
Server to Device	Host to Disk/Tape	Host-based mirroring, general access
Server to Server	Channel to Channel	CTC, IP on Fibre Channel, Clustering

storage networks. Fibre Channel SANs can now span distances of over 100km with extended buffer credits and long-range optics, including 80km GBICs, small form-factor plugs (SFPs), and DWDM. Farther distances are possible using Fibre Channel over WAN technology, including IP (iSCSI, FCIP, iFCP) and SONET/SDH-based bridges and gateways.

3.12.1 Server to device

Server to device includes local, metropolitan, and wide area access of devices from a server. A device could be a disk drive, LUN on a storage device or virtualization appliance, tape drive or tape library, optical media, Solid State Disk (SSD), high-speed printer, or other storage-related devices. Server to device could be local, in the same equipment room, network closet, or data center, as well as a server accessing a storage device elsewhere in a campus or metropolitan environment as though it were local, or remotely as a wide area device. Some examples include remote tape backups, host or server mirroring or replication (e.g., Veritas Volume Replicator [VVR], Volume Manager [VxVM]–based mirroring, IBM XRC, and Fujitsu Softex TDMF for S/390 and open systems) with a copy of the local data as well as the remote data with clustering for high availability. Another example would include a virtualization appliance accessed by a local server, which, in turn, could access different storage devices in different geographical locations to provide a common view of transactions, records, and other information for backup, recovery, journals, audit trails, and regulatory compliance. (See Figure 3.12.)

For the non-S/390 environments, storage access over long distances is a relatively new capability, which is being enabled today with Fibre Channel to extend a channel from one location to another to enable a CPU to access a remote storage device. For the S/390 environments this could include

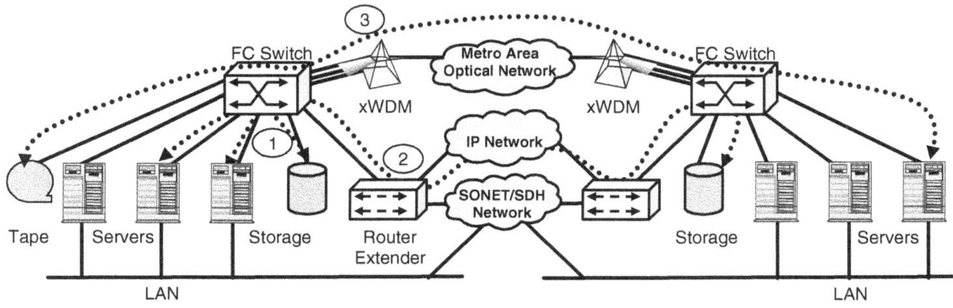

Figure 3.12 *Server-to-device storage networking example.*

FICON Cascade, Virtual Tape Subsystems (VTS), and Extended Remote Copy (XRC) for high-availability applications. In the open systems world, this could be host (server)–based mirroring using volume managers and virtualization tools, remote backup, and remote access to storage. In the past there have been point products to extend SCSI over proprietary Fibre Channel–derived solutions, as well as SCSI-to-Fibre Channel routers. With current-generation Fibre Channel technology able to support distances of 100km or more using SONET/SDH, FCIP, and iFCP distance extension devices, metropolitan SANs can be built to move data at high speeds, with high bandwidth over long distances, moving a step closer to a global storage network. The server to storage access model enables servers that are attached to a local SAN to perform LAN-Free backups to shared devices (disk or tape) locally, or remotely via an extended interface such as Fibre Channel over WAN or DWDM.

Some server-to-device storage networking applications include:

- Remote backup, Electronic Tape Vaulting (ETV), archiving to disk and tape
- Virtual tape, virtual disk, and virtual optical storage
- Remote storage access for application testing and Disaster Recovery (DR)
- Host-based mirroring, replication, and storage virtualization
- Consolidation of servers, storage, data centers, and SANs

Some server-to-device storage networking technologies include:

- Fibre Channel using FICON or FCP (SCSI over Fibre Channel)
- Gb Ethernet using FCIP (frame passing and tunneling) or iSCSI (SCSI over IP) or iFCP (Fibre Channel to IP gateway)
- DWDM metro optical networks and SONET/SDH
- Tape pipelining and grouped writes to optimize network bandwidth

3.12.2 Device to device (storage-storage mirroring)

Device to device, traditionally known as channel extension for remote mirroring and hardware replication, links two or more devices together locally or remotely. Some examples of device-based storage mirroring and replication are shown in Table 3.4. These interfaces traditionally have been ESCON based, with extension over various networking interfaces, and more recently Fibre Channel, and Ethernet with IP based. This would include IP/

Table 3.4 *Some Common Device-Based Mirroring Solutions*

	Synchronous	Asynchronous	Volume Snapshot	File Snapshot	Point-in-Time Snapshot
EMC	SRDF, MirrorView	SRDF/A, MirrorView	TimeFinder	SnapView	Replication Manager
HDS	TrueCopy	TrueCopy	ShadowImage	ShadowImage	ShadowImage, NanoCopy
HP	Business Copy XP	Continuous Access XP and EVA	—	—	Continuous Access
Network Appliance	SyncMirror	SnapMirror	SnapVault	SnapVault	SnapVault
IBM	PPRC	PPRC-XD	FlashCopy	FlashCopy	FlashCopy

GbEthernet cards such as those from EMC as well as use of channel extenders, bridges, and gateways that perform value-added functions such as compression, load balancing, and other features. (See Figure 3.13.)

Storage to storage is the traditional and one of the most commonly deployed wide area SAN applications to support business continuance. Storage-based mirroring using channel extension, also known as remote mirroring and remote copy, has in the past used ESCON as an I/O channel interface to various network interfaces, including Gb Ethernet, IP, Frame Relay, SONET/SDH OC-3, ATM, and others. More recently, Fibre Channel is being supported as an I/O channel interface to the previously mentioned network interfaces for channel extension and also to support the emerging SAN-to-SAN application market. The rudimentary method for device-to-device channel extension is frame passing, where frames are taken

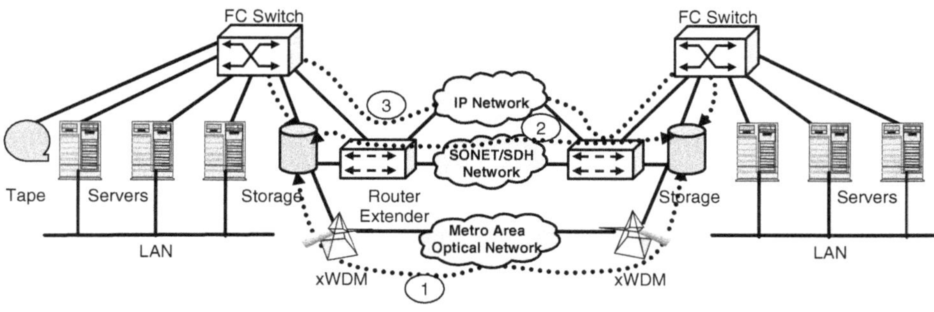

Figure 3.13 *Device-to-device (storage-to-storage) example.*

off the I/O channel at one end, mapped onto a LAN/WAN interface, and transmitted over distances where frames are placed on the remote channel. The effect is to create a virtual channel, or virtual storage network link, to interface the two sides together.

More advanced methods utilize compression on the channel side for maximum benefit, or on the network side to help reduce network costs and increase effective bandwidth. Depending on their environments and requirements, users can have the ability to mirror data synchronously (point in time) or asynchronously (point to point). Device-specific performance enhancements such as protocol spoofing and compression may exist in channel extension devices to further optimize performance over longer distances, ensuring data integrity. Data can be shared between geographically dispersed sites and can be accessed across the WAN/MAN. This approach can be deployed in enterprise environments to provide greater availability and access to data, to shorten recovery windows, and to minimize downtime in the event of a disaster. For metro area applications, DWDM can be used to connect storage devices together in lieu of, or in combination with, maximizing bandwidth and streamlining connectivity.

Some device-to-device storage networking applications include:

- Remote mirroring and business continuance
- Disaster recovery and prevention
- Data center migration and consolidation
- Synchronous and asynchronous data mirroring

Some device-to-device storage networking technologies include:

- Fibre Channel using FCP or FICON over dark fiber and DWDM
- Gb Ethernet using iSCSI or iFCP for Open Systems, and FCIP for FCP/FICON (open systems and mainframe environments)
- Wide area networks using SONET/SDH and IP

Some older implementations of hardware-based mirroring and replication had interfaces that did not support flexible Fibre Channel port types, including fabric (N_Port) and loop (NL_Port). The most common cause was a mismatch in port types that was solved by placing a Fibre Channel switch between the storage device and SAN extender device on each end with the WAN in the middle. Newer generations of SAN extenders have added support for more flexible port types, and Fibre Channel switches have also added wide area extension capabilities such as Fibre Channel over IP (FCIP and iFCP). Check with your storage vendor or systems integrator to see if you need to do anything special as part of implementing your wide area SAN and device-to-device SAN.

When connecting two storage devices together via switches with Inter-Switch Links (ISLs) running between them, the two switches are in the same fabric. Consequently, if you have a switch at Site-A and another at Site-B operating as two separate fabrics, by connecting them together to create a link for mirroring, you have joined the two fabrics into a single fabric. This may not be a bad thing, depending on how you have things configured and what your design objectives are; however, keep in mind that you now have one single fabric. So exercise care when connecting two normally standalone switches so as not to inadvertently create a single fabric out of what you may intend to be two standalone fabrics. Adequate bandwidth and traffic prioritizations combined with Quality of Service (QoS) may be needed for your ISLs to support the desired level of performance for mirroring operations. Performance is also going to affect whether you are going to do asynchronous or synchronous mirroring. Newer techniques, including compression, bandwidth optimization, and grouped writes, can help to reduce network bandwidth needs. For example, some storage subsystems can reduce networking bandwidth requirements by sending out grouped writes at variable intervals instead of in a constant stream. QoS and intelligent fabrics can leverage this sort of traffic flow with deterministic routing to optimize SAN traffic. Storage sub-system–based remote data mirroring is now available for enterprise, workgroup, and SMB environments for block, file, and object-based systems.

3.12.3 Server to server

For mainframe S/390 environments, server to server access would be Channel to Channel (CTC) over ESCON or FICON, and for open systems this could be Internet Protocol (IP), uDAPL, or Virtual Interface (VI) over Fibre Channel, Gb Ethernet, and InfiniBand. Server-to-server communications support data movement and processor-to-processor communications. The choice between using a traditional network interface such as Gb Ethernet or storage networking interfaces such as Fibre Channel and InfiniBand should come down to what the requirements are and what the best technology is for the given application. This method is most commonly deployed in environments where data needs to be shared among servers/processors.

Another description for server-to-server activity has been server area networks for clustering, grid computing, and other applications. For open

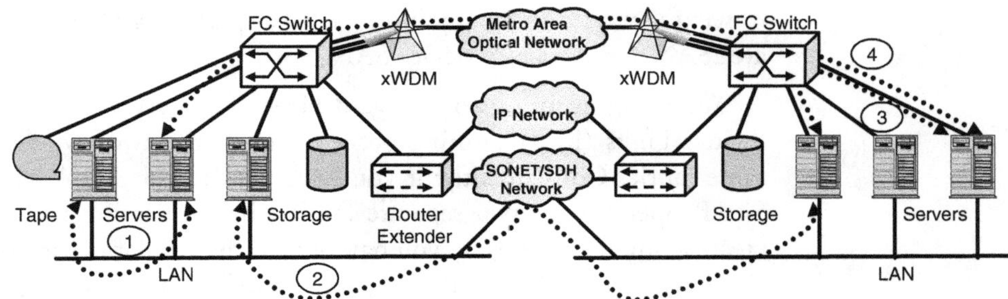

Figure 3.14 *Server-to-server storage (systems area) network example.*

systems, server-to-server traffic has been predominantly IP using Ethernet and Gb Ethernet. For specialized applications and environments, this traffic could be on dedicated subnetworks or storage channels.

For open systems environments, including Linux and Windows, server-to-server communication for cluster management is becoming more important, with the trend toward blade servers, blade centers, grid, and clusters of smaller, less expensive servers compared with traditional eight-way or larger processors. This approach works for applications that can be partitioned and segmented. For long-running and single-threaded tasks, a larger processor is still important. (See Figure 3.14.)

Some server-to-server storage networking applications include:

- S/390 CTC Infrastructure for Intersystem Communication (XCF-Cross-System Coupling Facility, VTAM and TCP/IP, and IMS reads/writes)
- Heartbeat for failover and distributed applications
- Geographically Dispersed Parallel Sysplex (GDPS)
- High-performance distributed filesystems and grid computing
- Clustering and high-availability software
- Grid computing applications and environments
- Distributed lock management (database, filesystems, virtualization)

Some server-to-server storage networking technologies include:

- Interfaces including Fibre Channel (1Gb, 2Gb, 4Gb, 10Gb), InfiniBand, Ethernet (10/100/1,000/10,000)
- Protocols including FICON, VI, IP, MSDA/RDMA/SDP (sockets), TDM over SONET, DWDM, DAPL

- RDMA for low-latency, direct memory access (DMA) without IP overhead

3.12.4 SAN to SAN (bringing it all together)

SAN to SAN can include and support the previous access models. SAN to SAN can be implemented using different approaches, including IP tunneling, bridging, protocol routing, backbone connection using DWDM over dark fiber, or SONET/SDH. Figure 3.15 shows an example SAN-to-SAN configuration that can be used to support server to server for clustering, server to device for remote access, device to device for remote mirroring, and SAN for wide area connectivity. This is an example of how MAN technology can be used to comply with certain regulations involving synchronous and high-speed recovery and survivability. For added protection, wide area technology is used to provide data movement and mirroring out of region and out of theater—for example, from the United State to Europe and Asia.

In this example (Figure 3.15) there are two main fabrics (Fabric-A and Fabric-B) that span two sites (New York and New Jersey) using DWDM to carry Fibre Channel FCP, VI, FICON (including Cascade), and IP traffic

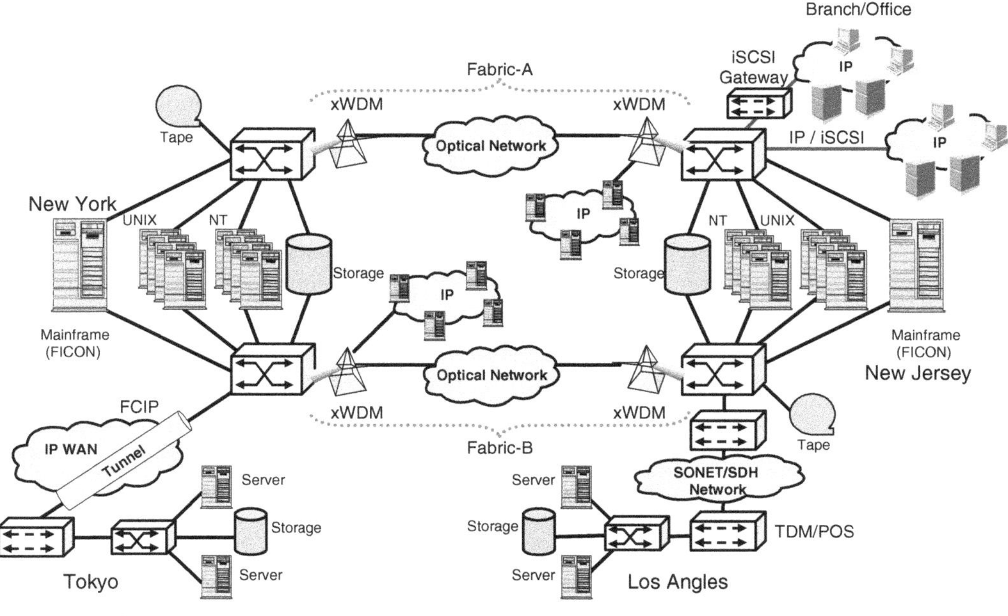

Figure 3.15 *Local, metropolitan, and wide area storage networks.*

along with Gb Ethernet LAN traffic. The two fabrics form a resilient SAN by creating dual fabrics between sites to guard against device, site, and network failure, providing fault containment.

Figure 3.15 shows multiple SANs, each of which is configured for redundancy using dual fabrics under a common storage network management. Each of the fabrics would be considered a domain, with two domains per SAN for redundancy. In this example none of the SANs is interconnected; however, they are under common management. This example could be modified to physically have the three SANs interconnected and logically isolated using zoning and other techniques. In that scenario, to provide redundancy, the A-path from each of the fabrics could be interconnected with the B-path. In Figure 3.15 the SAN on the left (SAN-A) could be made up of a pair of 16 port switches for redundancy and no ISLs. SAN-B, in the middle, could be made up of a pair of large port switches to provide hundreds of usable ports with redundancy and no ISLs. Finally, SAN-C is a collection of switches and/or directors configured as two separate fabrics using ISLs.

Two additional remote satellite SANs (Tokyo and London) connect to Fabric-A (for redundancy best practice is to attach to both Fabric-A and Fabric-B) via SAN-to-SAN links. These links could be FCIP tunneling devices, iFCP gateway, iSCSI, or SONET/SDH as a Fibre Channel backbone. Additional branch sites could access the primary sites in New York and New Jersey and the two satellite locations. The satellite SANs could be part of Fabric-A as a single domain, or, using autonomous regions, they could be physically attached to Fabric-A, yet logically isolated from each other to simplify management, with a configuration similar to how virtual LANs (VLANs) are used to segment LANs.

In this example, a variety of connectivity methods (network types and interfaces) are deployed to meet specific requirements and service objectives for performance, distance, and availability. The net result is that distance barriers are removed to enable continuous access to information and applications anywhere, anytime. As enterprise demands continue to grow, users will look to create global networks such as the one described, or similar to it.

Some SAN-to-SAN storage networking applications include:

- Regulatory compliance
- Data retention, archiving, and protection
- Departmental and workgroup
- Remote or branch office access

- Remote or distributed backup
- Consolidation of SAN islands
- High availability and disaster recovery
- Multitiered backup and recovery

An example of a multitiered backup and recovery scenario is shown in Figure 3.15, where data is mirrored synchronously (real-time) locally in a metropolitan area for business continuance. A second copy of the data is maintained elsewhere in the region using asynchronous (possible time delay) mirroring/copy techniques with off-line copies made and sent to disk or tape media at remote locations using wide area storage networking interfaces. The idea is to support nonstop operations using the synchronous copy while maintaining a rapid recovery for data. For example, the mirroring protects against loss of availability due to a site or hardware basis. Additional protection is needed in case files and data are deleted or corrupted.

Some SAN-to-SAN storage networking technologies include:

- Fibre Channel, InfiniBand, Gb Ethernet, WAN interfaces
- FCP, FICON, SRP, VI, IP, iSCSI, FCIP iFCP, TDM over SONET/SDH, DWDM
- SRP (SCSI RDMA Protocol) on InfiniBand for local cluster access
- Autonomous regions, VLAN tags, and border switches

With more storage, server, and SAN consolidation taking place, SAN-to-SAN configurations are increasingly being used locally as well as on a campus, metropolitan, and wide area basis. Some benefits of connecting SAN (either as a single SAN, or physically connected, logically isolated) include simplified management, improved resource usage, and benefits similar to physically interconnecting various LAN segments.

3.13 Chapter summary

Today, you have flexibility in implementing wide area storage networks with various technologies, including long-distance Fibre Channel, DWDM, SONET/SDH, Gb Ethernet–based frame passers and tunneling devices, and iFCP, FCIP, iSCSI to map SCSI onto IP networks. As with any building project, one can adapt a single tool to do all of the work; however, this may not be the most efficient approach and thus the right tool for the right job should be used.

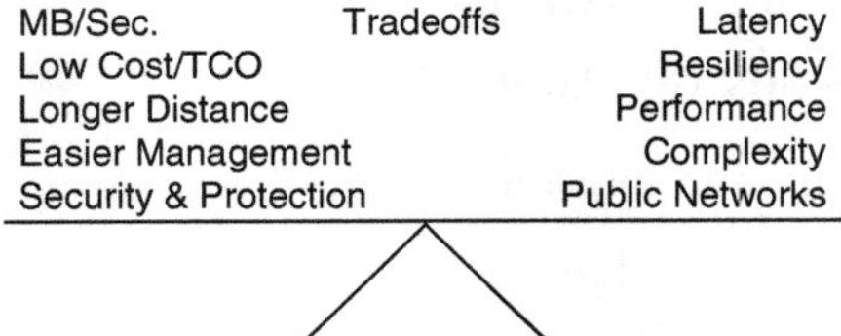

Figure 3.16 *Balancing costs and other tradeoffs.*

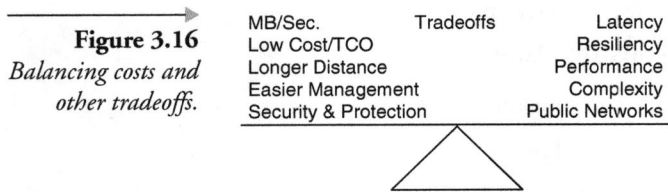

Understanding that distance is critical for a resilient storage networking environment to support a resilient enterprise, Figure 3.16 shows some tradeoffs between more localized (on the left) and more remote (on the right) access. The trade-offs will depend on what your business requirements and application service requirements are.

What This Chapter Will Do For You

This chapter will provide you with information about various storage and networking interfaces, and protocols, to help identify the appropriate technology for your requirements. Some of the items you will learn about in this chapter include:

- Clarifying myths and relationships between networking technologies
- Identifying technologies with different characteristics for specific applications
- How to leverage common infrastructures, including fiber optics, to reduce costs
- Improving design and management by better understanding core technologies

4

Storage and I/O Networks

4.1 Overview

This chapter covers various storage and I/O protocols and interfaces, commonly collectively called networks. This includes upper-level protocols, such as FICON, Fibre Channel SCSI Protocol (FCP), TCP/IP (IP), iSCSI, and lower-level physical interfaces (Fibre Channel, Ethernet, and InfiniBand). In Chapter 5 optical essentials are covered, and in Chapter 6 metropolitan and wide area storage networking interfaces, including Fibre Channel/FICON over IP (FCIP), SONET/SDH, Wave Division Multiplexing (WDM), and Dense Wave Division Multiplexing (DWDM), are covered.

4.2 Storage networking interfaces

Traditional LANs and WANs have been implemented using a variety of different interfaces, the dominant ones for LANs being various flavors of Ethernet (10/100/1,000/10,000Mbps), ATM, and to a lesser extent FDDI and Token Ring. These underlying networks support various upper-level network protocols, with the most common being IP (TCP/IP and TCP/UDP).

The storage path sits between a host computer I/O bus and storage devices (disk and tape). A storage interface enables computers to communicate with storage devices (send and receive data). A storage interface could be parallel IDE/ATA/SATA, SCSI, or Fibre Channel on open systems, or ESCON and FICON in an IBM mainframe environment. While not normally thought of as a storage interface, TCP/IP (IP)–based networks, including Ethernet (10/100, Gigabit and beyond) and FDDI, have been used as storage interfaces for file, clustering, and data sharing. New technology, including iSCSI, iFCP, and FCIP (storage over IP), are being used to enable TCP/IP-based networks to further expand storage networking. Parallel SCSI and Ultra SCSI are still being used for direct attachment of some storage devices to servers and some clusters. Fibre Channel is replacing parallel SCSI in cluster applications, providing increased performance, capacity, distance, and ability to scale beyond parallel SCSI address limits.

4.3 Performance and bandwidth

When dealing with storage, performance response time is measured in milliseconds. Networks are also measured in milliseconds; however, when dealing with WANs, instead of tens of milliseconds, that number could grow to 100 or more depending on latency, congestion, and other delays. End-to-end transmission time includes the time to send and receive data over a network from point-a to point-b. Table 4.1 shows some common units of measure and their relationship to each other, along with symbol and usage comment.

These units of measures have a bearing on response time and performance for local and wide area communications, including storage networking. To support global applications, network response time needs to be kept low to enable timely processing of transactions, messaging, reliable heartbeats for clusters, and storage access. Many different factors, including configuration, shared traffic, protocols, and others, can reduce the actual performance numbers. Something to keep in mind when comparing messaging networks and storage networks is that storage relies on predictable

Table 4.1 *Relative Comparisons of Speed*

Measure	Time	Symbol	Comment
Second	1	Sec	Real World
Millisecond	1,000ms = 1 second (1/1,000 of a second)	Ms	Storage and Networking Measurement
Microsecond	1,000usec = 1ms (1/1,000,000 of a second)	Usec	CPU and Networking Switching
Nanosecond	1,000ns = 1usec (1/1,000,000,000 of a second)	Ns	CPU and Switching

response time behavior associated with channels as opposed to nondeterministic behavior associated with traditional networking.

4.4 Storage and I/O interface

IP is used extensively today to support the Internet and its associated applications and has gone through many years of technology development to support these. Similar development is taking place today with storage over IP technology to enable storage networking to overcome distance barriers and be accessible by applications. IP-based storage networking exists today using NAS, iSCSI, FCIP, and iFCP protocols. IP needs a physical network to run on, for example, either an Ethernet with copper (traditional cabling), fiber optic, or wireless. Storage over IP may require additional bandwidth and, perhaps, a separate network unless your network currently has excess bandwidth.

Table 4.2 shows some common storage interfaces and interconnects in use today along with their characteristics. This is by no means an exhaustive list; rather, it presents some common external storage interfaces. The following text will cover these and other storage and networking protocols and interfaces in more detail.

Table 4.2 *Some I/O and Networking Interface Performance Characteristics*

I/O Interface	Full or Half-Duplex Mode	Bus Width (Bits)	Bus Speed (Clock Frequency)	Bus Bandwidth
10Gb Ethernet	Full	Serial	—	2,000Mbyte/sec FDX
10Gb Fibre Channel	Full	Serial	—	2,000Mbyte/sec
12x InfiniBand HCA	Full	Serial	30Ghz	6Gbyte/sec
4Gb Fibre Channel	Full	Serial	4.250Ghz	850Mbyte/sec
2Gb Fibre Channel	Full	Serial	2.125Ghz	425Mbyte/sec
4x InfiniBand HCA	Full	Serial	10Ghz	2Gbyte/sec
1x InfiniBand HCA	Full	Serial	100–2,000Mhz	500Mbyte/sec
1Gb Fibre Channel	Full	Serial	1.06Ghz	212.5Mbyte/sec
Gb Ethernet	Full	Serial	1.25Ghz	250Mbyte/sec
10/100 Ethernet	Half	Serial	4.100Mhz	1.25 to 12.5Mbyte/sec

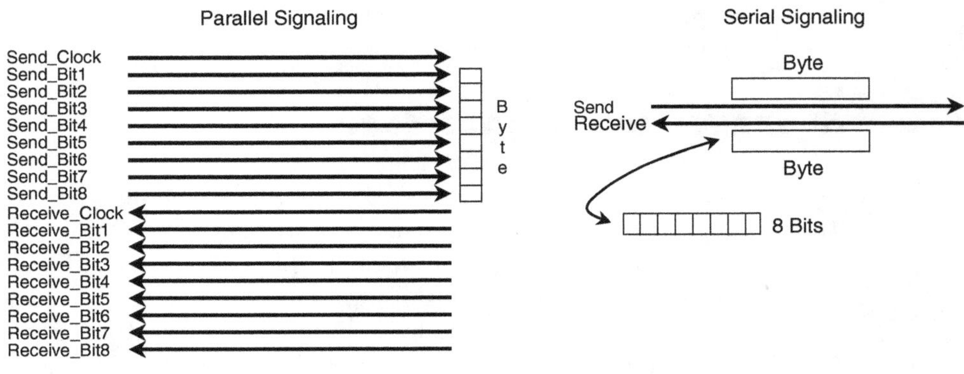

Figure 4.1 *Parallel and serial interfaces for communication.*

4.4.1 Serial and parallel interfaces

Traditional storage interfaces, including parallel SCSI for open systems and IBM S/390 mainframe Bus and Tag (also known as block mux), have utilized parallel signaling. Newer storage and I/O interfaces, including networks, have migrated to serial signaling, particularly when using fiber optics. Parallel interfaces rely on many pairs of wires organized in parallel for sending and receiving data, as seen in Figure 4.1. Separate wires are used for moving individual data bits, clocking for timing, data integrity checks, command, and control. The parallel signaling approach was robust for its time; however, it is also limited in distance and performance and complexity of cabling.

Parallel interfaces move bits of data in parallel, while serial interfaces move bytes of data (bit stream) serially one after another. Serial interfaces are common with optical interfaces, given the nature of optics and light to send a light stream very rapidly and to send a bit stream serially. Serial interfaces are much less complex, with simpler cabling and usually a send and a receive cable. Some networking interfaces and protocols support full-duplex data transmission, enabling data to be sent and received concurrently. Serial interfaces can also span longer distances, as is particularly the case with long-range optics. Serial interfaces enable long-distance capabilities, higher performance, lower cost, and simplified cabling.

4.4.2 Storage I/O basics

Servers access storage by performing input and output (I/O) operations, including reads and writes to peripheral devices over an I/O interface. Servers are referred to as initiators of I/O operations in that they issue reads and writes to devices that are called targets. From a storage standpoint, I/Os to and from storage devices are generally unsolicited in that a storage device typically does not say, "I want to do some I/O"; rather, the server decides it's time to do some I/O. The exception to this would be when a storage device needs to send a notification of some event to the server—for example, that it has a failed component, it needs to report a new device configuration, or another status type of information.

Depending on the storage protocol and interface being used, a device driver assembles the I/O commands and maps them to the specific addressing requirements of the interface and sends them to the storage device. Figure 4.2 shows a generic I/O example, with servers as initiators to send commands to a target device via a channel connection adapter, over a storage interface, or to a storage device via its address. In an open systems environment using the common SCSI I/O command set, the initiator accesses storage via its channel path (adapter and interface bus), device target address, and LUN (subaddress). UNIX and Windows-based system storage may be further accessed by the disk "slice" or partition number. For example, on a Solaris UNIX system an address might be c1t2d3s4, which would be channel c1 host bus adapter (hba) number one on the server; target device two (t2), known as the SCSI device target ID; LUN number three (d3); and disk partition slice number four (s4). Not all devices support multiple LUNs and subaddresses, so in those cases they would be left zero or blank. Servers also have an address that can vary depending on the operating system type, so care should be taken when placing two or more servers on the same storage interface to avoid address conflicts. For IBM mainframe environments I/Os are performed in a similar manner; however, the Channel Control Word (CCW) architecture is used with different terminology. A mainframe application builds a CCW program (I/O command instructions) and places it on a channel (bus) via a channel interface

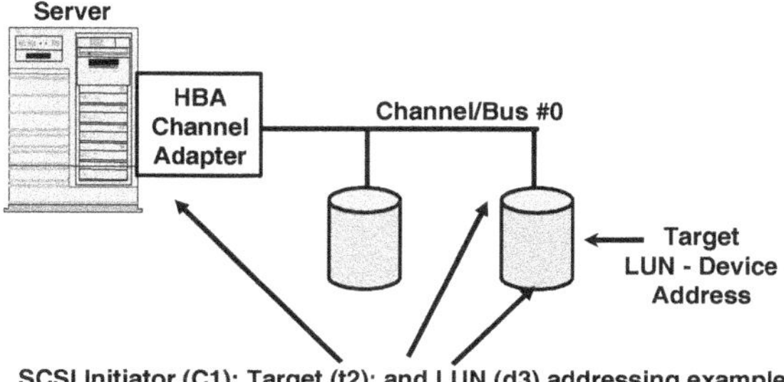

Figure 4.2 *I/O components.*

Figure 4.3 *Comparison of networking interface layers and OSI model.*

OSI Layer	Description	FC Layer	Fibre Channel SAN	Gigabit Ethernet Network	IP Routed Network
7	Application		Filesystem, FTP	FTP, Telnet	FTP, Telnet
6	Presentation		SCSI-3, NFS	HTTP, Telnet	HTTP
5	Session		CCW	NFS, iSCSI	NFS, iSCSI
			FCP, IP, FICON		
4	Transport		VI, AV, AE		TCP, UDP
		FC-4	ULP		
3	Network			TCP (IP & UDP)	IP
		FC-3	Services	MAC Client	LAN,WAN
2	Data link	FC-2	Framing, Flow Control	MAC Client	MAN
				MAC	
1	Physical	FC-1	Encoding, Link	Physical	Physical
		FC-0	Physical		

(adapter) to send it via a channel (bus) to a target storage device (control unit) address and subsequently to a specific device address.

To help put things into perspective, Figure 4.3 shows various network interfaces and protocols using the Open Systems Interconnection (OSI) networking stack model. Networking professionals may be familiar with the OSI model (stack) to depict and understand various networking layers. In Figure 4.3, a combined OSI and Fibre Channel stack model is shown to help understand the similarities and differences between the interfaces and protocols. This includes media, transport, network, and protocol layers to support different applications and functions. Layer 1 is the physical inter-

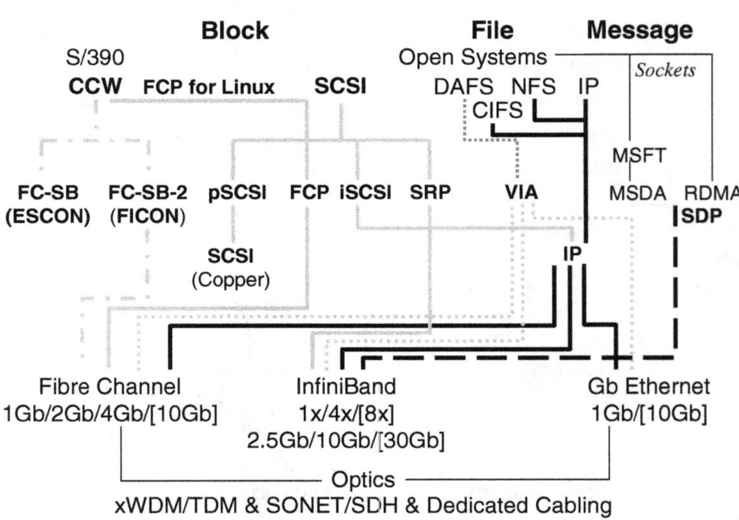

Figure 4.4 *Relationship between various (physical) interfaces and (logical) protocols.*

face (medium), which would be copper or optical cable. Layer 2 is the data link, which would be built on a physical interface (Layer 1).

Figure 4.4 shows the relationship between various physical networking interfaces and associated logical protocols. This helps to clarify some common confusion regarding Fibre Channel being compared with IP, which is comparing a physical (Fibre Channel) interface to a logical (IP) protocol. Looking at Figure 4.4 you can see that IP is a logical protocol, referred by some as a network, that can run on different media (copper, optical, WiFi, etc.) as well as different interfaces (Fibre Channel, Ethernet, ATM, etc.). Similarly, SCSI is a popular storage protocol that can run on parallel copper interfaces (commonly called and known as SCSI and pSCSI) as well as on Fibre Channel (FCP) and Ethernet/IP (iSCSI). There is a common association with FCP and Fibre Channel as being one and the same, similar to how IP and Ethernet are seen as one and the same.

4.5 Upper-level protocols for storage networking

Upper-Level Protocols (ULPs), sometimes also called or known as application layers (see OSI model), are sometimes confused as being the network. ULPs include SCSI, IP, FICON, and iSCSI, and physical interfaces include Fibre Channel, Ethernet, and InfiniBand. Applications interface to the ULPs and include block data movement, file sharing, Web access, terminal access, e-mail, clustering, video transfer, and so on.

4.5.1 ESCON for IBM S/390 and zSeries mainframes

Enterprise Systems Connection (ESCON) is a storage and I/O interface used on IBM S/390 and zSeries mainframes. ESCON implements the IBM S/370 Channel Control Word (CCW) architecture over a fiber-optic interface that is used for performing I/O on mainframes. Based on the S/370 I/O model, I/O is originated from a channel that sends a command based upon a CCW program to a control unit. The CCW is an I/O command packet similar in concept to a SCSI CDB, which tells the channel adapter and control unit on the I/O device what to do. A CCW, similar to a SCSI command sequence, may involve multiple exchanges of commands and information to complete a given I/O operation. ESCON combines CCW I/O with dynamic switched point-to-point fiber-optic interface based upon first-generation proprietary Fibre Channel, called Fibre Channel Single Byte (FC-SB), with a link speed of 17Mbyte/sec (half-duplex). ESCON interfaces can extend 2–3km without repeaters (channel extension) using single-mode fiber cabling. ESCON can be extended over DWDM and WAN interfaces, including E1/T1, E3/T3, 10/100 Ethernet (IP), ATM OC-3, and Gigabit Ethernet, to support device-to-device remote mirroring and replication. This extension capability can be between virtual tape systems (VTS) subsubsystems, storage subsystems, and remote tape for tape vaulting.

Prior to ESCON becoming available in the early 1990s, IBM mainframes utilized bulky Bus and Tag cabling, shown in Figure 4.5 (left), also known as a parallel channel, with speeds ranging from 1.5Mbyte, 3.0Mbyte, to 4.5Mbyte per second per link. IBM mainframe environments with parallel channels relied on complex cabling, which required dedicated connections between the mainframe and I/O devices. ESCON enables servers to attach to a switching device called an ESCON director, which in turn attaches to various I/O devices, including disk, tape, printers, communications, and other peripherals. This capability enables new devices to be added by attaching to open ports on the director and "gened" into the system (if not already done so), as opposed to establishing a dedicated link. In some ways ESCON can be considered an early proprietary storage network in that it enabled multiple IBM and Plug-Compatible Mainframes (PCMs) from Amdahl, Fujitsu, and Hitachi to attach and share storage devices. ESCON also enabled clustering of mainframes, called parallel Sysplex, for failover, shared workload, and creation of Geographically Dispersed Parallel Sysplex (GDPS) for business continuance. ESCON is not an open storage network environment; however, it is a good example of the idea of a shared infrastructure for storage resources. There are over 1 million ESCON ports installed, with some being migrated to FICON.

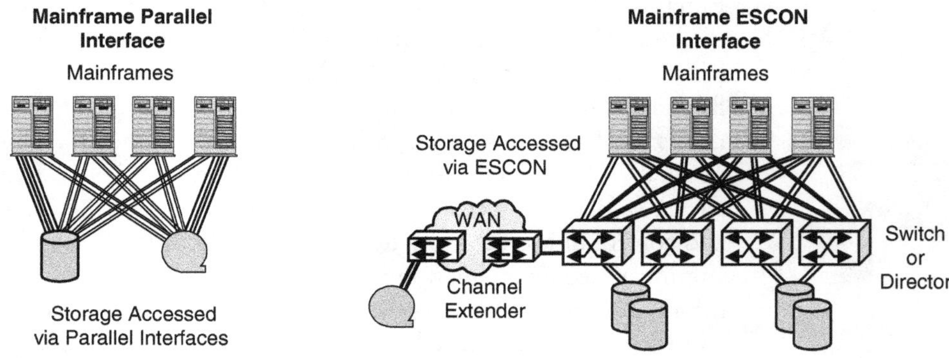

Figure 4.5 *ESCON configuration example.*

4.5.2 FICON—Fibre Channel

Fiber Connection (FICON) architecture is the latest I/O interface for IBM S/390 and zSeries mainframes. FICON (ANSI T11 standard FC-SB-2; SB = single-byte version two) is an FC-4 (Fibre Channel Layer-4) upper layer protocol (ULP) implementing the IBM CCW I/O architecture. Since FICON is a ULP, it can coexist on the same Fibre Channel network as other ULPs, including FCP. FICON is considered by some to be ESCON on "steroids" and thus ESCON on Fibre Channel, providing more performance, more addresses for devices, and more distance. FICON implements CCW I/O to access CKD and ECKD devices (disk and tape) similar to ESCON (FC-SB). With the advent of FICON-enabled storage, S/390 environments are now able to drive channel interfaces at over 200MB/sec (2Gb) versus traditional ESCON 17MB/sec, over distances of 100km, with expanded addressing. These benefits are further leveraged in that FICON utilizes the same physical networking interfaces and connectivity infrastructure as open systems Fibre Channel (FCP)–based storage networking. This capability is an important step toward the long-awaited promise of a shared storage network, storage utility model. The FICON–enabled processor (zSeries, 9672 G5 and G6) appears as N_Port (Node Ports) to the underlying Fibre Channel infrastructure that is used as the physical transport for FICON (FC-SB-2).

FICON is a full-duplex implementation of IBM S/370 CCW I/O architecture. FICON, without using the FICON Cascade feature, is a single-hop protocol. This means that unless the FICON Cascade feature is installed, only a single switching device (director) can exist between devices (processors, disk and tape subsystems). With ESCON you can have two directors between devices, with each director considered a hop. One of the directors is considered static, while the other is dynamic from an addressing standpoint. When the FICON Cascade feature is installed on IBM zSeries mainframe and a FICON-enabled switch, two directors can exist between devices to support various configurations, with both directors being dynamic. This enhanced flexibility enables FICON to be used for multisite and business continuance purposes applications. FICON Cascade is a feature that is implemented at the zOS server as a software enhancement and enables multihop FICON I/Os to occur over two FICON switches, which include directors. FICON Cascade is an optional software feature for zOS and for FICON switches. Fabric security is an optional feature that can be installed on switches to create a secure communication link for FICON using fabric binding. FICON utilizes fixed, server-based I/O addressing, unlike open systems environments using FCP that can exploit the underlying dynamic

Table 4.3 *Various FICON Operating Modes*

FICON Mode	FICON Characteristic
Bridged (FCV)	FCV stands for FICON conversion mode and enables ESCON devices to be attached to a FICON bridge for attachment to a FICON server. FCV mode operates as a subset of FICON, with some features, including full duplex, being disabled.
Cascade	Enables two multihop FICON I/Os to occur using two or more FICON switching directors daisy chained, cascaded together locally or over distance to support multisite configurations for business continuance and to increase horizontal scaling.
FCP (FCP)	Enables a FICON channel to be configured for FCP use to support native Linux on a zSeries processor.
FICON Express	Full-speed FICON at 100MB and now 200MB/sec or 200MB/sec and 400MB/sec in full-duplex mode. The actual throughput was raised from the original 65Mbyte/sec to about 165Mbyte/sec (half duplex).
Native (FC)	First native FICON implementation that operated at less than 100MB/sec, providing a steppingstone to full-speed FICON (Express) performance and capabilities.

addressing and pathing capabilities of Fibre Channel. FICON Cascade requires secure fabrics to ensure integrity of the underlying SAN fabric to prevent unauthorized switches and directors from interrupting the I/O path. Currently there are five types of FICON implementations that can be configured into different configurations; these are shown in Table 4.3.

The FICON Bridge exists in an ESCON director as a card that converts FICON commands to ESCON (FC-SB) commands to communicate with ESCON control unit device ports. Advanced FICON features, such as full-duplex (400Mbyte/sec at 2Gb) data transmission, mixed disk and tape traffic, and full performance and bandwidth are among those not supported with FICON Bridge. FICON (FC-SB-2) differs from other Fibre Channel–based Upper-Level Protocols (ULPs), such as SCSI_Fibre Channel Protocol (FCP), that provide dynamic addressing and resolution in that FICON

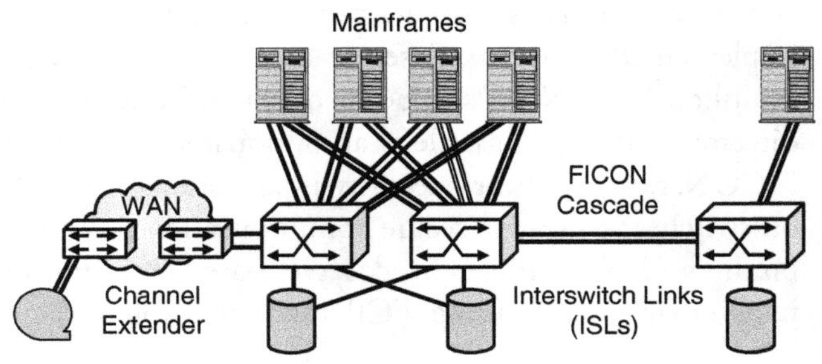

Figure 4.6 *FICON interface example, including FICON Cascade.*

relies on fixed addressing defined via HCD, IOCP mainframe software utilities. In Figure 4.6, there is a single FICON channel on the processor; however, multiple images, known as Logical Partitions (LPAR), and multiple control unit images share the same FICON link.

FICON supports multiple I/Os of various sizes on the same channel concurrently and utilizes full-duplex communication to improve throughput. Small and large block data can be intermixed on the same channel with impact to an application performance, enabling mixed workloads and device types. FICON, unlike ESCON, can coexist with other ULPs on the same storage network to enable open systems utilizing FCP and mainframes to share switching infrastructure.

Protocol Intermix Mode (PIM), shown in Figure 4.7, is a feature supported by IBM on zSeries and other FICON-enabled processors that allows FICON and open systems Fibre Channel (FCP) traffic to coexist on the same physical network. Traditionally, mainframe ESCON traffic and open systems traffic had to be isolated on separate physical networks. With FICON PIM, host traffic can coexist on the Fibre Channel/FICON switching director as open systems. To simplify cabling, PIM enables zOS, Linux, and other operating systems to coexist on the same network along with the AS/400, Windows/NT, and UNIX.

Some examples of PIM usage include:

- A small FICON and open systems environment with common storage network
- A zSeries processor that accesses storage via FICON and storage devices that utilize FCP to perform remote mirroring between devices instead of ESCON

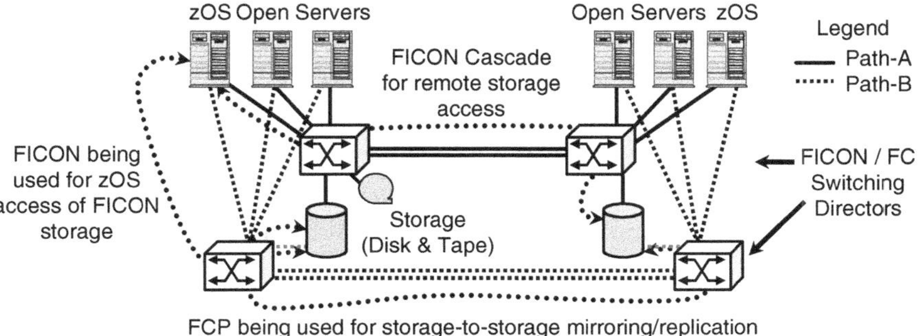

Figure 4.7 *FICON Protocol Intermix Mode (PIM) and Cascade.*

- Open systems servers accessing storage on the same storage network using FCP
- Linux on the zSeries located at either site using FCP to access storage
- The zSeries at both locations running zOS using FICON to access local storage
- Hardware-based remote mirroring between two locations using FCP as a transport
- The zOS servers accessing remote FICON storage via FICON Cascade

To intermix open systems and FCP traffic with FICON traffic depends on your environment, operating practices, and philosophies. While you may not want to intermix open systems and FICON traffic on the same SAN, you might have FICON and remote mirroring traffic using FCP coexisting, which is becoming more common.

A best practice, for Fibre Channel, ESCON, FICON, and parallel SCSI, is redundant and isolated paths. Another best practice when using PIM is to use a combination of Fibre Channel zoning and FICON port prohibit blocks. Utilize the FICON port prohibits to block FICON ports from open systems ports and then utilize zoning for the open systems and FICON ports. For example, place FICON ports in a zone separate from open systems ports. Always use a combination of zoning and port prohibit blocks for a PIM environment and follow vendor-specific guidelines. FICON and PIM can be used to support consolidation, including workload, data centers, server, and storage. It is important to understand the possibilities and caveats of using PIM and follow best practices. Ultimately, what is right for your environment depends on your needs, capabilities, and storage management philosophies.

Table 4.4 shows some comparisons between ESCON and FICON, including the increased number of devices, addresses, distance, and performance of FICON over ESCON. Table 4.5 shows various ESCON-to-FICON equivalency ratios of what is possible when consolidating ESCON-to-FICON interfaces. A word of caution: Your application performance and workload should be analyzed and reviewed to assess what is the appropriate equivalency ratio to be used. The equivalency ratio shown in Table 4.5 refers to how many ESCON channels can be converted to FICON channels under different workloads. For example, for light ESCON workloads, a single FICON channel could replace eight ESCON channels. For I/O-intensive workloads, a single FICON channel would replace fewer ESCON channels. Equivalency ratios are not unique to

Table 4.4 *ESCON and FICON Comparisons*

	ESCON	FICON
Bandwidth	17MB	200MB (400MB Full Duplex)
Command execution	Synchronous	Asynchronous
Duplex	Half	Full
Switching	Circuit Switching	Packet Switching
Distances (no repeaters)	3km	10–100km depending on optics (CWDM, WDM, DWDM, long-range GBICs, and SFPs)
Repeated distance	9km	100km+
Frame transfer buffer	1Kbyte	128Kbyte
Unit Address/Channel Devices per Channel	1,024 Devices	16,000+ Devices (architecture supports more)
Control Unit Images/Control Unit Link	16	255

FICON and ESCON; similarly, you can derive ratios for how many SCSI adapters could be replaced by a Fibre Channel (FCP) adapter. Actual performance and characteristics will vary, so careful planning is required, and, where appropriate, seek experienced assistance.

More material about IBM ESCON and FICON can be found at www.redbooks.ibm.com.

Table 4.5 *ESCON-to-FICON Equivalency Comparisons*

ESCON-to-FICON Equivalency Ratio	Channel Utilization	Application
8:1	100%	Tape processing
6:1	75%	Light I/O workload
4:1	50%	Mixed Workloads
2:1	25%	I/O intensive
1:1	13%	Channel to Channel (CTC)

4.5.3 SCSI command set

To many people the term *SCSI interface* means a thick, bulky cable with copper wires that could only extend to about 25m and performance in the 20–40Mbytes/second range. Well, that does describe a generation and implementation of SCSI on the SCSI Parallel Interface (SPI); however, the SCSI command set and architecture model have separated the SCSI protocol from different physical networks, as seen in Figure 4.8. This means that an application can issue I/O and that the operating system would use its SCSI drivers and associated hardware drivers to perform the I/O.

4.5.4 SCSI Fibre Channel Protocol (FCP)—Fibre Channel

The SCSI Fibre Channel Protocol (FCP) implements the SCSI command set on the physical Fibre Channel interface, as seen in Figure 4.8. FCP is a Fibre Channel Layer 4 (FC-4) ULP commonly used by open systems and other platforms, including IBM iSeries (AS400), UNIX, Linux, Windows, Novell, and legacy platforms such as OpenVMS. FCP is commonly referred

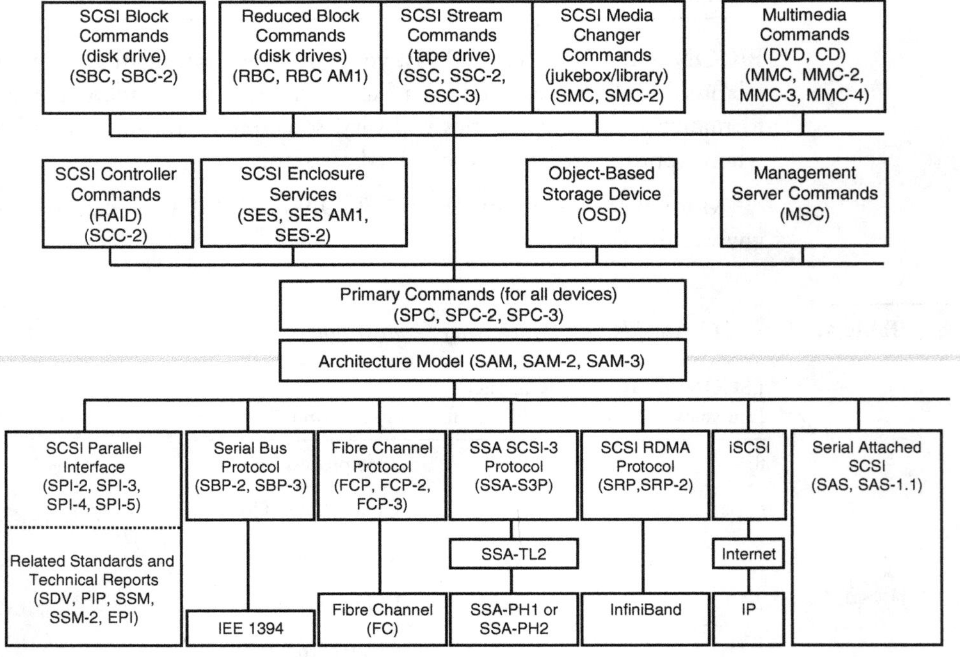

Figure 4.8 *SCSI protocol family utilizing different interfaces.*

to as simply Fibre Channel, with the perception that Fibre Channel and FCP are one and the same. Recently, IBM has added FCP support to zSeries mainframes running native Linux as an alternative to using ESCON and FICON. For zSeries mainframes running zOS (formerly known as MVS) they still utilize FICON and ESCON. Fibre Channel supports running multiple ULPs concurrently, including FCP and FICON, in what is called Protocol Intermix Mode (PIM). Since FCP is an implementation of the SCSI command set, bridges, also known as routers, can be set up to translate SCSI traffic from parallel SCSI to FCP, IBM serial storage architecture (SSA) to FCP, and iSCSI to FCP. Using FCP, SCSI block data traffic for disk, tape, and other devices can operate in full-duplex mode at up to 400MB/sec with 2Gb interfaces over distances of 100km and longer. FCP supports more devices per interface compared with parallel SCSI as well as more flexible topologies compared with simple point-to-point bus configurations. More information about FCP and Fibre Channel can be found at www.t11.org.

4.5.5 SCSI RDMA Protocol (SRP)—InfiniBand

Another example of the SCSI command set being mapped to an interface is SCSI RDMA Protocol (SRP) for use with InfiniBand. RDMA leverages 10Gb technology, including Fibre Channel, Gb Ethernet, and InfiniBand, to eliminate traditional hardware and software overhead as data is copied from application to application using kernel memory, software drivers, and I/O stacks (all adding latency, costing CPU cycles, and complexity). RDMA places DMA support at the NIC/HBA with an offload engine that supports a zero copy/overhead approach to moving data between memories of different processors. An application makes a call to the RDMA, which, in turn, can move data from the buffers of application memory to the remote NIC that can move the data into the application buffers without CPU intervention. There is a security mechanism; however, this is also all done without expensive processor context switching, network traffic, and overhead. Data is not copied over the network per se—rather, from buffer to buffer. The remote memory appears to be virtual for the operation being handled by RDMA. Other protocols that use RDMA include SCSI RDMA Protocol (SRP) and Direct Access File System (DAFS). Communications libraries such as DAPL or Direct Access Provider Library, Message Passing Interface (MPI), and Virtual Interface Provider Library (VIPL) support RDMA. These can be used for clustering, distributed filesystems, and grid computing. Databases can utilize RDMA via DAPL or VIPL for scaling and performance.

4.5.6 iSCSI (SCSI on IP)—SCSI/iSCSI/TCP/IP/Ethernet

Sometimes called Internet SCSI and IP SCSI, iSCSI converges a traditional block storage protocol and maps it onto TCP/IP as a virtual transport over various network interfaces, including Gb Ethernet and 10Gb Ethernet. iSCSI became an official standard in early 2003, and its development has been coordinated by the IETF iSCSI working group. Similar to other SCSI implementations, including parallel SCSI and FCP for Fibre Channel, iSCSI enables block data and SCSI commands to transmit over traditional IP-based networks, including wide area interfaces. Host processors with an iSCSI-enabled adapter and appropriate drivers can initiate I/O to iSCSI-enabled storage devices (targets), including bridges and gateways. An IP storage network using iSCSI can be set up using appropriate Ethernet Network Interface Cards (NICs), iSCSI-enabled Storage Networking Interface Cards (SNICs), and HBAs (along with drivers from various vendors, including HP and Microsoft).

An iSCSI storage network can use traditional Ethernet-based switches and places iSCSI packets inside IP frames, as shown in Figure 4.9. Care should be taken to assess your network infrastructure to determine what impact, if any, will be placed on it by additional iSCSI traffic, as well as what impact your network will have on your storage performance. The iSCSI Protocol enables traditional block storage applications, including database, e-mail, and backup, to be performed over longer distances for remote applications. Another use for iSCSI is small workgroup, departmental, and SMB, where block access is needed to share storage among servers and file servers; however, the cost and complexity of traditional storage networking interfaces such as a Fibre Channel are not applicable. As a popular networking protocol (IP) and storage protocol (SCSI) iSCSI is able to be

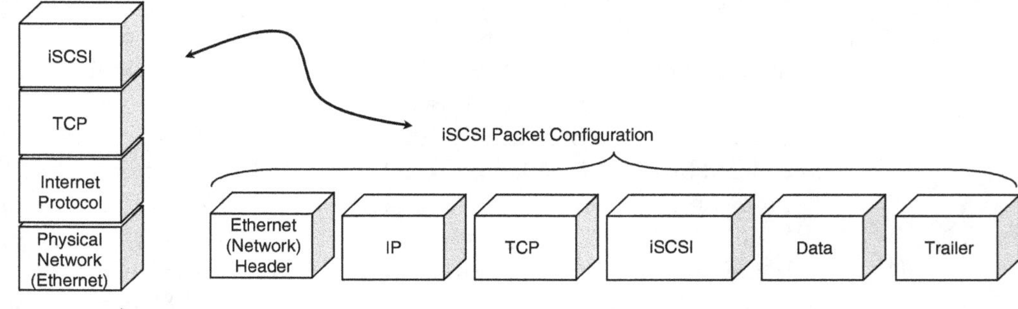

Figure 4.9 *iSCSI layers and packet configuration.*

positioned to be used for new applications and to redefine what is currently thought of as the cutting edge of the storage networking environment.

Some iSCSI benefits include:

- Leveraging a proven underlying physical networking infrastructure (Ethernet) and other IP-based networks and topologies
- Leveraging knowledge of TCP/IP and TCP/UDP networking protocols
- Leveraging higher speeds of 1Gb and 10Gb Ethernet networks and beyond
- Ability to map onto other IP-based networks, including WiFi, for flexibility
- Ability to align to different application needs, including distance, flexibility, and lower cost

Some iSCSI applications include:

- Server and storage consolidation using low cost and existing infrastructure
- Remote site access, data backup, archiving, and protection
- Alternative to NAS file sharing for storage sharing applications
- Provide sharing of storage for servers and NAS filers
- Enable remote systems to access core located Fibre Channel devices
- Enable network access for applications requiring block storage (e-mail, database)

Some iSCSI storage networking components include:

- Ethernet and IP-capable switches
- Bridges, routers, and gateways
- Storage devices (disk and tape)
- Servers with iSCSI interfaces and drivers

I/O size and loading may have to be monitored with iSCSI due to mapping sequential SCSI blocks on an Ethernet frame—for example, databases of 4.16Kbyte I/O sizes.

While iSCSI started out with a bang, including lots of hype, it has retrenched, matured, passed the standards process, and is now being deployed in different configurations and environments. To help jump-start the marketplace, leading storage vendors have made available Gb Ethernet multifunction blades for their enterprise storage subsystems that support iSCSI. Meanwhile, in mid-2003 Microsoft began shipping iSCSI drivers for certain Windows platforms, along with HP, for some HP-UX environments. The list of vendors offering iSCSI devices continues to grow, creating a new term called JAiD (Just Another iSCSI Device). For more information about iSCSI and IP storage, refer to www.ietf.org/html.charters/ips-charter.html.

4.5.7 IBM Serial Storage Architecture (SSA)

IBM Serial Storage Architecture (SSA) implements the SCSI command set on a serial interface similar to Fibre Channel loop topology with dual links and concurrent traffic flows. It's not coincidental that SSA and Fibre Channel have many similarities, including utilizing serial interfaces and the SCSI command. SSA has different link speeds, including 20MB/sec and 40MB/sec, with higher overall bandwidth derived from spatial reuse. Spatial reuse results in a much higher overall bandwidth by leveraging the ability of SSA to have multiple I/Os taking place concurrently. For example, a device could be sending and receiving while other devices are also sending and receiving elsewhere in the SSA environment, resulting in an overall performance boost. This is similar to a Fibre Channel switched environment where multiple I/O operations can take place concurrently for an overall higher bandwidth. The speed of an individual link determines how fast a specific I/O operation will operate. While SSA is still being deployed by IBM today and can be found as back-end storage on the enterprise storage subsystems such as the IBM ESS, it is generally giving way to other interfaces, including Fibre Channel and IP-based networks. More information about IBM SSA can be found at www.storage.ibm.com/hardsoft/products/ssa/.

4.5.8 Parallel SCSI—Parallel electrical cabling

The Small Computer System Interface (SCSI), pronounced "Scuzzy," and its derivatives are the dominant storage interface on Windows, UNIX, Linux, and other platforms today. SCSI is used to access peripheral devices, ranging from CD and DVD players, printers and scanners, and disk and tape devices. When you hear SCSI you may think of bulky cables, flat parallel ribbon cables, 50- and 68-pin connectors, and similar items. SCSI is a combination hardware interface and logical command set that can be combined, as is the case for parallel SCSI implantations, or separated, with the SCSI command set implanted on other interfaces.

The parallel SCSI interface and protocol combination continues to evolve from its initial 5MB/sec capabilities of the 1980s to being able to perform at hundreds of MB/secs today. For example, Ultra SCSI parallel interface can operate over short distances at up to 360MB/sec, and SCSI Fibre Channel Protocol (SCSI_FCP), more commonly known as FCP, can currently operate at up to 400MB/sec full duplex with 10GB (20GB/sec full duplex) on the horizon. Parallel SCSI, being a bus-based storage interface, is sensitive to reconfiguration when adding devices. Parallel SCSI is limited to less than 30m, depending on the speed, number of nodes, and devices. Parallel SCSI is also limited to the number of devices that can be attached and the topologies that can be used. Performance of parallel SCSI has increased well beyond traditional SCSI; however, it lacks the distance and scalability of new storage interfaces.

Parallel SCSI has been used in the past as a clustering and storage interface, called a multiinitiator configuration, shown in Figure 4.10. Care must be taken when configuring parallel SCSI-based storage to ensure that maximum distances and number of devices per SCSI bus are not exceeded. Another activity is to ensure that all addresses (computer and storage devices) are unique on each SCSI bus. In multiinitiator environments, care must also be taken that each host server has a unique SCSI ID and that proper termination of the SCSI bus does not leave it open.

The many implementations of parallel SCSI are shown in Table 4.6 and range from first-generation 5MB/sec SCSI to Ultra320 SCSI operating at up to 320MB/sec. The maximum distance of a parallel SCSI bus varies depending on the speed and number of devices. Older parallel SCSI host servers and devices can participate in a modern storage network using gateways or routers. The benefit of using Fibre Channel to SCSI routers is that existing IT assets (servers and devices) can be used for investment protection to reduce Total Cost of Ownership (TCO) and maximize Return On Investment (ROI). For example, existing IT assets can be redeployed to a

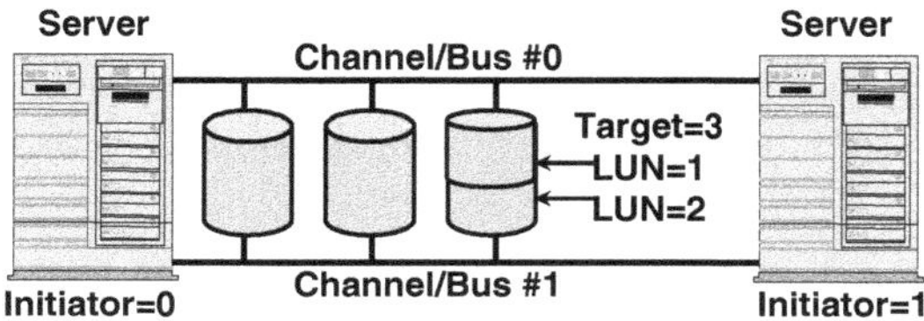

Figure 4.10 *Multiinitiator parallel SCSI example.*

Table 4.6 *Parallel SCSI Characteristics*

	Speed (MB/s)	Number Devices	Bus Width (bits)	SE Distance	LVD Distance	HVD Distance
SCSI-1	5	8	8	6m	*	25m
Fast SCSI	10	8	8	3m	*	25m
Fast Wide SCSI	20	16	16	3m	*	25m
Ultra SCSI	20	8	8	1.5	*	25m
Ultra SCSI	20	4	8	3	—	—
Wide Ultra SCSI	40	16	16	—	*	25
Wide Ultra SCSI	40	8	16	1.5	—	—
Wide Ultra SCSI	40	4	16	3	—	—
Ultra2 SCSI	40	8	8	—	12	25
Wide Ultra2 SCSI	80	16	16	—	12	25
Ultra3 SCSI or Ultra160 SCSI	160	16	16	—	12	—
Ultra320 SCSI	320	16	16	—	12	—

* 12m if all devices are LVD.

secondary site for disaster recovery. This would also enable older host servers to be backed up using LAN-Free and other storage networking backup techniques, as well as access shared Fibre Channel storage devices. More information about SCSI can be found at www.scsita.org.

4.5.9 VIA—InfiniBand/Ethernet/Fibre Channel

Virtual Interface Architecture (VIA) is a ULP that be implemented on various networking interfaces, including InfiniBand, Ethernet, and Fibre Channel, for low-latency, high-speed communication. VIA has been primarily associated with InfiniBand, although there are Fibre Channel and Ethernet implementations. VIA can be used for high-speed messaging applications for server-to-server communication, including distributed lock management, Channel To Channel (CTC), and distributed access filesystems such as DAFS.

4.5.10 DAPL—InfiniBand

DAPL and its various versions are ULPs for supporting high-speed, low-latency communication, including distributed and clustered database systems. There are user DAPL (uDAPL) and kernel (kDAPL) implementations of APIs being developed to support distributed storage networking applications, including databases, clusters, and high-performance filesystems. uDAPL is being driven by the DAT collaborative industry organization and is a transport-independent, operating system–independent API to leverage RDMA capabilities found in InfiniBand, Virtual Interface Architecture (VIA), and iWARP. By leveraging RDMA technology, uDAPL is being adopted by database and other application vendors to deploy scalable, high-performance distributed applications and clusters. The importance of DAPL and storage networking is to support distributed filesystems, parallel database, and clustered systems. Additional DAPL and uDAPL information can be found at www.datcollaborative.org.

4.5.11 Storage over IP

Storage over IP (SoIP) and IP storage generally refer to using an IP-based network as the underlying virtual infrastructure for supporting storage networking functions. There are a couple of things that can be done with IP storage; these include file (NAS), block (iSCSI), and distance support (iSCSI, FCIP, and iFCP). IP can be used and thought of as a virtual network layer that sits on top of other physical networks (Ethernet, FDDI, SONET/SDH, and even Fibre Channel) and is ubiquitous in its nature (being the lowest common denominator network).

Some of the benefits of utilizing storage over IP (SoIP) include:

- Providing enhanced distances greater than standard Fibre Channel
- Leveraging existing IP Ethernet LAN and WAN infrastructures
- Utilizing IP, Ethernet, and WAN networking skill set and knowledge base
- Providing interconnect between Fibre Channel–based (FCP and FICON) core SANs
- Enabling distance applications, including backup, clusters, and distributed storage
- Improving economics with different tiers of price/performance/functionality

Table 4.7 *IP Storage Characteristics Summary*

	iSCSI	FCIP	IFCP	NAS
File Access	—	—	—	Yes
Gateway	Maps SCSI onto different networks	Tunnel ULPs over IP	Yes	File Access
SCSI Block	Yes	Tunnel	Gateway	Via File
Tunnel	—	Yes	—	—

Table 4.7 shows some SoIP mechanisms and their functionality, ranging from file sharing using NAS to block storage access with bridging and gateway connectivity capabilities in the middle.

By building on channel extension and leveraging open interoperability, new gateways (routers) are enabling wide area storage networking beyond MAN distances. A difference between traditional channel extenders and storage networking routers is device and protocol independence. Storage networking routers provide tunneling of SANs over wide area networks regardless of server, HBA, storage, and application. Some examples are iSCSI routers (Fibre Channel to IP), FCIP and iFCP (Fibre Channel over IP), and FCBB (Fibre Channel backbone over ATM). Tunneling, on the other hand, enables all traffic (frames or packets) to pass from one network to the other over a wide area interface to bridge sites together.

4.5.12 TCP Offload Engines (TOEs)

This has helped reduce the cost of networking by enabling relatively low-cost hardware to be used while doing more in software. This relatively low-cost hardware has helped popularize IP and its value proposition as a storage networking interface. One of the criticisms of IP has been that it consumes a large amount of CPU overhead, particularly when processing storage-related functions. To overcome this issue, new technology, called TCP Offload Engines (TOEs), is being developed that will be implemented on new NICs for storage networking to offload the CPU. This could be a benefit to other IP applications as well as enabling storage networking over IP. More information about TCP TOEs can be found at www.10gea.org.

4.6 Storage and networking interfaces

The storage and networking interfaces, including Fibre Channel, InfiniBand, and Ethernet, along with metropolitan and wide area network technologies, will be covered in Chapter 6. Storage and network interfaces utilize physical interfaces, including fiber-optic cabling and copper/electrical networks. Various physical topologies can be implemented using different storage and networking interfaces to support the various ULPs. Chapter 8 provides a closer look at some topologies that can be implemented for different purposes. Storage and networking interfaces transform physical interfaces into transport mechanisms to support various ULPs in different applications.

4.6.1 Fibre Channel (1Gb, 2Gb, 4Gb, 10Gb)

Fibre Channel is the most commonly used interface for storage networking today. Fibre Channel is commonly thought of as both an upper-level logical network and a physical network; consequently, many people mistakenly make comparisons such as Fibre Channel versus iSCSI, FICON versus Fibre Channel, and so forth. As seen earlier in this chapter, Fibre Channel is the underlying physical network that supports various ULPs, including FCP, IP, and FICON. People commonly associate Fibre Channel and FCP as being one and the same; however, FCP is a ULP that runs on Fibre Channel—similar to IP running on an Ethernet network.

For resilient server-to-server communications, IP over Fibre Channel is being used for cluster heartbeat, NAS, and LAN-Free backup to offload network and server workloads. For S/390 environments, FICON on Fibre Channel is being used for access of disk, tape, and print resources up to 100km. Fibre Channel is being used in the open systems environment to access and share disk and tape resources as a resilient infrastructure. In some environments, IP, FICON, and Fibre Channel coexist on a common resilient infrastructure to support the resilient enterprise. Similar to parallel SCSI, Fibre Channel can automatically speed match between 1Gb, 2Gb, and 4Gb devices for compatibility. Various Fibre Channel speeds are shown in Table 4.8, with Mbytes/second and line rate. Fibre Channel interfaces of 1Gb, 2Gb, and 4Gb are interoperable with each other; however, they operate at the lowest common denominator speed. For example, if you intermixed 1Gb and 2Gb interfaces, the affected ports would operate at 1Gb. On a switch with 2Gb ports a port operating at 1Gb should not force all

Table 4.8 *Fibre Channel Link Speeds*

Speed	Throughput MBps (Full Duplex)	Line Rate (Gbaud)	Common Optical Connector Type
10Gb FC	2,400	10.5 or 3.1875	XFP
4Gb FC	800	4.25	SFP with LC
2Gb FC	400	2.125	SFP with LC
1Gb FC	200	1.0625	GBIC and SC

others to operate at 1Gb. With the interoperability of 1Gb, 2Gb, and 4Gb, newer adapters, switch ports, and storage interfaces can be intermixed for investment protection. Interfaces of 10Gb are initially targeted for use as ISLs, with proprietary implementations followed by open interoperable interfaces. A 10Gb server adapter and storage interface ports are in development to support faster data transfers in the future. Performance of Fibre Channel and Ethernet is commonly referred to in throughput of Megabytes or Megabits per second. Another method for measuring speed is the baud rate, which is the signaling rate between two devices per second. In the case of Gbit interfaces such as Fibre Channel and Ethernet, this is measured in Gbaud (Gigabits per second).

Fibre Channel is an ANSI standard supporting flexible topologies and multiple protocols. Fibre Channel supports several Upper-Level Protocols (ULPs), including SCSI, TCP/IP, FICON, and VI, for different application requirements concurrently. Fibre Channel can be configured into various topologies to meet different needs locally and over long distances, as seen in Table 4.9.

Fibre Channel contains properties of storage I/O channels with the flexibility of a network interface. I/O channels are predictable, highly reliable interfaces supporting high-performance deterministic behavior with high availability. Channels are not as general purpose as networks and thus tend to be more expensive—however, more robust. Fibre Channel supports many Upper-Level Protocols (ULPs) and applications. The predominant use of Fibre Channel has been for accessing open systems storage using the SCSI_FCP (SCSI Fibre Channel Protocol) ULP. SCSI_FCP (FCP) maps the SCSI-3 command set and addressing physical Fibre Channel interface. Fibre Channel enables multiple ULPs to coexist simultaneously on the same interface. Another Fibre Channel ULP TCP/IP (not to be confused with the iSCSI protocol) can be used for handling IP traffic between servers instead of over congested networks for LAN-Free backup and NAS. The

Table 4.9 *Fibre Channel Topologies*

Topology	Known As	Characteristics and application
Arbitrated Loop	FC-AL	Shared bandwidth loop environment with both public loop device (FCAL) and private loop devices (PLDA) using cabling from device to device in a ring or using a hub concentrator. Up to 126 devices (NL_Ports) can attach to a loop with one extra port (total 127) for attachment to a fabric (FL_Port). Loops were initially deployed for attachment of servers to storage, and some implementations still continue with the most common form of loop being used as a back-end storage interface in storage subsystems.
Point to point	Direct Connect	Direct connection from server-to-storage device without a switch or hub using an N_Port for simple environments with few servers and many ports on the storage device.
Switched	Fabric	Fabric with one or more switches configured together using an interswitch link (ISL) in various topologies, including mesh, ring, cascade, and core edge. Servers with fabric ports (N_Ports) and fabric loop (NL_Ports) attach to switch fabric and fabric loop ports (F_Ports and FL_Ports) to communicate with storage devices. Switches are interconnected with expansion ports (E_Ports). There can be maximum use of 239 switching devices in a fabric, also called a domain, with each switching device having a unique domain ID. There can be multiple fabrics isolated from each other logically or physically, similar to LAN subnet segments.

Virtual Interface Architecture (VIA) is another ULP that has been deployed on Ethernet, ATM, Fibre Channel, and InfiniBand for low-latency messaging applications. VIA applications include clustering, distributed lock management for databases, and distributed filesystems.

Fibre Channel implements a 24-bit (3-byte) address consisting of a domain (byte-0), area (byte-1), and port (byte-2). Nodes (servers, storage, and switches) are identified by a unique WorldWide Node Name (WWNN), sometimes also referred to as WWN, which is similar to a unique Ethernet MAC address. WWNNs are 8 bytes and are uniquely registered to each manufacturing vendor of the device or adapter card. WWNNs are generally fixed; however, some adapter vendors have special utilities to change a WWNN to facilitate maintenance and swapping of devices that have applications tied to a specific address. Many devices support more than one interface port, so there is a secondary address name called the WorldWide Port Name (WWPN). For example, a server can have an adapter, or an adapter with two ports, each with a unique WWPN and sharing a common WWNN. Storage devices would have a WWNN, and each path to a volume or LUN would have a unique WWPN, as seen in Figure 4.11.

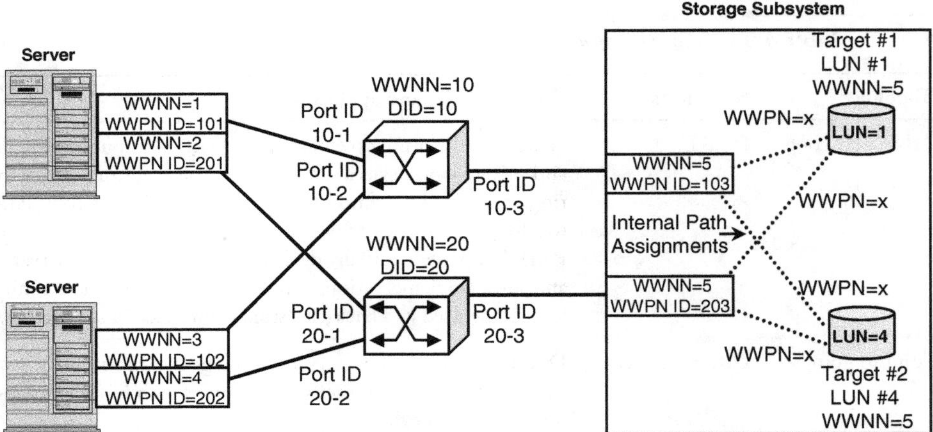

Figure 4.11 *Fibre Channel addressing with WWNN and WWPN.*

Fibre Channel IDs are 3-byte (Byte-0=switch, Byte-1=port on switch, Byte-2=subaddress up to 126 devices for loop) identifiers assigned by a switch when a device logs on to a Fibre Channel network. This ID is based on the Domain ID (DID) and port number of the switch port the device is attached to and is used in subsequent communications and by the FC-2 transport layer for routing. Fibre Channel frame headers carry a source ID (S_ID) to identify the sender and a destination ID (D_ID) addressing the port to receive the message. The ULP (FCP, FICON, etc.) and their associated drivers handle additional protocol-specific addressing and mapping. Switches also have a WWNN assigned to them, along with a unique domain ID.

Best Practices: A best practice is to fix or lock down the Domain ID on switches and directors to prevent conflicts. This also ensures that the Domain ID will be unique, since Domain IDs are used to base switch port addresses and for fabric binding security functions. There can be up to 239 Domain IDs in a fabric, and the values or range of numbers from 1 through 239 are vendor dependent. Similarly, the maximum number of switching devices supported and number of zones is also vendor dependent.

First-generation Fibre Channel products had limited buffer credits per port, which kept distances to 10km or less. Now it is common to see Fibre Channel devices with 64 or more buffer credits (BB_Credit). Buffer credits (BB_Credits) are used for buffer-to-buffer flow control. End-to-end

(EE_Credit) flow control is maintained using EE__Credits and EE_buffers. These extra buffer credits, combined with long-range optics, enable Fibre Channel and FICON to reach distances of 100km. This distance enables Metropolitan Area Network (MAN) resilient infrastructure to support the resilient enterprise; see www.fibrechannel.org.

4.6.2 Ethernet (10/100/1,000/10,000)

Originally developed at Xerox Palo Alto Research Center in the early 1970s, Ethernet has evolved from a performance of 2.94Mb/sec to 10Gb/sec. Today there are about 450 million Ethernet ports of various types in service around the world. The various Ethernet versions are based upon the IEEE 802.x standards. Ethernet can be deployed on different physical media, including fiber-optic and copper electrical cabling. Various versions of Ethernet include 10Mb/sec, 100Mb/sec (fast), 1,000Mb (1Gb E), and 10,000Mb/sec (10Gb E)—collectively referred to as 10/100/1,000/10,000 Ethernet. A 10Gb Ethernet, similar to 10Gb Fibre Channel, is being deployed in core-edge (tiered) topologies with 10Gb switches at the core and 1Gb and slower Ethernet switches and devices at the edge. For example, 10Gb Ethernet can be implemented as a backbone connecting two or more 10Gb-capable switched 1Gb and 10Gb trunks fanning out to 10/100/1,000Base T Ethernet switches. A 10Gb Ethernet can be utilized for storage networking environments supporting NAS and iSCSI block traffic. A 10Gb Ethernet can be utilized as an alternative to SONET/SDH for metropolitan area networking environments leveraging dedicated dark fiber and optionally DWDM technology. The various Ethernet implementations are interoperable with each other using common framing and formats. Ethernet can operate in half-duplex mode with Carrier Sense Multiple Access with Collision Detection (CSMA/CD) for slower speeds and full duplex for faster interfaces. Ethernet storage networking interfaces are implemented using copper (electrical) cabling, including Co-Axel (coax); Unshielded Twisted Pair (UTP) categories 5, 6, and 7 (CAT-5, CAT-6, CAT-7) and fiber-optic cabling. Gigabit Ethernet frame sizes can range from 64 bytes to 1,518 bytes and include 64, 128, 256, 512, 768, 1,024, 1,280, 1,518 bytes. Unlike 10/100 Ethernet, Gb E does not support hubs for connections; instead, it uses switched ports for core and fan-out connections with hubs being placed at edge and end points.

Figure 4.12 shows the Ethernet circle of technology as described by the 10Gb Ethernet Association (www.10gea.org), with various speeds ranging from 10/100 to 1,000 to 10Gb utilizing different physical interfaces to support different services, including IPV4, IPV6, TCP, IP, and UDP.

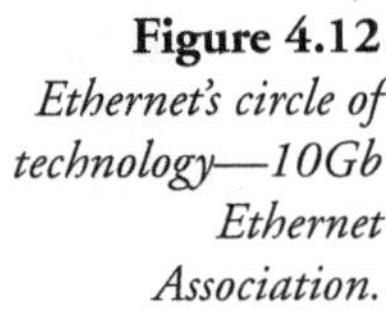

Figure 4.12
Ethernet's circle of technology—10Gb Ethernet Association.

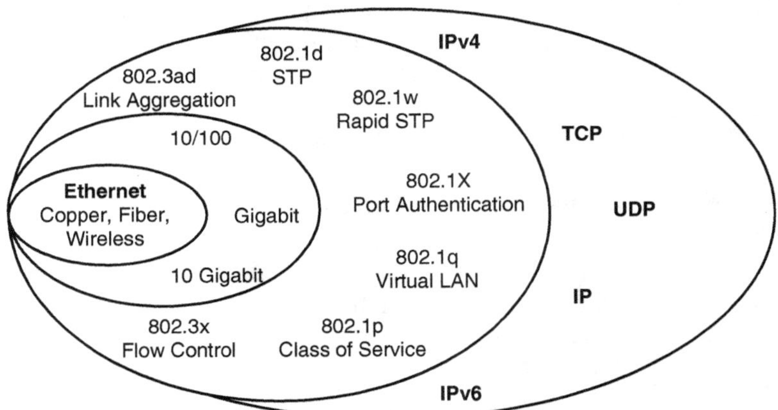

Optical-based Ethernet has been available for many years, utilizing fiber-optic cabling to support the various speeds and implementations of Ethernet. More recently, with the advent of 10Gb Ethernet and its improved distance capabilities with WAN PHYs, providers are deploying a new form of optical Ethernet at 1Gb and 10Gb into metropolitan areas. These initial deployments are expanding to leverage Ethernet as the networking interface to support IP as ULP- and IP-based applications, including Voice over IP (VoIP), file and data sharing (NAS), storage networking (SANs), and traditional LAN and WAN applications, including Web services. In the past these capabilities were provided using broadband Ethernet and IP services—for example, what you would have with a cable modem along with ADSL/DSL (xDSL) and ISDN over traditional copper telephone wires at much slower speeds. Another emerging interface to support IP is WiFi to enable wireless IP-based networking over various distances and speeds.

4.6.3 10Gb and beyond

The 10Gb technology today includes Fibre Channel, Ethernet, InfiniBand, and SONET/SDH. As has been the case in the past, with the introduction of faster interfaces, 10Gb is initially being deployed in core, backbone applications providing high-speed interconnects and ISLs between switches. The cost for 10Gb technology continues to decrease as do existing slower technologies, which helps to support different types of applications with the most cost-effective technology.

The 10Gb Fibre Channel (10GFC) is a good candidate for ISLs and is an alternative to trunking solutions as well as for building backbones (local and metropolitan). It borrows from 10Gb Ethernet (Table 4.10), similar to

Table 4.10 *Common Fiber-Optic Encoding Schemes*

	8B/10B Encoding	64B/66B Encoding
Gb Ethernet	X	—
ESCON	X	—
Fibre Channel	X	—
10Gb Ethernet	—	X
10Gb Fibre Channel	—	X

how Gb E borrowed from 1Gb Fibre Channel at the lower physical layers for commonality. Fibre Channel at 10Gb adopts the IEEE 10Gb transmission standards, similar to 10Gb Ethernet, with common cabling and transceiver technology.

Figure 4.13 shows a 10Gb parallel implementation using virtual lanes of 8 bits each to achieve 10Gb of bandwidth. Physical Media Devices (PMD) are used for attachment to local (LAN PHY) and metropolitan (WAN PHY) networks. There are multiple Physical Media Dependent Sublayers (PMD) for different types of fiber WAN PHY interfaces for 10Gb Ethernet to SONET/SDH OC-192 with an integrated SONET framer. Current 10Gb transceiver interface is the XENPAX and XPAX parallel optic interface evolving toward a common XFP serial interface. XPAK, also known as X2, implements four parallel lanes, each operating at 3.125Gb for a combined 10Gb interface. Initially the cost of multiple 2Gb interfaces and associated optics has been less expensive compared with 10Gb; however, this is changing. XFP is protocol neutral and will help drive costs down. XFP

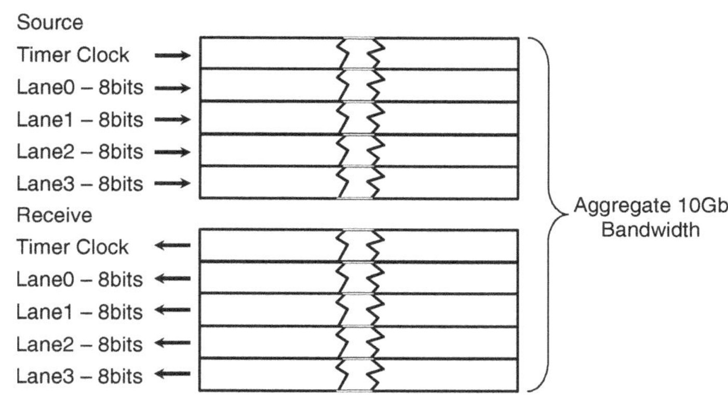

Figure 4.13 *The 10Gb Ethernet virtual lanes.*

specifications (www.xfpmsa.org) for ultrasmall form factor 10Gb/s modules are one-fifth the space and one-half the power of current 1Gb modules. In general, XFP-specified modules have an electrical interface, called XFI, that removes power and complexity associated with traditional approaches and places the electrical transceivers inside versus using other modules to reduce space, power, and cost.

4.6.4 InfiniBand

InfiniBand (IBA) is a unified interconnect that can be used for storage and networking I/O as well as interprocess communications. IBA is being developed under the guidance of the InfiniBand Trade Association (www.ibta.org) as a standard for I/O and storage interfaces. IBA can be used to connect servers to storage devices, storage to LANs, and servers to servers primarily within the data center applications. As a unified interconnect IBA can be used as a single adapter capable of functioning as multiple logical adapters. IBA enables a channel to extend outside of a single server up to about 100m (longer distances may be possible with future iterations), while current busses are measured in inches. IBA enables memory-to-memory (DMA) transfers to occur with fewer overheads to improve storage, networking, server clustering, and other activities.

For those familiar with memory channel interface from the early 1990s or with proprietary mainframe channels, IBA has some similar characteristics; however, the differences are that it is open, fiber-optic based, and supports multiple ULPs. IBA features high performance, availably, scalability, and reliability as primary characteristics. IBA-enabled servers (Figure 4.14) have Host Channel Adapters (HCAs) that attach point to point to an IBA device with a Target Channel Adapter (TCA). IBA servers can also attach to TCAs using IBA switches configured as a single network, or as part of a subnet in various topologies.

To support interprocess (server-to-server) communications for sockets, clustering, distributed lock management, and filesystems IBA features low-latency, high-throughput capabilities. IBA utilizes channel-based message passing architecture over switched interconnects to avoid memory coherency and latency associated with store and forward models. IBA packets are variable in size from 256 bytes to 4Kbytes, and a single message stream combining multiple packets can be up to 2Gbyte in size. IBA is not intended for long-distance applications; rather, it is for data center and small campus environments to maintain low latency and data reliability capabilities.

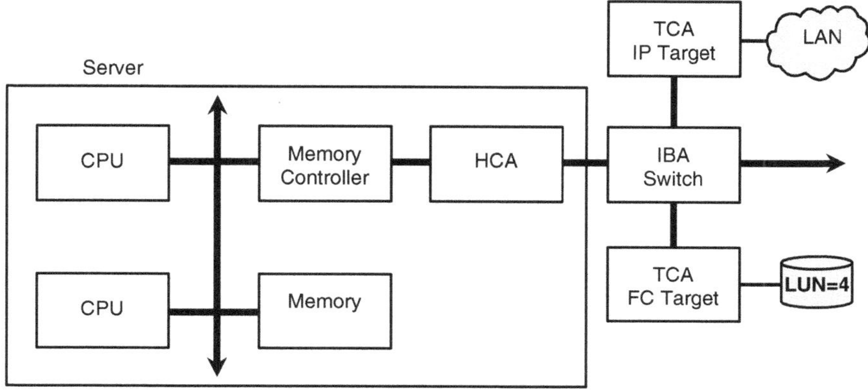

Figure 4.14 *InfiniBand architecture.*

IBA is a full-duplex, bidirectional interface, meaning that 1X (2.5Gb/sec) provides 5Gb/sec combined in both directions. A 4X IBA at 5Gb/sec provides 10Gb/sec in both directions, and 12X IBA provides up to 60Gbs/sec in both directions. IBA can also support many nodes (servers and storage devices) attached to IBA switches and routers configured in various topologies including subnets. IBA is also a serial interface, resulting in smaller cables and simplified connectors using copper or electrical cabling. Using optical cabling, IBA can reach distances of 10km; however, most practical applications will be measured in meters and under 1km in distance. IBA allocates its bandwidth into virtual lanes using byte striping, so that a common set of wires can carry data from different I/O packets based upon their priorities and flow control. IBA lanes are numbered 0–15 (16 lanes), with lane 15 being reserved for management and housekeeping activities. The IBA 4X interfaces can speed-match to support 1X interfaces and devices without losing data or impeding other high-performance traffic. Some IBA ULPs include IP over IBA (IPoIB), Shared Resource Protocol (SRP), Winsock Direct Protocol, Sockets Direct Protocol (SDP), SCSI Remote Direct Memory (RDMA), and Microsoft protocol for plug-and-play channel bus interfaces including USB and IEEE-1394. Remote Network Driver Interface Specification (RNDIS), for clustering applications such as DAPL, is being adopted by various vendors including database providers and DAFS.

4.6.5 ATA, SATA, and SAS

Serial ATA (SATA) is an evolutionary replacement for the parallel IDE/ATA physical storage interface traditionally used for internal server storage.

SATA is scalable and can be used for internal and external connections. SATA simplifies cabling over traditional ATA ribbon cabling by using a simpler four-wire cable to reduce cost and complexity. The thinner SATA cabling requiring less space helps to improve airflow within servers and to facilitate smaller designs and lower power consumption (250mV) using 8B/10B signaling and can be configured in point-to-point and star topologies. ATA and SATA are being used as alternatives to tape architecture for archiving and data retention, and as second tiered storage. Storage solutions utilizing ATA/SATA disk drives are available with ATA/SATA, Fibre Channel, and iSCSI interfaces for block access. NAS and CAS storage systems utilizing ATA/SATA storage devices are also available.

SATA and SAS both utilize a smaller form factor cable that is more flexible and takes up less space in servers. This helps to improve airflow and to enable the drives to consume less power to help lower costs of the server and storage. SATA has already gained market acceptance at the consumer level and workstation level as well as for back-end storage in high-end solutions. SATA/ATA solutions are being deployed to leverage low cost of the storage as a stepping-stone to SATA (www.serialata.org).

4.6.6 IEEE 1334 (Firewire) and Universal Serial Bus (USB)

IEEE 1334 Firewire is a network interface that is used for attaching disk drives, digital cameras, scanners, printers, and other things to computers. Firewire is a more complex protocol to meet time constraints for high performance than USB and is thus more expensive; it is suited for video processing and other high-performance applications. USB is very common today on computing products as well as consumer products, including digital cameras, printers, laptops, PDAs, computers, and so on. USB can be deployed as point to point or in hub configurations using USB hubs to share a common adapter among multiple devices. While USB can be configured into hub configurations with up to 127 devices, distance is limited to about 5m for fast devices and 3m for slow devices. Further distances to about 30m can be accomplished by daisy chaining multiple hubs together; however, there would be increased latency and more points of failure for the data to traverse.

So what does a perceived low-end interface such as USB have to do with implementing a resilient storage network? Good question. For one it is the interface commonly used today on PCs, workstations, and other devices for attaching local peripheral devices, including backup storage, archiving,

DVD/CD writers, and so forth. USB- and Firewire-based storage devices with RAID data protection for small home offices (SOHO) and SMB environments are becoming more common. So while it may not be used as the backbone, it's worth discussing, since some data that is stored on these devices could prove to be critical. More information about Firewire and USB can be found at the 1394 trade association Web site (www.1394ta.org).

4.6.7 Legacy storage and networking interfaces

There are many legacy storage interfaces still in use today that are worth mentioning, since you might encounter them. For many of them, dealing with these interfaces means ignoring them and leaving them where they are. If it's not broke, why fix it? You may actually have more issues trying to integrate some of these older systems and their interfaces than leaving them alone. A simple strategy can be to fence these older systems and interfaces off, protect them, and let them do what they are doing until you can phase them out. Some of these legacy storage interfaces include, but are not limited to, Hewlett-Packard (formerly DEC DSSI, CI, and MI), IBM Bus and Tag (Block Mux), HIPPI, and IPI. FDDI is a 100Mb/sec network interface that was popular in the early 1990s as a follow-on to Ethernet and a challenger to ATM; in many ways it was surpassed in terms of performance by Ethernet and Fibre Channel to name a few. FDDI and its copper-based sibling, CDDI, have been used for storage applications, including supporting DEC's mass storage control protocol (MSCP) for block storage on VMS Clusters.

4.7 Chapter summary

Various storage and I/O protocols and interfaces exist to support different applications. Upper-Level Protocols (ULPs), including FCP, FICON, IP, iSCSI, and RDMA, are implemented on several interfaces, including Fibre Channel, Ethernet, ATA/SATA, USB, PCI, InfiniBand, and parallel SCSI.

What This Chapter Will Do For You

Fiber optics are at the core of local and wide area communications, and support voice, data, and IP-based networks on a public and private basis. Some of the items you will learn about in this chapter include:

- How to protect your infrastructure investments now and in the future
- How to improve your purchasing capabilities with improved knowledge of fiber services
- What not to do with fiber in order to maintain resiliency and performance
- Techniques to delay purchasing extra bandwidth while increasing performance

5

Fiber-Optic Essentials

5.1 Overview

This chapter takes a look at fiber-optic communication components, including cabling, connectors, transceivers, and structured cabling. Fiber optics, and in particular cabling, can be taken for granted with regard to building storage networks, but an outage or performance degradation can occur from bad or misconfigured fiber optics.

5.2 Fiber-optic essentials

Fiber optics are an enabling technology for wide area communication for both voice and data. New network bandwidth being installed around the world is based on fiber optics to support voice and data. Fiber optic technology is at the core of traditional IP networks and storage networks. Benefits of fiber-optic communications include increased bandwidth, capacity, distance, resilience, and scalability.

The cost of fiber will vary, depending on whether it's dedicated (dark) or another type of shared service, and other factors including distance, bandwidth needed, availability, and location. Another determining factor pertaining to cost and availability of fiber access and services is who else in your neighbored or vicinity has or needs fiber access. If you are the first and only one in your area with a fiber-optic need, you may expect to pay more for fiber-optic access. You may also find that perhaps your needs are not seen by the fiber bandwidth providers as significant; therefore, you can expect to pay a larger dollar amount. An alternative is to have the fiber installed on your own using a contracted service, where you own and provision the network. The latter approach has more cost, however, it gives you complete control and access to all bandwidth.

The presence of fiber does not mean you can do what you want to with it. For example, there may be fiber running up to a data center; however, it may not be compatible with your networking needs. There are several forms of compatibility, including cable, connector types, and light sources using lasers and Light-Emitting Diodes (LED). Another compatibility item is how the fiber-optic cabling supports different networking interfaces and protocols. For example, the same type of fiber-optic cable could be used to implement FDDI, ATM, Gigabit Ethernet, Fibre Channel, ESCON, or FICON, however, not at the same time. Typically, network interfaces require dedicated use of the fiber-optic cable, supporting multiple upper-level protocols. DWDM can be used to aggregate and extend multiple optical-based networks between locations. Fiber-optic cabling has grown in popularity because of its support for distances, immunity to electrical noise in harsh environments, high performance, and multiplexing capabilities to create additional bandwidth. An example is that a piece of fiber-optic cabling being used for Gb Ethernet or 1Gb Fibre Channel could be multiplexed using DWDM to create hundreds of gigabits of bandwidth. Some tests have shown that with fast 10Gb transceivers, advanced optics, and ultradense multiplexing the bandwidth of a piece of fiber-optic cabling could be as much as 100Tbps per fiber cable pair. Now think about all of the potential bandwidth that is not being utilized when you see multiple fiber-optic cables supporting 10/100 Ethernet or even Gb Ethernet networks. There are protocol and interface technology limitations that result in performance of less than the speed of light for fiber optics. There is also latency associated with fiber optics that works out to be about 5usec per kilometer or about 2msec per 100 miles. Regardless, 1Gb, 2Gb, 4Gb, and 10Gb are plenty fast today—with 40Gb out over the horizon, including OC-768 interfaces for even more performance.

An Ethernet network could be built on the same type of fiber-optic cabling as Fibre Channel. The Ethernet network could support a TCP/IP network along with router devices to bridge Fibre Channel SANs and other networks over wide area interfaces. The Ethernet could also support storage networking protocols such as iSCSI for block data movement to back up departmental servers using the IP network and a central Fibre Channel–based SAN.

Normally, each network has its own dedicated physical fiber-optic cable. As the number of fiber pairs per network increases, so would the amount of fiber-optic pairs between sites. DWDM enables fewer physical optical cables to be used between sites as well as increasing bandwidth by creating new virtual circuits (channels). In Figure 5.1, there would be six pairs of

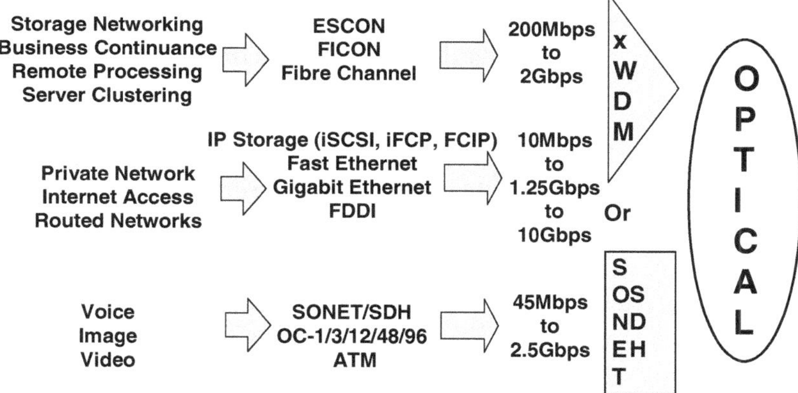

Figure 5.1 *Various networks converging on fiber optics.*

fiber-optic cables (one per network interface) attached to DWDM devices. Between the DWDM devices, the various networks are multiplexed onto a single common fiber-optic cable.

Figure 5.1 shows how various networks and interfaces converge with their use of fiber optics and how multiplexing can be used as a common cabling schema, particularly for long-haul, as well as other concentrated applications.

5.3 Fiber-optic basics

Fiber optics are available as dedicated (dark) and as an optical service (lit) using public optical networks. Dark fiber is used to build private optical networks, which allow full control over the network and management. This also means that you have to implement the network, including redundancy for failover, monitoring, and management. The benefit is that by using WDM technology including DWDM you can scale the amount of bandwidth and the number of networks that can share the physical fiber-optic cabling. Dark dedicated fiber can also be obtained from local, regional, national, and global fiber-optic service providers, including local telephone carriers.

Sometimes dark dedicated fiber-optic cabling may not be available on its own without also acquiring the required networking (WDM) components and management services from the provider. There are other situations where the provider may place limits on the number of lambdas (light wavelengths) that can be utilized on the fiber cable to control bandwidth. In other situations a provider may only offer a lambda service where it provides one of the lambda wavelengths split out of a WDM service. While a lambda service gives you the ability to fully utilize the bandwidth of that particular wavelength, it does not enable you to further multiplex and create additional lambdas. A solution for this situation can be to use Time Division Multiplexing (TDM) to aggregate various slower networking interfaces onto a single lambda or SONET/SDH interface, sometimes called a clear channel. Multiplexing technologies for resilient storage networking will be covered in more detail in the next chapter.

If a telecommunications carrier provided you with fiber, it would be lit (SONET/SDH, ATM, or IP) or it would be dark dedicated. A service offered as lit or gray fiber could be a SONET/SDH clear channel, TDM offering, WDM lambda offering, or an Optical IP interface using metropolitan Ethernet. There is a variation of lit fiber, when using SONET/SDH, called a clear channel. A clear channel appears to be dedicated for your use; however, it is a fraction of a larger SONET/SDH network. Since it is not dedicated, clear channels can only be used with special networking equipment and protocols such as Time Division Multiplexing (TDM) and are not full bandwidth, as a dark fiber would be. What is important about understanding which type of fiber service you are getting is to make sure that it can support your needs.

The reason service providers may be reluctant to offer dark dedicated fiber or charge large sums is that by using WDM technology, you can provision your own additional circuits to increase your bandwidth. Now, granted, fiber optics, particularly dedicated dark fiber over long distances, can be expensive; however, by using WDM and DWDM you can amortize the cost by spreading it out over more usable bandwidth, which you can create and control. This is where the convergence of different networking physical interfaces being able to coexist on the same physical fiber-optic cable can be achieved without having to remap everything onto IP. Keep in mind that IP is a protocol that requires some type of physical network interfaces. The most common form of physical medium to support network interfaces is fiber optic. For distances farther than WDM and DWDM metropolitan networking SONET/SDH can be used to travel regional and global distances. It should be pointed out that SONET/SDH networks themselves utilize carrier class SONET/SDH switches, TDM, and DWDM technology to turn dark fiber into carrier networks.

If you are not able to get dark fiber from a provider, you might consider having your own installed. This can be expensive in terms of physical installation and process. This process can involve complex negotiations for right of way, issues with various municipalities, and other potential difficulties. While not for everyone, this can be an option for some companies even if it is to install your own fiber to the carrier or provider's access point. For those who can look at the cost from a business ennoblement standpoint, it can be well worth it in terms of the bandwidth and control over the network.

Caution: As with any laser or high-powered light-emitting device, do not look at the light source or point it into your eyes or other people's eyes, since this can cause serious eye damage. There are different types of light-generating devices, including lasers for long-distance and LEDs for short-distance transmissions. Open Fiber Control (OFC) is a mechanism that is part of the transceiver to detect disruptions (breaks) in the link and disrupt normal data transmissions. When interrupted, an OFC device transmits short pulses of light at low repetition rates for safety purposes. OFC, while providing a safety capability in case fiber-optic cables are unplugged during use, are more expensive and sensitive to interoperability timing. Using smart GBICs and SFP transceivers provides interoperability between OFC and non-OFC devices.

5.4 Fiber-optic cabling types

Not all fiber-optic cabling is the same, and the presence of a fiber-optic cable can have different applications and performance characteristics. There are two types of fiber-optic cabling: Single-Mode Fiber (SMF), also known as long-wave or long-distance fiber, and Multimode Fiber (MMF), also known as short-wave or short-distance fiber. For short distances, as in data centers and campuses, MMF fiber-optic cable is used. MMF fiber-optic cable includes 62.5- and 50um fiber, which, depending on the upper-level protocol, GBIC (usually LED based), and speed, will determine its distance.

MMF is used for short distances and SMF is used for long distances from 1km to 100km. Fibre Channel utilizes the same cabling scheme as Gigabit Ethernet, ESCON, and others. In addition to cable type (MMF for short distances, SMF for long distances to 100km), there are different connector types for 1Gbit and 2Gb. These include SC and ST connectors for 1Gb applications and Small Form-factor Pluggable (SFP). The SFP connector for 2Gbit provides improved port densities similar to those used by traditional Gigabit Interface Converters (GBICs).

Fiber-optic cabling, as seen in Figure 5.2, is made up of a pair of fiber-optic cable strands—one for transmits and one for receives. The fiber-optic cable strands consist of a very thin core wrapped by cladding and an outer

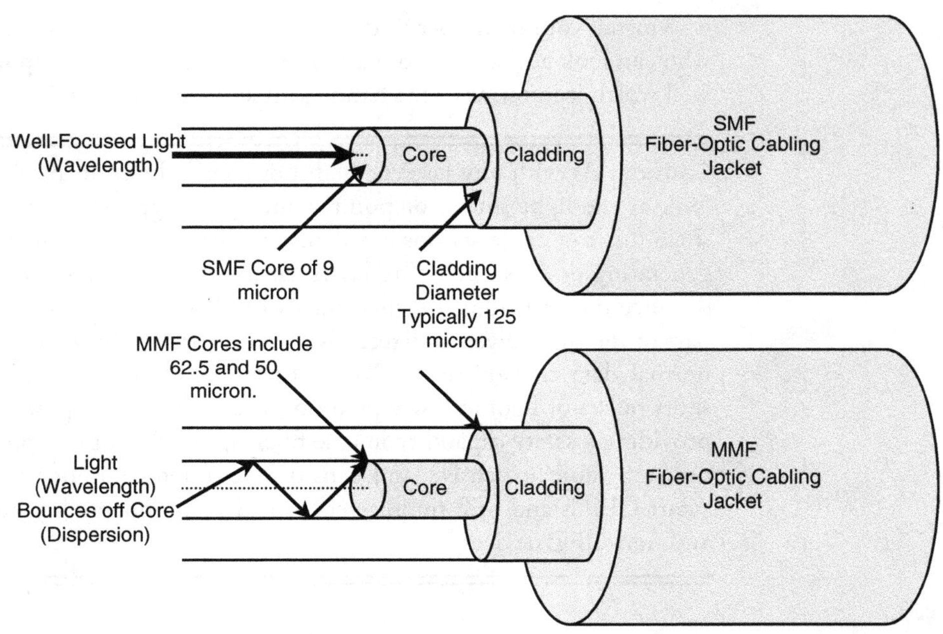

Figure 5.2 *Closer look at fiber-optic cabling pair.*

jacket material that provides protection to the inner layers. The core can vary in size from less than 9 microns (um) for single-mode fiber to 50um to 62.5um in diameter for multimode fiber. To put this into perspective, a typical human hair is about 75um in diameter. The core is surrounded by a cladding layer, typically about 125um in diameter, that is used to reflect light back into the core. The outer jacket of the fiber cable provides external protection and strength for the cable. Typical single-mode fiber-optic cable will have a yellow jacket, and multimode fiber will be orange.

Cabling is identified by its mode (SMF and MMF), which defines how light travels through the fiber-optic core. With MMF cabling there are many light propagation paths, defining how the light travels down the cable, while SMF has only one light path. In simpler terms, SMF has a more precise path that the light takes through the core, with fewer bounces off of the cladding; this results in less intermodal dispersion (the time it takes different modes of light to travel through the fiber), which means better performance over distance. Consequently, SMF provides the bandwidth and long-distance support for long-haul applications, including campus, metropolitan, and regional carrier networks. Long-distance carriers, as well as Incumbent Local Exchange Carriers (ILEC) (also known as the Baby Bells), utilize SMF optic cabling in their networks.

From a cost standpoint the higher tolerances in fiber-optic cabling quality and coupling means SMF is more expensive. MMF is less expensive from a cabling and connector standpoint, with very good performance over shorter distances, and is most commonly used for short applications, including LANs. With MMF the cabling is referred to by its core and cladding diameters—for example, 62.5/125 is a core of 62.5um diameter with cladding of 125um. For SMF the diameter is referred to as the Mode Field Diameter (MFD), describing the optical power in the fiber by providing equivalent diameter, sometimes called the spot size. The MFD is larger than the core, with values ranging between 8 and 10um, with the core being 9um or less. Some common storage and networking interfaces and cable distances are shown in Figure 5.3.

Graded-index 62.5/125um multimode fiber (500MHz * km) can support various distances depending on the networking interface and the speed of operation. Using short-wave optics the multimode port can transmit light at an 850-nanometer (nm) wavelength at distances of 300m at 1Gb. MMF cabling is typically orange. Graded-index 50/125um multimode fiber (200MHz * km) can provide transmission distances of up to 500m; it

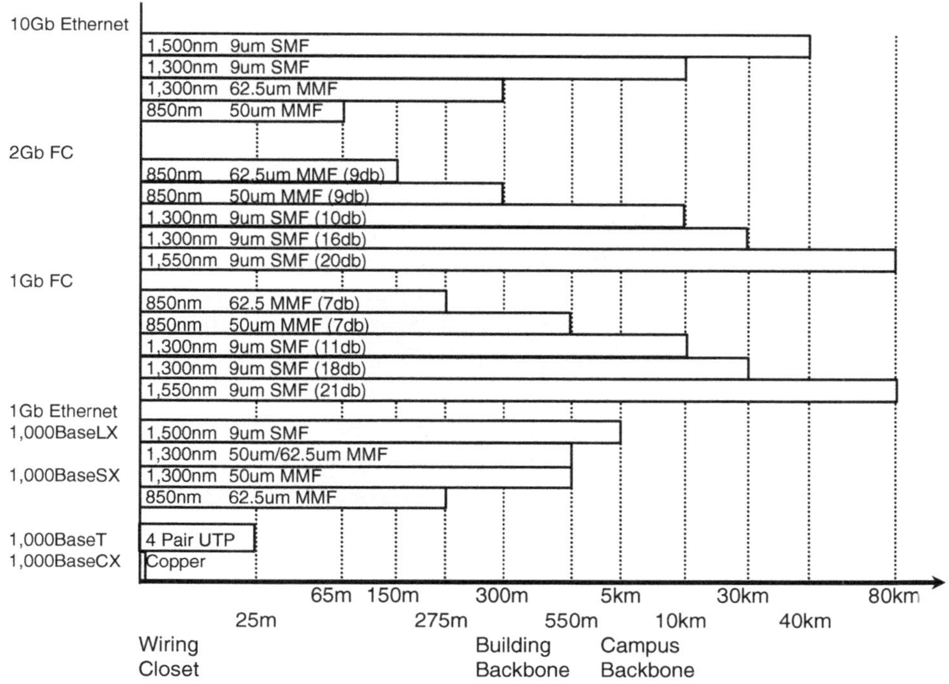

Figure 5.3 *Fiber-optical cabling distance.*

connects to short-wave multimode ports at an 850nm wavelength and looks similar to 62.5/125um cabling. Step-index 9/125 single-mode fibers provide distances between 2m and 200km, connecting to long-wave optic ports that transmit light at 1,310nm or 1,550nm wavelength. Single-mode fiber-optic cabling is usually yellow in color. The optical loss on single-mode fiber cabling depends on the wavelength being used; typical losses are 0.5db/km for 1,310nm and 0.33db/km for 1,550nm cabling. For example, using ultra-long-wave GBICs and good SMF fiber-optic cable with minimum db loss (signal degradation) plus sufficient buffer credits (40–64), distances of 80 km can be achieved for Fibre Channel. Using DWDM, distances of 100km and beyond can be achieved with Fibre Channel IP and WAN interfaces, providing even longer distances.

5.5 A word about wavelengths

The International Telecommunications Union (ITU) is a standards organization that oversees various fiber-optic standards documents, including wavelength spacing. If you have ever seen a rainbow after it rains, or the multiple colors seen through a prism when light is shown on it, you are viewing light wavelengths. These wavelengths in optical terms are called lambdas, so each wavelength corresponds to a different lambda. The ITU defines the spacing in nanometers (nm) at which different light wavelengths are spaced and at which optical transceivers and fiber-optic cabling operate. For example, 1,300nm 9um SMF fiber has a core diameter of 9um or less operating in single mode (long wave, long range) with the light source aligned to 1,300nm. To complete the optical interface a 1,300nm SMF GBIC or 2Gb SFP would be paired with the fiber-optic cable. Mode conditioners can be used to adjust and interconnect various cable types—for example, reusing 62.5/125 and 50/125 MMF ESCON cable for 1Gb FICON. The common cabling and optical transceiver (GBICs and SFPs) wavelengths are 850nm, 1,300nm, and 1,550nm. Coarse Wave Division Multiplexing (CWDM) may use a loose or wide separation spacing of about 20nm, where each wavelength is 20nm apart from the other. Wave division multiplexing technology utilizes successively tighter (narrower) wavelength spacing with more sophisticated optics and components, which, in turn, cost more. The benefit of more dense spacing is the ability to create more wavelengths and thus circuits for bandwidth. DWDM and other wave division multiplexing technologies are covered in more detail in Chapter 6.

5.6 Fiber-optic connectors and transceivers

Fiber connector types include SC and ST for 1Gb Fibre Channel, Gigabit Ethernet, ESCON, and FICON. A smaller form-factor GBIC, about the size of a networking RJ45 (Ethernet) connector, is the Small Form-factor (SFF); a Small Form-factor Pluggable (SFP) connector is used with 2Gb and 4Gb Fibre Channel, although some products utilize SFPs for 1Gb applications. SFF and SFP are sometimes referred to as LC connectors. Fibre Channel supports copper and fiber-optic interfaces (most implementations are now optical). Fibre Channel utilizes various cable types, including 62.5 and 50um Multimode Fiber (MMF) and 9um Single-Mode Fiber (SMF). Trunk cable is used to physically combine multiple cable strands into a single cable bunch that fans out at each end or has a special connector to attach a fan-out cable. Some common fiber-optic connector types are shown in Figure 5.4. Duplex connectors have two connections attached to each other (pair), where as simplex has individual connectors.

In Figure 5.4, some common fiber-optic connector types are shown, including LC, SC, simplex (single connector), and duplex (a pair of fiber connects). Two other fiber-optic connector types are ESCON Duplex and MIC (FDDI), which are used for ESCON and FDDI configurations, respectively. Various cable and jumper configurations are available, includ-

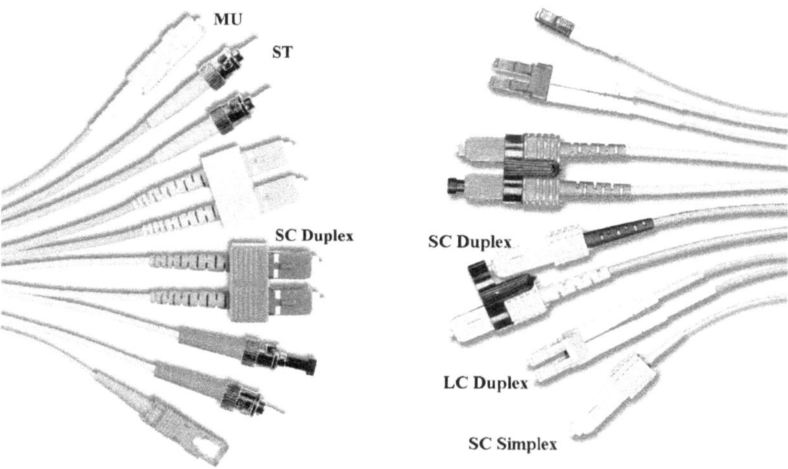

Figure 5.4 *Fiber-optic connectors. (Photo courtesy of Siemon Company, www.siemon.com.)*

ing SC to SC, SC to LC, LC to LC, SC to ST, Simplex, Duplex, and LC to MT-RJ, to name a few. There are also mode conditioners, which enable different types of fiber-optic cabling to coexist—for example, using existing ESCON cables for 1Gb FICON. Connectors, cables, and other accessory optic items are available from a variety of different sources.

Caution: *Fiber-Optic Care and Handling:* Fiber-optic cable is relatively flexible compared with traditional bulky storage interfaces and even Unshielded Twisted Pair (UTP) copper cabling used with networking. However, fiber-optic cabling is sensitive to bending and sharp turns as well as dust and dirt. Keep your fiber-optic connectors clean and if you plan on making many changes resulting in unplugging and replugging connectors, invest in a quality cleaning kit. As part of managing your fiber-optic infrastructure avoid sharp bends and twists in your cabling to prevent damage to the core. Cable bend radius guides can be used to help protect cabling.

Fibre Channel and Ethernet borrow and leverage technologies from each other, particularly at the physical layer. 1Gb Ethernet utilizes fiber-optic transmission (8B/10B encoding) technology borrowed from Fibre Channel, with Ethernet operating at a faster clock rate. A 1Gb Ethernet has a slight wire speed theoretical bandwidth advantage of 1.25Gbps compared with 1.0625Gbps Fibre Channel, which is about 150Mbps difference. Some Fibre Channel and Ethernet 1Gb GBICs are interchangeable and support dual clock rates; however, this varies by manufacturer and vendor-supported configurations. At 10Gb Fibre Channel borrows from Ethernet using a common encoding and transmission scheme, including virtual lanes and common coding (65/66B).

Similar to fiber-optic cabling having different types for short- and long-haul applications, fiber-optic transceivers also have different characteristics and capabilities. Table 5.1 shows some common fiber-optic transceivers and their characteristics, including cable type and connector type along with supported distance. Fiber-optic transceivers include Gigabit Interface Connector (GBIC) for 1Gb, SFPs (called SFFP by some) for 2Gb, and eXtended Fiber Plug (XFP) for 10Gb applications. Note that some fiber-optic transceivers, including 1Gb GBICs, 2Gb SFPs, and 10Gb XFPs are interchangeable between Fibre Channel and Ethernet devices; however, consult the manufacturer's material for specific guidelines and supported configurations. Media interface adapters (MIA) can be used to convert from copper electrical to optic.

Table 5.1 *Some Fiber-Optic Transceiver Characteristics*

	Cable Type	Cable Type	Connector Type	Distance Supported
1Gb GBIC				
Electrical	Copper	N/A	DB9	30m
Electrical	Copper	N/A	HSSDC	30m
850um SWL	MMF	850nm	SC	275m
1,310um SWL	MMF	1,310nm	SC	550m
9um LWL	SMF	850nm	SC	10km
9um LWL	SMF	1,310nm	SC	35km
9um LWL	SMF	1,550nm	SC	80km
2Gb and 4Gb SFPs				
850um SWL	MMF	850nm	LC	150m
1,310um SWL	MMF	1,310nm	LC	300m
9um LWL	SMF	850nm	LC	10km
9um LWL	SMF	1,310nm	LC	35km
9um LWL	SMF	1,550nm	LC	80km

Transceivers are also used on DWDM technology for sending and transmitting light over various distances and for using different wavelengths. For diagnostic, monitoring, and test purposes there are also loop-back transceivers that simply take the transmit signal and loop it back to the receiver. There are also snoop transceivers, which have an extra connection pair for attachment of optical test tools, sniffers, analyzers, and performance probes. Snoop GBICs bleed off a small amount of the light source and send it to the extra monitoring port for use by diagnostic and monitoring tools. This allows fiber-optic and interface analyzers to look at and collect traffic information for diagnostic and troubleshooting applications. Performance analyzers and probes can also be attached to these ports to collect detailed session-level statistics at the network interface up to the protocol layer. This would include SCSI, IP, VI, and FICON reads, writes, I/O size, source, destination, response time, signal and synchronization loss, and other pertinent data to aid management, storage resource management, and capacity planning. Another technique for tapping into a fiber-optic stream without using snoop GBICs and SFPs is to use a "Y" splitter cable, sometimes called a pigtail cable or splitter device, which is essentially a "Y" in a small connector box.

An emerging trend is to have extra ports, called mirrored ports and spanning ports, available—similar to Ethernet switches. Another emerging trend is to have the information from the port itself sent in-band to management software. Analyzers are good for collecting very detailed state information with some retention capabilities, while probes and sniffers tend to take a higher-level view, providing analysis capability, long-term retention of data, and reporting/display capabilities. Depending on your specific needs, you may need both, one or the other, or perhaps neither. From an educational standpoint, it certainly helps to have at least some exposure and training—even if it's a demonstration regarding what these tools can do and how they can be used to help you better understand your storage networking environment and troubleshoot things.

There is another specialized type of transceiver, which is a wavelength (lambda)–specific GBIC or SFP—sometimes called CWDM GBICs and SFPs. Regular transceivers transmit light at a common wavelength or light level. By using CWDM technology different transceivers can have different wavelengths assigned to them—for example, at 20um ITU grid spacing. Each wavelength must be aligned with its corresponding wavelength or the transceivers will not communicate. By using Optical Add-Drop Multiplexer (OADM) devices the various wavelengths are combined to create a multiplex light source and transmitted over a single-mode fiber-optic cabling. The light is demultiplexed at the far end back into the individual wavelengths and sent to the wavelength-specific transceiver.

Figure 5.5 shows an example of wavelength-specific transceivers based upon CWDM technology with an ITU grid spacing of 20nm and an OADM. In this example a server on the left has a wavelength-specific transceiver operating at 1,470nm spacing—that is, multiplex with other wavelengths for long-haul transmission using SMF optical cabling. On the right, we see that the combined light source is demultiplexed by the OADM and the appropriate wavelength is sent via fiber-optic cable to the storage on the right. In this example there is a jumper cable between the server and the OADM on the left, an SMF cable between the OADM on the left and right, and a jumper cable between the OADM on the right and the storage device.

Another example, based on Figure 5.5, would be to introduce a switch (Ethernet, Fibre Channel, FICON) that servers and other devices would attach to on both sides. The switches would then connect to an OADM device using the wavelength-specific transceivers to multiplex their signals over a common SMF fiber-optic cable. Consequently, multiplexing can be

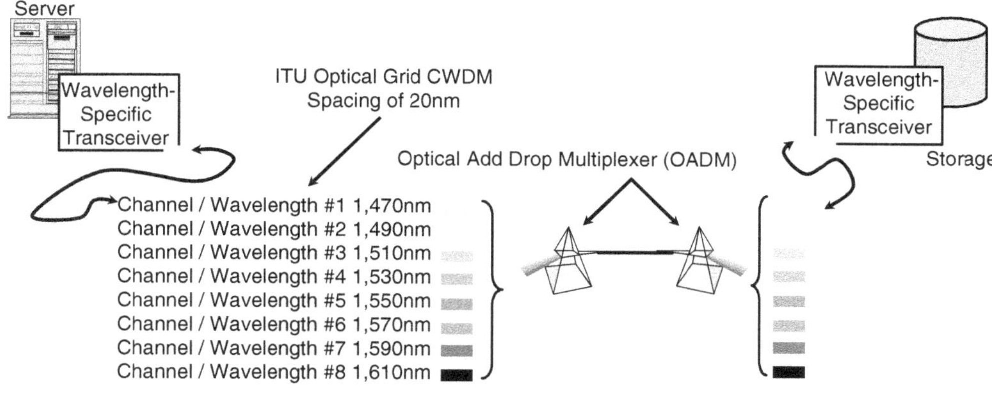

Figure 5.5 *Wavelength-specific transceivers and multiplexing.*

used to combine Fibre Channel, FICON for storage access, and Ethernet for server access and clustering heartbeat over a common fiber-optic cable for long-distance applications.

5.7 Fiber-optic distance and performance topics

Distance is an important component in building a resilient storage network, and while fiber-optic interfaces, including Fibre Channel, and Ethernet, can span long distances, there are some underlying items that need to be understood. While it is possible for SMF fiber to span distances of 10–80km and more, that is what it is capable of. What can actually be achieved can vary, depending on the quality of the fiber-optic cabling, strength and quality of the lasers, db (signal) loss, and protocol droop. There is a power budget, and when there is a break in a cable, another connector, or other factors, this all adds up. There is a certain amount of margin that you work into your budget to offset these, but after that distance starts to decrease, which can impact performance and quality. It is important to understand that if you have a fiber-optic infrastructure, even a short one, if link loss and other things are not considered, you could see link loss, intermittent problems, and other things that do not belong in a resilient infrastructure.

5.8 Link loss and power budgets (db loss)

Early generations of fiber-optic cables encountered significant db (signal) loss over distances of up to 20db per kilometer. This restricted distance, or necessitated repeaters (regeneration amplifiers) to boost the optical signal.

Fiber-optic cabling has improved and now 0.2–0.3db loss per kilometer distances of 100km using 9um can be accomplished. For long-haul applications SMF 9um is used, while 50um MMF is preferred for short haul. Distance is also a factor of the protocol being used and speed of the interface. Table 5.2 shows some sample db loss for 9um single-mode fiber cable. For example, typical 1,310nm long-wave 2Gb SFP, which has a transmit minimum link loss budget of 9.5db per meter and worst case receive loss of 20db per meter, would have a link budget of 10.5db. Using 1,310nm cable (shown in Figure 5.2) would allow about 20km distance. Any farther distance would require a more powerful SFP optic device with larger optical power budget. At 100km you would need at least 30db power budget (100 * 0.3db/km = 30db) using 1,550nm optics. Link attributes include allowances for splices and so on. These values are for example purposes only, with actual end-to-end values being measured to be accurate.

When dealing with long-distance communications, latency and performance issues are certain to pop up, since these are natural occurrences. There are, after all, some physics involved, and latency increases over longer distances. Even fiber optics, which use light to transmit information, have latency issues that affect all networks, including wave division multiplexing and IP networks. The speed of light is about 5usec per kilometer, which can be used to figure out transmission times and round trips. For example, a distance of 20km round trip would add [5usec * 20 (distance) * 2 (round trip)] or 200usec, which does not include any added latency from other components along the way. So at the magic number for distance—for example, 80km for a GBIC—does light just stop? Figure 5.6 shows how electrical signals (top) deteriorate over distance, as does the light signal. The light continues to travel; however, it loses its efficiency and begins to disperse.

Note that 2Gb, as well as faster transmission speeds, result in shorter distances due to the dispersion effects of light on the optical cabling and higher speeds. The number of connections, splices, grade and quality of fiber-optic cable, device restrictions, buffer-to-buffer credits, flow control,

Table 5.2 *Sample 9um SMF db Loss Example*

Cable Type	Attenuation Coefficient Cable Attributes	Link Design Factors
1,310nm	0.4db/km	0.5db/km
1,550nm	0.35db/km	0.3db/km
1,625nm	0.4db/km	0.35db/km

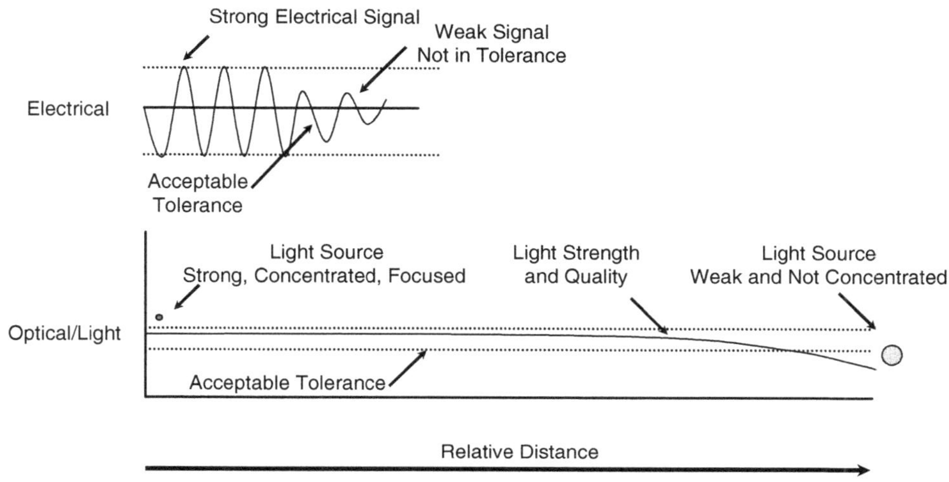

Figure 5.6 *Impact of distance on electrical and fiber optics.*

and quality of optics can impact distance and performance. An important note about faster speeds and distances is to keep your fiber-optic connectors clean, use appropriate powered optics, and factor in your db loss and link loss budget.

5.9 Protocol droop

Performance over distance can be impacted by the type of fiber-optic cabling being used, type and power of optics being used, configuration (including number of splices and connectors), latency from distance being covered, and the type of network being used on the fiber-optic cabling. The latter is what is called protocol droop, which may not be specific to fiber optics; however, I'm covering it here, since it is appropriate before we go to the next chapter to discuss metropolitan and wide area storage networks.

Droop is what occurs with some protocols over distance, resulting in a loss of bandwidth and increased latency. An example of this is the ESCON IBM mainframe I/O interface, which utilizes fiber optics. ESCON, known as FC-SB (not to be confused with FICON FC-SB-2), utilizes standard fiber optics in the same way as Fibre Channel, FICON, and Gigabit Ethernet. While the type of fiber being used (MMF or SMF) and the GBICs will determine physical transmission limits, it is the networking protocol or interface that regulates the actual speed and distance. That is why the same piece of MMF fiber that supports 100Mb Ethernet, or ESCON at 17MB, can support FICON,

Fibre Channel, or Gigabit Ethernet at 100MB or 1Gb per second. The clocking rate of the lower-level networking protocol also contributes to speed, while the flow-control mechanism affects distance.

Interfaces such as Fibre Channel that provide deterministic or predictable behavior rely on some sort of flow-control mechanism to ensure timely delivery of information. Fibre Channel uses buffer credit systems similar in concept to your checking account; in principle, you can only write checks (send data) for the amount of funds (buffers) you have available. When you run out of funds (buffers) you have to (or you should) stop writing checks (sending data) until it is safe to resume. From a performance standpoint, if you have enough buffers (buffer credit count) you can keep the channel or "pipe" full while sending over long distances to compensate for propagation delays.

In Figure 5.7 (top) traditional flow control is shown, where acknowledgments are received before sending additional data takes place. This approach can lead to loss of total bandwidth due to delays waiting for acknowledgments to take place, particularly over longer distances. Flow control (bottom) shows how multiple outstanding I/O operations can take place to improve bandwidth utilization. Enough buffer credits can compensate for distance by supporting more I/O operations "in-flight" to enable continued sending while waiting to receive. Fibre Channel accomplishes flow control using Class-2 (end to end), and Class-3 (buffer to buffer) service classes. Ethernet has a similar flow-control mechanism to support windows of outstanding I/O frames. At 1Gb, Fibre Channel requires roughly one buffer credit per 2km for full frame transfers. Smaller frames

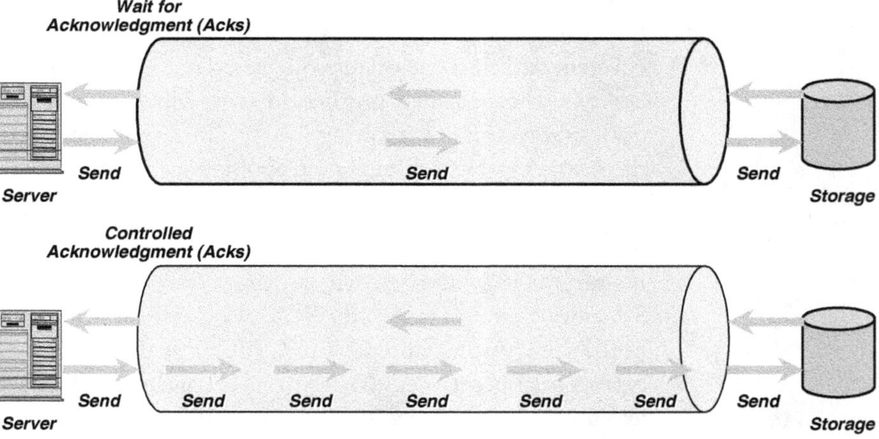

Figure 5.7 *Buffer credits and flow control.*

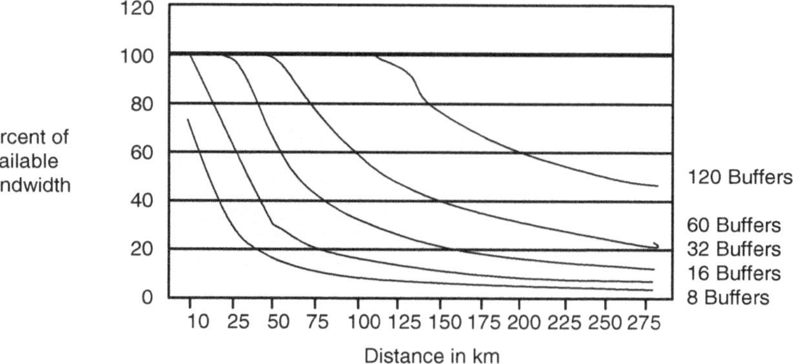

Figure 5.8 *The effect of protocol droop on data transfer performance.*

and partial transfers can consume buffer credits faster. At 2Gb, Fibre Channel and FICON require roughly 1 buffer credit per kilometer, so to reach 100km you would need 100 buffer credits, as can be seen in Figure 5.8.

ESCON suffers from droop in that it is a unidirectional (half-duplex) interface that is susceptive to droop. Fibre Channel and FICON are susceptible to droop when insufficient buffer credits exist to maintain elasticity in the fabric. Fibre Channel, FICON, and Gigabit Ethernet can operate in full-duplex mode (send and receive simultaneously) to boost performance. First-generation Fibre Channel products, including switches, had a limited number of buffer credits, which made going beyond 10km difficult. Sixty-four to 100 or more buffer credits per port are becoming a standard feature to enable long-distance applications without severe impact of droop. While these buffer credits do not eliminate droop, they do delay the impact so that distances of over 100km at 2Gb can be achieved to build resilient infrastructures. Networking interfaces such as Gigabit Ethernet and IP are not as susceptible to the impact of droop, since their applications tend to be nondeterministic, where as storage applications rely on deterministic behavior channels.

5.10 Chapter summary

Fibre optics are at the core of storage networking today on a local, campus, and metropolitan basis. There are different types of fiber-optic cabling for different applications, including short-haul multimode and long-haul single mode. Fiber-optic cabling can be configured into various networks, including IP LANs, SANs, MANs, SONET/SDH, and is available as dark dedicated and shared fiber for building your own private optical network to support resilient storage networks.

5.10 Chapter Summary

What This Chapter Will Do For You

This chapter looks at MANs, WANs, and associated communications techniques, including SONET/SDH, FCIP, iFCP, ATM, and DWDM, which are essential to support storage access and communications over various distances. Some of the items you will learn about in this chapter include:

- Demystify the communication cloud in order to enable storage access over distance
- Understand alternatives and characteristics to better deal with bandwidth providers
- How to enable distance for survivability and data protection with continued access
- Make sure you have true redundancy with wide area networks and providers
- Manage the appropriate technology to meet different service requirements

6

Metropolitan and Wide Area Storage Networks

6.1 Overview

This chapter takes a look at metropolitan and wide area storage networking interfaces, including Wave Division Multiplexing (WDM), Dense Wave Division Multiplexing (DWDM), SONET/SDH, Fibre Channel over IP (FCIP and iFCP), and other wide area networking interfaces for implementing resilient storage networks.

6.2 Metropolitan and wide area networking

Metropolitan and wide area networks are designed and implemented in a series of layers. An implementation may include multiple networking interfaces (SONET/SDH, ATM, Frame Relay, Ethernet, DWDM) and different physical media (copper and optical) to support IP and other ULPs. With a network, the various characteristics of different technologies can be extended and leveraged to meet different service requirements and SLAs. Incumbent Local Exchange Carrier (ILEC), Competitive Local Exchange Carrier (CLEC), and International Carrier (IXC) are examples of telecommunication bandwidth services providers.

Metropolitan and wide area storage networks enable distributed data centers to support resilient business processing of information. By using metropolitan, intercity, regional, and global storage networking technology, businesses can interconnect data centers to share information resources, address storage management from a central perspective, implement business continuance and recovery schemes, and facilitate consolidation. Metropolitan and wide area storage networking builds on Local Area Networks (LANs) and traditional storage networking, spanning longer distances that could range from 10km to thousands of kilometers using different networking technologies. Generally speaking, a Metropolitan Area Network (MAN) utilizes dedicated dark fiber with long-wave optics, including long-range GBICs and SFPs as well as WDM and DWDM technology.

MANs can also be implemented using SONET/SDH Optical Carrier (OC-x) network interfaces provided by a service provider or implemented on your private Optical Transport Network (OTN). From a distance perspective, MANs using SONET/SDH can span hundreds to thousands of kilometers; however, for practical purposes, a MAN typically covers distances of 100–150km. MANs can support both asynchronous and synchronous applications. The caveat is that storage- and server-based applications are typically sensitive to latencies involving distances of greater than 100km when in synchronous mode. Longer distances are possible in asynchronous and semisynchronous applications as well as vendor-specific variations of multistage copies and mirroring using MAN and WAN interfaces.

6.2.1 Why metropolitan and wide area storage networks?

Metropolitan and wide area storage networking can be used to support:

- Remote backup and restores
- Disk to tape (D2T), disk to disk (D2D), and disk to disk to tape (D2D2T) backup
- Remote archiving and data movement to disaster recovery locations
- Remote mirroring and replication using hardware and software
- Clustering for high availability applications and systems
- Workload consolidation of servers, storage, SANs, and resources
- Data center and workload migration and consolidation
- Business continuance and disaster recovery
- Regulatory compliance and data preservation/protection
- Unified management of storage resources

Metropolitan and wide area storage networking have evolved in conjunction with storage and networking technologies. Similar to the increases in computer performance and storage capacity, network bandwidth has increased along with ability to support more interface types over longer distances. The cost economics of long-haul networking technologies have improved in most cases, with the exception being some older, slower interfaces that have seen cases of price increases. The diversity of available long-haul communication options, ranging from high-speed SONET/SDH to low-speed Frame Relay and fractional bandwidth services, enables you to select the right technology for your needs and applications.

In the past, metropolitan and wide area data protection involved:

- Locally managed SANs with no interconnect
- Tape-based backups over the LAN to the mainframe or both
- Poor resource sharing and utilization of assets
- File and data transfers using copies
- Channel extension for remote storage (disk and tape)

Currently, metropolitan and wide area storage networking is characterized by:

- SAN interconnection and interoperability
- Locally managed SANs and SAN islands
- Private lines and dark fiber availability
- Carrier services for storage

Moving forward, storage networking in general should be widely distributed with central management and shared resources. Other characteristics include:

- Intelligent routing and resource sharing
- Carrier-managed storage interconnects and services
- Networking aware and agnostic storage devices
- Improved bandwidth and wavelength allocations

6.2.2 Local and long-haul storage interface characteristics

Distance choice depends on application performance and availability requirements, distance, budget, and availability of services locally and remotely. An important point regarding survivability and business continuance is distance—whether across the computer room, across the campus, across town, in the region, or globally. Resilient storage networks leverage metropolitan and wide area storage networks to span distances between locations and sites. So why the need for different networking interfaces including dark dedicated fiber and MANs if they can only be useful to 100–150km? Why use SONET/SDH and why not just utilize IP for everything? Hopefully, at the end of this chapter you will have the answer to these and other common questions.

There are different I/O and network interfaces with various characteristics, ranging from dedicated dark fiber, which can be used to implement networks including InfiniBand, Fibre Channel, Ethernet, and SONET/SDH. These interfaces, as seen in Chapter 4, can support different ULPs, including RDMA, FCP, FICON, IP, and ATM. Figure 6.1 shows various networking interfaces, protocols, and technology, including dedicated dark fiber, which can be used for implementing metropolitan and wide area storage networks.

Figure 6.1 shows how bandwidth scales from left to right across the bottom axis, while costs increase from bottom to top on the left axis. This figure shows various networking interfaces, including traditional WAN (T1/E1, T3/E3, Frame Relay, and ATM) as well as SONET/SDH with Optical Carrier (OC-x) interfaces. Also shown are dedicated dark fiber with TDM, CWDM, WDM, and DWDM, which can be used for building SONET/SDH, Ethernet, and Fibre Channel networks. These networks can then be used to support IP and other protocols as well as to support tunneling of various interfaces over wide area distances. There are trade-offs with the different interfaces—for example, while more expensive, dedicated dark fiber, particularly when combined with multiplexing, has the highest bandwidth capability. Storage networks need some sort of network to support longer distances—for example, a SONET/SDH network that could support IP

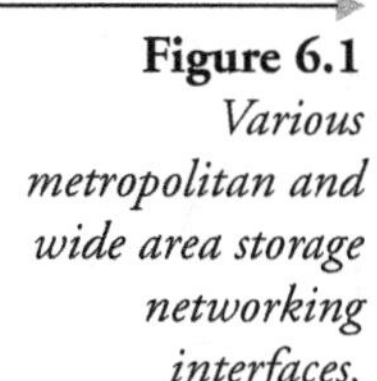

Figure 6.1 *Various metropolitan and wide area storage networking interfaces.*

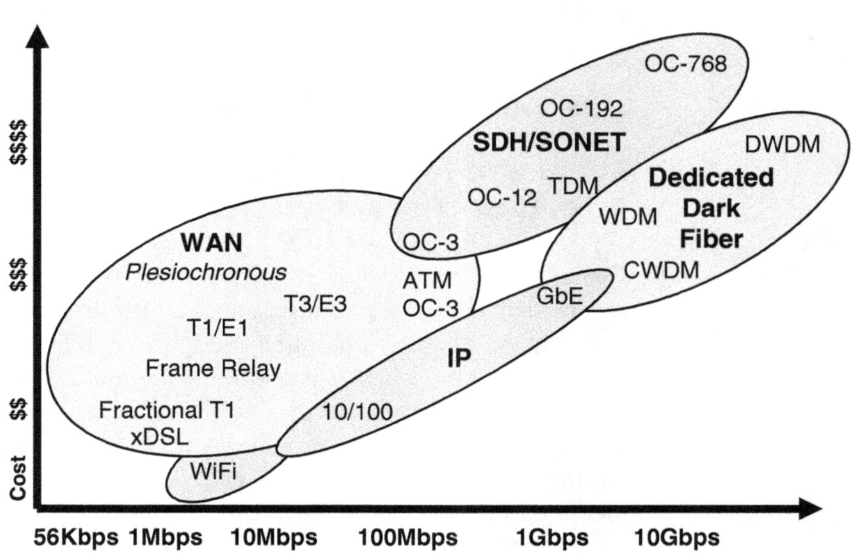

services, Ethernet, Fibre Channel, ATM and others. An IP network needs some form of underlying network, with an interface such as Ethernet, ATM, SONET/SDH, Fibre Channel or similar, to move IP packets over various distances. These different network interfaces can be characterized as short haul for local applications and long haul for long distances.

Some examples of combining different technologies include:

- Channel extension for device-to-device and server-to-device communication
- SAN-to-SAN interconnection over various distances and performance characteristics
- Fibre Channel, including FICON and FCP over IP (FCIP and iFCP), ATM, and SONET/SDH
- ESCON over IP, ATM, and SONET/SDH as well as Frame Relay
- Fibre Channel (FCP, FICON), ESCON, Ethernet, SONET/SDH, and ATM over WDM
- Storage over IP including use of wireless and Wi-Fi and WiMax

6.2.3 Broadband and baseband commutations

The term *broadband* today is generally used to describe high-bandwidth networks and interfaces for voice and data. High bandwidth is loosely characterized, particularly for consumer and mass-market applications, as something faster than a dial-up telephone connection. Some examples of broadband networking technology in use today include high-speed cable modems, xDSL, ISDN, and traditional high-speed long-haul networking, including SONET/SDH. For example, a SONET/SDH network provides a high-bandwidth network interface (pipe) to support an ATM, IP, or other network service between locations. A more refined definition of broadband communication is a transmission medium capable of supporting many frequencies as different channels for voice, video, and data. The channels are derived by dividing up the total capacity into multiple independent bandwidth channels that operate at specific frequency ranges. Consequently, the term *broadband* today is used more commonly to describe a fast data network interface as opposed to its more formal definition. Baseband communication network interface transmits data via digital signals without shifting frequencies and subdividing the bandwidth. Only one communication channel is available at any given time on a baseband network interface. Ethernet is an example of a baseband network interface.

6.2.4 Connection-oriented and connectionless transport modes

Two different modes for communication and transmission of data across networks are connection oriented and connectionless. These communication modes characterize how different networks and protocols handle data transmission. A connection-oriented transport mode is the opposite of a connectionless transport, which sends data in a continuous stream from one source to another—for example, from one server to another or from a server to a storage device. The transport guarantees that all data will be delivered to the other end in the same order as it was sent (in-order delivery) without data loss or duplication of data. The data transmission occurs through a defined process, including connection establishment, data transfer, and connection release. A common example of a connection-oriented transport is the Transmission Control Protocol, more commonly known as TCP.

In a connectionless transport mode, data is transferred between source and destination with no previous setup (connection establishment, transmission, session close). Individual data packets can take divergent routes between the source and destination, whereas in a connection-oriented mode data takes the same route unless there is a disruption to the route. Each packet is individually routed to its destination in a packet switching (connectionless) transport mode using the most expedient route determined by some routing algorithm. The packets are reassembled at the destination into their appropriate sequence. An example of a connectionless transport mode is User Datagram Protocol (UDP). Connectionless transport modes are also called packet switching networks—for example, an X.25 network.

6.3 Storage over IP for distance

In Chapter 3, various storage access models, including server to device, server to server, device to device, and SAN to SAN, were covered. This section looks at channel extension; SAN over WAN, sometimes called Storage Wide Area Networks (SWANs); and SAN-to-SAN connectivity. The function of the channel extenders is multifaceted, including:

- Various methods, such as WDM, FCIP, iFCP, IP, SONET/SDH
- Handling device-specific interfaces
- Supporting synchronous, asynchronous, and semisynchronous transfers

- Compression and bandwidth optimization
- Network translation to WAN and IP interfaces
- Failover and dynamic bandwidth allocation

Figure 6.2 shows how various applications accessing different ULPs can leverage storage over IP to span distances. On the left, S/390 systems can perform CCW I/O using FICON over Fibre Channel, which can also be extended over distance using FCIP. For FCP traffic, FCIP or iFCP can be used. Also shown is iSCSI for native block data movement over IP-based networks using the SCSI command set. In the past, hardware-based mirroring solutions have used ESCON—more recently, Fibre Channel FCP—and device-specific command sets to communicate with each other. Channel extenders have enabled hardware-based mirroring to be implemented in LAN, MAN, and WAN environments over a variety of network interfaces, including IP.

To support a resilient enterprise, channel extenders can be configured for redundancy and failover in an active/passive or active/active mode. To achieve optimum performance, channel extenders are fine-tuned for specific storage devices. For wide area resiliency, distances of 1,000km and beyond are supported in asynchronous modes. As a general rule of thumb, synchronous mirroring should be kept to under 100km for good performance and data integrity. Longer distances can be accomplished using store and forward buffering technology, where the data being transmitted is buffered to help smooth out traffic flow. This can be combined with compression to help optimize network utilization and traffic flow.

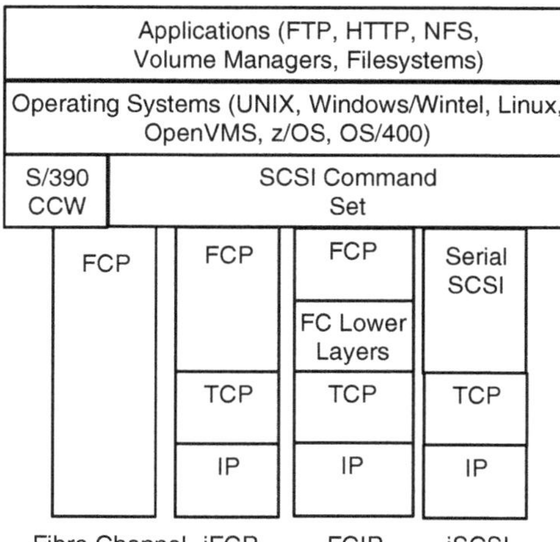

Figure 6.2 *Storage and networking layers.*

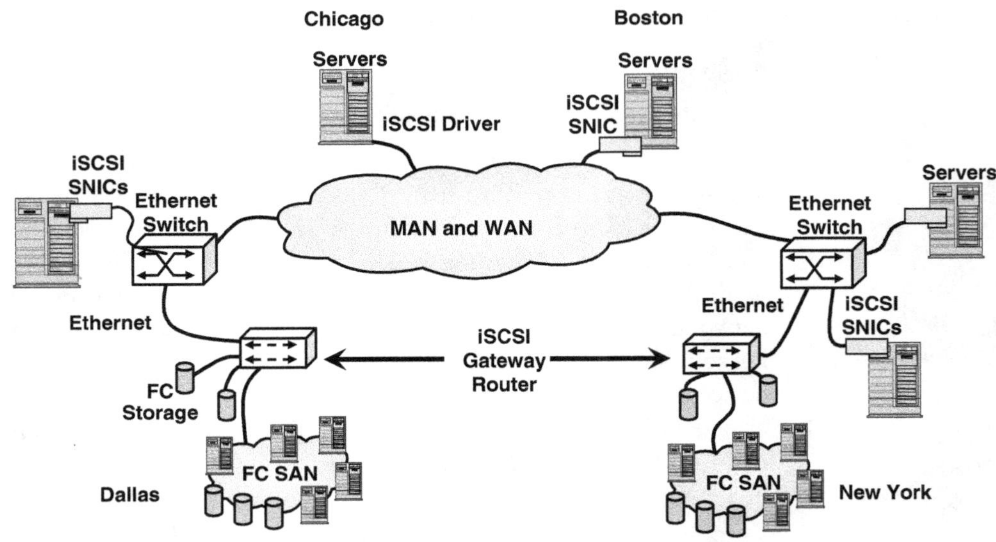

Figure 6.3 *An iSCSI metropolitan and wide area example.*

6.3.1 SCSI for remote storage access

iSCSI can be utilized for metropolitan and wide area applications to enable block storage I/O to be performed over distance. While not intently targeted as a SAN-to-SAN interface, or device channel extension, iSCSI-based storage networks can be used for various distance applications. One of the main benefits of iSCSI is the ability to leverage an IP-based network interface for accessing block storage, as opposed to using NAS file-based access. This capability makes iSCSI an attractive interface for distributed environments, branch offices, satellite office locations, and SMB environments. Using iSCSI-enabled servers at remote locations (Figure 6.3) can access centralized storage resources and local iSCSI-enabled devices. For example, in Figure 6.3 local data in Boston or Chicago can be backed up to the larger data center SANs in Dallas and New York. Storage in the main data centers that are attached to the Fibre Channel SANs can be accessed by remote systems at the various locations using iSCSI gateways.

6.3.2 Fibre Channel IP gateway—iFCP

iFCP is a protocol to enable Fibre Channel devices (servers and storage devices) to attach to and use an IP network as a fabric switching infrastructure in place of Fibre Channel.

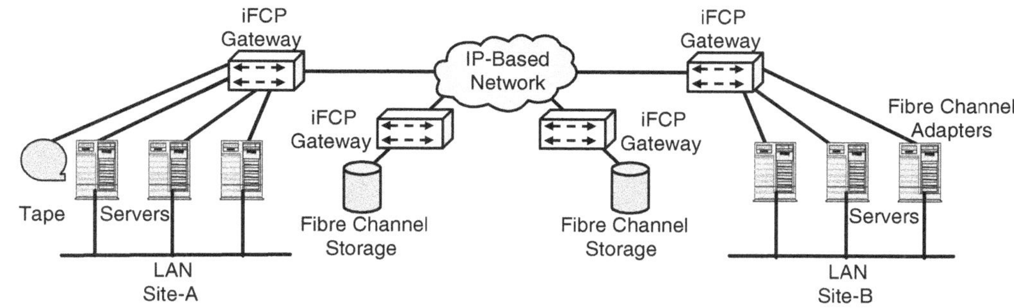

Figure 6.4 *An iFCP example.*

iFCP can be used to interconnect various SAN fabrics together; it can also be used as a device-to-device distance extension device. Both iFCP and FCIP enable Fibre Channel traffic to be transmitted over an IP network for connecting SANs together and supporting device distance extension. FCIP is a tunneling protocol in that Fibre Channel frames, regardless of their content and ULP (FCP, FICON, IP, etc.), are placed into IP packets and sent across a virtual Fibre Channel interface (tunnel) using IP and the underlying network as the interface. iFCP functions as a gateway (Figure 6.4), with devices attaching to an iFCP switch gateway to attach to an IP-based switching network.

iFCP has been slow to catch on widely compared with FCIP and iSCSI. iFCP provides a gateway-to-gateway interface leveraging an IP switching network infrastructure. The IP network provides the basic services that normally would be handled by a Fibre Channel switching infrastructure. With storage vendors implementing storage-to-storage remote mirroring extension capabilities, it's difficult to say if iFCP will gain popularity and acceptance.

6.3.3 Fibre Channel over IP (FCIP)

Fibre Channel over IP (FCIP) is a technology for interconnecting Fibre Channel–based storage networks over distances using IP. FCIP implements tunneling techniques to carry Fibre Channel traffic over IP networks. Fibre Channel frames are placed in IP packets and sent over an IP-based network to span distances. Tunneling is transparent so that it is ULP transparent, meaning that FICON and FCP traffic can be sent via the tunnel over an IP-based network. This is similar to writing a letter in one language, and putting it in an envelope to be sent through the postal system to some other destination in the world. At the receiving end, the envelope is opened, and

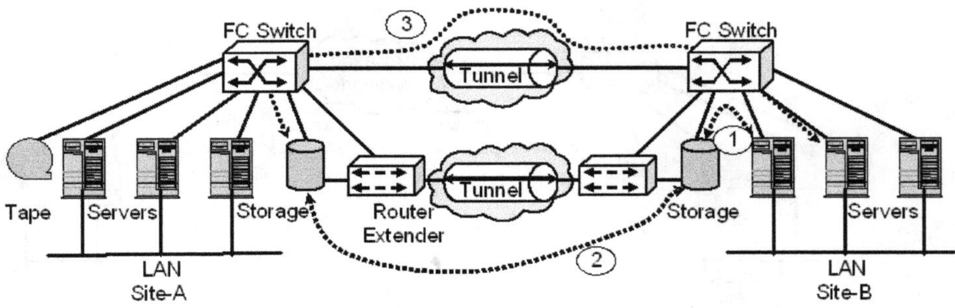

Figure 6.5 *FCIP tunneling example.*

the contents of the letter are read. Along the route those handling the letter do not have to understand the contents of the envelope, only where it's intended destination is and where it came from. FCIP takes Fibre Channel frames regardless of what the frame is for (FCP, FICON, IP, etc.) and places these into IP frames (envelopes) for transmission to the receiving destination. At the receiving destination, the envelopes are opened, and the contents are placed back on the Fibre Channel network to continue their trip.

In Figure 6.5, the two Fibre Channel switches at each location on the left and right are connected using FCIP. Two implementations are shown: one using switches with integrated FCIP capability (top path [3]) and another (bottom path [2]) using an FCIP extension, or bridge device connected to a 10/100Gb Ethernet, SONET/SDH, or ATM network. In this example servers on the left can access local storage as well as remote storage, and storage can be mirrored to companion devices at each site.

In Figure 6.6 Fibre Channel frames carrying FICON, FCP, and other ULP traffic are sent from the SAN on the left to the SAN on the right. The

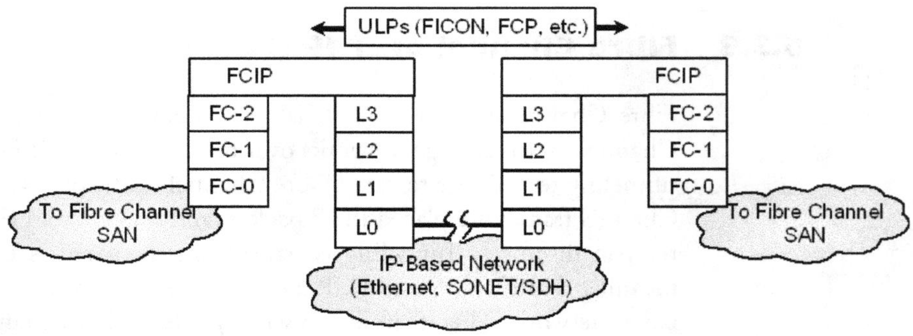

Figure 6.6 *FCIP mapping to move data between Fibre Channel SANs over IP.*

frames are placed into IP wrapper packets and transmitted over an IP-based network that could use 10/100Gb, 10Gb Ethernet, SONET/SDH, or ATM as underlying interfaces.

Gateways are also known as channel extenders and bridges; their function is to establish a tunnel between Fibre Channel environments and pass all frames with different ULP traffic between the locations. FCIP is in the ANSI IETF standards body process and is widely deployed by many different vendors, however, these devices typically have to be paired with like devices.

6.4 Wave division multiplexing

Wave Division Multiplexing (WDM) is a technology to implement optical networks by increasing the overall usable capacity and number of simultaneous networks that can use a common fiber-optic cable. There are different types of WDM that vary in cost, capacity (density), distance, and management capabilities, ranging from Coarse Wave Division Multiplexing (CWDM) to WDM and Dense Wave Division Multiplexing (DWDM). For carrier environments and building backbone networks, including SONET/SDH, carrier class DWDM technology is available. WDM, CWDM, and DWDM, collectively, are called DWDM—with differences being density, distance, cost, and management capabilities, as shown in Table 6.1.

Some benefits of using DWDM include:

- Business continuity (mirror, remote backup, vaulting)
- Increased performance and capacity
- Support for multiple interfaces and networks
- Lower total cost of ownership by doing more with less

Table 6.1 *CWDM, WDM, and DWDM Comparisons*

	Density	Distance	Management	Other
DWDM	Very dense	Long distances	Yes	More expensive, more flexible, more interfaces and options
WDM	Moderate	Long distances	Varies	Less expensive and flexible than DWDM
CWDM	Limited	Medium	Limited	Less expensive than WDM

- Self-provisioning to reduce lead times and increase performance
- Increased performance and capacity for all interfaces
- Providing some level of added security with own network
- Protocol-independent physical interface
- Simplified fiber management and cabling

Some networks that can leverage DWDM technology include:

- 10/100 Fast Ethernet, Gigabit Ethernet, and 10Gb Ethernet
- FDDI, ATM, and SONET/SDH OC-x services
- IBM Coupling Link (ISC) and IBM Sysplex Timer (ETR)
- Fibre-Channel, including FCP and FICON ULPs

DWDM is more commonly deployed in European countries, the United Kingdom, and other parts of the world, where dark fiber is more readily accessible. In certain areas of the United States there are large amounts of fiber—the catch is getting access to it. If there is dark fiber between sites, performance, distance, and bandwidth can be improved using DWDM. By using optical amplifiers to regenerate the light source, longer distances of 150–200+km can be achieved with DWDM.

DWDM is used to build carrier (SONET/SDH) and enterprise networks. Thus, when you are using a metropolitan or wide area service with an optical infrastructure or possibly an IP service, there most likely is some form of multiplexing being used. Communication carriers and backbone network providers utilize multiplexing technology to increase their own available optical networking bandwidth. For enterprise customers, DWDM enables simplified management by being able to self-provision new circuits to support multiple network interfaces. In Figure 6.7, Fibre Channel, FICON, ESCON, and Gigabit Ethernet are all using DWDM technology for MAN applications between different sites. For example, a LAN might be made up of a combination of Gigabit Ethernet, 10/100 Ethernet, and ATM to support IP traffic. DWDM technology can be used to support physical network interfaces in a MAN environment, and IP-based bridging can be used to interconnect over global distances.

6.4.1 Wave division multiplexing basics

Optical networks use light to send data serially by turning light on and off. This on and off sequence maps to a digital or binary state used for communications. This is similar to using a flashlight to send a signal to someone

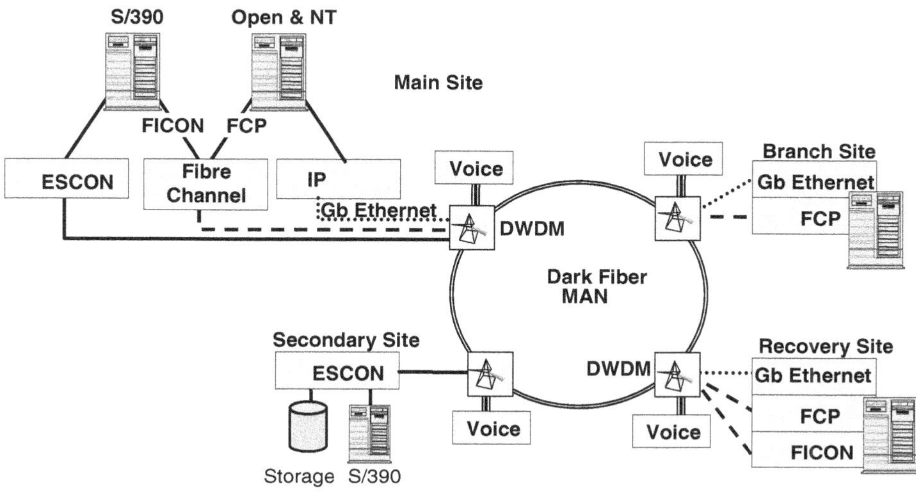

Figure 6.7 *Wave division multiplexing metropolitan network.*

using Morse code. By turning the light on and off in different patterns (protocol), a message is sent. DWDM, for all of its sophisticated components (electrical and optical) and flexibility, in its simplest form is relatively easy to understand. If you have ever seen a rainbow after it rains, or have seen light pass through a prism, you are seeing different wavelengths—also known as lambdas. The basic premise of DWDM involves sending light through an optical device creating virtual channels (lambdas) using different wavelengths from the light spectrum and then multiplexing them together for transmission, as seen in Figure 6.8.

Each light wave represents a separate lambda that corresponds to a virtual channel, the equivalent of a dedicated fiber to support different network interfaces. For example (Figure 6.9), FDDI, Gigabit Ethernet, ATM, Fibre Channel, FICON, and ESCON could each be mapped to a different lambda. Each network functions as though it has its own dedicated piece of fiber, when in reality unused bandwidth is being used to create a virtual

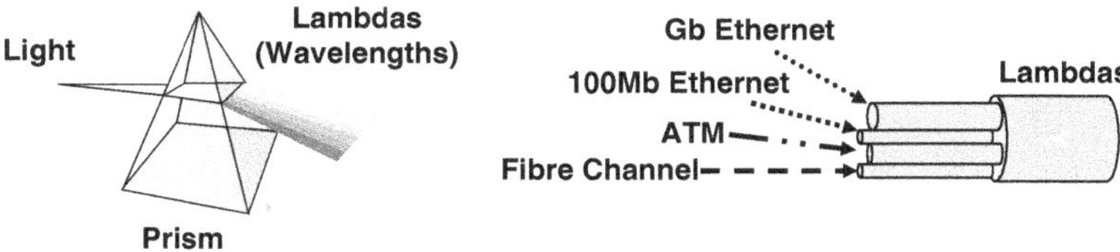

Figure 6.8 *Wave division multiplexing fundamentals.*

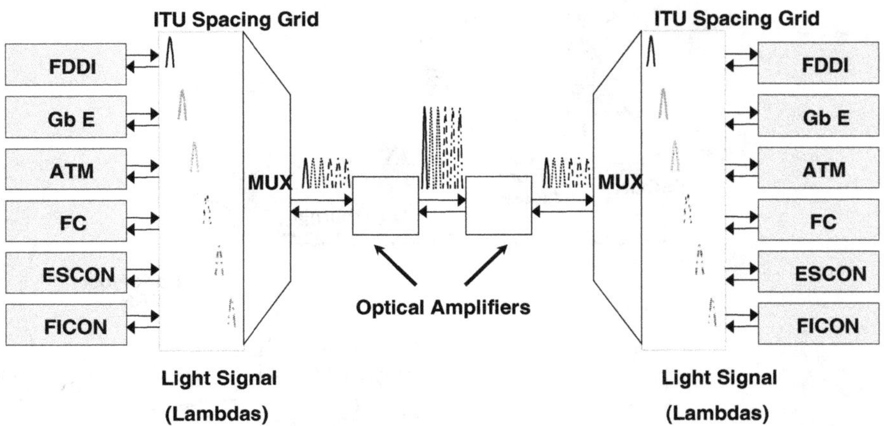

Figure 6.9 *Fiber optics supporting multiple networks with multiplexing.*

fiber. Consequently, performance of the different networks is not impacted and additional bandwidth can be created (self-provision) by enabling more lambdas (adding port cards). The limit to the number of lambdas is device and vendor dependent; however, 16 to 64 ports are available for enterprise DWDM devices, with larger devices being available for carrier applications.

DWDM technology can be configured in point to point, ring, and multi-drop to support multiple sites. DWDM technology supports many more channels to enable more bandwidth. The speed of each channel could range from 2.5Gbps to 10Gbps depending on equipment being used. There are two classes of DWDM devices: enterprise class and carrier class. Enterprise DWDM devices have different levels of availability and redundancy features, management tools, and interfaces. Carrier class DWDM devices have higher levels of availability, bandwidth density, and management features. These devices also have high availability and diagnostic and monitoring features (along with more ports).

6.4.2 Reducing cost of fiber

A valuable advantage of DWDM is that while a dark pair (send and receive) of fiber strands (cable) can be very expensive, when you start to multiplex at 8 times (8×), 16 times (16×), or 32 times (32×), or even higher, you effectively reduce the cost of the fiber by how many channels or lambdas (light colors) you are able to create. For example, if you were using 16 lambdas, the cost of the fiber would be fiber cost plus DWDM technology cost divided by number of lambdas (16). Thus, while a single dark fiber could be expensive and support only a single network interface, by using DWDM additional network protocols and interfaces can be supported and bandwidth self-provisioned.

6.5 Time division multiplexing

Wave division multiplexes multiple wavelengths together using wave division, separation multiplexing. Time Division Multiplexing (TDM) multiplexes traffic based on time intervals to aggregate traffic for transmission. TDM can be used to aggregate multiple slower networking interfaces together to more effectively utilize a dark fiber link or map onto a SONET/SDH network. TDM can be used to feed slower networks such as 10/100Mb Ethernet and 17MB/sec ESCON interfaces into WDM-based solutions to make more effective use of dark fibers. TDM can also be used to aggregate slower networks as well as aggregate bandwidth from other network interfaces onto SONET/SDH OC-12 and faster WAN interfaces. For example, multiple 1Gb Fibre Channel interfaces operating at 50 percent utilization would only require 50MB/sec each and not fully utilize the bandwidth of a dark fiber or lambda service. By aggregating underutilized or slower network interfaces using TDM, WAN interfaces can be more effectively utilized and help lower networking costs. TDM devices that support Fibre Channel and FICON to SONET/SDH as well as packet over SONET/SDH can be used to build wide area storage networks as an alternative to FCIP.

6.6 When to utilize multiplexing

Multiplexing is traditionally thought of for use between locations and when cost and distance are a factor. Multiplexing can also be used in a building as a means to simplify and enhance the scalability of cable plants. For example, instead of running large bundles of fiber optics between floors in a building or between buildings in a campus, multiplexing can be leveraged to simplify and recover the cost of optics. There may be a lot of fiber in the ground; however, it may also be older than 50um, which may not be suitable for higher speeds. Multiplexing can also be used for fan-out applications, normally implanted with smaller 8- and 16-port switches.

While not a network interface or protocol, DWDM can be thought of as an extension and expansion to physical dedicated fiber-optic cables by increasing the available bandwidth, supporting longer distances, and utilization of the fiber. Various optical network topologies can be built, including point to point and add-drop rings for redundant paths. Amplification can be used to regenerate, boosting the optical signal and cleaning it up if needed to span ultralong distances of hundreds of kilometers.

From a campus and MAN perspective dark fiber provides great flexibility for bandwidth, performance, and ease of management. While potentially expensive, once you have access to the dark fiber, you can control the actual amount of bandwidth you want, or are willing to pay for, using DWDM. Self-provisioning enables you to create bandwidth when you need it rather than waiting for the carrier to provide it. This capability also enables the cost of the physical fiber to be spread out over more interfaces.

Some carriers are reluctant to provide dark fiber, particularly without restrictions on the number of virtual circuits (lambdas) to control bandwidth. The reason is that some carriers are concerned customers may leverage the capabilities of dark fiber to create their own subcarrier networks and thus the carriers will lose revenue. Some providers place restrictions on the number of lambdas, self-provisioning, and types of protocols used. Some providers only allow dark fiber as a total service (DWDM equipment, management, dark fiber). This is similar to broadband providers requiring that their modems and devices be rented to gain access to their services. In the United Kingdom, Europe, and other parts of the world, fiber can be more easily acquired than in the United States.

6.7 Asynchronous Transfer Mode (ATM)

Asynchronous Transfer Mode (ATM) is a common backbone networking technology used in the core, as well as at the edge of many telecommunications systems for voice, video, and data at high speeds. Carriers and other network providers commonly utilize ATM as the basis for allocation of bandwidth services over various distances and speeds. ATM integrates with other technologies and features sophisticated management for QoS and guaranteed delivery of data. ATM has different layers as part of its protocol design, with integrated management controls and diagnostics. ATM is a cell-based networking protocol that can be used to carry traffic (data, voice, video) using fixed packet frames, called cells, over long distances and can be used to interconnect various networks. ATM utilizes short, fixed-length packets, called cells, to transport data between locations. For example, IP frames and their contents can be mapped into an ATM cell and sent across an ATM network with reassembly at the other end to create a seamless IP traffic flow. ATM is a layered networking interface, which can be deployed on different physical media and networking interfaces, including dedicated dark fiber and SONET/SDH OC-x interfaces.

The first ATM layer is referred to as the adapter layer; it holds the majority of the data transmission, including the 48-byte payload. An ATM cell is 53 bytes, with 48 bytes as payload and 5 bytes as control information. The control information can be thought of as overhead, since it is not used for moving data; rather, it is used to describe the data and where it is going. The 48-byte payload section of an ATM cell is where data and information being carried over the ATM network are placed for transmission. The ATM physical layer is the interface to the networking interfaces (optical, electrical), including SONET/SDH and Frame Relay. ATM includes diagnostics, called operations, administration, and management (OAM). ATM can be used to connect storage networks together as well as to support device-to-device communications for remote mirroring and access. The industry trade association concerned with ATM is the ATM Forum (www.atmforum.com).

6.8 SONET/SDH

Synchronous Optical Network (SONET) and Synchronous Digital Hierarchy (SDH) describe an optical network for global networking. SONET (United States and some foreign countries) and SDH (Europe and other parts of the world) are synonymous to create carrier backbone networks. SONET/SDH specifics how data is organized, framed, and transported synchronously across fiber-optic transmission links. SONET/SDH also enables the various nodes and links to have different clocking frequencies out of phase (not synchronized). SONET/SDH networks carry data in frames at speeds in multiples of 51.84Mbps using Optional Carrier (OC-x) networks, where "x" is the multiple. For example, an OC-1 is a 51.84Mbps interface, while an OC-12 is a (12 × 51.84) 622Mbps interface. SONET/SDH supports multiple frames being sent together as a superframe. SDH networks also refer to the interface in terms of the multiple, with an STS-1 network being 1 × 51.84Mbps, an STS-3 being 3 × an STS-1, an STS-12 being 12 × an STS-1, and so on. SONET/SDH networks are metropolitan and wide area, with bandwidth varying between locations depending on topology. SONET/SDH is used for carrying voice and data traffic on different channels on the same physical cable. SONET/SDH are Layer 2 interfaces that networks (IP, ATM, Fibre Channel) use as long distance transports. SONET/SDH bandwidth is allocated to different users and workload depending on the type of service being used or purchased. Technologies such as Fibre Channel Backbone (FCBB) gateway and channel extension devices can use SONET/SDH as an alternative to IP for wide

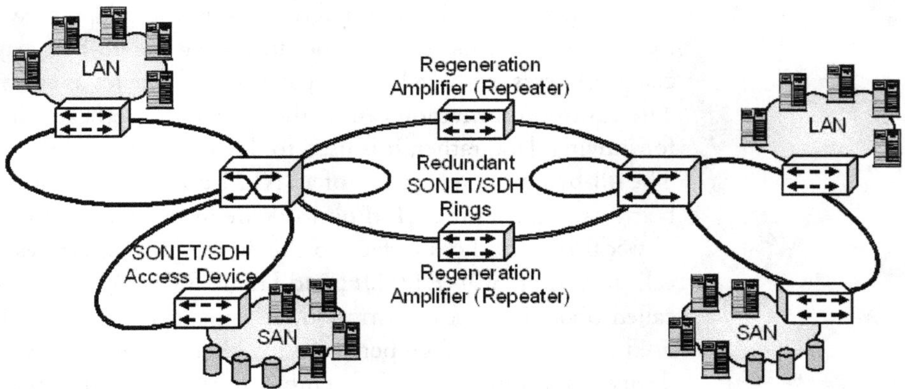

Figure 6.10 *An example SONET/SDH network.*

area communications to bridge storage networks beyond the 100–200km distance.

Figure 6.10 shows a SONET/SDH network with multiple rings that could connect different cities including redundant rings. In Figure 6.11, the bandwidth is subdivided into smaller, lower bandwidth allocations including

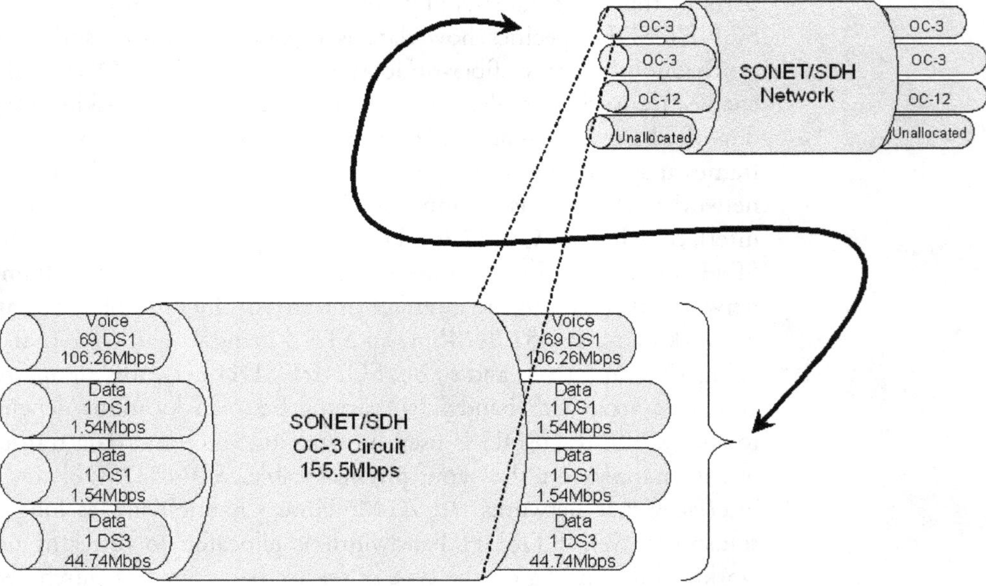

Figure 6.11 *SONET/SDH high-speed circuit allocation.*

OC-3 and OC-3. The OC-3 SONET/SDH bandwidth is further subdivided into various channels for voice and data usage. The dark fiber that SONET/SDH networks are built on utilizes carrier class DWDM technology to increase bandwidth and available channels.

A SONET/SDH network can similarly subdivide a physical cable into multiple circuits, each operating at different Optical Carrier (OC-x) rates, as shown in Table 6.2.

Synchronous transport module level 1 (STM-1), also known as OC-3 and STS3, is the lowest bit rate expected to carry ATM traffic. A truck and airplane are shown because, while they do not provide real-time recovery, there are still many sites that rely on some form of physical transportation of data on tape or other medium. Large amounts of data can be transported in a truck over a freeway with large amounts of bandwidth; the truck also has latency associated with retrieving tapes or data from a storage facility, transportation to the destination, unloading, and, if needed, acclimatizing and restoration.

Table 6.2 *SONET/SDH Characteristics*

Optical Level	SDH Equivalent	Electrical Level	Line Rate (Mbps)	Payload Rate (Mbps)	Overhead (Percentage)
OC-1	N/A	STS-1	51.84	50.112	3.33
OC-3	STM-1	STS-3	155.5	150.336	3.33
OC-9	STM-3	STS-9	466.560	451.008	3.33
OC-12	STM-4	STS-12	622.080	601.344	3.33
OC-18	STM-6	STS-18	933.120	902.016	3.33
OC-24	STM-8	STS-24	1,244.160	1,202.688	3.33
OC-36	STM-12	STS-36	1,866.240	1,804.032	3.33
OC-48	STM-16	STS-48	2,488.320	2,405.376	3.33
OC-96	STM-32	STS-96	4,976.640	4,810.752	3.33
OC-192	STM-64	STS-192	9,953.280	9,621.504	3.33
OC-768	STM-256	STS-768	39,713.120*	38,486.016*	3.54*
DWDM	N/A	N/A	Varies	Varies	N/A

* Estimated.

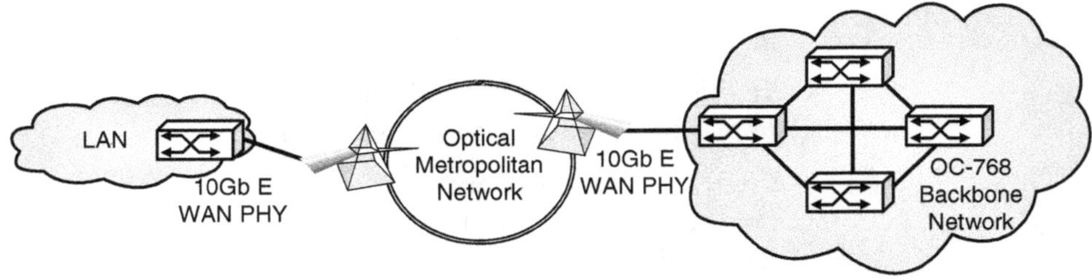

Figure 6.12 *A 10Gb Ethernet with metropolitan area network and SONET backbone.*

Various networking interfaces, as seen in Figure 6.12, include Gb Ethernet, optical networking with wave division multiplexing, and SONET/SDH; these can be combined to create metropolitan and wide area networks to support bandwidth needs of 10Gb.

6.9 Public switched telephone network

The Public Switched Telephone Network (PSTN) is a collection of interconnected systems operated by various telephone, telecommunications, and administrations around the world. Also known as the Plain Old Telephone System (POTS), the PSTN provides the basis for analog circuit switching to support voice, video, and data communication. In contrast to POTS, newer technology based on digital transmission includes xDSL and ISDN networks for voice and data. Today, much of the PSTN has at the backbone been switched over to digital technology; however, the last mile(s) transmission commonly remains analog using a twisted pair of copper electrical cables. The basic unit of measure in a telecommunications (telco) system is a DS0, which is made up of 8,000 samples per second, with 8 bits per sample, to yield 64Kbit/sec data stream. Multiple DSO data streams can be combined (24 in the United States for a T1, 31 in Europe for an E1) to create higher bandwidth. The T1 and E1 circuits can be further combined to create even higher bandwidth.

Some WAN interfaces are shown in Table 6.3, including service name, transport speed in Mbit/sec, payload size, ATM equivalency, and average latency for various I/O sizes. The data rates shown in Table 6.3 are those that can be found, or are available, via PSTN providers.

The values shown in Table 6.3 are specifications (wire speed) shown by interface type, Mbits/second, Mbytes/second, and network protocols used with the interface. While DWDM is not really a network interface, it is a very useful tool that is used to extend and create additional bandwidth for

Table 6.3 *Various Wide Area Storage Interface Comparisons (shown in milliseconds)*

Service	Transport (Mbit/sec)	Payload	ATM	4k block (msec)	8k block (msec)	16k block (msec)	27k block (msec)
E1	2	1.92	—	16.67	33.33	66.67	112.50
E2	8	7.68	—	4.17	8.33	16.67	28.13
E3	34	30.72	—	1.04	2.08	4.17	7.03
T3	45	41.30	—	0.77	1.55	3.10	5.23
STM-1	155	149.76	135.63	0.24	0.47	0.94	1.59
STM-4	622	599.04	542.53	0.06	0.12	0.24	0.40

these interfaces as well as to build them. Thus, it can be considered an interface using dark fiber as well as a complementary technology for networking and storage networking.

The values are shown in milliseconds (msec), with one-way transfer and latency caused by basic WAN clock rates and traffic. Compression can help reduce the transfer times. The values show the average time it takes to transfer various block (I/O) sizes over telecommunications lines. Wire and fiber latency is 5usec/km, and a synchronous copy will require an acknowledgment of completed write operations—therefore adding 10usec/km for round-trip delay. Latency of WAN multiplexes and PDH/SDH cross-connects add navigable end-to-end delay.

Plesiochronous Digital Hierarchy (PDH) networks, including Frame Relay, utilize plesiochronous synchronization and multiplexing for network transmission of voice and data. Integrated Subscriber Digital Network (ISDN) is an example of a PDH network. Bandwidth for PDH networks is described as DS0, DS1, T1, and so on, as shown in Table 6.4. A DS level and associated framing specification for synchronous digital streams in North America at T1 transmission rate is 1,544,000 bits per second (baud). Multiple DS0 channels are multiplexed together to create high DS levels—for example, DS1 consists of 24 DS0 channels. DS0 circuits can carry 800 bytes per second (64,000 bits per second). ISDN networks can be implemented on single wire (electrical) and optical-fiber networks to carry voice and data using Public Switched Telephone Network (PSTN) switches at various bandwidths. ISDN is available in Australia, parts of Europe, Japan, and Singapore, with limited availability in the United Kingdom and the United States. A T1 circuit requires two twisted pair lines, one for each direction. PDH-based networks are being replaced by SONET and SDH networks.

Table 6.4 *Plesiochronous Digital Hierarchy Network Characteristics*

Hierarchy Level	Channels (DS0 Equivalency)	Line Rate (Mbps)	Payload Rate (Mbps)	Overhead Rate (Percentage)
DS0	1	0.064	0.064	N/A
DS1-T1	24	1.54	1.54	0.52
DS1C-T1C	48	3.15	3.07	2.54
DS2-T2	96	6.31	6.14	2.66
DS3-T3	672	44.74	43.008	3.86
DS4-T4	4,032	274.2	258.05	5.88
E1	30 or 31	2.048	1.984 or 1.944	3–6
E2	120	8.448	8.056	4.64
E3	480	34.368	30.720	10.61
E4	1,920	139.264	122.880	11.76
E5	7,860	565.148	503.040	10.99

6.10 Inverse multiplexing

Another approach to improving performance of data transmission is to divide the data stream into multiple concurrent streams that are transmitted across separate I/O interface channels (e.g., a T-1 or E-1) and then reconstructed at the far end. This is similar to disk stripping to improve performance and what is being done with fabrics in the form of trunking. Data integrity is very important, as is in-order delivery. This is an approach to overcome bottlenecks of slower interfaces by combining multiple data streams. Ideally you would use a faster interface; however, if this is not available, then this is not feasible. Another trade-off or benefit is that multiple slower interfaces may be less expensive than faster ones.

6.11 Free space optics and wireless communication

Free space optics are a variant of optical networking, but they do not utilize fiber-optic cabling. As its name implies, free space optics transmit a light beam through the air between two locations within relatively close proximity to each other, as in a city center. Free space optics are an alternative to when fiber-optic cabling is not available between buildings and higher speeds are not needed. Free space optics can be a fit for distances of about 1km and speeds under 1Gbit/sec to create IP networks. Free space optics can also be used as an alternative to metropolitan microwave applications. Wireless communications have a potential as a storage networking metropolitan interface given improvements in bandwidth and distance. WiMax, a new wireless interface standard (IEEE 802.16), provides support for distances of about 31 miles and is well suited for some MAN environments. The WiMax supports 70Mbit/sec or about 7 percent of a 1Gb interface. While this is not as fast as other interfaces, including Gb Ethernet and DWDM MAN technology, various wireless interfaces provide support for remote access. A key capability for using wireless interfaces for storage networking will be enhanced security techniques and tools.

6.12 Chapter summary

So what is the right interface for you? The right interface for you is what is applicable for your business needs, recovery and survivability requirements, and budget constraints. Be sure that your wide area and other service providers are using unique paths so that you have no single points of failure in your network design and configuration. Combined with autonomous regions and state change management, iFCP and FCIP can be used to physically interconnect different SAN fabrics, yet isolate traffic. IP-based and other networks utilize underlying networks locally as well as over long distances. DWDM and SONET/SDH are at the core of many local and wide area networks. For redundancy and availability concerns ensure that your alternate communication paths actually take divergent paths, as opposed to converging in the same central office switching facility and on the same path.

What This Chapter Will Do For You

This chapter looks at various storage networking devices, including servers, adapters, switches, and storage devices (disk and tape). Some of the items you will learn about in this chapter include:

- The different classes and types of storage devices needed to meet your requirements
- Tape is still alive, however, the economics of using disk retention are improving
- Your storage investment may not be fully usable without server upgrades
- How much feature and function do you need and what can you pay extra for?

7

Storage Networking Devices

7.1 Overview

What good is a network with nothing to use it? What good is storage if you cannot get to it? This chapter takes a closer look at various storage networking devices and components, including storage devices (disk and tape), adapters, switches, and gateways.

7.2 Storage networking devices

Storage networking devices, also known as nodes, attach to storage networks to communicate with storage resource. Storage networking devices include servers, adapters, I/O paths (storage interfaces), switches, intelligent switches, storage devices (disk, tape, and SSD), as well as gateways, routers, and bridges for protocol conversion and distance support. The different servers could support different applications, including domain name services (DNS) for network name services and authentication, file, print, Web, and data warehouse to name a few.

Figure 7.1 shows a storage network with two separate fabrics for redundancy (Path-A and Path-B), with some servers attached to both paths and some servers attached only to one. In this example servers are shown along with I/O adapters known as host bus adapters attached to switching devices that have storage attached to them. This example also shows how one of the fabrics (Path-B) spans two locations for resiliency and access of remote servers and storage devices over a wide area network.

7.2.1 Servers, processors (nodes)

Servers supporting different applications and functions vary in shape, size, and characteristics from IBM (and compatible) mainframes running MVS,

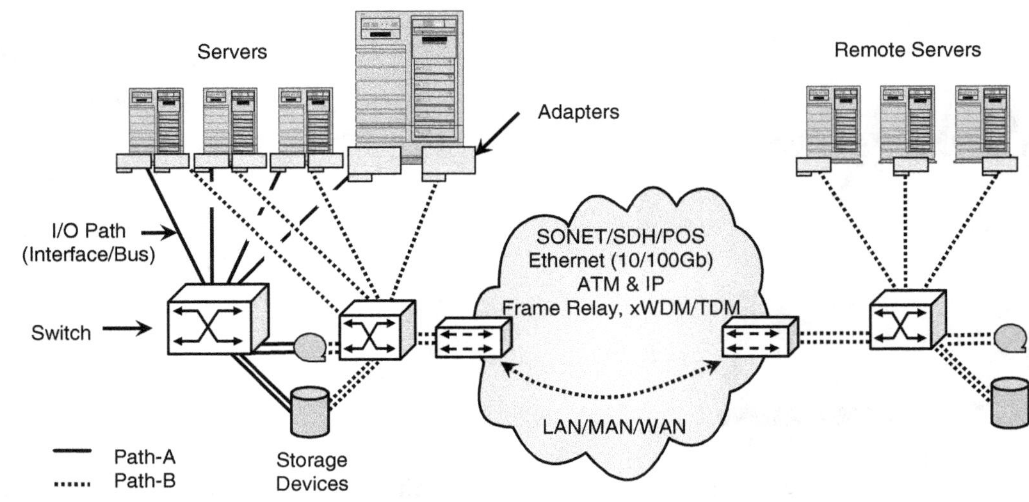

Figure 7.1 *Storage networking devices and components.*

zOS, and Linux to large UNIX and open systems servers supporting many partitions and small servers running UNIX, WinTel, and Linux systems. Some IBM servers and operating systems include IBM AS/400s (iSeries) running OS/400, IBM pSeries (RS/6000 and SP2) running AIX (IBM's UNIX), and IBM S/390 mainframe (zSeries) running MVS, zOS, VM, and Linux. Intel-based servers from Dell, Unisys, NCR, Bull, Gateway, IBM (xSeries), and HPQ, to name a few, run WinTel, Linux, OS/2, and NetWare. Sun Sparc–based systems run Solaris, HP OpenVMS, and Tandem systems among others.

Servers can be large frame-based systems with large memory capacity and compute power as well as corresponding large I/O capabilities. Servers can be rack mounted with a couple of small servers per cabinet, many ultrasmall form-factor servers in a 19" rack cabinet, or high-density configurations with many blades per shelve with multiple shelves per cabinet. Servers can be configured as standalone systems or clustered with other servers for high availability in standby as well as active failover modes. Servers can be single processor based (uniprocessor) and multiprocessor based. A server can be configured to support one copy and instance of an operating system or be partitioned into logical processors (domains) to support multiple instances and different operating systems. Clusters of servers can be in the same cabinet; however, for improved resiliency they are best located in separate cabinets to eliminate single points of failure. For added resiliency, server clusters should be located some distance apart in the same facility or at separate locations to create geographically dispersed and metropolitan clusters.

Servers attach to storage networks using adapters that interface to the server's internal I/O bus, which could be proprietary (e.g., HP HSC, Sun Sbus, IBM STI) or open interfaces, including PCI, PCI-X, and IDE with support for hot swap of devices. The adapters interface to the server's bus as well as attach to the external storage networking using a storage interface (Fibre Channel, SSA, and SCSI among others). Adapters can provide simple attachment of the server to the storage network interface as well as perform more advanced functions, including providing host-based RAID (mirroring and protection). Servers may have multiple storage interface attachments for redundancy and performance, as well as attachment of different devices. For clustered systems, heartbeat interfaces may use shared interfaces or have dedicated interfaces for redundancy and robustness of the cluster.

Many servers have internal (dedicated) storage as well as expansion slots to add more storage as well as host bus adapters. Some servers come with a minimum amount of internal storage to support the base operating system, applications, and functions, while others have more storage. For your environment, you will want to assess if the value of having dedicated storage available in the different servers offsets the cost in terms of management and support of storage in the servers. For smaller environments this may be a simple analysis and decision while for larger ones it may be more complex. On one hand you have storage that is available for use, so why not utilize it, while on the other it incurs costs in terms of people, time, and management tools, including backup to support the multiple instances of storage.

Some other characteristics of servers include the ability to boot over a network, including storage network from remote storage to eliminate or reduce the need for internal storage. By utilizing diskless servers or servers that rely on a minimum amount of internal based storage swapping, replacement of servers becomes much simpler. Some models of blade servers have dedicated storage as well as optional embedded Fibre Channel and Ethernet switches to facilitate attachment to larger storage networks. Combining storage networking and blade servers can provide a high degree of scalability and flexibility. For higher availability and resiliency, some servers now support mirrored and RAID-protected memory for redundancy (in addition to standard parity protection techniques).

A question that comes up is how many servers to configure per storage device or per storage interface, and the answer, as might be expected, is that it depends. One approach is a connection-based approach based on a rule of thumb that defines the number of servers per amount of storage or devices. A more practical approach is to base this decision on performance (throughput/bandwidth, I/O operations, or a combination), also known as activity. This can be based on averages, knowledge of your applications and workloads, and vendor-supplied information. One simple example is that if your servers average 10–20MB/sec on a sustained basis (meaning over time the sustained active average), on a 1Gb Fibre Channel interface with a need to operate at 80 percent bandwidth, four to eight servers could be on the same interface. Of course this is only an example and later in Chapter 10 additional examples and discussion will be covered.

7.2.2 Storage networking adapters (HBAs, SNICs, and HCAs)

HBAs and Storage Networking Interface Cards (SNICs) are an important part of storage networking. Host servers use Host Bus Adapters (HBAs) to attach to the storage network, while storage devices use their port adapters. Without an HBA, a server does not have access to a storage network and its resources. This is similar to how servers use Network Interface Cards (NICs) to attach to networks. HBAs attach to the host I/O busses (including PCI and Sun Sbus) and system device drivers. For example, a Fibre Channel HBA will use a SCSI (FCP) driver to initiate (issue) I/O requests from a host to a SCSI target/LUN on a storage device. In addition to providing a physical interface between the host bus and Fibre Channel interface, HBAs can support various protocols, including SCSI (FCP), FICON (FC-SB-2), IP, and VI. For storage over IP, instead of an HBA a Storage Networking Interface Card (SNIC) similar in function to a standard NIC could be used or an iSCSI driver on a supported network NIC—for example, an Ethernet TCP/IP iSCSI–enabled adapter.

Figure 7.2 shows three examples of adapters with dual ports for attachment to I/O path interfaces. The top example in Figure 7.2 shows a dual port (two I/O path interfaces) and a single controller chip for attachment to a server I/O bus. The middle example in Figure 7.2 shows a dual port adapter with two controller chips for improved performance attaching to a single server I/O bus. The third example (bottom) shows a single port adapter with an attachment to a server I/O bus.

First-generation Fibre Channel SAN HBAs had a single port or interface, with current-generation HBAs having two or more ports either connected to a common ASIC or controller chip, or multiple ASIC controller

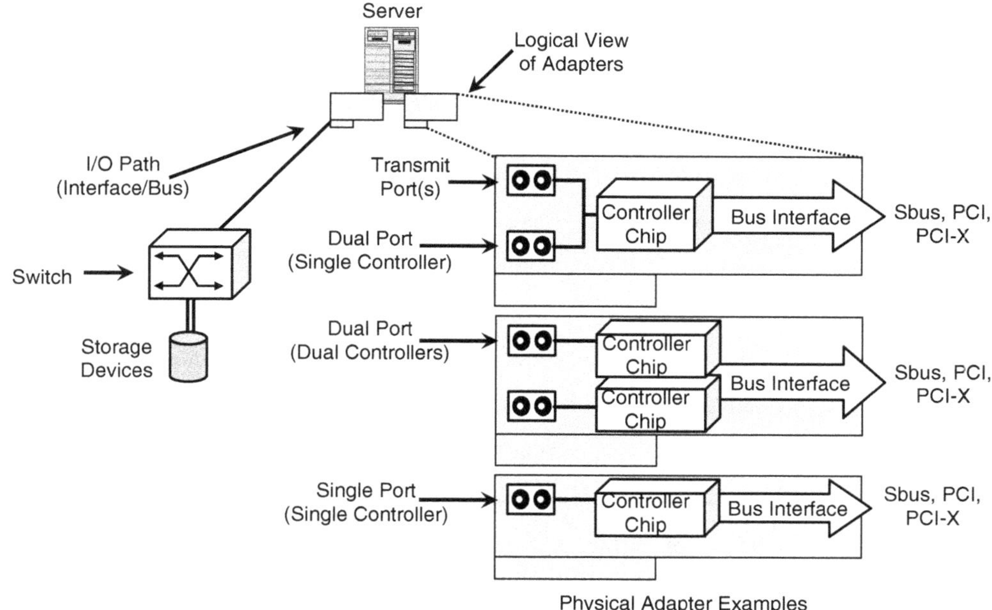

Figure 7.2 *Host adapter example.*

chips for added performance. HBAs can also have multiple WWN and/or World Wide Port (WWP) names and identities. The good news is that by using an HBA with two or more ports you can have port or path failure isolation and possibly performance benefits. The downside is that the HBA is still attached to the host server via a single PCI interface, which is a single point of failure.

On larger servers this can be overcome by using two or more PCI or bus slots for attachment of multiple HBAs. Ideally this would be done placing each HBA on a separate bus for performance and improved resilience as well. On smaller servers, which only have a few or limited number of PCI or bus slots, a multiport HBA may provide some negligible performance and redundancy up to the server level in case something happens to a path. However, this does not fully protect the server or provide complete fault isolation. Path managers can be used to utilize the paths for dynamic failover, load balancing, and some volume management functions. Unless there is not a need for resiliency, dual or multiple HBAs should always be used and attached to redundant fabrics. In addition to providing redundancy and resiliency, multiple adapters and I/O paths can also improve availability by supporting failover during mainte-

Table 7.1 *Storage Networking Adapter Names*

Common Name	Descriptive Name	Interface and Protocol Supported
Adapter RAID	Host-based RAID controllers	SCSI, ATA/SATA
Channel Adapter	Channel Adapter	FICON
HBAs	Host Bus Adapter	Fibre Channel and SCSI
HCAs	Host Channel Adapter	InfiniBand
NIC	Network Interface Card	Ethernet and Networking
SNIC	Storage Network Interface Card	iSCSI
TNIC	TCP/TOE-enabled Network Interface Card	iSCSI

nance of different components. Table 7.1 shows some types of storage networking adapters with their common name (or alias), descriptive name, and supported protocol interface.

In Figure 7.1 some storage networking adapters are shown for different protocols and interfaces along with their common names. Besides HBAs, there are also Host Channel Adapters (HCAs) for InfiniBand and SNICs (modified Ethernet NICs) with TOEs and security performance accelerator functions. The TOEs handle TCP and, optionally, IPSec offload functions to free up CPU cycles on a server. New adapter implementations will support RDMA for high-performance memory-to-memory transfer between systems over a Gb Ethernet network interface.

TCP Offload Engines (TOEs) are special processing chips that can be added to an Ethernet network card to offload the server CPU from TCP handling. Normally a server CPU would perform extra work to process TCP traffic, which would consume CPU resources, resulting in busy servers or perhaps a premature server upgrade. By having an adapter card with a TOE the TCP processing functions can be offloaded to the adapter card, saving the server CPU for processing other workloads and applications. All Fibre Channel adapters perform lower-level protocol processing to reduce server CPU consumption. The server CPU still processes device driver software; however, the adapter cards provide protocol offload and I/O assistance.

Some common host adapter and storage networking interface card characteristics include:

- Type of bus interface (PCI-33/66MHz, PCI-X 66/100/133MHz, CompactPCI [cPCI] 66MHz, Sbus, HSC, S/390 STI) as well as hot swap capability
- Type of storage interface (Fibre Channel, GbE, InfiniBand, SSA, ATA/SATA)
- Type of protocol (FCP, FICON, SCSI, iSCSI, RDMA, uDAPL)
- Port speeds (1Gb, 2Gb, 4Gb, 10Gb) and interface medium (GBIC, SFP, electrical)
- Number of ports per adapter (single, dual, quad)
- WWN spoofing for security and clustering as well as swapping of interfaces
- Load balancing (automatic or manual) and multipathing (path management software)
- Buffer credits and data buffers per adapter and per port for distance
- Variable buffer and frame sizes (extra large frames for IP) for speed and distance
- Trunking of adapters for aggregation of performance and load balancing
- State change management and RSCN isolation to minimize disruptions to adapters
- Variable number of devices and volumes (LUNs) that can be addressed
- Remote boot support for servers, including x86 BIOS and Fcode for Sun Solaris
- Reloadable drivers and auto recognition of devices by operating systems
- Support (including plug and play) for different operating systems (WinTel, NetWare, Linux, Solaris, AIX, HP-UX, OS/400, S/390, OpenVMS)
- Different media interfaces (single-mode Fiber, multimode Fiber, copper)
- TCP Offload Engines (TOEs) to offload servers from processing TCP traffic

Some storage networking adapter topics and recommendations for scaling resilient storage networks include path managers to be used with HBAs for automatic failover and load balancing. While most HBAs can coexist with various vendors' devices, zoning can be used (fabric or host persistent binding) to isolate HBAs when needed. LUN mapping and masking on storage devices should also be used in conjunction with other forms of zoning to prevent unwanted, unauthorized access to storage. Most Fibre Channel HBAs today are fabric capable. However, some (mainly legacy models or those being used with older servers) only support loop. By using redundant HBAs, attached to separate switches and/or directors, storage systems can be configured to isolate against HBA failure, cable failure, and failures at the switch, or I/O controller level. Fibre Channel's distance and performance capabilities enable many applications to benefit from increased redundancy and resiliency, including in-house disaster recovery. Some vendors still recommend as best practice to isolate certain adapters from others as well as to isolate storage devices (disk and tape) from each other. This can result in a need for many small zones, which can add complexity to management. Some older tape devices, particularly those with FC-AL ports, can be disruptive to other servers and storage devices. Newer storage devices, including tape that utilizes a Fibre Channel fabric (N_Port) interface port type, tend to behave and coexist better. You may choose to isolate disk and tape traffic by placing tape devices on a separate storage network. There is a performance benefit to this in addition to isolating devices in that data can be read in from a storage device on one interface and adapter while written to tape (or disk) on another interface path.

7.2.3 NAS appliances, servers, and gateways

First-generation NAS and file serving implementations were based on existing servers with file sharing enabled. Second-generation implementations were based on dedicated appliance servers using a dedicated PC or processor with customized software tuned to specially handle file and data sharing with dedicated direct attached storage. The decoupling of dedicated storage from NAS appliances has resulted in what is called a NAS "head," which is the NAS server and software minus dedicated direct attached storage. A NAS head may utilize proprietary vendor-supplied storage or leverage and utilize existing customer-supplied storage via a storage network (SAN). NAS devices can range from enterprise class large-capacity, high-performance products to very compact devices for small office and even home environments.

Figure 7.3 shows, on the left, a general-purpose server using general-purpose servers with local and SAN attached storage with NAS file sharing software. In the middle is a NAS appliance, sometimes called a filer, that is

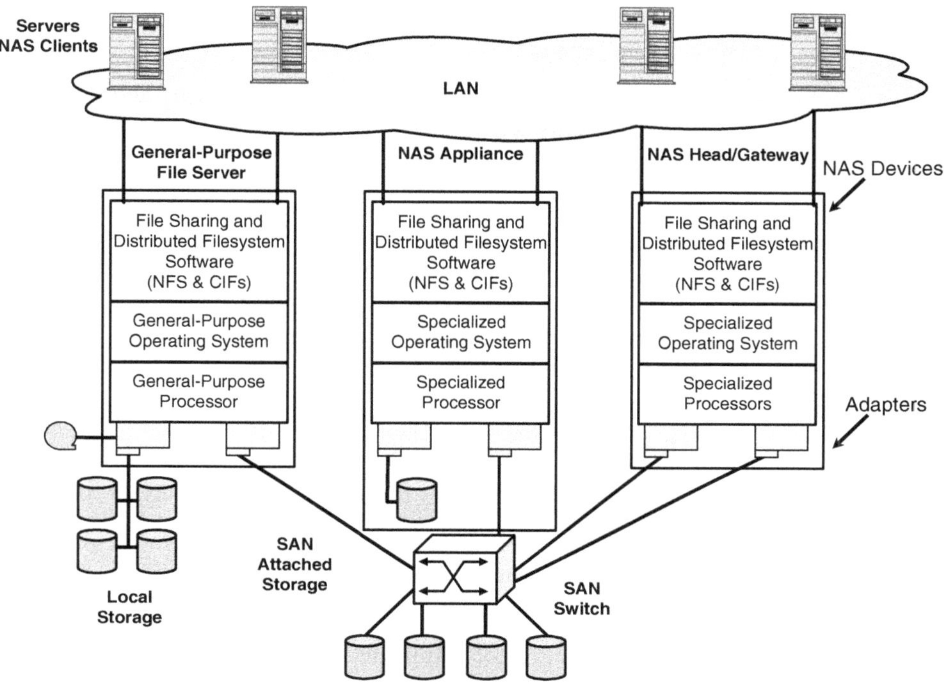

Figure 7.3 *NAS configurations (general server, NAS appliance, NAS head).*

a self-contained specialized processor with operating system, NAS file sharing software, and local and SAN attached storage. On the right in Figure 7.3 is a NAS head, also known as gateway, that is essentially a NAS appliance, specialized processor without integrated storage. NAS devices, in addition to providing file-based access via NFS and CIFS, can support iSCSI-based block access. Some NAS devices also support the Direct Access File System (DAFS) as an alternative to NFS and CIFs access. Historically, NAS storage has not been recommended for use with some database and e-mail-based systems, including Microsoft Exchange. This is changing now, with some database vendors supporting NAS access and devices; however, check with your supplier to see what it supports. Microsoft is also now a NAS software vendor, providing a developer and deployment kit, so the current restrictions with Microsoft Exchange should go away. However, as a word of caution, check with your supplier to see what it supports for your configuration.

Some common characteristics of NAS devices include:

- Distributed access methods (NFS, CIFS, and DAFS) for filesystems

- How many filesystems can be supported and what the maximum file system size is
- Snapshot backup and journaling capabilities with NDMP backup support and WORM functionality
- Integrated NAS filer with storage or detached NAS head using SAN-based storage
- Caching capabilities for file, Web, and other functions, including a SAN cache
- Supported RAID levels and automatic drive rebuilds using hot spare disks
- Ability to turn software RAID off to utilize hardware subsystem RAID
- Journalized filesystems for snapshots as well as to speed up recovery and reboots
- Networking interfaces (10/100 Ethernet, Gb E, 10Gb E, FDDI, ATM) supported
- Network protocols supported (TCP, UDP, FCP, iSCSI)
- Storage interfaces (Fibre Channel, parallel SCSI, ATA/SATA) supported
- Access control lists, security and policy management features
- Support for database, e-mail, and other specialized application access
- Clustering, remote mirroring and replication, and failover capabilities

Physical NAS devices can vary in size, functionality, and capabilities, including integrated appliances with dedicated storage and controller as well as NAS heads serving as gateways to SAN-attached storage. NAS functionality can also be implemented as a layered software application available from different providers.

7.2.4 Storage devices (the storage in storage networking)

Storage is one of the essential components of storage networking, with the other being networking and I/O interfaces. Storage devices and media include embedded processor-based cache, direct Random Access Memory (RAM), Read Only Memory (ROM), nonvolatile RAM (NVRAM) and ROM (NVROM), rotating (spinning) disk media, magnetic tape, and optical. These can be combined into different combinations to derive various storage and I/O subsystems. An I/O or storage subsystem is the collection of components commonly referred to as a storage array that includes I/O interfaces, cache, controllers, and physical media (disk, tape, memory, optical).

Storage devices include disk, tape, and bridges (router or gateway) and are typically accessed using SCSI_FCP (S/390 uses FICON). A Fibre Channel disk device (DASD) could be a RAID array or Just a Bunch Of Disks (JBOD) in a cabinet. FICON disk or storage could be in the same cabinet as Fibre Channel storage accessed via the FICON ULP over Fibre Channel. Thus, storage can be shared between S/390 (FICON) and open systems (SCSI_FCP) over a common medium (Fibre Channel). Note that this is storage sharing and not data sharing. Data sharing requires additional technology (NAS) to handle the addressing and locking of data. Table 7.2 shows some characteristics of enterprise, modular, and JBOD storage subsystems; this is by no means a comprehensive list.

Table 7.2 *Characteristics of Various Storage Architectures*

	Enterprise Monolithic Frame Based	Modular Midrange	JBOD Disk Array
SAS/ATA/SATA interface	—	Yes	Yes
Cache for performance	Yes	Yes	—
Count Key Data (CKD) format	Yes	—	—
Drive rebuild	Yes	Yes	—
ESCON	Yes	—	—
FCP	Yes	Yes	Yes
FICON	Yes	—	—
Fixed Block Access (FBA)	Yes	Yes	Yes
Hot spare drive	Yes	Yes	—
Individual volumes	Yes	Yes	Yes
iSCSI	Yes	Yes	Yes
Logical volumes (LUNs)	Yes	Yes	—
LUN/volume mapping	Yes	Yes	—
Mirroring and replication	Yes	Varies	—

Table 7.2 *Characteristics of Various Storage Architectures (continued)*

	Enterprise Monolithic Frame Based	Modular Midrange	JBOD Disk Array
RAID support	Yes	Yes	—
Redundant controllers	Yes	Yes	—
Redundant power/cooling	Yes	Yes	Varies
SCSI	Yes	Yes	Yes
Swappable interface	Yes	Yes	Varies
Variable drive rebuild	Yes	Yes	—

Over time the distinction between frame-based and modular storage is blurring; it used to be based primarily on physical attributes. Enterprise class subsystems are adopting some of the modular and high-performance architecture design that has been available on a smaller scale with modular devices.

7.2.5 JBOD and disk array subsystems

The basic storage device is a disk drive or tape drive that can be combined and configured into various configurations with different features and interfaces. Figure 7.4 shows a basic disk drive attached to a server and an expanded detail view of the inner components. Disk drives are manufactured by vendors that are listed in Appendix A. You can go to their web sites and see specific details about the various types of drives, including performance, availability, capacity, rotational speed, and other characteristics. While this is an oversimplified and generic view, it shows a number of platters, also known as spindles, that spin driven by a motor. Read/write heads are controlled by a controller to store data and send data to the server via a disk drive interface, which could be Fibre Channel, SCSI, ATA/SATA, or SSA. The disk drive platters can be different diameters that continue to decrease, while the capacity increases. Different disk drives, for example, SCSI/SAS/Fibre Channel and IDE/ATA/SATA, have different characteristics, including performance, cost, capacity, and reliability. Using the appropriate disk drive technology for the proper application is an important component for resilient storage networks of all sizes.

Just a Bunch Of Disk (JBOD) is a term that is used to describe disks that are accessible directly and individually without using a storage controller or

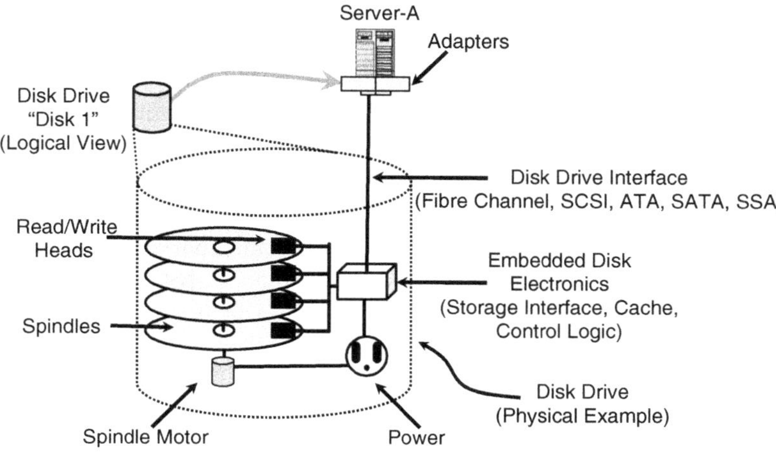

Figure 7.4 *Individual disk drive.*

logical volumes. A JBOD device could be an individual disk drive in an enclosure (packaging) with power, optional cooling, and a storage interface to attach to a server. In Figure 7.5, a more sophisticated JBOD example is shown with multiple disk drives, each with a dual shared interface for attachment to servers directly or via a switch or hub.

In Figure 7.5 six disk drives are shown attached to two separate interfaces, with each disk appearing as an individual disk device with a unique

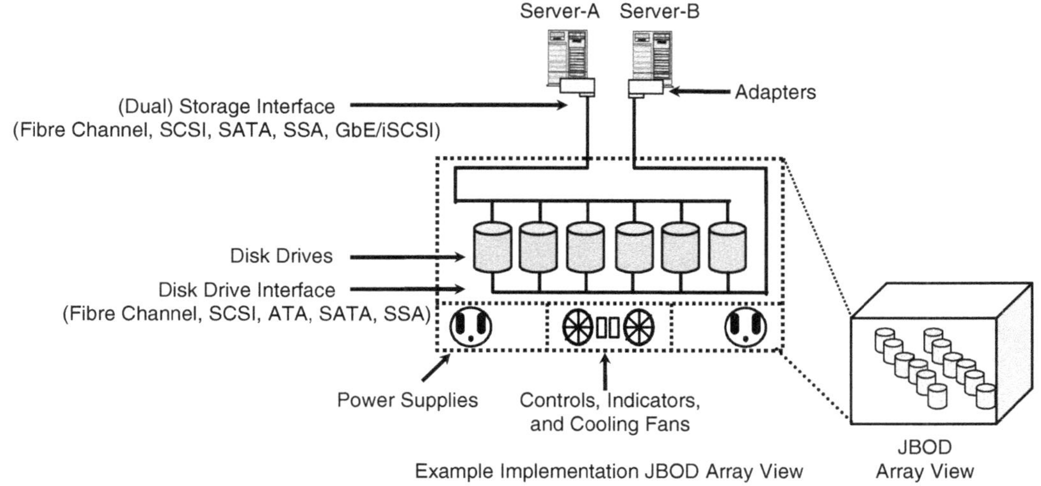

Figure 7.5 *JBOD storage array example.*

address. Some JBOD disk arrays may have a simple protocol converter interface to enable a server with a different storage interface to access them. For example, a server using iSCSI with Gb Ethernet could access a JBOD storage array with an internal protocol converter that has serial ATA (SATA) physical disk drives. The address of the disk drives could be, for example, the SCSI target ID assigned to the device via setup and configuration. Also shown in this example are power supplies and cooling fans. A simpler version of this JBOD example could have a single storage interface, single power supply, and single cooling fan. JBOD systems can be used for simple individual storage devices as well as serving as the storage modules for larger modular and enterprise frame-based subsystems.

7.2.6 Modular storage subsystems

JBOD storage devices, also known as storage arrays, provide enhanced packaging for individual disk drives and, with some implementations, storage interface protocol conversion. JBOD and storage arrays can be combined with a storage controller to provide enhanced performance, disk aggregation (also known as device virtualization), data protection, and availability features. This combination is sometimes called RAID arrays and intelligent storage controllers, depending on the amount of features and functions supported. RAID arrays, also known as storage subsystems, are

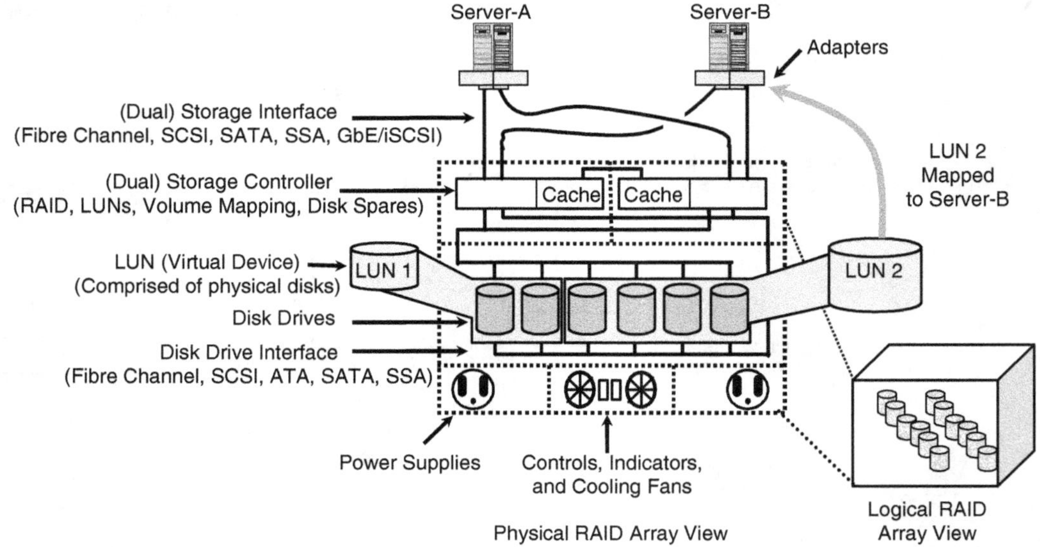

Figure 7.6 *Modular storage subsystem example.*

available in different shapes, sizes, configurations, and available features. A storage subsystem array can be a self-contained, fully enclosed device with hot swappable disk drives for replacement but with fixed expansion capabilities. Fixed-base storage subsystems can be small form-factor, with two or more disk drives, up to large enterprise class systems (also known as storage frames). Similarly, a storage subsystem can be a highly scalable and modular device expandable by attaching more JBOD storage arrays, also known as drive shelves, to a controller. A modular storage subsystem is shown in Figure 7.6, with a pair of controllers for redundancy and mirrored cache for performance and data availability. The modular array utilizes JBOD storage shelves, which could be physically enclosed or removable for expansion. In Figure 7.6 two of the disk drives on the left are grouped together using the controller RAID capabilities to create a larger higher-performance LUN that is mapped to Server-A. Another LUN is created and RAID enhanced as LUN 2 and is mapped and allocated to Server-B. Both servers utilize a high-availability configuration to attach to redundant controllers on the modular storage subsystem over separate paths.

While the difference is blurring from a performance and packaging standpoint between enterprise and modular storage subsystems, some common characteristics of modular storage subsystems include:

- Typically do not support ESCON and FICON access or CKD formatted data
- High bandwidth and I/O (performance) utilizing fast disk subsystems instead of depending solely on cache to accelerate performance
- Mirrored cache with battery backup
- Hot swappable redundancy components (power, cooling, controllers, drives, cache)
- Modular in design with detached controllers and storage shelves
- Blade and shelf-based modular storage for ease of handling and maintenance
- Integrated as starter storage networks, including "SAN in a Can" configurations
- Variable volume sizes and LUN assignment addressing
- Multiple RAID (0, 1, 0+1, 1+0, 3, 5) levels for data protection and performance
- Variable size from small form-factors to large and expandable systems

- Many LUNs and variable volume sizes accessed from different operating systems
- Mirroring and replication support, including to enterprise class storage systems
- Advanced features similar to those found on traditional enterprise storage

7.2.7 Frame storage subsystems

Frame-based storage subsystems are also known as monolithic. In terms of basic functionality the distinction between large monolithic frame-based architecture products, such as the EMC Symmetrix, HDS Lighting, and IBM ESS "Shark," is blurring compared with modular products. A couple of major differences are that the large frame-based storage subsystems support both S/390 mainframe with ESCON and FICON as well as open systems platforms using parallel SCSI and Fibre Channel. Some of these devices are also now adding Gb Ethernet interfaces with support for iSCSI and/or FCIP for remote mirroring and replication support. Another characteristic of these devices is that they tend to be physically very large and expensive while providing many functions (software features).

In Figure 7.7 an enterprise frame-based storage device is shown with different interfaces and access protocols on the left. In the middle are the storage controllers and cache supporting high-performance and feature-rich functionality. To the right are the various storage devices that can be implemented using different interfaces, including ATA/SATA, SSA, Fibre Channel, and SCSI devices.

Some of the advanced function support on enterprise class storage subsystems include:

- Physical and logical mirroring (synchronous, asynchronous, and semisynchronous)
- Business continuance, snapshot, and journal volumes for data protection
- Variable size volumes, including CKD and FBA formatted data
- Interface support (Fibre Channel, Gb E, ESCON, ESCON)
- Protocol support, including (FICON, FCP, iSCSI)
- Various storage access port interface speeds (1Gb, 2G, 4Gb, 10Gb)

- Data movement and migration tools via the internal controllers
- Advanced caching and data optimization firmware
- Device emulation and addressing capabilities
- Back-end disk drive interface (SCSI, Fibre Channel, ATA/SATA, SSA) and disk drive type.
- Multiple management interfaces (APIs, SNMP MIBs, SMIS)
- Hot spare disk drives with automatic rebuild and adjustable rebuild parameters
- Redundant controllers, interfaces, and cache with on-line firmware updates
- Availability characteristics (power, cooling, controllers, cache, spare drives, etc.)
- RAID levels supported (0, 1, 1+0, 3, 5) and other protection schemes

The various capabilities of enterprise as well as modular storage subsystems have been summarized and are by no means all encompassing. Rather than place dated material in this book, more detailed and vendor-specific information regarding enterprise, modular, and JBOD subsystems is located on the accompanying Web site for this book: www.storageio.com.

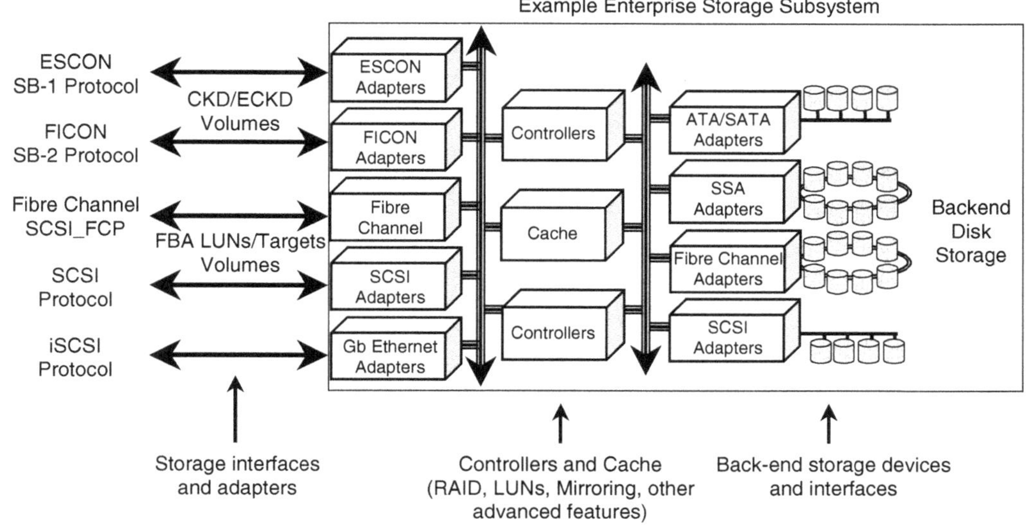

Figure 7.7 *Enterprise frame-based storage example.*

7.2.8 Magnetic tape devices

Magnetic tape is a storage medium that has been around for about 50 years in different formats and with various characteristics. While utilizing similar techniques and basic principles over the past 50 years, magnetic tape has evolved along the lines of other technologies, with increased densities, reduced physical size, better reliability, faster performance, ease of handling, and lower costs. Tape today is being challenged by lower-cost, high-performance disk-based storage, including ATA/SATA devices to perform disk to disk (D2D) and disk to disk to tape (D2D2T) backups and archives to support data life-cycle management. This is not to say that tape is dead, since it still continues today to be the most cost-effective medium for long-term and off-line data retention. Consequently, tape storage will remain in use for some time, but its usage is changing. The tape medium is still being used for performing backup/recovery as well as archiving and portability. With the advent of improved networking and data interchange capabilities, the need for sending tapes containing data between different locations has decreased.

In Figure 7.8, a typical tape device is shown attached to a server for performing backup and other functions. This example shows a logical view of the tape devices as well as a generic physical example, including the tape medium along with the tape transport mechanism. Also shown are the read/write heads for reading and writing data and a controller that tells the transport mechanisms in which direction to move the tape and the read/write heads what to do. There are also a power supply and external tape

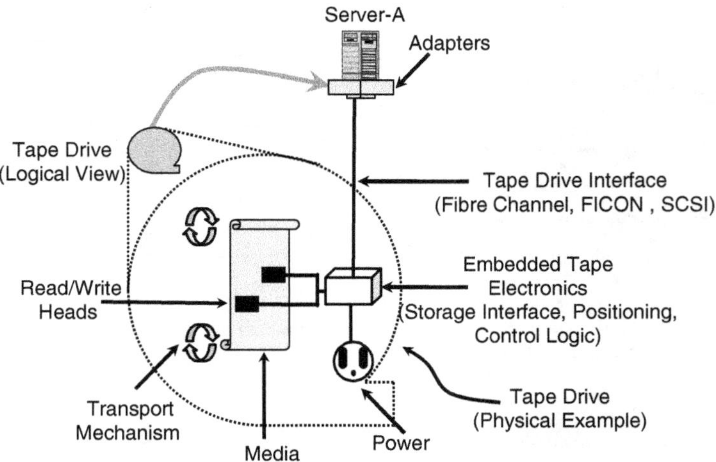

Figure 7.8 *Individual tape drive.*

storage interface, which could be Fibre Channel, FICON, ATA/STA, or SCSI. Also shown are the media, which could be of different sizes using various physical packaging and recording techniques.

Individual tape drives can be attached to servers, attached to a back server (which in turn receives data from other servers to perform backups), or in a tape library. A tape library can be a small tape stacker with a tape drive (transport) and a number of tape cartridges (media) that are sequentially loaded into the tape drive as needed. A tape library can also be a robotic jukebox, varying in size from small to very large with a robotic mechanism to automatically load and remove tape. Another tape device is a virtual tape subsystem, which emulates and appears as multiple tape drives while in fact containing a small number of actual tape drives. Some virtual tape subsystems utilizes memory and disk drives to create a cache to hold data being written from the server to what are virtual tape drives created in memory and later written to tape. This helps to improve overall tape efficiency as well as enhance performance of backups and recovery. Tape devices and tape libraries can be dedicated to specific servers or shared among many servers using specialized library management and backup software.

Figure 7.9 shows a typical tape library with multiple tape drive transports and robotic or mechanized capability for loading and unloading tapes.

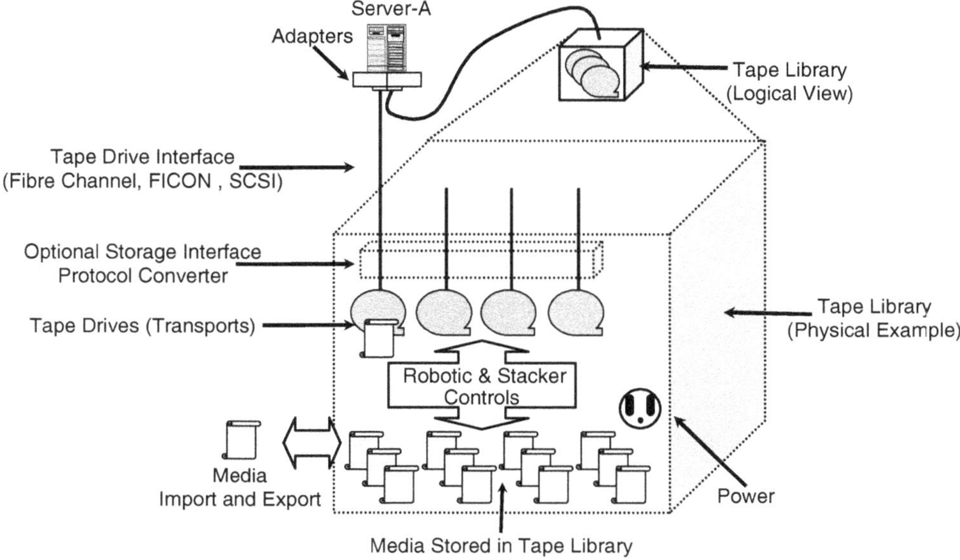

Figure 7.9 *Tape library example.*

Also shown are optional protocol conversion capabilities for tape access interfaces (Fibre Channel, FICON, SCSI) as well as hold locations (slots) for tape and import and export slots. Alternative media include CDs, DVDs, and other variations of optical media for data storage, transport, and retention. Some other alternative media include memory sticks with thumb drives for data movement and protection. Many disk-based tape alternative technology using ATA/SATA and Serial SCSI disk devices are available today. These devices range from arrays of very large capacity, low cost ATA-based storage to specialized appliances optimized to work with various backup media servers. Some devices have additional features to protect data while being stored, as well as reduce the actual amount of physical capacity needed to store data—what generically could be called compression of data at rest. These various devices are changing the economics of storing and managing data. An important thing to keep in mind is that technology needs to be refreshed from time to time. Regardless of using tape or disk, data needs to be migrated from one medium to another as part of on-going data maintenance. Look for solutions that will help move the data and assist with data maintenance functions.

7.2.9 Solid-state disk, memory disks, and SAN cache

Solid-State Disk (SSD) features high I/O rates with very low latency for I/O-intensive applications compared with traditional spinning media devices. SSD can achieve low latency by utilizing Random Access Memory (RAM) to provide access to storage, eliminating the latency associated with data seeks on spinning media. SSD is well suited for applications with high I/O rates as opposed to those with high bandwidth (throughput) demands. Since SSD utilizes RAM to reduce or eliminate latency, it is best suited for latency and I/O-intensive applications, including OLTP, journaling, indices, paging, and small frequently accessed files.

Figure 7.10 shows an example SSD device that contains RAM memory for storing data to reduce latency and response time. A controller has a storage interface (Fibre Channel, SCSI) for access from a server as well as performing emulation of storage devices and LUNs. For data protection a battery-backed power supply is shown, along with an optional disk drive for protecting data when the power is turned off.

Some SSD characteristics include:

- Parity and CRC data protection with battery-backed power supplies
- Integrated hard disk for data retention to store data when device shuts down

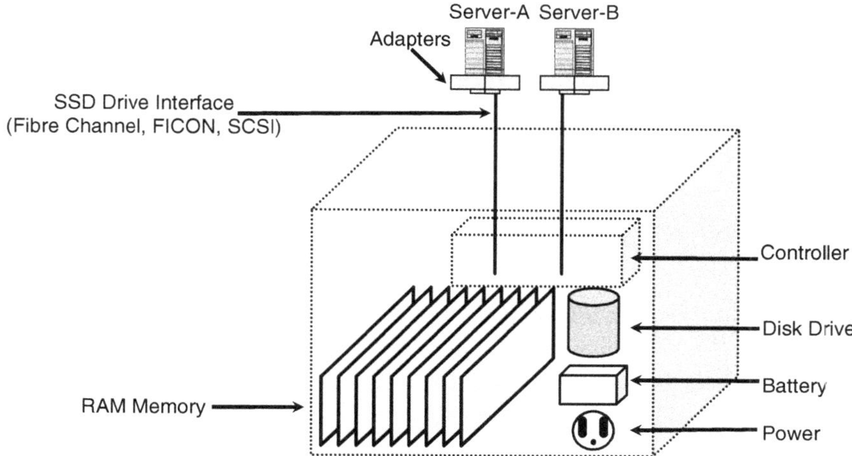

Figure 7.10 *Solid-State Disk (SSD) example.*

- Automatic staging and destaging from hard disk to memory
- LUNs and volume allocation and device emulation
- Performance indicators and classification software
- Various storage interfaces (Fibre Channel/FCP, SCSI)
- Operating system support and performance optimization tools

7.3 Networking components

Storage networking devices include servers (including adapters), storage, and networking components, which are used to provide the interface between servers and storage. These networking components include hubs (also known as concentrators), switches (also known as directors), and bridges, routers, and gateways (sometimes called appliances).

7.3.1 Hubs and concentrators

Hubs and concentrators are utilized in storage networking to support different interfaces for low-cost, low-performance shared bandwidth applications. Hubs and concentrators traditionally have been deployed as early shared access devices with networks and storage networking interfaces until switching functions became available. While not yet extinct from the storage networking landscape, hubs are not as commonly used and are being replaced by switches and embedded switches (switch on a chip).

First-generation storage networks were built using loop hubs, similar to how early networks were built with shared bandwidth. Hubs were used because of their relative low cost and ability to provide shared connectivity. Fibre Channel Arbitrated Loop (FC-AL) topology enables up to 127 (including ports for attachment to fabric) servers and storage devices to share a common interface. Hubs are mainly used in storage back-end applications for connecting Fibre Channel disk drives to RAID storage controllers. These, however, are being phased out over time by embedded switches. Another use is to enable multiple slower devices (older tape, storage, or servers) to attach to a fabric via a hub, which in turn attaches to a fabric, reducing the number of switch or director ports (fan-in/fan-out). Hubs can also be used to attach loop devices to fabric devices that do not support native loop.

While most server adapters (Fibre Channel) support fabric access and topologies, some older servers do not support fabric device drivers or fabric HBAs, forcing use of loop or Private Loop Device Addressing (PLDA). Similarly, today most storage devices and gateways support fabric access and topologies, while some older devices may be limited to loop access. For recovery purposes compatibility with existing devices should be particularly considered at alternate sites.

Some characteristics of hubs and concentrators include:

- Low cost per port and shared bandwidth
- Can be used as part of tiered or fan-in/fan-out
- Relatively easy to implement
- Traditionally early-on adoption curve

Hubs and concentrators have been used to deploy simple, small, low-performance, low-cost LAN and storage networks with Ethernet, FDDI, Fibre Channel, and USB. There have also been some specialized devices, including SCSI hubs.

7.3.2 Switches and directors

Switches and directors, also known as fabric devices, can be used as standalone or single-device fabrics, in pairs to create multiple single-device SAN islands, or connected together to create a fabric. Storage networking switches include traditional storage-related devices—for example, ESCON, Fibre Channel, and FICON—as well as traditional IP network Ethernet-based switches. Most Fibre Channel switches support multiple protocols, including FCP for open systems, FICON for IBM mainframes, iSCSI, FCIP (or iFCP) for distance, and IP over Fibre Channel. Some Ethernet devices support FCIP capabilities, with iSCSI being designed to utilize the Ethernet switching infrastructure. Fabrics or networks are used to increase the number of ports beyond what is physically available on fabric devices and to support different topologies for various applications and environments. Switches and director ports can also isolate local traffic to particular segments, much like traditional network switches isolate LAN traffic. Storage networking switching devices can range from simple 4 ports to large multiprotocol devices of 256 to 512 ports, with larger devices to come. Storage network fabric devices such as switches and directors are the basic building blocks for creating a SAN or fabric. A Fibre Channel switch provides the same function as a standard network switch as well as providing zoning and name services. A Fibre Channel switch provides scalable bandwidth between various subnets, segments, or loops. A switch provides scalable bandwidth as users and devices are attached and range in port count from 8 to 32.

Figure 7.11 shows a simplified example of a switch with server access storage (disk and tape). Shown in the example are send and receive ports (transceivers and optics), power supply, and cooling. Also shown is a controller processor, which interfaces with the switching chips that move data

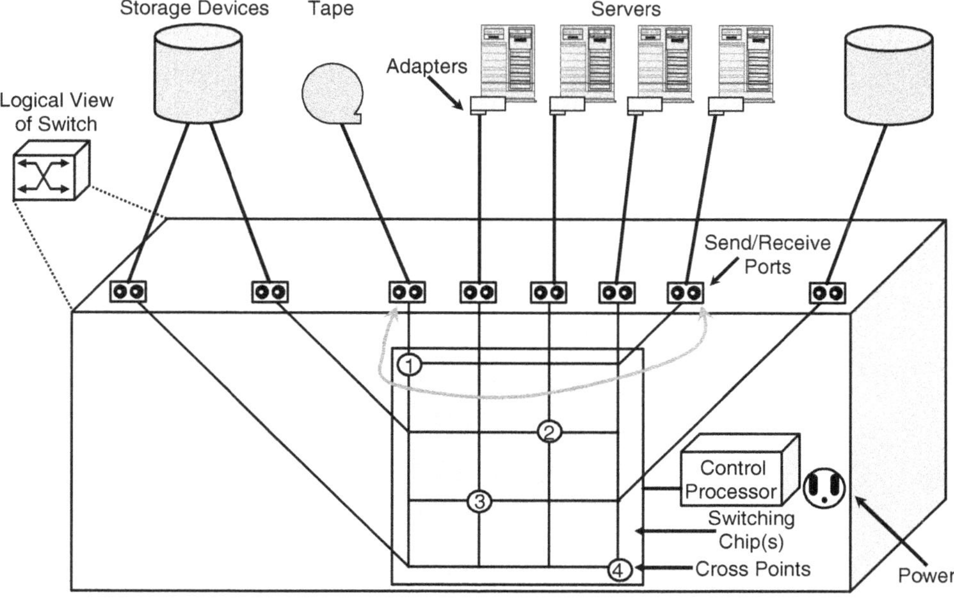

Figure 7.11 *Switch example.*

from port to port as well as performing other functions. A switch can be implemented using a single switching chip for smaller switches or using multiple chips, also known as Application-Specific Integrated Circuit (ASIC), and Field Programmable Gate Array (FPGA) chips. The difference between ASICs and FPGAs is cost and in some cases performance for ASIC and flexibility for lower production runs and to make changes for FPGAs.

A Fibre Channel director is a highly scalable, fully redundant switch supporting blades, with multiple interfaces and protocols, including Fibre Channel, SCSI (FCP), FICON, and IP (including FCIP, iSCSI, iFCP, NAS)—similar to a large network switch. Switching directors vary in size from 4 to 512 ports and can replace or supplement fabrics of smaller switches. Fabric devices, including directors and switches, can be networked into various topologies to create very large resilient storage networks of hundreds to thousands of ports. Inter-Switch Links (ISLs) are used to connect switches and directors to create a fabric or SAN. An ISL has a port on each switch or director to which the ISL is attached, and for redundancy ISLs should be configured in pairs. So for every ISL needed, you will use up at least one port per switch or more for redundancy.

There are many different terms that are used to describe the different switching devices, some of which are shown in Table 7.3. In the examples shown in this book, a switch can also refer to a director and vice versa.

Some common characteristics of switches (including directors) are:

- Number of ports per switch and ports per blade
- Port interfaces (Fibre Channel, GbE, InfiniBand)
- Port types (E_Port, F_Port, FL_Port, TL_Port, trunking)
- Port interface speeds (1Gb, 2Gb, 4Gb, 10Gb, auto sensing, speed matching)
- Port WAN interfaces (10/100 Ethernet, Gb E, 10Gb E, SONET/SDH)
- Port media types (SMF, MMF, LC, SC, GBIC, SFP, HSSDC, copper, RJ45)
- Protocols supported (FCP, FICON, IPFC, FCIP, iFCP, iSCSI, RDMA, SRP, etc.)
- Redundant components (cooling, power, controllers)
- Hot code load and code activation (NDCL and NDCA)
- Environmental items (physical dimensions, weight, cooling, power consumption)

- State change management, including RSCN and Simple Name Servers (SNS)
- Security, including authentication (RADIUS), IPSec, and zoning (WWN, WWPN)
- Power-on Self-Test (POST), diagnostics, and test tools
- Virtual switches, domains, partitions, and fabrics, also known as VSANs and LSANs
- Quality of Service (QoS) and Virtual Output Queue (VOQ) for performance, load balancing, and elimination of head of line blocking from slower devices
- Performance features, including cut-through routing and store and forward
- Security and management interfaces (CLI, SNMP MIBS, FC-GS3/4, SMIS-S)
- Adequate number of zones to support server and storage consolidation needs

Table 7.3 *Various Names for Different Types of Switches*

Device	Description	Characteristics
Core Switch	Core fabric switch, fabric switch. A switching device that sits at the core of a storage network as a single device or with other switching devices attached in various topologies, including those shown in Chapter 9.	Same functions as switch and director
Chassis Switch	Same as director class	Same as director class
Director	Storage networking switching director switch, supporting multiple protocols, interfaces, high availability, and advanced functionality. Other characteristics are large port counts ranging from 64 to 512 ports or more, similar to large Ethernet frame switches. New products are also supporting advanced functionality blades for storage services and virtualization.	Same functions as switch Expansion capabilities Common components Part of a family of products Supports multiple interfaces Supports multiple protocols High-availability features High port count High performance Nonblocking between ports

Table 7.3 *Various Names for Different Types of Switches (continued)*

Device	Description	Characteristics
Edge Switch	A smaller switch that can sit at the edge of a storage network, also known in the networking world as a stackable switch.	Same functions as switch An edge switch does not have to be small, since a director class device could also be utilized as an edge switch.
Embedded Switch	Switch chip or small switch physically integrated into a storage subsystem at the controller level or on a server blade or motherboard.	Same functions as switch Physically part of server or storage device at board level
Fabric Switch	A collection of switches preconfigured together to create a fabric network with more ports than a single switch device might have.	Same function as switch Multiple switches networked together with ISLs
Modular Switch	Switch that can be expanded or part of a family of switching devices utilizing common components, including power supplies, port blades, and controllers.	Expansion capabilities Common components Part of a family of products Supports multiple interfaces Supports multiple protocols
Multiprotocol Switch	Switch that can handle multiple protocols (FICON, FCP, iSCSI, FCIP) and multiple interfaces (Fibre Channel, Gb E, and SONET/SDH)	Same function as switch and director class Supports multiple protocols Supports multiple interfaces
Switch	A device that performs Layer 2 switching functions between storage networking devices. Unlike a hub concentrator with shared bandwidth between ports, a switch provides dedicated bandwidth between ports.	High-speed switching Store and forward or cut-through routing Supports different port types (E_Port, F_Port, FL_Port)
Stackable Switch	Switch with various numbers of ports that can be physically stacked on top of other switches or mounted in 19" racks. Special interswitch ports, sometimes called spanning ports, using high-speed interfaces—for example, 10Gb interconnects the switches without loss of user ports.	Same function as a switch Small form-factor

7.3.3 Bridges, gateways, and router devices

Bridge, gateways, and routers provide the ability to migrate existing SCSI or other devices to a Fibre Channel SAN environment. On one side of the bridge are one or more Fibre Channel interfaces and on the other side are one or more SCSI ports. The bridge enables SCSI packets to be moved between Fibre Channel and SCSI devices in a storage network performing protocol routing. Other new bridges include Fibre Channel to iSCSI for accessing storage over Ethernet and Fibre Channel to ATM gateways for SAN/WAN. Other examples of bridges include Fibre Channel to an Ethernet iSCSI device. Routers play a role in building the resilient infrastructure by enabling existing SCSI servers and older SCSI devices to participate in a Fibre Channel storage network. An example of this is to enable an older Fibre Channel tape device to be attached to a fabric and accessed by servers. Another example is to enable SCSI hosts to access Fibre Channel devices using target mode to share storage and resources. New routers enable existing SCSI devices to be accessed via Ethernet using iSCSI for remote access to disk and tape.

Some gateways, bridges, and appliances include:

- SAN over WAN devices (channel extenders)
- Protocol routings (FCP to iSCSI, SCSI to FCP, ESCON to FICON)
- Security and encryption devices
- Filesystems and content caching others
- Storage services and virtualization

Note that this functionality can exist in a switch as a specialized blade, embedded in the switch in silicon, or as a standalone device.

Figure 7.12 shows various gateways, routers, bridges, and appliances supporting different functions. These include clockwise from top left:

- iSCSI (Gb Ethernet) to FCP (Fibre Channel) for access to Fibre Channel storage
- NAS head gateway to access Fibre Channel storage
- Security appliance, providing encryption and authentication
- Storage over IP (SoIP) router for FCIP and iSCSI access
- Storage virtualization appliances for mirroring and data movement

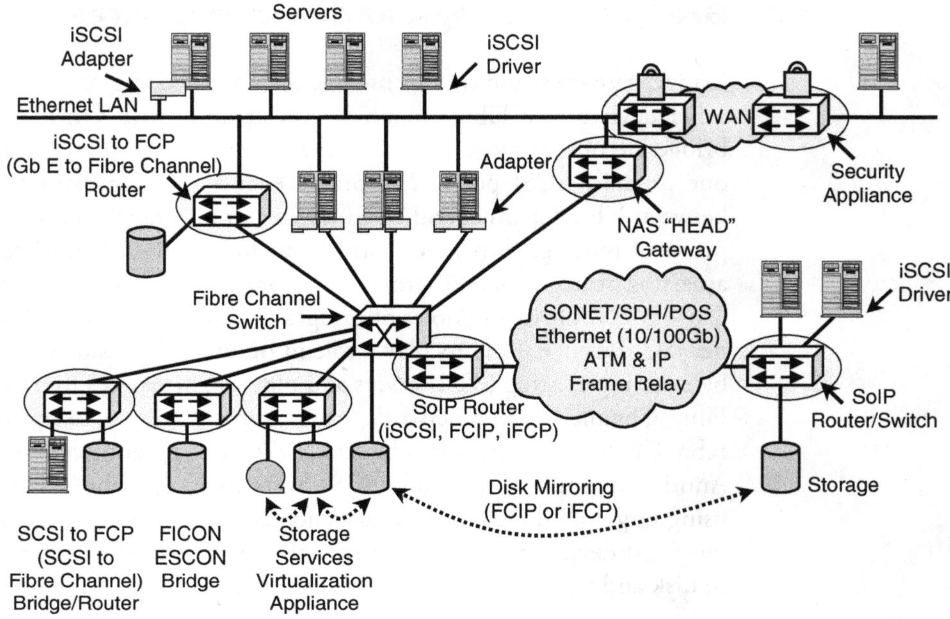

Figure 7.12 *Various gateways, routers, bridges, and appliances.*

- FICON/ESCON bridge for access of ESCON storage by FICON processors
- SCSI (parallel SCSI) to FCP (Fibre Channel) router

7.3.4 Intelligent switches, multifunction switches, storage domain controllers

Intelligent switches are known by different names, including storage networking servers, multiprotocol switches, storage appliances, fabric appliances, and storage domain managers. These products differ from traditional switches that simply move frames and packets from source to destination by adding intelligence to perform more specialized functions requiring heavy thinking. Heavy thinking means that the device needs to perform more functions than simply moving frames through the network—consequently, these devices require more processing power, memory, and I/O bandwidth. These functions can be called storage services as well as storage virtualization.

Some examples of functions that can be performed by these intelligent devices regardless of where they physically exist in the fabric include:

- Data movement for mirroring (business continuance) and migration
- Security, including encryption during data movement and at rest
- Data protection (backup and copy) as well as retention
- Data and storage pooling for improved utilization and provisionment
- Hardware assists for storage tasks, including backup to offload processors
- Interoperability between various storage devices for data movement
- Volume mapping and storage security
- Data and content caching for performance enhancements
- Wide area data movement and communication interfaces and protocol conversion

Figure 7.13 shows some examples of where intelligence can exist in a storage network, including in the server and operating system, in the network or fabric, and within storage devices. Servers can support intelligence within applications, filesystems, volume managers, operating systems, adapters, and device drivers. Intelligence in the network (fabric) can exist in appliances, routers, bridges, gateways, and switches. Intelligence in storage devices can occur in disk subsystems and tape libraries, including advanced data protection with RAID, device-to-device remote mirroring, snapshots and high-speed backup, LUNs, virtual volumes, virtual disks, and virtual tape subsystems.

In Figure 7.14, a single switching device is shown representing an intelligent, multifunction storage switch supporting various functions. These functions could include backup/recovery, HSM, archiving, remote mirroring, and data movement. Additional functions could include volume man-

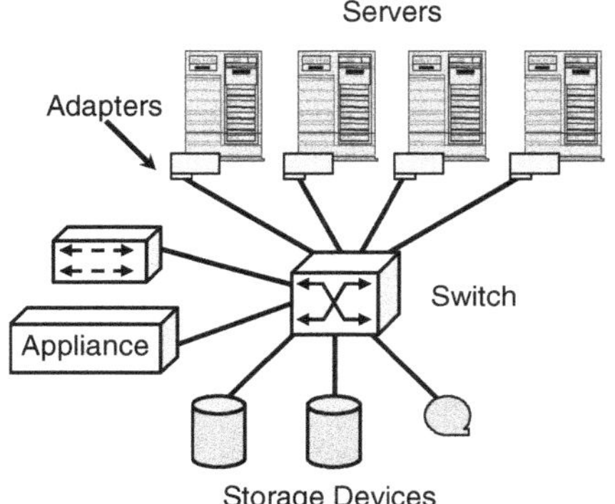

Figure 7.13 *Where intelligence can exist in a storage network.*

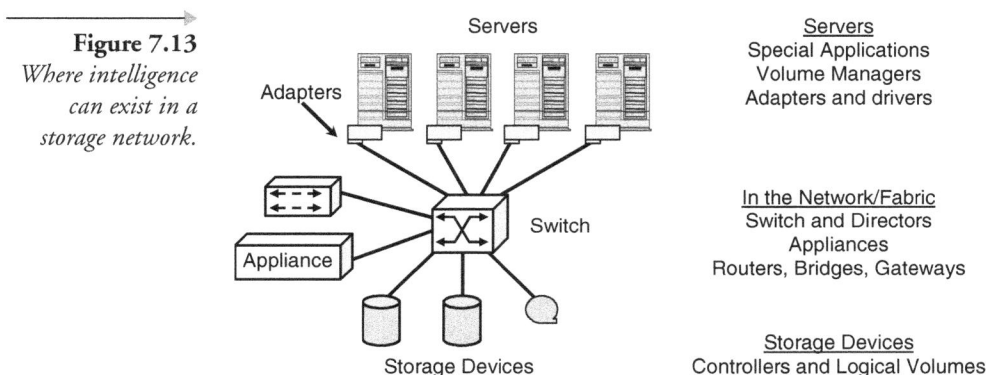

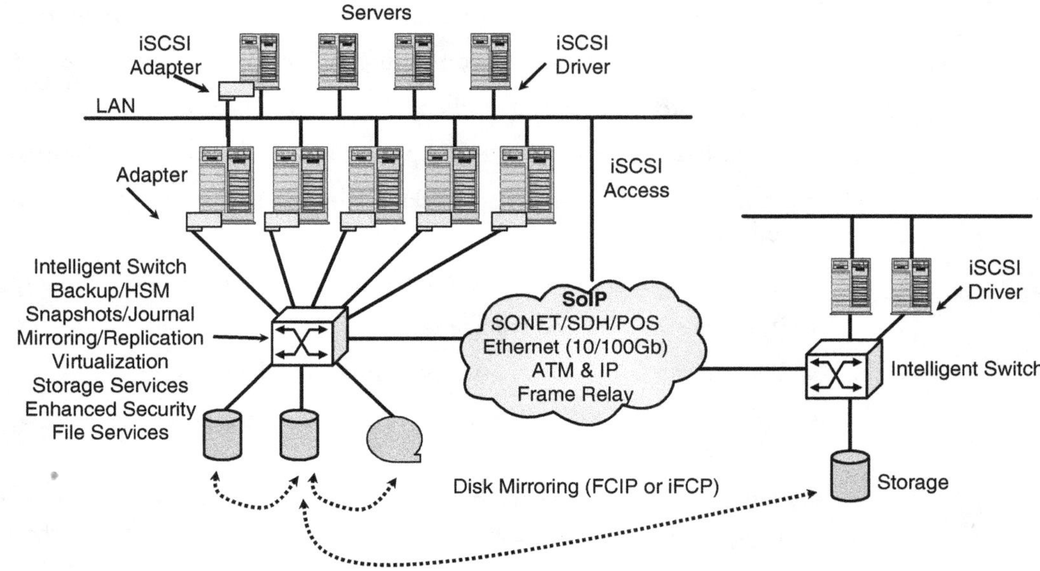

Figure 7.14 *Intelligent, multifunction storage switch.*

agement, LUN and storage pooling, provisioning, security encryption, volume mapping, and masking, as well as file access and protocol conversion. An alternative approach would be to utilize multiple devices for SAN over WAN, security, virtualization and storage services, and switching.

The next generation of storage networking switches should combine convergence features of storage, networking, storage applications, and storage I/O functionality. First-generation storage networking switches, including directors, were designed to support level-1 switching functions to move packets and frames from source to destination at wire speeds. The next generation of storage networking switches built on this capability—similar to how LAN/WAN networking switches have evolved to have more functions and intelligence. Some storage applications and functionality being added to switches include backup, file serving (NAS), mirroring and replication, thin provisioning, point-in-time (PIT) copies, security, and storage pooling. An open interface to support storage networking switching devices and intelligent switch platforms to complement the SNIA SMI-S interface is the Fabric Application Interface Standard (FAIS). The FAIS API should enable more application and storage vendors to support different switching equipment while utilizing open interfaces. These level-2 and level-3 switching platforms should not be confused with Fibre Channel classes of services.

Additional coverage of storage services and virtualization can be found in Chapter 11.

7.3.5 Test and diagnostic devices

Not to be forgotten or diminished in their importance as storage networking devices are test and diagnostic devices. These include protocol analyzers, performance probes, network sniffers, and fault and error detection equipment. Some other examples include network and physical cable monitoring and diagnostic devices and workload generators. Some of these devices are protocol based while others work at the networking interface layer and others at the physical cable level. These tools can be integrated and complemented by additional management software tools as part of an overall storage and storage networking management solution set.

Some functions and capabilities of testing and diagnostic equipment include environmental monitoring and recording devices to track power, cooling, and ventilation fluctuations over time. Sniffers, analyzers, and probes can be used for collection of event and activity data, including errors, utilization, and performance of various storage networking components. This information can be utilized to provide a historical perspective to develop a picture of what is normal and abnormal behavior under different workloads. These capabilities can be utilized to diagnose and isolate faults and errors by looking at upper-level protocol activity down to networking interface. To avoid disruption to your storage network, if possible design into your storage network the ability to perform testing and diagnostics. This can involve implementing diagnostic ports and access points that are secured from unauthorized access ahead of time. This can also be accomplished with switching devices that support external mirror ports and internal trace functions. Workload generators and fault inducers can be utilized to see how the network is performing under different conditions. This can be useful for determining baseline performance under various workloads as well as regression and stress testing of components and the overall storage network.

Network and link error detection and monitoring of local, metropolitan, and wide area links, including signal quality, are important. This can include monitoring of event and error counters of the link on networking equipment and comparing results across different devices utilizing the same network link. This is particularly useful for WAN environments in that if you see errors on multiple devices utilizing the same WAN interface, this can be a clue as to where to continue your diagnostics.

Fiber-optic test, diagnostic, maintenance, and repair equipment can be utilized to verify the signal quality of a fiber-optical connection. This can be helpful in determining the actual distance being traversed, the number of connections, and overall loss of efficiency (db loss) over distance independent of the protocol (droop). Maintenance and repair equipment include connect and terminator connection devices and polishers to clean and ensure quality connections. Note that good preventive maintenance for your fiber-optic infrastructure includes use of quality fiber-optic cabling, terminator connections, and clean optic surfaces. To ensure long cable life, adhere to manufacturer recommendations on cable bend radius, including use of radius bend guides, fiber conveyance systems, and proper use of cable tie wraps.

Testing and diagnostic equipment can be utilized for design and development of components as well as testing of components individually and as part of an overall storage network. For example, a component may work fine by itself and with other devices under certain conditions; however, when additional devices and workloads are added, things may change. Unit and component testing for verification and validation and stress testing of the entire system under various workloads may uncover other issues not seen in normal testing, such as impact on memory, memory and network leaks, and so on. The combination of various equipment, operating systems, patches, and device drivers can add to the complexity of testing and diagnostics and in some cases finger pointing.

One approach to working around this is to stick with one vendor for all components—from applications, to servers, to networking and storage if you are comfortable with a single vendor in your environment. Another approach is to utilize multivendor certified solutions where a group of vendors certify and support different solutions among themselves or under a public forum such as the SNIA Supported Solution Forum (SSF). Another approach is to perform your own testing and validation, or leverage a combination of vendor capabilities and inputs, your own resources and test, and independent test and analysis organizations. Ultimately, what is applicable for your environment will depend on many other things with storage networking for your specific requirements and needs.

7.3.6 Interoperability topics

With any new technology there will be growing pains and interoperability issues. Fibre Channel, ATA/SATA, iSCSI, FCIP, iFCP, storage services, and virtualization are no different, but things appear to be improving with time and with the cooperation of vendors. Is there interoperability with storage and storage networking today? The answer is a qualified yes and a qualified no, with the qualifier being what your expectation and perception of interoperability are. For example, can HBAs from different vendors communicate with each other? The answer is that it varies. Can different switch vendors interoperate? The answer is yes; however, there are different configurations required, which may be disruptive—so, again, it varies.

Interoperability occurs at different layers and has different levels of meaning—for example, two different storage subsystems from two different vendors can coexist in the same fabric and zone on the same HBA, which to some would mean interoperability. Yet these different subsystems may not interoperate with each other to perform, for example, mirroring and data migration without an additional device to perform the data movement. More recently, some storage vendors have been working with others to exchange APIs and other information to support some level of data exchange and movement to help address interoperability.

Types of interoperability include vendor certified and tested; these may include end to end, component, workload, and nonworkload. Is the application tested with all of the components or only certain components? There are alliance and partnership certifications and joint certifications. Interoperability can be a marketing tool for vendors to determine what will work with what. Vendors should listen to their customers and this is a good way to influence what gets tested. The permutations become complex, so there also needs to be some reality and common sense applied to testing.

The good news is that there are various levels of interoperability today, including FC-SW2 for switch-to-switch communications and FCIA SANmark certification programs for Fibre Channel. There is the SNIA SMI-S for management interface for hardware, software, and networks. There is the FAIS initiative for storage services and virtualization for interoperability between various products. With new technology, the time to develop and mature shortens (SCSI took many years, Fibre Channel a few less), so hopefully storage over IP interoperability and stability can leverage this trend and be ready sooner than later.

7.4 Chapter summary

There are two main components involved with storage networking: storage and networking. This chapter has covered some storage devices that are involved with storage networking utilizing different storage networking interfaces. Is there interoperability among storage and storage networking components today? The answer is: It depends on your perception and requirement for interoperability, but there is plenty of room for improvement. For more detailed information abut the different types of storage devices discussed in this chapter, as well as storage device vendors, refer to this book's Web site (www.storageio.com) and Appendix A.

Resilient Storage Networks

What This Chapter Will Do For You

This chapter looks at important aspects involved with designing a storage network of various sizes, including assessment, analysis, and design. Some of the items you will learn about in this chapter include:

- A bad design can lead to a bad implementation, which impacts data availability
- Understand your needs and objectives so that you know when they have been met
- Good information leads to good decisions; know your storage environment
- Get your partners to work with and for you and reward them for helping to meet your objectives
- Obtain management endorsement and buy-in, and determine what they need for success

8

Storage Network Design

8.1 Overview

This chapter looks at storage networking design from simple to complex and from local to wide area. Design of a storage network can be as varied as the environments and applications they will support. Storage networking design involves having clear objectives, understanding business needs, assessing resources, analyzing information, documenting the design, and implementing it. This chapter contains many lists that can be used to create checklists, information worksheets, and comparison sheets for evaluating technology.

8.2 Getting started

As part of the storage networking design process, depending on what the scope is, you may decide to assemble a team of people from different groups, including networking, storage management, server management, applications, database management, and security. For smaller environments, perhaps you are the person responsible for pulling everything together. For larger storage networks a team can be useful to divide up the assessment activities as well as to provide subject matter expertise on the topic areas. If storage networking is new to you and the group you have assembled, certainly educating yourselves by reading books such as this is important. So don't be shy about telling your friends and others that they too should buy and read this book. You and your team may decide to attend conferences and seminars as a group or divide up the events for more coverage. There are also many on-line Webinars and articles that help to provide basic education about storage networking as well as updates on new and emerging technologies. You can also go to the Web site (www.storageio.com) to learn more about some of the technology covered in this book, as well as sources for seminars, conferences, articles, and more information.

8.3 Storage networking design influences

Storage networks have evolved from simple single vendor test configurations to multisite, multivendor local and wide area storage networks. Storage networks can vary in size and complexity using different interfaces and protocols to meet various needs. Storage networks can range from a simple single storage device with dedicated point-to-point Fibre Channel connections to a few servers to those supporting hundreds to thousands of servers and storage devices. Storage networks can support S/390 mainframe environments running ESCON and FICON to open systems using NAS, FCP, and iSCSI as well as intermixed environments. Careful planning and design can enhance the scalability, stability, management, and resiliency of a storage network. A storage network design consists of planning, understanding needs and requirements, identifying where resources (people and technology) are available, and being aware of technology trends. A poor storage networking design can lead to lack of stability; poor performance; unplanned outages for maintenance; and disruptions for future growth, regardless of which hardware, networks, and software are used.

Some influences on storage networking design include:

- What your business drivers, requirements, and needs are
- What your regulatory (government and industry) and compliance concerns are
- What your availability and survivability objectives are
- What your operating philosophies, paradigms, and principles are
- Which existing technology you have and how long you will retain it
- What is the existing skill set (knowledge base) pertaining to storage and networking
- What the storage network scope (how small, large, or complex) is
- What your budget and project constraints and ability to justify what you need are
- How your storage is being used, or how it will be used

8.4 Which type of storage network is right for you?

Your storage network design may also have to balance other factors as design trade-offs impacting choices to be made. Some examples of trade-offs and things to balance include availability versus performance, distance versus cost, legacy support versus new features and functions, budget constraints versus efficiency, and so forth. Other factors that will have an impact on your storage design include availability of technology, interoperability with existing hardware and software, and the skill (knowledge) base of those who will be working with and supporting the design.

A storage network could be simple integrated solutions, sometimes called a "SAN in a Can," with storage and some servers attached. A storage network could be many individual SAN islands using Fibre Channel or Gb E with iSCSI or a NAS solution. A storage network could be a large FICON environment with some large switching directors and remote distance support for mirroring. A storage network could also be a large, complex environment spanning locations using multiple technologies and interfaces. Storage networks can be a combination of these different implementations depending on what your needs are.

A SAN island is typically a single switch with multiple servers and storage attached and with no connection to other switches. SAN islands could have as few as 4 ports or as many as 512 (more with next-generation switches) on a single switch. For high availability SAN islands may be deployed in pairs for redundant paths (dual pathing) or multiple pairs (quad pathing). A SAN could be made up of many switches, servers, and storage devices using multiple protocols and interfaces. A SAN could also be made up of many SAN islands interconnected physically yet logically isolated using routers.

Some reasons for isolating and segmenting storage networks in separate regions or what could be considered subnets include:

- Different applications (production, Internet, test, database, OLTP, development)
- Different customer data (isolate internal and external customers from each other)
- Different vendors and equipment (isolate different technologies from each other)

So there are as many different applications and needs for storage networks as there are different types of implementations. Some types of storage networks include:

- Individual isolated islands to isolate different devices, vendors, and applications
- Simple SANs for small environments, including "SAN in a Can" solutions with iSCSI for block, and NAS for file sharing.
- Business continuance and disaster recovery SANs
- Segmented SANs to tie multiple SAN islands together
- Integrated and SAN consolidation, including mixed vendors and applications
- Complex wide area storage networks using different interfaces and protocols

8.5 Know your objectives and requirements

An important factor in designing a resilient storage networking environment is to understand needs and objectives. This is similar to building a sturdy house; it is necessary to know what the requirements are for the house before you can define the supporting infrastructure. Similar to LANs and networks, storage networks can be configured into different topologies to meet specific needs and requirements. An underlying principle with storage networking, as with traditional networking, is to simplify and remove complexity to reduce the chances for infrastructure failure and increase fault containment. The following questions may be intuitive; however, let's go over them to help better clarify what needs to be understood to design a resilient storage network.

- What are your requirements?
- What are your resources (people, budgets, time)?
- Do you have management-level sponsorship and endorsement?
- Do you have a storage plan?
- Do you have a backup plan?
- Do you have a disaster recovery and security plan?
- Will your storage network be used for SAN-to-SAN activity?
- Will your storage network be used for server to storage?

- Will your storage network be used for storage to storage?
- Will your storage network be used for server to server?
- How many ports do you need?
- Which locations are involved and what is needed at those sites?
- Do you need block, file, object access, or a combination of these capabilities?
- Do you need backup, failover, clustering, and continuous availability?
- How much performance do you need; what type of response time is needed?
- How many and which types of devices need to be supported?
- How many servers, how many ports per server, how much bandwidth per server?
- How much security do you need and where do you need it?
- What are the storage requirements in terms of capacity, performance, and availability?
- How much storage (real and usable) do you have and do you need?
- What are your data protection strategies, including mirroring, backup, and security?
- How many switches, bridges, gateways, and routers do you have or will you need?
- How much availability do you need for different applications and locations?

8.6 Storage network design

One of the benefits of storage networking is flexibility to meet various needs and support diverse applications locally and over wide areas. Consequently, a storage network design needs to be flexible and adaptable to support change in business requirements and technology enablement. Similar to traditional networks, a storage network can be built in a "flat" manner or a "segmented" manner. A flat approach would have all servers able to access all devices as one large SAN or fabric. The other approach is to segment the storage network into a group of two or more subnets that may be physically isolated from each other under common management, or physically interconnected, logically isolated, and under a common management schema.

The most common storage networking implementation is a storage device with servers attached via Fibre Channel, with Gb E and iSCSI becoming more common, as well as NAS solutions. These simple storage networks may have a switching device to support additional growth as well as a bridge or routing capability to allow access of iSCSI-enabled servers to Fibre Channel storage. The next most commonly deployed storage networks involve islands of switching devices with servers and storage attached. These islands could be individual switches and directors, or they can be made up of multiple switches networked together to create more complex storage networks.

8.7 The design process

The design process for storage networks can be relatively simple to rather complex. The process can be selecting a storage device with the appropriate amount of storage, with enough ports to attach servers directly or via a switch. The process can also involve assessments, analysis, and design to support complex global storage networks with many interfaces and protocols. The basic process is similar to that used for server and storage design and capacity planning, involving:

- Assessment (fact gathering)
- Analysis of assessment results
- Classification and life-cycle management
- Design and implementation topics
- Performance topics
- Maintenance and growth considerations
- Security topics
- Availability topics
- Reevaluate these items

In Figure 8.1, a simplified diagram shows the flow from assessment of needs, business requirements, capabilities, available resources for analysis and design, implementation, and validation. This is shown as a continuous process of assessment, analysis, design changes, implementation, and reassessment. This could be a constant cycle, annual cycle, or when appropriate for your requirements. One of the objectives of a good design and the continuous improvement process is to minimize surprise and alleviate risk from disruptions and unplanned outages.

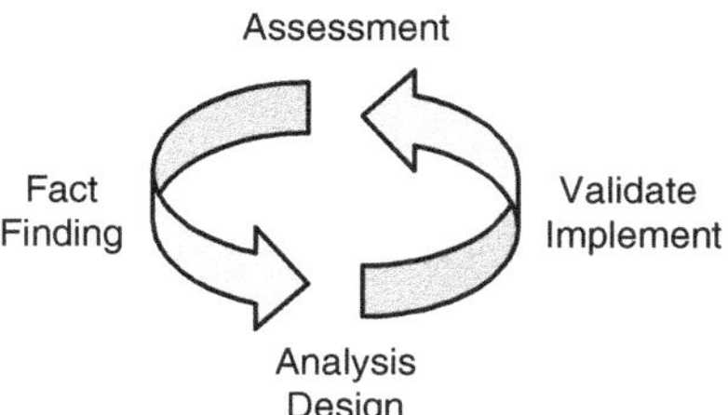

Figure 8.1 *Storage networking design: an ongoing process.*

If the process seems rather simplified, straightforward, and intuitive, it is! The process can be as complex or as simple as your needs dictate, including formalized processes and sophisticated tools. The process can also be rather simple to adjust to your needs. This theme should also carry over into your design in that simple yet robust designs can scale and be highly resilient. The old adage of "Keep It Simple Stupid" (KISS) should apply to the design process as well as to the actual design and implementation. Capacity planning will be covered in a subsequent chapter, as will be security and various topologies.

8.7.1 Assessment (fact gathering)

The assessment process can be very involved, or quite simple, depending on what your needs and objectives are. For example, having a good inventory of your equipment, how it is configured and utilized, and what your needs are greatly simplifies the process. Similarly, if the design objective is for a relatively simple storage network, that reduces the complexity of the assessment process. More involved assessments can be broken up into separate projects for backup, storage, disaster recovery, server and networks, or they can be combined. As part of your assessment process, you may want to employ the services of an outside consultant, analyst, or vendor to assist with the process. Look for service providers that are objective, thorough, and willing to work for your best interest. You may also, as part of an assessment, put together a rough request for information from vendors and partners to learn about their capabilities and plans. This can be as important as understanding your own needs as you move into the analysis and design phase. By understanding your needs, capabilities, and resources, as well as what those of the industry, suppliers, and business partners are, you can formulate all of these into capabilities and plans for moving forward. The trick is to balance your needs with what technology is able to do for you now, and then moving forward.

In general, the assessment process consists of:

- Taking inventory of existing resources (hardware, software, networks, vendors)
- Understanding objectives and requirements
- Determining people skill set, training, and knowledge base
- Determining service requirements (response time, throughput, availability, etc.)
- Determining business and application needs and growth
- Setting up a capacity forecast and performance plan
- Identifying procedures, practices, and policies
- Documenting findings and results

While storage networking enables any server to conceivably access any device, in practicality you may want to isolate, segment, or fence off certain systems and devices from others. Reasons for doing this are similar to why and how you isolate and segment a network into various subnets and include security; application isolation; customer isolation; and backup/recovery from production, protocol, and so forth. Some factors that need to be considered, in addition to those previously mentioned, when designing your storage networks, are shown in the following list. Keep in mind that depending on the type of your storage network and your specific needs, the following questions may be more than what you need to address, or they could represent an outline that needs further details.

In addition to the previous questions, some additional business and application items to look into and understand include:

- What is your processing growth plans?
- What is the overall business growth plans?
- Do any applications need to be isolated from others?
- Which applications and data are absolutely essential for the business to operate?
- What is the profile of busy periods, shifts, end-of-month, and seasonal activity?
- What are your legal and other regulatory obligations?
- Which external systems or data feed sources are needed to support the application?

While not an exhaustive list, the preceding questions help to establish a framework of the types of questions and things to be aware of from a business and application perspective. Moving from business and applications into the server, some common questions about servers and associated components, including adapters, are:

- Which servers are being used (blade, diskless, Intel, proprietary, make, model)?
- Which servers are partitioned into logical domains and what are their configurations?
- Which type of bus interface exists on the servers (PCI, PCI-X, Sbus, HSC, FICON)?
- What is the configuration of the servers (memory, processor, version, bus, adapters)?
- Where are the servers located and are they owned or leased (when is the lease up)?
- Which servers are set up for failover and clustering and with which other servers?
- Which clustering and HBA path failover tools and software are being used?
- What are the security needs and requirements for the servers?
- What are the backup and recovery requirements for the servers?
- Which servers exist at outsourced or collocation facilities?
- Are the servers and applications storage (capacity) or I/O intensive?
- What are the network interfaces for the servers and how many?
- What are your guidelines for number of servers per storage port?

You may already have some of this information in various formats, and, depending on the scope of your storage networking needs, this will determine the level of detail. The previous information is valuable not only for storage and storage networking design but also for general planning and asset management. Moving from business to applications to servers, let's look at some storage items. Storage and storage allocation, including volume management, questions include:

- Which type of storage (make, model, vendor, and configuration) do you have?
- Which medium (disk or tape) is utilized in the storage systems?

- Which volume managers and volume management tools are being used?
- What are the volume characteristics (RAID level, speed, redundant paths, backup)?
- What are the volume mapping and masking configuration and security requirements?
- How is the storage accessed (file, block, object)?
- Which data and storage are shared among which servers?
- Which tape and off-line media devices, including optical, do you have?
- What are your data classification policies and data retention plans?
- How is the cache on storage subsystems and buffers on VTS devices being used?
- Which devices and volumes are being mirrored to alternate locations?
- Where are the storage devices (disk and tape) located?

Storage networks enable storage to be utilized and accessed with more flexibility, including over long distances using public networks. Storage has been relatively safe in the confines of data centers and other isolated habitats. With storage traversing public and not so friendly networks, security becomes more important, as does maintaining data protection for business continuance. The following are some questions and things to look for with regard toward data protection and security (backup and business continuance):

- Which type of mirroring and replication is being used or is needed?
- Where is host, appliance, and storage-based mirroring and replication being used?
- What are your backup plans, schedules, and policies?
- What are the characteristics of the backup data (small versus large files, many versus few)?
- How much tape medium and which type do you have?
- How much time is spent on doing file and volume restoration and for which reasons?
- What are your data retention polices?
- How far away do the various types of data need to be?

Networking is an import component for storage networking; in addition to storage, the following items should be considered with regard toward networking (fabric, LAN, SAN, MAN, WAN) during an assessment:

- What are the storage and networking interfaces and protocols being used?
- What is the overall storage and networking topology?
- Which type of cabling and fiber optics exist or can be obtained?
- Can you obtain dedicated dark fiber between locations if needed?
- Can you share bandwidth (dedicated or service) with others between locations?
- Which type of optical connectors (GBICs, SFPs) do you have and need to support?
- What are the network growth plans in terms of more servers, storage, and bandwidth?
- What do you currently have in terms of switches, bridges, routers, and gateways?
- How many ports do you need for sparing, diagnostics, and growth?
- Which legacy devices do you have; do they need to be incorporated into a design?
- Do you plan to isolate legacy devices from newer devices?
- Do you need to support loop (public and private) devices such as older tape devices?
- Which type of access (any to any, any to many, many to many) is needed?
- Which ratios do you have or need to convert from slower interfaces to faster interfaces (e.g., how many ESCON channels need to be replaced by FICON channels)?
- Which storage networking tools are you currently using and for which functions?
- What are your current storage networking challenges and needs?
- Which equipment is leased and when does it need to be replaced?

Management of storage and storage networks is an ongoing task that may require multiple tools from different vendors. Some questions and things to consider regarding management tools and utilities include the following:

- What are your system and component monitoring requirements and needs?
- Which storage utilities, including backup, reporting, and configuration, are being used?
- Who is being notified, including vendors, of which events?
- Who has access to the tools and interfaces, including e-mail and dial-in/dial-out?
- Which maintenance and configuration tasks do you need to have the vendor perform?
- What are your people resource skill sets and knowledge base (experience)?
- Which test and diagnostic capabilities, including probe and data collection points as well as fault insertion and profile capabilities to assess normal or abnormal conditions and behavior to develop profiles, are available?

The previous is by no means an exhaustive list of things to look at, but consider that it provides a framework to help with your assessment. Keep in mind that the level of detail needed for your assessment is proportional to the scope, size, and complexity of your storage networking needs. Some items to consider with regard toward storage and storage networking assessments include:

- Are you utilizing an xSP, co-location, carrier, or data hotel to host part of your SAN?
- What are your MTTR and MTTB considerations and requirements?
- Which current challenges do you have with regard to fault containment?
- What are your needs for enhancing resiliency and fault isolation?
- Which areas are currently requiring extra management and support and why?
- What are your maintenance windows and opportunities for hardware, software, applications, data conversions, and migrations?

One of the most important things when doing an assessment, either by yourself or with outside assistance, is to be objective and keep an open mind; don't jump to conclusions on what is good or bad. This will help you to see what you have as well as to start assessing what you need and what you can do differently or better. The assessment process is really a chance to leverage what you have learned.

8.7.2 Analysis of assessment results

The term *business partner* has many different meanings, ranging from that of a vendor that is a trusted supplier to that of an independent third party that does not sell any hardware, software, network, or support services. This latter definition can be expanded to those who do assessments, analysis, design, and implementations and those who oversee the projects and other suppliers on your behalf. A business partner can be independent as well as represent various vendors, simplifying the process of you having to deal with different vendors. There are business partners whose value is getting you the lowest price on all of the components, essentially a reseller of equipment that you need. There are business partners who represent and can offer you different equipment, software, and services, along with managing the vendors who might not otherwise want to work together. If you have a large organization, vendors may be very willing to work directly with you and provide different services. On the other hand, if you are not seen as a large opportunity, they may hand you off to one of their business partners or resellers. Regardless of whom you utilize to assist in the different aspects of storage networking, seek out a resource who has experience with what you need to do and who is willing to work with and for you. Talk with others who have implemented storage networks—especially those who have similar requirements and needs. User groups and conferences can provide a good venue to learn more and meet others who have perhaps done what you are looking to do.

With the assessment information in hand and an understanding of requirements, now it's time to analyze and interpret it. By reviewing the results you have from your assessment or existing information, a quick analysis may determine that your needs fit some predetermined design solutions, also known as templates. Later, in Chapters 14 through 17, various storage networking examples are covered. These solutions can be combined with others and modified to meet your different needs and provide a guide to give you ideas on what you can do.

A simple analysis would be a scenario where you identify a few servers that need to share some storage and perhaps be clustered. You know the server types, their operating system and bus adapter requirements, and their expected performance requirements and amount of storage needed, as well as growth plans. From this you could determine that a storage system with enough ports to attach the server is needed, or that a switching device is also needed. Assuming that your assessment and analysis indicate that you need new equipment and software, your next step would be to talk to vendors and business partners. For a simple environment, the vendors may offer a simple solution; or they may decide to utilize your assessment information to put some proposals together based on some different designs.

For more complex and larger projects you may want to ask the vendors and business partners for a request for information if that was not done during the assessment phase. You may also seek out a business partner or consultant to review your assessment information and perform an analysis of it, including data classification and organization. The analysis could include a life-cycle classification to determine how storage is utilized and accessed. This can be useful for deriving various design alternatives utilizing different storage technology to help address management of increasing amounts of data. The analysis process can be separated from the design process or combined, depending on your specific needs and requirements.

8.7.3 Classification and life-cycle management

Classification of data is an optional step you may decide on as part of a storage network design or as a follow-up task. This activity may be done on an ongoing basis as part of a data life-cycle management task or as part of an overhaul to develop a storage strategy and plan. Table 8.1 shows some terms that are commonly used to describe data, storage and information life-cycle classification, and management.

The actual processes you utilize to analyze and classify data to determine design alternatives and results are varied. The process can be simple, using pen and paper to identify common associations and categories based upon

Table 8.1 *Terms Relating to Classification*

Term	Full Name
DLM	Data Life-cycle Management
ILM	Information Life-cycle Management
SLM	Storage Life-cycle Management
xLM	Generic use of the life-cycle management term, where "x" refers to data, information, storage, and so on

similar requirements, or the process can be involved, utilizing spreadsheets, databases, and analysis tools to obtain the results. Some companies, such as large multinational outsourcing companies, have created sophisticated, patented algorithms to analyze, profile, and characterize application needs. The results of these processes determine what is needed to support the applications and workload and to help derive a design.

To help profile and characterize data and storage, some tools exist from different vendors or as part of services. These tools can look at your storage and data access patterns to determine when they are accessed, in some cases who accessed them, and other information. This information can be utilized to determine which data is frequently accessed and which data is seldom accessed to help develop policies and storage placement strategies. Not all data is equal, with some having higher priority and importance than others. Where tools are not available, the brute-force approach can be used to utilize standard operating system and other vendor-supplied tools to see which storage and data have been accessed recently.

8.7.4 Design and implementation topics

First-generation storage networks, like their early networking counterparts, tended to dictate the environment based upon the available technology at that time. More robust and larger devices are enabling larger and less complex heterogeneous storage networks to be built—similar to how LANs and traditional networks grew. For medium to large enterprise environments, multiple large megafabrics of switches and directors can scale to support thousands of ports.

Some design considerations include:

- Any to any, many to few, few to many access of servers and storage devices
- Logical and physical isolation and segmentation of fabrics and devices
- Centralized versus distributed architecture
- Support for legacy equipment or working from a clean sheet of paper design
- Multiple platforms, devices, and applications versus isolated environments
- Large SAN versus small SAN, local versus wide area
- Plans for expansion and maintenance as well as fault isolation

- Consolidation of servers, storage, SAN islands
- Design for implementation in phases and design for change

Avoid starting with a technology design to drive your technology plan—rather, develop a design that technology will adapt to. Configure for upgrade and maintenance, including redundant path availability as well as support for access during changes. Leverage vendors and consultants as resources for input, but develop a plan that meets your requirements and leverages existing and emerging capabilities; avoid one that simply meets vendor agendas.

Your plan should be the convergence of what you need to do to support the business and what technology is capable of. This is for now and for the future. So since the business will be growing and technology will be evolving, the plan should account and leverage both. Your plan may not be fully deployable on day one; however, not all of your business requirements may be ready for the plan, so have a phased and flexible plan that can be used as a guide and input into the continued plan and revise it as needed to support changes in business and technology capabilities and economics.

To help in the design process, identify which type of storage network in terms of access (block, file, object) is needed. In Table 8.2, various applica-

Table 8.2 *Application and Storage Access Methods*

Application Type	Object (CAS)	Block	File (NAS)
Archiving and retention	Yes	Yes	Yes
Backup and recovery	—	Yes	Yes
Data sharing	—	—	Yes
Database	—	Yes	Yes
E-mail and attachments	Yes	Yes	Yes
File sharing	—	Yes	Yes
High-performance compute	—	Yes	Yes
OLTP	—	Yes	—
Reference data (images, documents)	Yes	Yes	Yes
Video server	Yes	Yes	Yes
Web server	—	Yes	Yes
Workgroup and office functions	—	Yes	Yes

tions are characterized with different storage access methods, including object (CAS), block, and file (NAS). This by no means a definitive list, and I will leave it to the vendors to debate which applications fit on which technology.

Part of designing a storage network is determining which protocols to use for different applications, environments, and functions. In Table 8.3, various storage networking protocols are shown, with their suitability for different functions.

Another component to storage networking design is to identify local, metropolitan, and wide area needs and determine the appropriate interface. In Table 8.4, various metropolitan and wide area storage networking interfaces are shown.

Develop a plan that meets your needs and requirements but that is also flexible to change and grow. Utilizing the information from the assessment and analysis process, enlist the assistance of others, including vendors and consultants, to identify alternatives. You may want to utilize and request for information activity to collect feedback and information to impact your design and analysis as well as to validate it. Develop a plan, either small or complex, that supports growth, stability, maintenance, and ease of management.

Table 8.3 *Determining Storage Interfaces and Protocols*

	FCP	iSCSI	FICON	SCSI	NAS	CAS
Block access	Yes	Yes	Yes	Yes	—	—
File access	—	—	—	—	Yes	—
High performance	Yes	Yes	Yes	—	—	—
Long distances	Extend	Yes	Extend	—	Yes	—
Many devices	Yes	Yes	Yes	—	Yes	—
Medium distance	Yes	Yes	Yes	—	Yes	—
Object access	—	—	—	—	—	Yes
S/390 CCW support	—	—	Yes	—	—	Yes
Short distances	Yes	Yes	Yes	Yes	Yes	—
Utilize Ethernet	Extend	Yes	Extend	—	Yes	Yes
Utilize Fibre Channel	Yes	Bridge	Yes	Bridge	Yes	Yes
Utilize SONET/SDH	Yes	Yes	Yes	—	Yes	Yes

Table 8.4 *Designing for Distance*

	Long-Distance Optics	xWDM	SONET SDH	IP	Traditional WAN
0–100km+	—	Yes	Yes	Yes	Yes
0–80km	Yes	Yes	Yes	Yes	Yes
Across campus	Yes	Yes	Yes	Yes	Yes
Across towns	Yes	Yes	Yes	Yes	Yes
Bandwidth service available	—	—	Yes	Yes	Yes
Between buildings	Yes	Yes	Yes	Yes	Yes
Beyond 100km	—	Limited	Yes	Yes	Yes
Dedicated fiber available	Yes	Yes	Yes	Yes	Yes
Global	—	—	Yes	Yes	Yes
In the same building	Yes	Yes	Yes	Yes	—
Regional	—	Limited	Yes	Yes	Yes
Shared fiber available	—	—	Yes	Yes	Yes

Which topology is best for resilient storage networks?

So what is the best topology for SAN or fabric? Well, that really depends on your needs and environment. Ultimately it should be the topology that meets your needs, not one that forces you to adjust to the technology capabilities. Another factor to consider is whether you need any-to-any access from all servers to all tape and storage devices. A simple cascade solution would be two switches or directors—each with attachments to all servers and storage. Should a component fail, there would still be connectivity. Multiple E_Port ISLs to support FSPF routing and redundancy need to be configured in as well. Finally, reducing the complexity of your topology will simplify management and help to improve the resilience of your storage network. In Chapter 9, various storage networking topologies are covered in more detail; these can be used with different interfaces and combinations to implement your storage network design.

Best Practices: For high availability, a best practice is to have dual or multiple paths between the host server and storage devices. This entails having redundant HBAs, resilient fabrics, and dual attachment of storage devices. Dual Ethernets enable clients to access the servers, and communicate between servers. Path management software on servers enables HBA failover, and some also support load balancing. Path management software is available from server, adapter, storage, and data management vendors.

One of the benefits of SANs is to remove the physical interface dependence between a server and a dedicated drive. This helps with disaster recovery and high availability by being able to disassociate the storage with a server and place the two in different locations. Faster network interfaces are also enabling greater distances between servers and storage devices. Redundancy should be considered to ensure that the fan-in and fan-out are not impacted due to loss of an ISL. A variation of the fan-in and fan-out approach is to connect switching hubs to provide loop support for public and private loop hosts and devices. This could also be done by placing a switch into hub mode and then connecting it to the core via a loop port or an E_Port.

8.7.5 Performance topics

There are many components to performance, as well as capacity planning involving storage and storage networking. Performance similar to availability is the sum of all components working together. Performance can also be tied to availability in that the system and storage network may be available, but if performance degrades to a point where applications are not able to function, availability is impacted. Similarly, you can have the most robust storage and storage networking environment, but if it is not available, that impacts your overall performance. Table 8.5 shows some performance impacts on different storage networking components.

Data can be collected from the fabric, from devices, from servers, and from HBAs. While performance is a relative point with respect to the workload or application, it is still something that must be considered, particularly for disaster recovery. The level of performance you may need is going to be in part a function of your pain threshold for recovery. Put another way, how long you can afford to be down versus the cost for more performance

Table 8.5 *Components That Impact Storage and Storage Networking Performance*

Component	Impact
Servers	Application characteristics include database locking, volume manager and filesystem configuration, lack of buffers, memory usage and activity, paging and swapping, CPU busy, I/O activity and type, bus and adapter activity.
Network	Available bandwidth of interfaces, source and destination activity, congestion of switches, flow control buffers, MAN and WAN interface utilization.
Storage	Cache utilization and efficiency, device load balancing, configuration, and allocation of storage to devices.

capability to expedite recovery. For example, if we assume that a truck carrying 5Tbytes of backup tapes can arrive at a recovery site in nine hours and, within an hour of arrival, restoration can begin, the amount of recovery bandwidth will determine how much more time will be required.

Performance is an easy thing to talk about until it comes time to actually measure it, prove it, or otherwise quantify it—whether it is for usage, capacity planning, or performance tuning and measurement. Other than basic metrics such as frames received or transmitted per second and error counts, more meaningful storage and I/O types of metrics have been elusive in storage networking. This is now changing, with various tools and techniques becoming available and continuing to emerge to help provide metrics or statistics, such as megabytes/second, bytes sent, bytes received, utilization of ports, and so on; these can be used for configuration and design, problem isolation, and performance tuning. Something that needs to be considered when looking at performance is how it is actually measured and reported. For example, are we dealing with 1 million bytes or a megabyte? There is a difference between the way storage is reported and measured and the way data communication is measured. An example is 1,000,000 bytes versus 1,024,000 bytes.

Some performance metrics include:

- Equivalency ratios for migration from slower interfaces to faster ones
- S/390 mainframe SMF and RMF records
- UNIX SAR, iostat, and timex tools
- Automated Resource Monitoring/Management (ARM)
- SMI-S-enabled performance and capacity planning tools

- Tape handing and volume mount, rewind times
- Buffers and cache allocation, utilization, and effectiveness
- Channel busy and delay, resulting in queues and elongated service times
- I/O types, including random, sequential, reads, writes, full volume and device (large), cylinder (medium), sector (small) access
- I/O patterns, including transfer length and duration and frequency of access
- Throughput and bandwidth and transfer time (MB/Mb/sec)
- Latency and response times, including seek and access
- Device and channel resets and errors, including network line errors
- Number of servers to storage ratio, based on workload activity versus connections

Traditional storage wisdom is to reduce response time in terms of a few milliseconds while the interface behaves in a deterministic manner. From a traditional IP networking perspective, storage interfaces may appear over-configured and expensive, with an excess toward minute incremental response time improvements. From a traditional storage thinking standpoint, IP-based networks are thought of as being designed with lowest cost in mind and performance and data integrity as secondary. A difference in paradigms between traditional storage practices and IP network practices is summarized in Table 8.6.

Table 8.6 *Traditional Storage Practices versus IP Network Practices*

Storage	IP
Perspective is that storage may be configured based on capacity versus performance and activity.	Networks may be configured to optimize costs and share bandwidth.
More conservative with regard to performance.	How many connections can you have with an eye on reducing costs?
Storage and I/O have deterministic behavior, dropped packets are not an option, and data integrity is paramount.	Packets can be dropped and resent. Data integrity is important, but so is utilization important.
$/MB	$/Port

Table 8.6 is presented to put in context the different approaches, thinking, and needs of storage and general networks. Understanding these differences helps to put different performance characteristics into focus, particularly when comparing apples to oranges.

Vertical scaling

Vertical scaling refers to scaling by increasing the physical size of a single device to increase capacity and performance. Some examples would be a larger processor, larger storage device, and larger network switch.

In Figure 8.2, some examples of vertical scaling are shown, ranging from a small port count device on the left to a large port count device on the right. While this example shows vertical scaling of switch ports, this model of vertical scaling applies equally to servers and storage devices. For example, you could have a small storage subsystem with few access ports and limited capacity, or you could have a large frame-based storage subsystem supporting many servers with large amounts of storage capacity and features. An example of server-based vertical scaling could be small servers at one extreme and a large powerful server that could be partitioned (similar to mainframes and UNIX superservers) at the other extreme.

Horizontal scaling

Another approach to scaling would be horizontal scaling, which relies on networking or aggregation of multiple devices to create the combined resources of a larger device. Some examples of horizontal scaling include clustering of servers for availability or supporting parallel workloads. Other examples include grid computing to combine multiple servers to increase

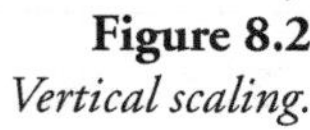
Figure 8.2
Vertical scaling.

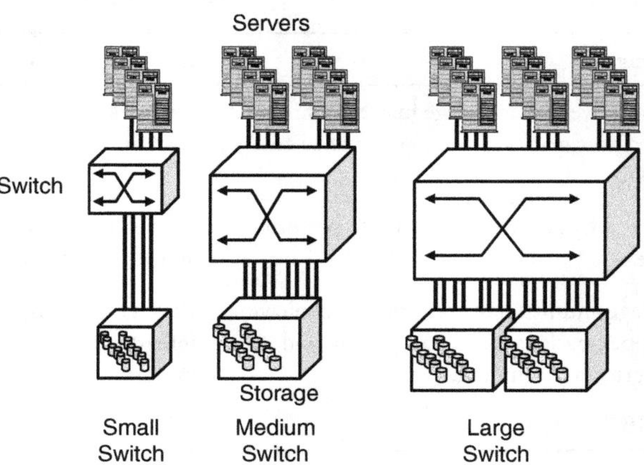

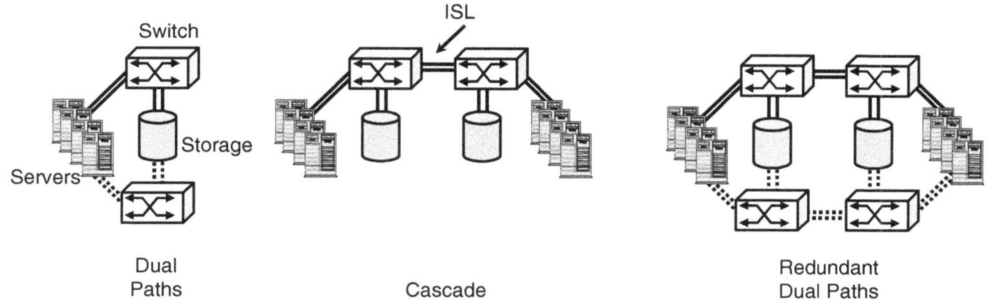

Figure 8.3 *Horizontal scaling.*

overall computing power. A storage example would be multiple smaller, or even larger, devices using volume managers and virtualization appliances to create larger storage pools. From a switching and network standpoint, examples of horizontal scaling would be networking multiple switches together to create more ports and to span geographical distances for HA and business continuance.

In Figure 8.3, some examples of horizontal scaling for storage networking that could exist in the same facility or across multiple sites are shown. Utilization of networking or fabrics of two or more switches/directors in various topologies across one or more locations can provide adequate numbers of ports, performance, redundancy, and meet application service requirements. Various topologies can be implemented to meet different needs, including core-fabric switch, cascade, mesh, tiered, ring, core-edge, and so on. FICON Cascade is an example of vertical scaling for DR and resiliency.

There is a misnomer that ISLs are bad, when the reality is that there is no such thing as a bad ISL. However, there can be bad implementations of ISLs as opposed to using other scaling and design techniques. For example, ISLs are useful to create expanded (Figure 8.3) and resilient storage networks as well as scaling for thousands of ports. A bad implementation of an ISL would use ISLs to increase the complexity of a storage network where ISLs are not needed. Table 8.7 shows some different characteristics to help assess what type of scaling (vertical, horizontal, or combination) is best for your needs.

Placement and locality

There are two extremes when it comes to locality: one being 0 percent locality, when all devices and servers are not on the same switch or director, and

Table 8.7 *Utilizing Vertical and Horizontal Scaling*

	Vertical	Horizontal
Network to other devices (core-edge)	X	X
Scale across locations	Network	X
Scale as a single device	X	—
Scale beyond a single device	Network	X
Scale into thousands of ports	X	X
Scale using multiple devices	X	X

the other being 100 percent locality, with all devices and servers on the same switch or director. There can be a balance between the two in a production environment, particularly depending on what the workload requirements are and how the applications behave. When all devices and storage are local, you do not need to be worried about placement, extra hops, congestion, and other items.

With a low percentage of locality, which is how much traffic is local to a switch or device compared with traffic that spans multiple switches, other issues can occur, including increased latency and congestion over ISLs. The tradeoff between high locality and low locality can be performance over cost. Some side effects of poor locality include blockage (delays or congestion from more workload than available bandwidth to handle it), oversubscription (excessive delays similar to a constant busy signal when no cell phone circuits are available), and added complexity (load balancing, placement, security, configuration).

A key piece to locality is the size of the device. Smaller devices are configured into a fabric having lower locality than a higher port count device. The idea of locality can be seen with LANs and the migration from small switches to larger core devices with fan-in and fan-out edge devices. In Figure 8.4, the left panel shows a switch with all ports being local (100 percent locality), resulting in a single hop.

In the middle panel, there is a partial mesh with a server and storage device attached to the top and another storage device attached to the bottom. For the server to access the local storage device (the one on the same switch) there is only one hop involved and traffic stays on that switch or fabric device. For the server on the top to access the storage device attached to the bottom right switch the data has to flow across or through multiple

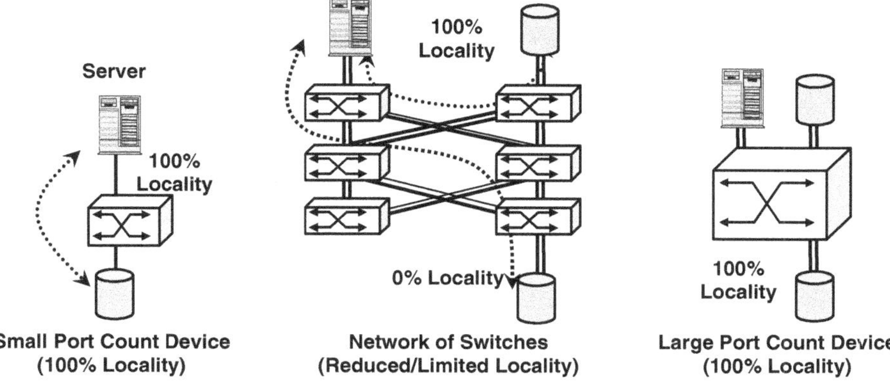

Figure 8.4 *Locality example.*

switches and over ISLs, adding to latency. While some applications may be immune to the extra few microseconds of latency with each hop, some applications (backup/restore, database) can be enhanced with attention to device placement and performance. In the example on the right, a large port count device provides the same locality of the smaller switch on the left but with many more ports. The benefit is reduced complexity by not having to worry about placement of devices for optimum performance and improved locality.

Placement is concerned with where we attach host servers or storage devices to the SAN with regard to performance, latency, and other items that affect availability. In addition to performance, placement in a SAN is important for recovery as well as where the device is for continuous access. First-generation SANs relied on placement due to the size of devices, similar to early LANs and storage controllers. As LAN devices became larger, more servers and devices could be attached locally, and, as larger storage devices supported more performance, locality was not as much an issue as it was with early RAID devices.

8.7.6 Maintenance and growth considerations

Planning for maintenance and growth up front can help minimize disruptions in the future. Allowing for growth and maintenance can mean planning multiple paths that can be utilized for high availability and workload balancing. By having multiple paths and components, scheduled maintenance can be performed if needed on one path while another path is kept in service. Note that you might want to perform maintenance on alternative paths during a scheduled maintenance period just to be safe and to minimize impact on applications and the business. For growth you may want to preposition extra fiber cabling and have spare ports for expansion use to avoid reconfiguration later. Careful naming and addressing strategies can also help avoid surprises in the future when you expand or consolidate servers, storage, or switching components.

While not an exhaustive list, some maintenance and growth tasks to plan for include:

- Firmware updates for HBAs, switches, gateways, storage, and servers
- Hardware upgrades and expansion (cache, memory, ports, disks, bandwidth)
- Failover of devices to alternate paths or locations
- Network changes internally or in the carrier environment
- Movement of data from one storage device to another for replacement and upgrades
- Testing, diagnostics, and troubleshooting
- Expansion of capacity (bandwidth, ports)
- Plan for vendor access (dial-in, dial-up, e-mail, access to secure networks)
- Determine what is normal, what is abnormal
- How to test and verify distance
- Change control and management
- Staged changes with fallback

8.7.7 Security topics

There are many methods for implementing security and zoning in a storage network, and these will be covered in more detail in Chapter 13. These range from server (HBA binding), fabric based (WWN, port, and hardware), and storage based (volume/LUN mapping/masking). There are different practices for zoning; some are carryovers from first-generation SANs. Current-generation storage networks have different vendor storage devices in the same zone, including different HBAs. Regardless of zoning strategy, consider storage-based zoning as the last line of defense to secure data in a storage network. Some items to consider when designing a storage network for resiliency include:

- Zoning and networking isolation
- Security of management tools and interfaces
- Security of wide area storage networking interfaces
- Security of storage devices

8.7.8 Availability topics

One of the keys to building a resilient storage network for resiliency is to have dual or redundant SANs or fabrics, with each providing a separate and isolated path between the host server and the storage devices or other host systems. Avoid overconnection or the temptation to have everything connected to everything. There is a tradeoff in that in order to prevent blockage or congestion, various switches in a fabric may have to be interconnected to provide adequate bandwidth using the Interswitch Links (ISLs). The preferred method is to create two fabrics or SANs, each with their devices interconnected; however, the SANs themselves are not interconnected.

High-availability configurations might have multiple switches or directors for redundancy and increased bandwidth. The servers could be all the same operating system type, or they could be a mix of UNIX, NT, Novell, Linux, and others. Some things to be concerned with include firmware levels and any enabling keys, as well as principal switch selection and domain IDs. Zone merge and zone sets need to be considered, as well as placement, port types, and intermixing of public and private loops.

Plan and build redundancy into your fiber infrastructure. Be aware of where the fiber goes and where it is on shared bandwidth and infrastructure. Make sure that you have unique paths and that your alternate vendors are not converging on the same fiber-optic cable and connection points. In spring 2003 during the "Big Dig" in Boston, which involved a lot of digging to relocate expressways underground, a fiber-optic cable supporting an OC-48 SONET/SDH circuit was accidentally cut when a pipe fell on it. For those who had no alternate path, or whose alternate path from a different provider was on the same cable, this resulted in loss of bandwidth or accessibility. Another precaution is to physically isolate and separate where external fiber connections come into your premises so that they are better isolated from cable cuts. There have been numerous outages around the world (some that are publicized, many that are not) where a back-hoe or some other digging device cut a fiber-optic cable along with the standby circuit that happened to be in the same trench.

Something to consider with any type of fiber-optic service or communication mechanism is failover and redundancy. This can vary based on the type of service and who is providing the service and equipment. For example, if you are using DWDM with your own fiber or dark fiber supplied by a provider, you will be responsible for configuring your equipment to utilize multiple fiber cables for failover. If you are using a managed service, or your provider is doing a managed service for you, then part of the fee you pay may include redundant network and telecommunications links as well as the equipment to automatically handle failover on a network failure. Assess your components, and in particular storage devices and host HBAs/SNICs, to see how they are configured to tolerate timeouts and state changes from RSCNs should there be a disruption to the physical cabling somewhere in the network. For example, an ATM SONET/SDH circuit may take up to 50ms to fail over, which may be acceptable for an IP circuit handling Internet traffic but is a long time from a disk I/O standpoint.

Use good quality cabling, transceivers, patch panels, and cabling techniques to support a scalable, stable, and manageable resilient storage network. If you are looking to save costs, avoid cutting corners with regard to cabling and connectors—particularly for high-performance and long-distance applications. While you might get by in some instances with cutting corners or stretching fiber-optic technology beyond what it's rated for, you are also inviting random and mysterious events to occur. For example, a fiber channel SMF cable that worked fine as an ISL at 1Gb all of a sudden quits working or loses connections randomly when upgrading to 2Gb. The solution could be as simple (assuming the proper cable and connectors are being used) as cleaning the fiber-optic cable at the connection points. If you recall, SMF cable has a core diameter of 8um or less, and a human hair is about 75um in diameter. Imagine what a piece of dirt or dust can do if on the connector.

Also make sure that your cable runs are within tolerance over long distances by using fiber-optic test equipment to measure db loss. You may find that your cable is within limits for distance, but due to cable breaks for connectors, jumpers, and paths through various other components your combined db loss has an adverse effect on performance and stability. This is similar to pushing a parallel SCSI bus to its maximum length with several devices attached and placing a heavy workload on it. It might work for a while, but at some point you may find yourself perusing random and mysterious events with an analyzer and diagnostic equipment.

Distance and redundancy are very important in creating a wide area resilient enterprise. The tradeoffs with distance and redundancy are cost and performance; costs go up with distance while performance decreases. By the same token, the more redundancy, the higher the cost. However, this cost, particularly for sensitive applications (backup, clustering), may be offset by the impact of not having it in place.

While distance brings protection and added resiliency to the enterprise, distance also brings additional exposure to security breaches and other network attacks that can disrupt the enterprise. Interfaces should be isolated so that if there is a failure in the network core, there is no impact. For example, if you have multiple network interfaces between your sites, these should be isolated from each other and never traverse the same physical network. If at some point they converge and utilize a common physical network interface such as shared fiber optics, and that cable is disrupted in any way, you have a single point of failure. It is also important to know the routing or physical path that is being taken by the network and what redundancy is built into the network.

Habitats for storage networks

A resilient storage network is flexible as well as producing a stable platform and infrastructure to support business information needs. Consequently, resilient storage networks can be deployed in different sizes, using a variety of interfaces and protocols to meet different needs. A resilient storage network for a single location could exist in an equipment room or perhaps a secure communications closet. A larger storage network could span multiple locations, with equipment in different computer rooms, data centers, and communications closets. From a physical security standpoint, keeping equipment in locked and secured facilities is a best practice. Depending on the size and complexity of the storage network, the storage network can exist in different habitats.

Some infrastructure items concerning addressing habitats (physically, where resilient storage and storage networking will reside) include:

- Establishing security and environmental zones, sectors and perimeters
- Hardened bunkers, vaults for tape, data storage, and retention
- Tag and label fiber cables at both ends for identification and tracking purposes
- Have a cabling topology schematic and keep it updated
- Component racking and cabling to simply maintenance, replacement, diagnostics
- Cable harnesses, cable trunks, cable raceways, and conveyance trays

- Redundant and backed up Network Operation Centers (NOCs) and command centers
- Office space and meeting rooms, for staff, vendors, and contractors
- Adequate cabinetry and equipment racking space
- Separate networks for command and control functions
- Humidity control devices to protect equipment from static discharge
- Enhanced cooling for higher-density equipment (blade servers, switches, storage)
- Protection against flooding and water damage (note that while fiber optics are relatively immune to water, the optics to electrical equipment generally are not)
- Air exchangers and ventilation for smoke, odors, chemical, and other containments
- Fire and smoke monitoring, detection, suppression, and protection
- Electrical power (primary and backup)
- Protection from electromagnetic interface and electromagnetic pulse
- Redundant and isolated power sources from separate grids
- Self-generated generators with sufficient fuel and cooling
- Battery maintenance and services for UPS, motor generators, conditioners
- Adequate and proper grounding and static dissipation
- Protected and maintained fuel supplies and other consumables for generators
- Test generators regularly with a heavy workload on them as part of maintenance
- Line surge protection and isolation technology from lighting
- Adequate power and right type of power (voltage, amperage, phase)
- Proper connector types for power requirement, country location

Some testing items include:

- Testing the entire configuration beyond basic connectivity
- Testing with various patches, configurations, and topologies
- Performance and regression testing of components and entire system

- Determining baseline to understand what is normal and abnormal
- Document your plan and design including topologies, configurations, and who the implementer is

Avoid starting with a technology design and plan that you then need to adapt to your business—rather, identify what you need to support your business, which technology you have or need, and then develop a plan to support the business with available technology as well as what is on the horizon. Work with your vendor partners to identify what they are working on that might help shape what you will be able to factor into plans and time frames. Avoid developing plans based on road maps—rather, leverage the road map and vision of your partners with yours. Your vendors should also be aware of what you need to do down the road so that they can be prepared to support you.

8.8 Chapter summary

Storage networks can be implemented for many different applications and business needs. Storage networks can be big, small, complex, local, and wide area. Understanding your specific needs, knowing your available resources, and having clear objectives combine to create a stable and flexible storage networking design.

What This Chapter Will Do For You

This chapter looks at various topologies that can be used for implementing storage networks. You will learn how to use different topologies to span distance and optimize for performance and resiliency to meet your data protection needs. Some of the items you will learn about in this chapter include:

- How complexity can increase cost and management activities
- What *not* to do to in your effort to create a scalable and flexible access infrastructure
- The right topology is one that works for you instead of you working for it
- Locality and performance can be at the root of many storage challenges

9

Storage Networking Topologies

9.1 Overview

This chapter looks at various storage networking topology configurations that can be implemented using different interfaces for diverse needs. The topologies discussed in this chapter can be combined with others and are not specific to any one protocol or interface unless otherwise noted. Some of the examples in this chapter are shown as a single fabric to simplify the illustration; however, a best practice is to implement redundant paths and redundant networks (fabrics).

9.2 Storage networking topologies

Storage and storage networks can be deployed into many different environments and for a wide range of applications. Storage networks, similar to traditional networks, can be implemented in varying topology configurations using different interfaces and protocols. Consequently, storage networks need to be flexible to meet the needs of these environments and align to their specific requirements, ranging from simple to complex, local to metropolitan to global. What is the correct storage networking topology for your environment? That depends largely on what your needs and requirements are. Various storage network topologies to meet different needs are discussed in this chapter. Later, in Part IV, various topologies are shown for different applications as examples. When building a storage network, there are many options and choices as to what the topology or configuration will be. Ultimately the best topology will be one that is resilient, redundant, simple to manage, and matches the needs of your environment and requirements.

There are many different topologies for storage networks, including SAN and NAS, that can be used to scale storage networks beyond the limits of the physical fabric devices. In addition to scaling to support larger storage networks, flexible topologies and interconnects are also being used to connect various SAN islands or first-generation homogeneous SANs into heterogeneous storage networks to simplify backups/restores and resource sharing. Flexibility and scalable storage networking topologies are also needed to span distances for resiliency and business continuance. In this chapter, a switch and switching director are generically referred to as a switch. Similarly, the topologies discussed in this chapter are technology and interface independent unless otherwise noted.

9.2.1 Dedicated, point to point (bus architecture)

A basic and simple topology would be a direct connect, also known as point to point, between a server and a storage device. This could be accomplished using Fibre Channel, SATA/ATA, SSA, parallel SCSI (Ultra SCSI), USB, or another storage interface. For a single server and storage device, this is referred to as direct attached and dedicated storage. This is a common approach for laptops with internal hard disks and servers with internal and external dedicated storage. An improvement on this approach would be to use modular or enterprise storage devices configured in a point-to-point topology, shown in Figure 9.1, or in a combination of point-to-point and switched attached storage.

Some examples of point-to-point and bus topologies include:

- Internal server storage using SCSI, SAS, SATA, or IDE interfaces
- External storage using SCSI, ATA, SAS, SATA, USB, SSA, Fibre Channel, or iSCSI
- Attachment to shared storage using dedicated interface paths

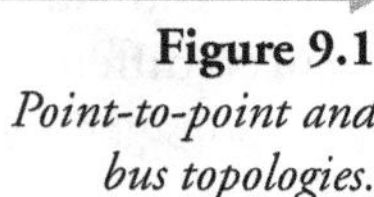

Figure 9.1
Point-to-point and bus topologies.

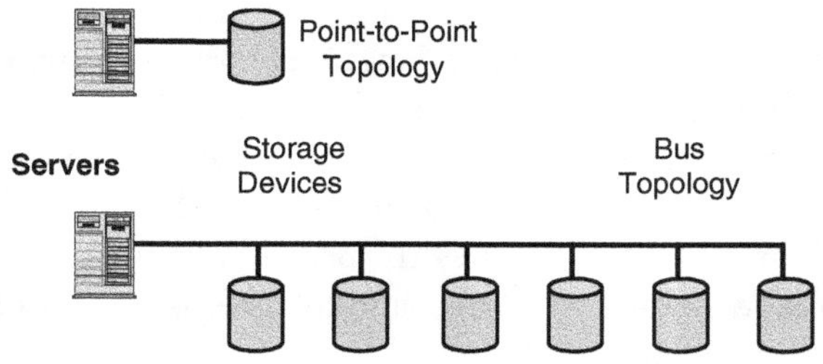

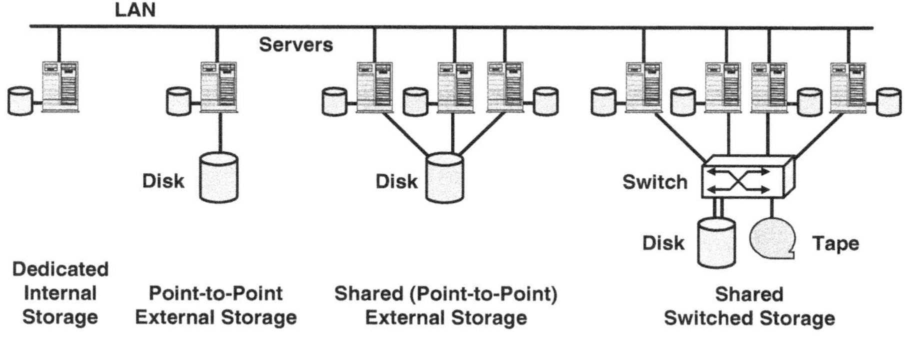

Figure 9.2 *Various storage topologies.*

A variation of a point-to-point and bus topology is a shared bus with two servers attached, both functioning as initiators to the target devices. An example of this would be multi-initiator SCSIs, with each server being a unique initiator (SCSI ID) communicating to SCSI target devices on the shared bus. Another example would be two servers with a dedicated Ethernet to support IP traffic between them, including cluster heartbeat, as would a crossover cable for point-to-point Ethernet.

A simple non-point-to-point topology involves a single fabric device (switch or director) providing 100 percent locality for servers and storage attached to it. Depending on the size of the fabric device, various topologies or configurations may be needed to increase or scale the SAN, similar to the LAN world. One approach is to use multiple smaller fabric devices, such as 16 port switches, and have them networked into different topologies. Another approach, also similar to LANs, is to use larger port count devices, which can also be networked into different topologies to scale.

In Figure 9.2, various topologies are shown, including dedicated, internal attached storage on the left and point-to-point dedicated external and internal storage. In the center a shared external storage topology is shown, and on the right we see a shared external storage configuration attached via a shared switch topology.

9.2.2 Simple storage networks ("SAN in a Can")

A simple storage network, perhaps thought of by some as not even being a storage network, is an integrated solution sometimes called a "SAN in a Can." The term "SAN in a Can" comes from the concept that all of the components are preintegrated, preconfigured, and ready for use in a single

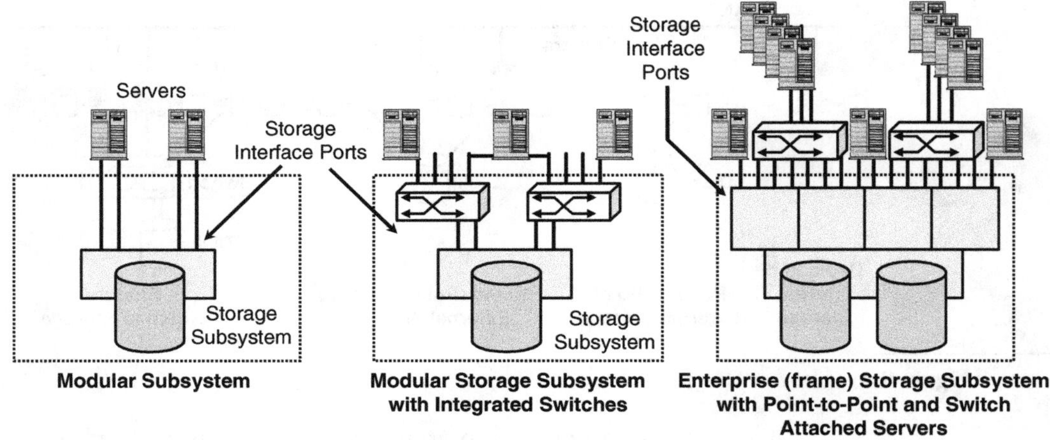

Figure 9.3 *Some "SAN in a Can" examples.*

box or cabinet. In Figure 9.3, some examples of integrated "SAN in a Can" solutions include marketing bundles to simplify selling and ordering of diverse components. These components are pretested and qualified (perhaps certified) to work as a solution. Also shown is an integrated storage subsystem with adapter ports integrated into the controller and integrated Fibre Channel and Ethernet switches (Fibre Channel or Ethernet) in the same cabinet. A SAN in a CAN can be a NAS device, block, or object (CAS) device.

Integrated SAN solutions, including those depicted in Figure 9.3, can vary from small departmental to large enterprise class systems. Enterprise class storage subsystems can have many interface ports (SCSI, SATA/ATA, Fibre Channel for FCP and FICON, ESCON, and Gb E for iSCSI or NAS) that can be attached directly to servers for point-to-point connections or via a switched network (Fibre Channel or Ethernet). Midsize, modular storage supporting two or more host servers sharing storage in a point-to-point topology or via a switched network is an example. A common packaging technique has been to utilize a modular storage device with integrated Fibre Channel interfaces, and more recently Ethernet switches for iSCSI and NAS storage devices, in the same cabinet as a "SAN in the Can" solution. SMB solutions may also have SATA/ATA, USB, or Firewire ports. This simplifies installation and implementation in that the storage network switches are configured and cabled to the storage in a common cabinet at the factory. Depending on the implementation, scalability could be a challenge, depending on what the vendor supports for expanded networking and interoperability with others.

Small rack-mountable modular storage arrays can support two or more storage interface ports on a much smaller scale than midsize and frame-based storage subsystems. This would include entry-level storage arrays targeted for small Windows-based and Linux clusters as well as other environments that do not require a large amount of storage and that have few servers to attach to the storage. Some of these devices have removable interface ports to change from SCSI to Fibre Channel to Gb E for iSCSI as your needs evolve.

Some might assert that a point-to-point connection to a shared storage device is not a storage network, or is not a SAN. I'll leave that decision up to your own interpretation; however, keep in mind that multiple servers attaching to a storage device using a storage interface sure sounds like a network to access storage or a network for storage.

9.2.3 Loop and shared access topologies

Much has been written about loops, particularly Fibre Channel Loop (FC-AL and PLDA), device login, and communication protocols, in other books, so I'm going to spare the details in this book and focus rather on implementation as a topology. In Appendix A, some useful Web sites and URLs contain additional information about Fibre Channel Loop and other items. There are still many loop devices attached to hubs and switches that support loop, particularly for tape drives. Newer tape and storage devices, along with servers, support fabric attachment and provide more flexibility. While tape drives can attach to Fibre Channel–based storage networking without using loop support, it is still a good practice to isolate tape devices from other traffic. At a minimum, port zoning (zoning and security are covered in Chapter 13) should be used to isolate tape ports from storage ports. For added performance and device isolation, separate adapters on a server with a unique path to tape devices may be appropriate. One approach is to use separate adapters on servers for tape and disk traffic attached to the same switch. The tape and storage devices would then be zoned away from each other. Another approach, which entails more costs but more performance and isolation of devices, is to utilize separate switches and networks for disk and tape traffic. Note that as you scale the number of tape devices and server attachments, the number of zones may also increase depending on what your zoning strategy is. By using logical switch partitions, ports on a switch can be partitioned to create a virtual switch for disk and tape. These added costs include hardware, software, and management; however, the cost should be balanced with your need for having separate environments.

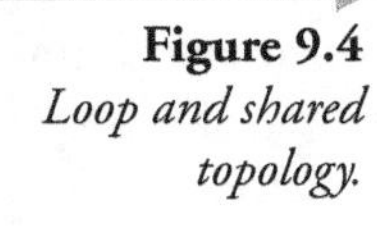

Figure 9.4
Loop and shared topology.

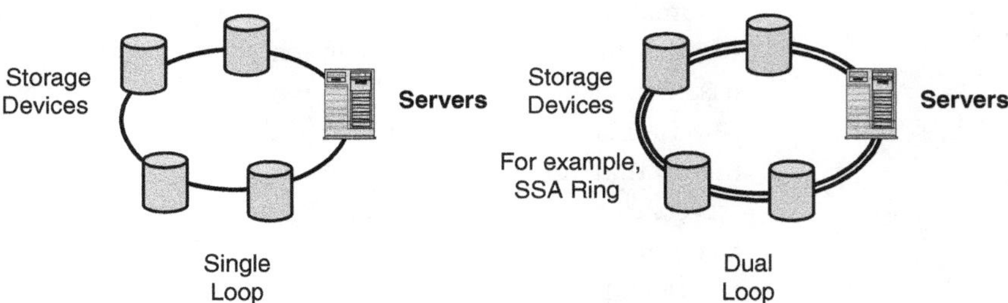

A loop can be implemented by physically connecting each device together in a daisy chain fashion (Figure 9.4), or by implementing a hub concentrator. With either a daisy chained loop or hub, all devices have shared access and shared bandwidth. Consequently, if a device needs to utilize the interface to communicate with another device, it must wait until it becomes available. Similarly, all devices that are attached to it share the bandwidth of the interface, which differs from a point-to-point and switched environment where all devices have equal access and bandwidth.

Loop along with hub implementations can have fairness algorithms to ensure that all devices get access to the interface. For example, Fibre Channel Arbitrated Loop (FC-AL) has an arbitration mechanism to enable devices to acquire the storage interface and give it up when others need it. Typically, loop configurations only support one device communicating with another at the same time—for example, with Fibre Channel, Ethernet, or FDDI. A variation on this is with the IBM SSA storage interface, which supports multiple devices communicating on different segments of the loop (called spatial reuse) to increase overall bandwidth. Some loop devices can be configured to isolate ports from each other and avoid loop disruptions caused when devices are added and removed. A loop can be implemented by connecting each of the devices with cabling as a single or redundant loop. A hub concentrator (Figure 9.5) device simplifies the wiring and cabling by integrating them onto a printed circuit board.

Figure 9.5
Hub and concentrator shared bandwidth topology.

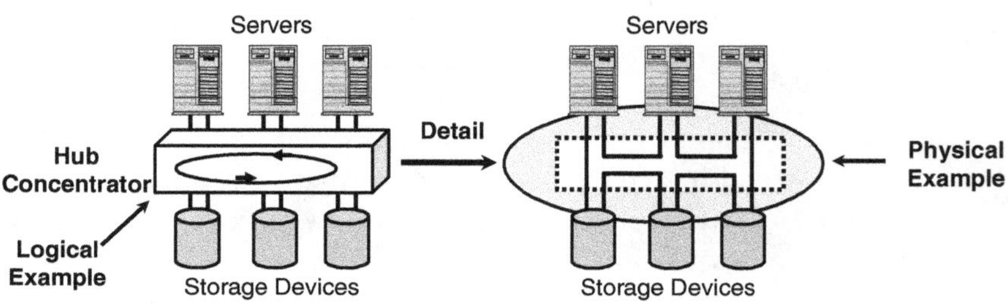

A hub concentrator device implements on a printed circuit card the connections (trace points) that go between each port for transmit and receive. A hub chip, or chip interface, to these trace points implements the associated signaling protocol. Hubs can also implement port bypass technology to isolate a port from the loop should it fail. Without port bypass capabilities, a failed port splits the loop and can render it inoperable.

There are still implementations of Ethernet hubs as a low-cost connectivity device for slower devices to create a network and to share faster switch ports. Fibre Channel initially was deployed with loop using both public (FC-AL) and Private Loop Device Addressing (PLDA) modes with hubs. More recently Fibre Channel, like Ethernet, implementations have utilized switches or point-to-point dedicated topologies for connectivity. There are still Fibre Channel loop implementations today, primarily for attachment of older loop devices, including tape drives, some storage devices, and first-generation server adapters. Fibre Channel loop is also used as the back-end interface on some storage subsystems that utilize Fibre Channel devices using hubs, hub chips, and physically integrated connections on printed circuit cards.

This could be an IBM SSA ring with dual paths implementing spatial reuse (all paths supporting concurrent data transfer) to increase overall bandwidth. This could be a Fibre Channel loop topology with a cable going from each device to another creating a ring or utilizing a shared hub. Hubs, also known as concentrators, have shared bandwidth and access between the devices being attached to them. Some examples of hub configurations include Fibre Channel arbitrated loop, USB hubs for attaching various peripherals to a server, Ethernet hubs, and FDDI concentrators.

9.3 Storage network and fabric network

Building on the simple storage networks already covered in this chapter involves building network fabrics (networks) with switches. Networks are built to support an increase in the number of available ports beyond what a single physical device can support, as well as to support distributed configurations. Networks may be distributed to support business continuance as well as for attachment of devices located in different physical locations. This could include devices in different parts of a computer room, different floors in a building, different buildings in a campus, or in a distributed environment. Networks may also be built to consolidate and interconnect SAN islands that have been deployed to share resources and hopefully enhance management. Consolidating multiple switches into a common storage network might help with physical management, but it can add to the logical management.

Fabrics in storage networking terms, and particularly for Fibre Channel, are called SANs. Consequently, the term *SAN* can mean an individual fabric of one or more switches networked together; however, it is also used interchangeably to mean a storage network of one or more networks. As a result, there can be confusion as to whether a SAN means individual fabrics or the collection of all fabrics. A way to put things into perspective is to think of a storage network as having one or more fabrics, with each fabric having one or more switches with some number of ports. A storage network can also be implemented using different interfaces and protocols in various combinations. A storage network can be implemented as a single, large flat network, similar to LANs, as well as segmented into different subnet fabrics (also called regions). A storage network can have one or more SAN islands, each with one or more devices that are not interconnected, or they could be interconnected via a backbone configuration. Management of the storage network can be aligned with the physical topology—for example, each region managed separately with different tools or all managed centrally but logically and physically isolated.

The decision to place everything into a single large (preferably at least two for redundancy) fabric or multiple fabrics includes:

- How you wish to manage the overall storage network
- Which devices and components are part of the configuration
- Vendor requirements, including certifications and support
- Application and workload requirements
- Security and fault isolation needs
- Your operating philosophies and policies
- Age of existing technology (hardware and software)

While it is tempting to merge storage and traditional networks into a single, unified physical network, as well as a logical entity coupled with common management, caution should be exercised. While there are cost savings associated with reduced hardware and software expenses by moving to a common network, there are also management costs and complexity associated with doing so. You may find yourself having to install secondary networks to support storage and traditional networks, and perhaps storage can be a justification to do so. Storage Area Management (SAM) can be an approach to utilize various management tools that present a logical unified view of separate and isolated storage networks. This can be thought of as virtualizing storage management and typically at a minimum includes visualization (the ability) to see different devices and components across networks from a single window.

So how big a storage network could you build? As probably expected, the answer is that it depends on the variables balanced between theoretical limits, vendor claims, and actual supported configurations. You can have many fabrics, either standalone or interconnected using backbone routing—for example, Autonomous Regions (AR) and device mapping. By using AR implemented as part of a switch or in a standalone routing device, sometimes referred to as border switches, multiple fabrics can be interconnected but logically isolated, similar to a VLAN in a LAN network, as seen in Figure 9.6.

Similar to a traditional network, a storage network, regardless of the interface, could be configured into a large flat network, as seen in Figure 9.7. While this may be tempting, as was the case with first-generation LANs, lessons learned have resulted in segmenting the network into logical subnetworks, as seen in Figure 9.8.

By using routing techniques and technology, including AR, the different physical storage networks and SAN islands can be interconnected but isolated and kept as separate local storage networks, as shown in Figure 9.9.

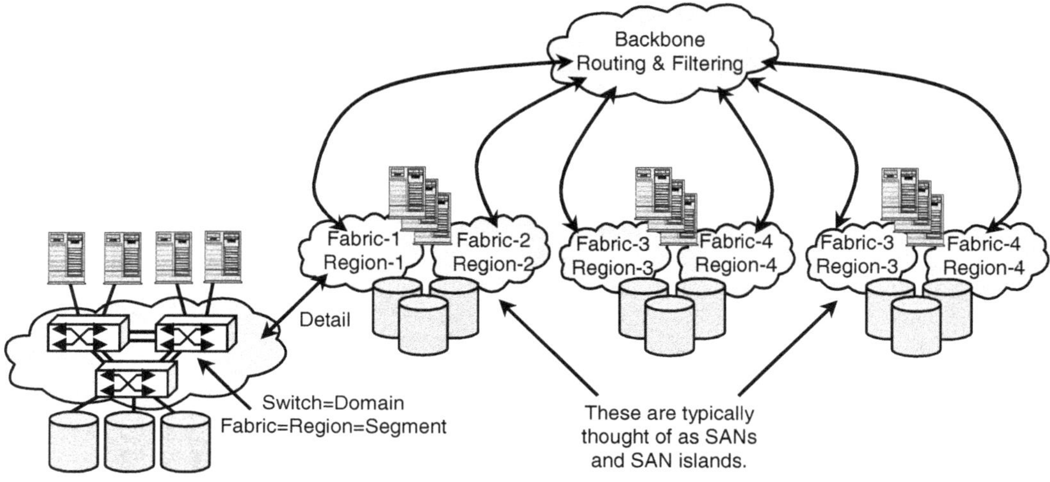

Figure 9.6 *Storage networking hierarchy.*

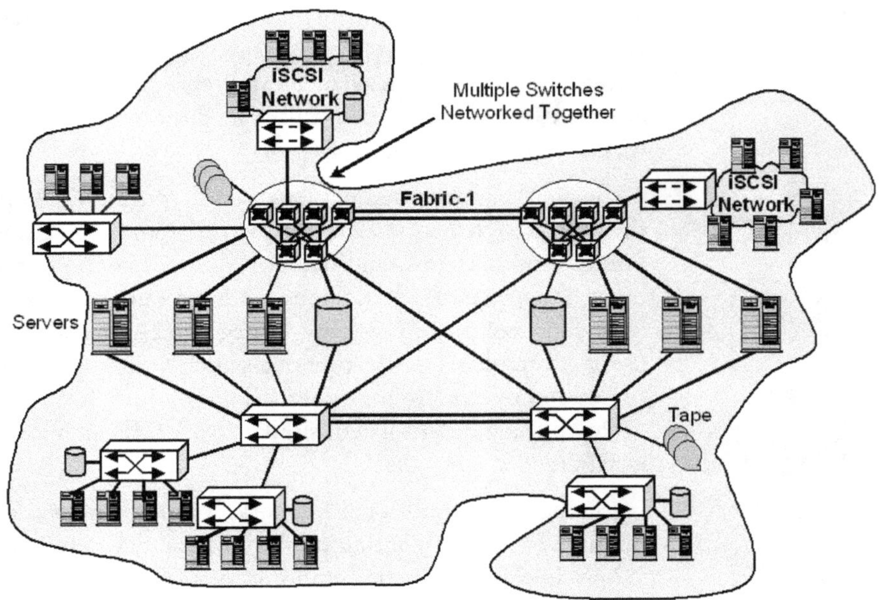

Figure 9.7 *Single fabric storage network.*

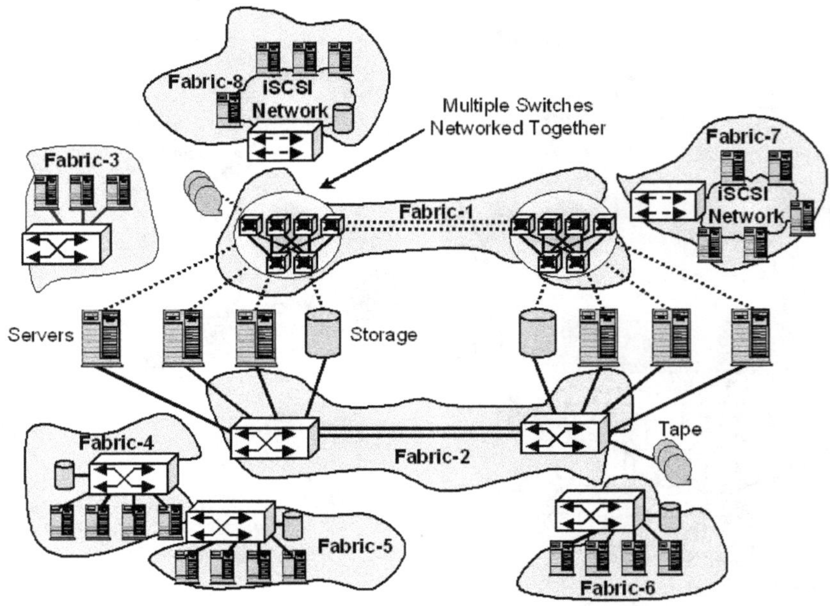

Figure 9.8 *Independent (isolated) fabric storage network.*

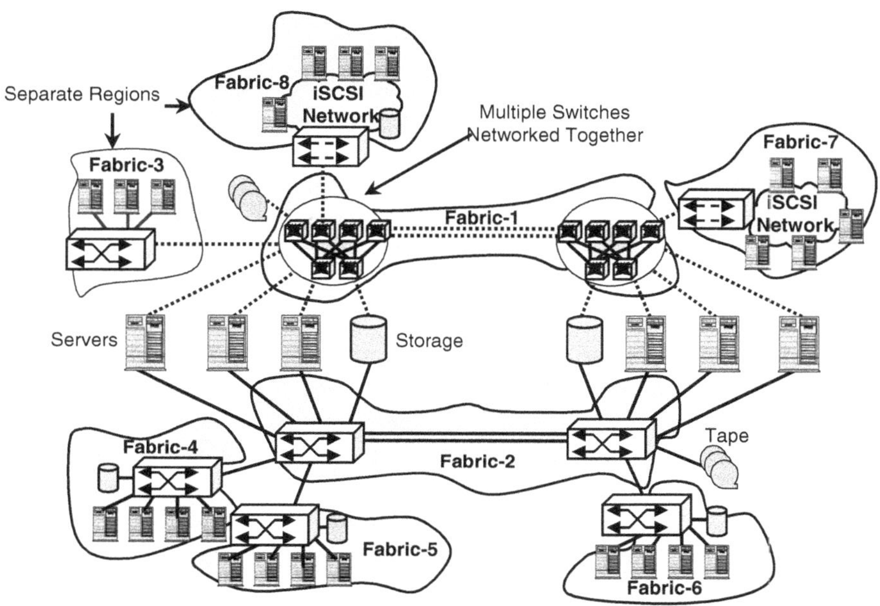

Figure 9.9 *Separate logical fabrics (regions).*

In the past, the term *edge* with regard to Fibre Channel storage networking (SANs) has been used to define a particular type of switching product. For example, an 8- or 16-port switch has been called an edge switch, since it could sit at the edge of a Fibre Channel core-edge SAN. With iSCSI storage networks, the term and concept of edge have been refocused from being small Fibre Channel switches to leveraging low-cost IP-based networks using Ethernet for attachment of servers.

The number of standalone SAN islands that each could have is 239 (theoretical limit of the current Fibre Channel standard) switches (domain), each with their own Domain ID (DID). Each switch could have from 4 to over 512 ports (1,000+ port switches are on the drawing board), enabling fabrics of thousands of devices. This might not seem that big from a traditional networking standpoint, but go back about 15 years when a 1,000-port LAN was perceived as being very large. To scale even larger, or to support distributed environments, multiple fabric segments can exist—either connected physically and logically isolated or as standalone islands. The caveat is that different vendor implementations will vary as to how many ports they support in a fabric and how many switches per fabric.

9.3.1 Interswitch links (ISLs) and cascades

Interswitch links (ISLs) are used to connect two or more switches to create a network. ISLs can span various distances to meet different needs. ISLs are used to connect Ethernet, Fibre Channel, and other networking and storage networking switches. ISLs can be used to increase the number of ports by connecting more switches together as well as to connect multiple locations spanning distances. ISLs can also be increased and configured to increase the available bandwidth to support traffic between the switches. Similar to first-generation networking, first-generation storage networking involved extensive use of ISLs to create fabrics and fabric switches made up of multiple smaller switches in order to scale. Storage networks have become larger in terms of available usable ports, with a large port count device (vertical scaling) and using ISLs (horizontal scaling). Figure 9.10 shows an example of horizontal scaling using ISLs to increase port capacity and support geographical and multisite needs.

A cascade consists of two or more switches or directors connected in a flat or daisy chain topology. A cascade provides a simple fabric at the expense of resilience; should ISLs fail, the fabric will become partitioned or isolated. This poses a data integrity risk and can cause end devices to be isolated. Cascade topologies are best kept to as few switches or directors as possible.

Cascade (Figure 9.11) can be configured locally as well as remotely using xWDM with dedicated dark fiber and over wide area distances using SAN over WAN technology, including Fibre Channel over IP (FCIP) gateways and bridges. Other solutions include Fibre Channel over SONET/SDH to leverage carrier bandwidth. Cascade configurations are well suited for high-availability and business continuity configurations that must span locations. For high availability and redundancy, a pair of cascades would be configured to have two separate fabrics isolated from each other.

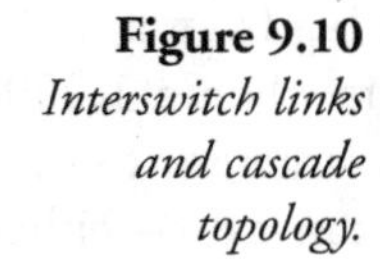

Figure 9.10 *Interswitch links and cascade topology.*

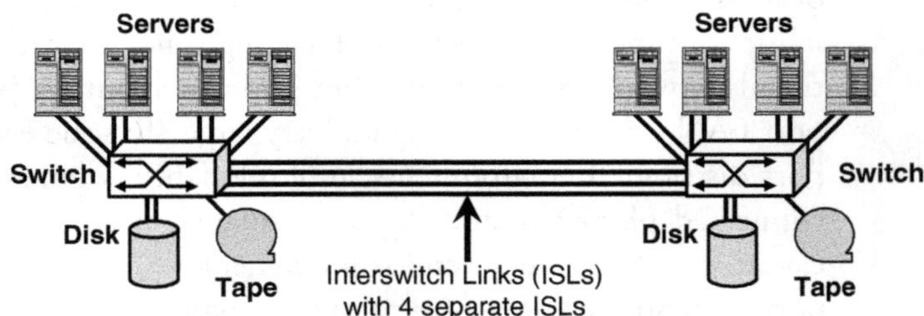

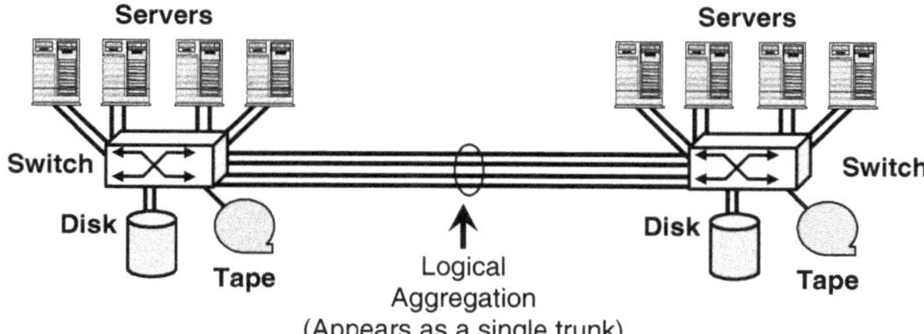

Figure 9.11 *Cascade with trunking.*

9.3.2 Virtual interswitch links

With the availability of various implementations of virtual switches, virtual fabrics, and virtual (logical) domains it makes sense to also introduce virtual interswitch links. In general, partitioning of a switch enables different logical switches to be created that could be used as standalone or networked with other switches into a fabric. A difference between other approaches to isolate traffic and ports, including zoning, separate fabrics, port prohibits, and blocks, is to be able to have a separate name server running in each partition. With a unique name server running in each fabric, you create a unique fabric for workload allocation and isolation. There are many vendor-specific implementations accomplishing the same or similar results, including VSANs, LSANs, virtual switches, and logical partitions to name a few. With large port count switches (directors) with the ability to carve up the ports into subsegments or subnets, it is now possible to more effectively manage traffic and workload. A virtual ISL eliminates the need to physically connect a cable between two external ports to interconnect the different partitions. By using a virtual ISL, the different partitions are connected via the hardware switching core, sometimes called the backplane. The benefit of this approach is that there is no loss of usable ports to create the ISL and no extra latency for exiting and then returning to the same physical switch.

9.3.3 Fan-in/fan-out

Fan-in is used to attach more host systems or servers to a storage device than there are available physical ports. This helps to build a resilient infrastructure in that multiple host systems can access and share storage for clustering and other applications. Fan-out is similar to fan-in and can be thought of as the opposite or inverse. By using fan-in and fan-out, device ports can be shared across more host or servers, which helps with disaster recovery and access.

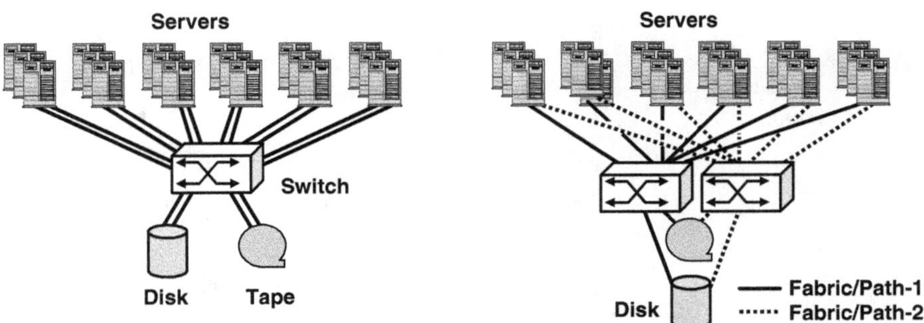

Figure 9.12 *Fan-in/fan-out example.*

In Figure 9.12, a simple single switch fan-in (many servers to a few devices) is shown, along with a redundant configuration with multiple switches creating dual access paths. Looking at Figure 9.12 from a server standpoint, this would be a fan-in topology; if viewed from a storage perspective, it would be a fan-out topology (few devices to many servers). Another variation, not shown, would be to have a few servers accessing many storage devices or many servers accessing many storage devices. For increased residency and scalability, additional switch pairs could be installed to create quadpaths and other configurations for any-to-any access to all devices. Note that the switches themselves are not interfaced, in order to create separate and isolated fabrics for high availability.

Two scaling variations are shown in Figure 9.13, including partitioning a large switch into two or more logical domains to create the separate switches. Another example, on the right, is leveraging two separate fabrics made up of multiple switches isolated together using topologies from this

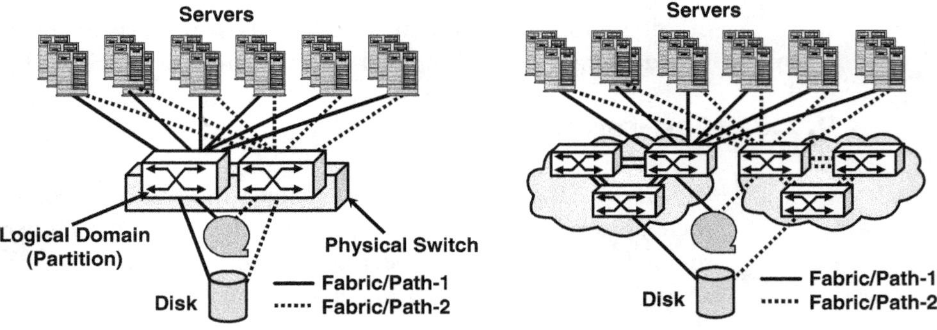

Figure 9.13 *Multipath scaling.*

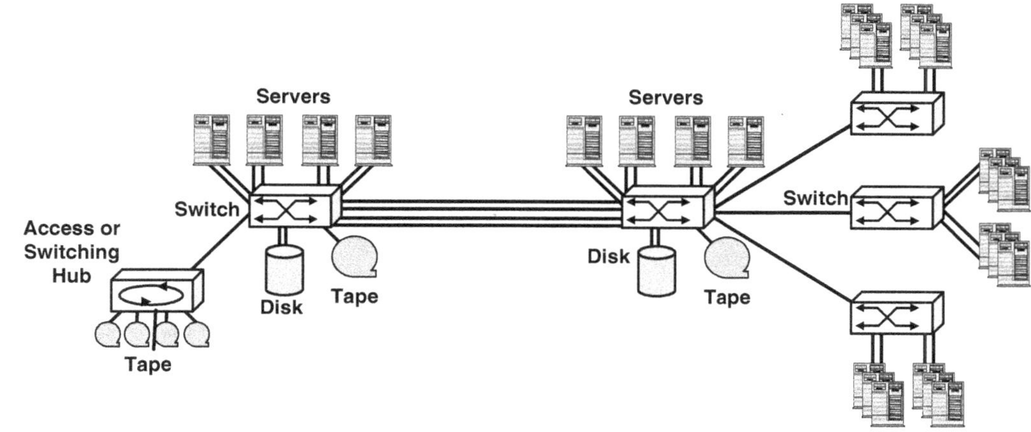

Figure 9.14 *Cascade with fan-in and shared hub.*

chapter. If your concern is simply to isolate traffic and leverage the high-availability features of the switch hardware for good availability, your risk is that the hardware itself may be the single point of failure. A better approach would be to have a pair of switches that could be partitioned to support different SAN islands but isolate the traffic (physical consolidation of switches) and still provide redundant access paths.

A combination of cascading switches and using fan-in/fan-out with switches and hubs is shown in Figure 9.14. This could be a Fibre Channel implementation with 10Gb ISLs between the switches in the middle (core) and 1, 2, or 4Gb ISLs extending from the core switches out to the edge switches and hubs. This could also be an Ethernet implementation with 10Gb Ethernet at the core, and slower 10/100 hub ports on the left and 10/1000 or 1Gb Ethernet switches on the right. This configuration could also be an intermix implementation (FCP and FICON) with FICON Cascade with edge switches on the right and a hub on the left for attachment for FCP-based storage devices.

To increase availability and resiliency, a pair of cascade networks is shown in Figure 9.15 to provide redundant paths between locations. This implementation could be in the same computer room, building, campus, or metropolitan or wide area environment. As the distance between the switches is increased, design considerations to accommodate for distance delay, bandwidth costs, and fault isolation items need to be considered. This type of topology is a good fit for clustering, failover, and related applications for high availability and survivability.

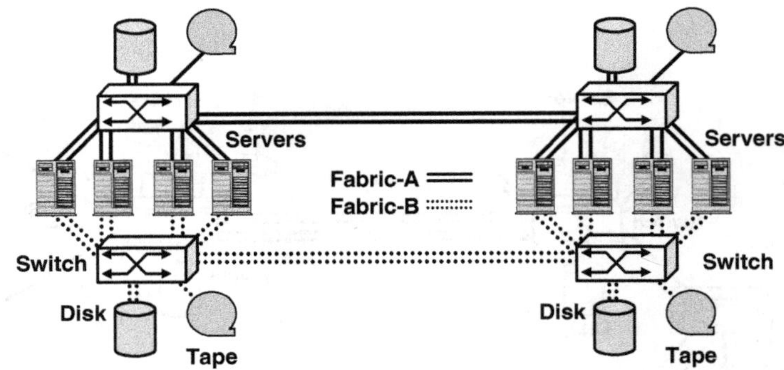

Figure 9.15 *Redundant cascade topology.*

The number of ISLs between the switches will be a function of how much bandwidth is needed for your applications, as well as how much reserve (standby) bandwidth you want to factor into your design. For example, if you determine that you need 7Gb/sec bandwidth between the two switches, then you would need at least that amount of ISL bandwidth. This could be accommodated with seven 1Gb ISLs, 4 × 2Gb ISLs, 2 × 4Gb ISLs, or a 10Gb ISL. Depending on the level of performance you need in a failure situation (loss of an ISL, loss of a switch, loss of a communication circuit), this will determine how to spread your ISLs across the two fabrics. For example, if you can run in a degraded mode, then you may simply balance the ISLs between the two fabric paths. On the other hand, if you need to plan for full performance, then you would need twice the amount of bandwidth equally spread between the two switches on both fabrics. For example, in Figure 9.15, a pair of 4Gb ISLs would be created on Fabric-A between the switches, and similarly for Fabric-B, to support 7Gb between the switches. For your specific environment you need to balance the cost with the desired level of performance and availability to meet your service requirements.

9.4 ISL performance topics

To increase the bandwidth and address performance bottlenecks between switches additional ISLs can be implemented. In addition to increasing the number of ISLs, faster ISLs, including 4Gb, 10Gb Fibre Channel, and 10Gb Ethernet, can be implemented to improve bandwidth and performance. In some circumstances simply adding more interfaces is not sufficient if they cannot be effectively utilized. An example of this would be if the routing algorithms do not load balance evenly across the interfaces. Fibre Channel utilizes the FSPF routing algorithm to handle routing, performing load balancing when connections are initiated between servers and storage devices. This results in traffic flowing across the same interface until that interface becomes unavailable or the connection is terminated. This can result in some ISLs becoming overutilized while others may be underutilized. Some techniques that can be implemented to increase bandwidth and improve performance include:

- Hardware- and software-based trunking and multiplexing
- Aggregation (trunking) of multiple ISL interfaces into a logical ISL
- Multiplexing of physical interfaces using CWDM, WDM, or DWDM technology
- ISL grouping, load balancing, and enhanced routing to enhance quality of service

The number of ISLs supported on a switch varies depending on vendor implementation, as does the number of zones supported. While it might seem obvious, keep in mind that the larger the number of ISLs in your configuration, the larger the number of switch ports being used for networking. This results in a loss of usable ports and adds to the cost of deploying the storage network. For performance-intensive environments and applications, when using an ISL to interconnect switches, make sure that you have enough ISLs to support the workload to avoid oversubscription and blocking in the network.

9.4.1 Star and ring topologies

An improvement on a simple cascade is a ring, shown in Figure 9.16, where three or more switching devices are connected with ISLs. If the ring is broken, the topology turns into a cascade or, possibly, multiple cascades. An issue with both ring and cascade topologies is locality and impact on performance. To reduce the impact on performance by a server having to access storage devices via multiple switches (hops), careful placement of devices is important. As the ring becomes larger, management becomes more complex in terms of security and where to physically locate or place servers and storage devices for optimum performance and reduced latency. Advanced topologies have enabled large, resilient, and high-performance fabric storage networks to be built.

Another example of a ring topology is shown in Figure 9.17, where three sites are connected over various distances using two separate fabrics, each configured as a ring. This redundant configuration enables storage to be

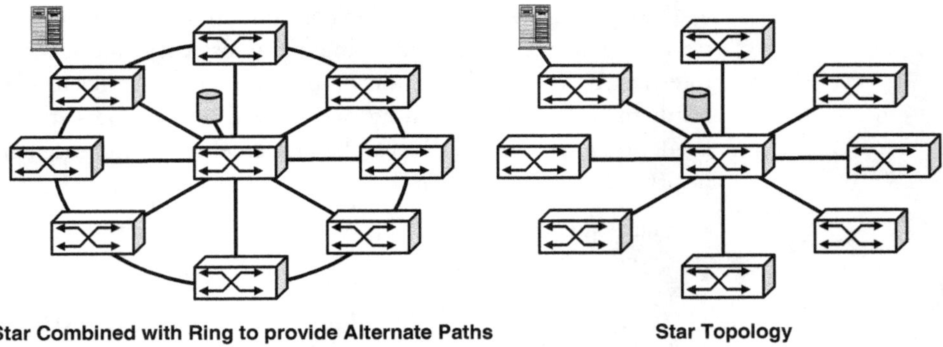

Figure 9.16 *Various star topologies.*

mirrored (replicated) between locations as well as backed up to one of the sites designated as a primary recovery location. In Figure 9.17 there are two fabrics (Fabric-A and Fabric-B) shown with redundant ISLs to enable traffic to flow between locations as needed. Local servers at Site-A have redundant paths to storage at Site-A using either Fabric-A or Fabric-B. Servers at Site-A can also access storage at Site-b and Site-c using either path (Fabric-a or Fabric-B). Storage at Site-A can also communicate at Site-B and Site-C for performing remote mirroring for business continuance. Tape drives can be attached at the different sites for direct server-to-tape backups (LAN-Free backup) to offload LANs from backup traffic.

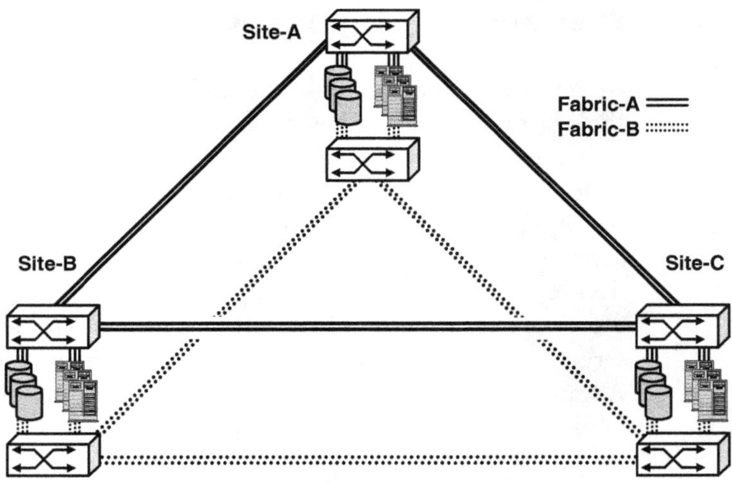

Figure 9.17 *Multisite redundant topology.*

Best Practices: A best practice for a mesh environment is to split large complex meshes into two or more smaller meshes (fabrics) and replace large complex fabrics with directors and core-edge topologies

9.4.2 Mesh topology

To improve performance and resilience, partial mesh (Figure 9.18) ensures that each switch has an alternate path to the other switches. While a partial mesh does not provide a direct path between all switches, it offers improved resilience over cascade and ring topologies—with lower costs. More complex, yet providing better performance and resilience than a partial mesh, a full mesh (Figure 9.18) has an ISL between all switches in the fabric. A full mesh becomes very complex to manage as more switches are added—impacting locality and troubleshooting.

9.4.3 Core-edge, multistage, and tiered topologies

Core-edge provides more scalability than the previous topologies and can be built using switches as both the core and edge devices for about 100 ports, switches as edge devices and directors with an integrated fabric of switches as the core, or a mix of switches and directors as edge devices and directors as the core—supporting thousands of ports and devices. A core-

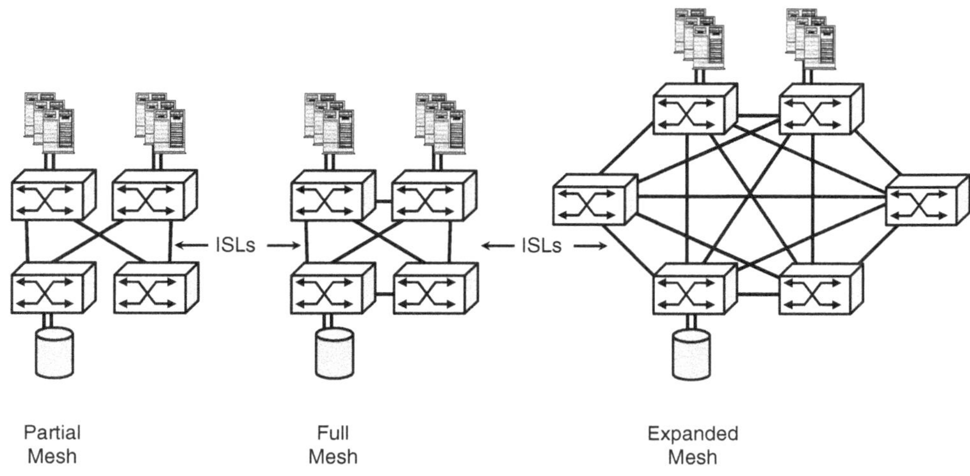

Figure 9.18 *Mesh topologies.*

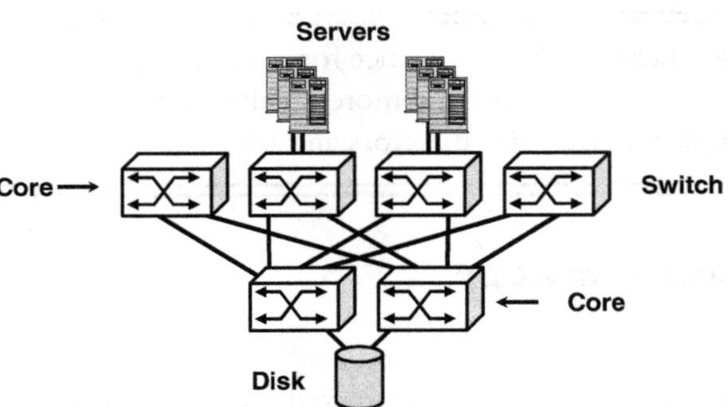

Figure 9.19 *Simple core-edge (tiered) topology.*

edge (Figure 9.19) resembles how many LANs are built today, with large frame-based switches at the core and smaller edge devices in a star type of configuration. Tiered and expanded core-edge can support even larger numbers of ports or devices. With a tiered approach, servers may attach to the top edge devices, while storage devices attach to the bottom edge. For improved performance and locality, larger fabric devices, such as a director, can be placed at the edge or top to keep traffic local between servers and storage.

For better resiliency, two separate fabrics should be configured. These separate fabrics could be any combination of the previously discussed topologies. A simple redundant storage network has each server with dual HBAs that are attached to different switches. This topology provides a dual or redundant path to isolate against HBA, cable, or switch failure to help provide fault containment. The on-line storage has attachments to both paths for redundancy and performance, while the tape devices are single attached. Note that there can be two separate fabrics isolated from each other (no ISLs between them) for redundancy.

A skinny tree architecture (Figure 9.20) has fewer ISLs between the edge and core switches, while a fat tree has more ISLs to scale the bandwidth through the network. This topology can be scaled in size by replacing the switches with larger port count directors or building a fabric using one of the topologies previously discussed. While the storage device is attached to both of the switches, the switches are not connected with ISLs, so that two separate domains (fabrics) are created. If ISLs were placed between two fabric devices (switches and directors), there would be a cascade.

In Figure 9.21, a single fabric is shown with redundant paths and edge switches supporting multiple servers in a fan-in/fan-out topology. Depending on the sizes of the switches being used at the core and edge, hundreds to

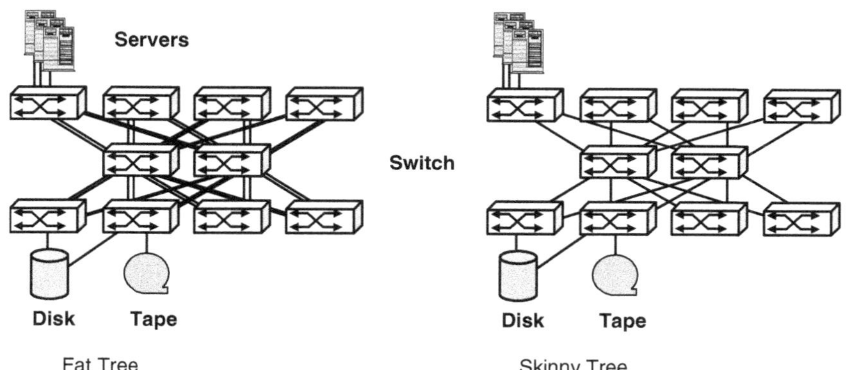

Figure 9.20 *Core-edge topologies.*

thousands of ports could be configured. This type of topology could be used to support distributed environments, where servers are located in different locations, and storage consolidation.

In Figure 9.22, a variation of the previous example is shown utilizing larger switches at the core to reduce the number of ISLs, switches, and overall complexity while scaling capacity and performance.

Figure 9.23 shows a core-edge tiered with redundant fabrics for scaling purposes to support high availability and simplified management.

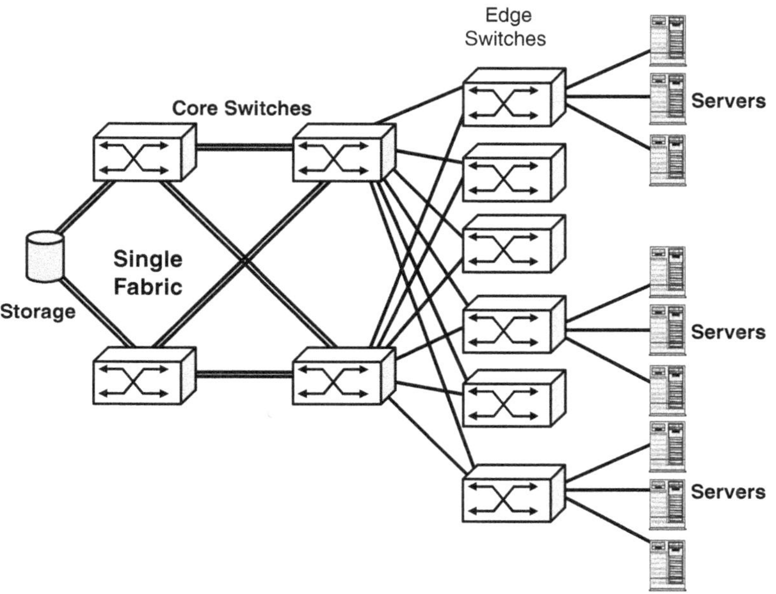

Figure 9.21 *Single fabric mesh with fan-in/fan-out.*

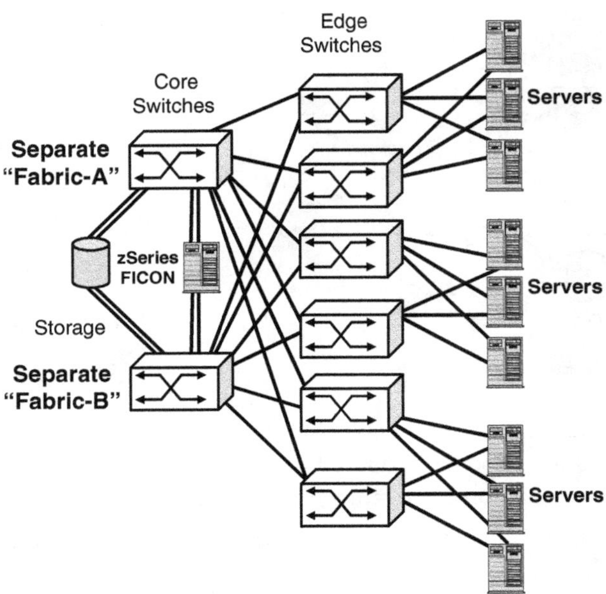

Figure 9.22 *Alternative approach for scaling fabric.*

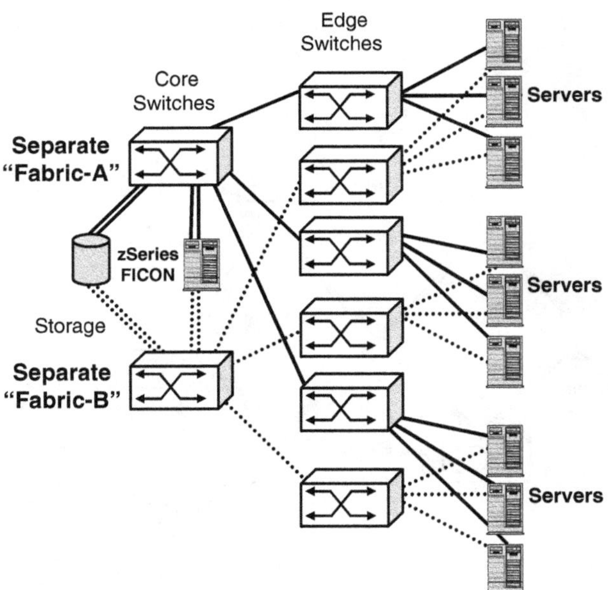

Figure 9.23 *Alternative approach for dual fabric for redundancy.*

Best Practices: For high availability, a best practice is to have dual or multiple paths between the host server and storage devices. This entails having redundant HBAs, resilient fabrics, and dual attachment of storage devices. Dual Ethernets enable clients to access the servers and communicate between servers. Path management software, including dynamic multipathing software on servers, enables HBA load balancing and failover to alternate paths. Advanced path management software can also provide a level of virtualization by providing volume management capabilities.

One of the benefits of SANs is to remove the physical interface dependency between a server and a dedicated drive. This helps with disaster recovery and high availability by being able to disassociate the storage with a server and place the two in different locations. Faster network interfaces are also enabling greater distances between servers and storage devices. Redundancy ISLs should be used to ensure that the fan-in and fan-out are not impacted due to loss of an ISL between switches or to devices. A variation of the fan-in and fan-out approach is to connect switching hubs to provide loop support for public and private loop hosts and devices. This could also be done by placing a switch into hub mode and then connecting it to the core via a loop port or an E_Port.

In the previous scenarios, multiple ISLs could be connected between the fabric devices to increase performance and reduce congestion or oversubscription. A best practice is to reduce the complexity by using a pair of larger port count devices at the core to reduce the number of ISLs, improve locality and security, and simplify management and troubleshooting. ISLs are not bad; however, there can be bad or poor uses of ISLs to implement storage networks.

Best Practices: A best practice for device fan-in is to connect devices that do not need full bandwidth to an edge switch, hub, or 1Gb blade on a director. Some examples include tape devices, smaller and slower servers, older storage devices, and some gateways.

9.5 Chapter summary

By using the various topologies shown in this chapter in different combinations you can derive countless derivations to meet different needs and scale. Today, storage networks can be scaled into thousands of ports, whereas only a few years ago 100 ports was considered to be large.

Table 9.1 gives a summary of several networking topologies.

The storage network topology that is right for you is the one that works for you, one that enables scalability and stability, and one that enables your business to meet its needs. Topologies do not need to be complex; however, they do need to be extensible to meet your complex and diverse requirements. Allow room for upgrades, expansion, maintenance, and management in whatever topology is implemented. From a physical networking and hardware standpoint, today it is relatively easy to build storage networks consisting of thousands of ports using large port count devices. Management of the number of ports will be impacted on the design and implementation.

Table 9.1 *Summary of Some Storage Networking Topologies*

Example	Where to Use	Comments
Ring	Connecting multiple locations together, scaling the number of ports in a fabric using switches of various sizes.	As with any topology, high availability is achieved with redundant fabrics. The number of ISLs is determined by the given workload and service requirements.
Cascade	Heartbeat, clusters, geographically dispersed, simple scaling configuration, storage-to-storage support, DWDM, FCIP, others.	This is a common configuration for local as well as distributed environments to scale the number of available ports as well as for availability.
Full Mesh	Can be used for SAN island consolidation, scaling redundant links between sites and devices.	This can be used for interconnecting multiple locations as well as multiple switches in close proximity.
Tiered (Core-Edge)	Can be used for scaling the number of ports available, SAN island consolidation, interconnecting multiple sites and locations together.	This can be used for tying multiple smaller switches together, interfacing multiple sites together, or for scaling large storage networks together.

What This Chapter Will Do For You

This chapter looks at performance and capacity topics pertaining to storage networking. Adequate performance and capacity are essential to a resilient storage network, regardless of the size of the business it is supporting. Some of the items you will learn about in this chapter include:

- How lack of performance and capacity can negatively impact business revenues
- Understand the relationship between availability, performance, and capacity
- How to manage storage and storage networking resources and performance
- Cost impact of simply adding more hardware and the hidden management cost
- How to more effectively acquire technology by knowing what you need and when to add more

10

Performance and Capacity Planning for Storage Networks

10.1 Overview

What do you mean we need more, what happened to what I just bought? Have you encountered the feeling regarding storage that you need more, yet you just bought more and wonder where it went? This chapter looks at performance and capacity planning for storage networks, building on the material covered in previous chapters. This chapter leverages design items covered in Chapter 8 (storage networking design)—in particular, assessment of resources. Performance and capacity planning are associated with storage networking design and storage resource management. Performance and capacity planning are important for resilient storage networks to ensure adequate performance under different workloads and available resources when needed.

10.2 Performance and availability for storage networks

For those who are familiar with performance engineering, tuning, Storage Resource Management (SRM), capacity planning, hardware planning, and configuration, much of this will be review in terms of processes and principles. For the reader who is new to capacity planning and performance tuning, this will provide an overview of processes and principles and focus on specific storage and storage networking topics.

On the surface there may not appear to be a synergy between availability and performance and capacity planning. However, there is a direct correlation in that if a resource is not available, performance is impacted. Similarly, if a resource has poor performance, then availability and accessibility are impacted. If resource exhaustion (running out of something) occurs, then there can be both availability and performance impact—thus, there is a correlation among these. Put another way, what do capacity planning and performance have to do with availability and resilient storage networks? If a system or component is not available when needed, or if performance is impacted due to a component failure, performance is impacted.

Some performance and capacity planning impacts on performance include:

- Someone goes to a different Web site to make a purchase if yours is too slow.
- Users call and complain that the system is not available when it really is available.
- Backups are not completing in time, causing delays to other scheduled processing.
- Batch workloads cannot complete within their time-frame window.
- Someone invokes a failover or component replacement under a false alarm, thinking that the device failed.
- Applications are not able to work, since the server is too busy or experiencing I/O delays.

Capacity and performance planning should accommodate expectations for service during degraded performance—whether planned, scheduled, or unexpected—as well as peak processing periods. For example, if your business generates most of its revenue during a particular time of the year, you want your systems available and with the proper resources during that time. Performance and capacity planning activities have occurred in the enterprise environments for S/390 mainframes and open systems platforms for many years. These activities have for the most part focused on large (expensive) components, including processors, memory, network interconnects, and storage subsystems (disk and tape). As with other computer resources (CPU, memory, and storage), storage networks have grown to the point where they need to be managed, measured, tuned, and leveraged. This falls in line with shifting from reactionary to tactical to strategic management and operation of a storage network. Why the concern and emphasis on performance and capacity planning—after all, hardware is cheap, why not just buy some more? While hardware in relative terms has become more powerful and economical, the associated costs, including management tools, application software, and people to manage and support it, have not decreased in cost.

10.3 Performance and capacity planning overview

Performance and capacity planning can be combined as complementary activities, along with Storage Resource Management (SRM) and utilization, as well as handled as separate tasks. Performance tuning and optimization can initially be seen as a reactionary task to respond to specific situations. A performance plan and ongoing performance tuning initiative can support a shift from reactionary to tactical and longer-term strategic management approaches. For example, shifting to a performance plan approach, where performance and usage are analyzed and optimized as part of an overall growth plan, can help maximize and optimize spending. Capacity planning can be a one-time exercise to determine how much and what types of resources are needed to support a given application. A non-tactical approach to resource needs assessment and sizing would be to simply acquire some amount of resources (hardware, software, networks, and people) and buy more later as needed. A strategic approach would evolve from the tactical to help make more informed decisions and timed acquisitions. For example, by knowing your resource needs (forecast) ahead of time, you might be able to take advantage of special vendor incentives to acquire equipment that suits your needs on your terms. Similarly, if the terms are not favorable and resource usage is following the plan, you may choose to wait and delay your purchase. The following are some common questions and statements with regard to performance and capacity planning.

1. *Hardware is cheap, people are not, why tie someone up doing tuning?*

   While hardware is becoming less expensive, management (people and software) is not.

2. *Your staff is already busy, if not overworked, why give them more to do?*

   With planning, you can utilize your resources (people, hardware, software, networks, and budget) more effectively.

3. *Why not buy more and have the vendor manage it for you?*

   This may be an alternative if you can afford it from a dollar and business perspective. However, keep in mind that if you simply add more resources, you still have the expense of managing them.

4. *Your environment is not growing, so why be concerned with planning?*

   If your environment is stable, now is a good time to institute a plan for the future.

5. *Your environment is dynamic, so why do tuning and capacity planning?*

   During the dot-com bubble this was a practice that led to purchases of excess capacities, and the vendors absolutely loved it! Some sites overbought at what turned out to be higher prices than now and had excess capacity that was consuming power and cooling and that resulted in extra management.

A storage networking performance and capacity planning initiative can help to plan for as well as answer the following, and other, questions. These items can be incorporated into a questionnaire or a worksheet as part of an assessment and planning process.

- How many Gbyte/Tbyte/Pbyte of storage do you have?
- How much of your storage is allocated and actually in use?
- How many storage devices (disk and tape) do you have and where are they located?
- How many switch ports on how many switches do you have and where are they located?
- How many switch ports are being utilized for trunking and ISLs?
- What are your bandwidth requirements between switches and locations?
- Are you currently experiencing application I/O–related slowdown impacts?
- Do you know where your performance bottlenecks, or possible bottlenecks, are?
- What is the cache utilization and effectiveness on storage systems?
- How many transactions and how much workload are being supported?
- How do transactions and workload translate into I/Os, frames, and packets?
- Why do backups and recovery take as long as they do?

Figure 10.1 shows resource usage and capacity trends over a period of time. While this chart shows activity in months, it could also be shown in quarters or years. The resource usage could be CPU, memory, disk, or network bandwidth to support applications and business functions. Also shown in the chart is a line depicting available capacity (top line) with a line mirroring it (below) for a capacity threshold. This threshold line indicates

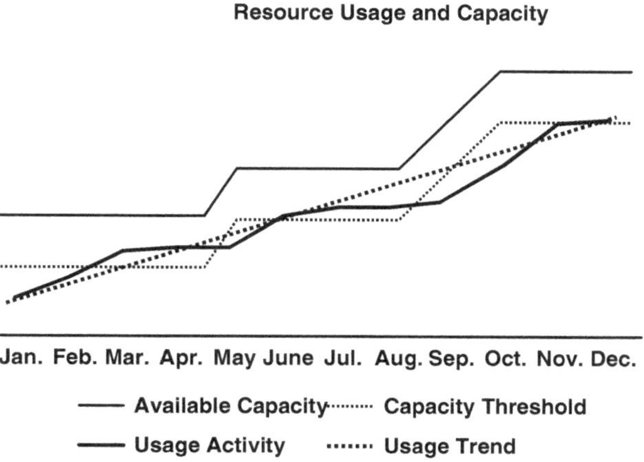

Figure 10.1 *Resource usage and capacity trend for some period of time.*

the logical capacity limit—for example, 80 percent of disk being full, 90 percent CPU utilization, and 75 percent network busy or some other value. This is a logical line in that utilization can exceed this value without resource exhaustion; however, above this threshold performance could suffer. An example would be exceeding the threshold and having response time increase as well as I/O contention and queuing, resulting in application delays. These delays, if severe, might manifest themselves as application unavailability, resulting in user phone calls asking if the system is still available or an on-line Web shopper going to another Web site to buy something. Also shown in the chart is a resource usage line as well as a trend line, which could be interpreted as a forecast or indicator of future usage.

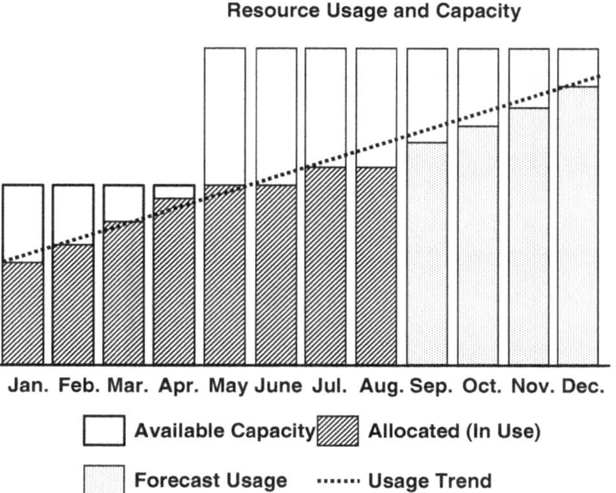

Figure 10.2 *Resource usage and capacity trend.*

Similar to Figure 10.1, in Figure 10.2 available resource capacity is shown along with allocated or consumed (in use) and forecasted usage together with a trend line. This could be, for example, showing disk capacity, I/O bandwidth, the number of switch ports available, or other resources. This shows over a period of time how resources are being utilized as well as the planned utilization of resources. This chart also shows when an upgrade is needed or planned.

10.4 Assessment—determining how what you have is being used

The assessment process identifies what you have available for resources, how they are being utilized, and what your requirements are. This is an important step, since it lets you know what you have to work with from a performance and capacity planning standpoint. Performance and capacity planning leverages information gathered from the assessment process as a basis of how resources are being utilized. The level of sophistication for your storage network will have a bearing on how much detail your performance and capacity planning activities will involve. For example, your needs may simply be to know that you will require 1Tbyte of storage with at least four Fibre Channel ports capable of being expanded. Additionally, your environment may require more detailed assessment and analysis, including tying business transactions to IT resource consumption to ensure that adequate resources are available to support the business. For example, you may know or be able to determine that a bank customer accessing an ATM cash machine transaction results in some number of database accesses, resulting in some number of disk operations. You may have identified that a particular Web activity results in some number of servers being accessed, resulting in some number of Mbytes of data, some number of transactions, and other data movement occurring. Another example is how many e-mail messages are sent each day and the average, maximum, and median size of the messages and attachments and the corresponding impact on the storage network. To protect data and ensure availability, you may need to understand how often data changes each day and thus is backed up locally and remotely, as well as how much data is mirrored between locations and how long it takes.

Some assessment questions include:

- Do you have detailed configurations and topology information?
- Do you have an inventory or list of which equipment and software you have?

- Do you have profiles or information about your workloads and what is normal?
- Do you have information about business and application growth factors?
- Do you have any reporting and trending capabilities (pen and paper, Excel, Web, SAS, XML, etc.)?

10.5 Analyze, model, and forecast—determining your plan

Once you have done an assessment as to which resources you have and how they are being used, you can analyze, interpret, model, and put together a forecast plan. Some tasks that are done during the analysis and data interpretation phase include:

- Identifying trends and patterns based on history, present activity, and projections
- Understanding business, applications, and hardware and software activity
- Creating supporting reports and charts showing trends and activities
- Tracking resource consumption (ports, memory, processor, storage)
- Tracking resource activity (frames/packets/loss, queuing, delay, bandwidth)
- Forecasting using tools or pencil, paper, and calculator

By using the assessment and analysis results, you can identify various options and alternatives to support business needs, including:

- What is needed for upgrades and expansion to add more resources
- Tuning and conservation to extend useful life of resources
- Identifying costs for upgrades and acquisitions for budget and funding
- Combination of above items

10.6 Storage networking performance and capacity concerns

Part of the assessment and data analysis process involves understanding the cause, effect, and how various components behave by themselves as well as with others. These components include the server, I/O channel (interface), and storage subsystems (disk and tape). These components are measured, assessed, and planned for in terms of resources that are consumed to support business applications. For example, server resources include amount of available CPU processing power and its utilization, amount of memory available, and its utilization and effectiveness. Some I/O interface resources include the amount of bandwidth available and its utilization and latency. Some resource examples for storage devices include the amount of capacity available for storing information and bandwidth for storing and accessing the data.

In Figure 10.3, a generic storage and I/O access model is shown with a server attached to a LAN network that is accessed by other systems, applications, and users. The server accesses the storage devices (disk and tape) via the storage and I/O interconnect (interface) using redundant paths (Path-A and Path-B).

Understanding what resources are needed is also important, particularly for SMB and small office home office (SOHO) environments. I often hear people tell me they are out of memory when, in most cases, they have enough memory, its disk space they are out of. Assuming they have the expansion capability, they are very pleased when they learn they do not need to buy that new computer just yet. Storage is often discussed in how many Gbytes or Tbytes of storage a subsystem has or perhaps how many connections (servers) that can attach to the storage. This type of discussion lends itself to comparisons of dollar per Mbyte or dollar per Gbyte. A more effective and reflective way to look at storage is in terms of bandwidth and performance available to access some amount of usable and protected storage. Consequently, resource consumption and usage is looked at in terms of capacity (how much resource you have) and activity (how the resource is being used and consumed).

Latency and delay compared with throughput, bandwidth, and megabytes per second refer to activity from two different viewpoints. Throughput is more exciting as an indicator of speed and movement, similar to I/Os per second and frames per second. Throughput is concerned with how data

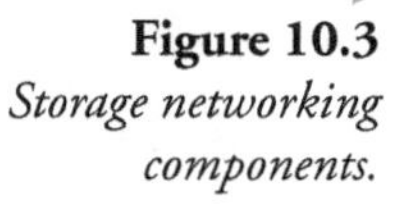

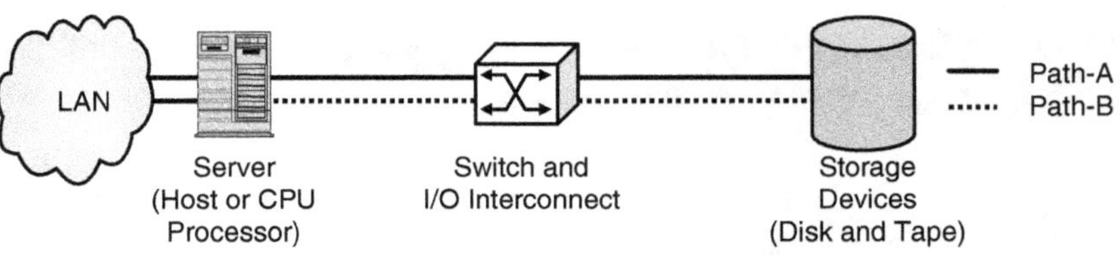

Figure 10.3 *Storage networking components.*

is being moved (transferred), while I/O rate is concerned with how data is being required (operations) of various sizes. There is a correlation in that as I/O operations increase with larger I/O size, so too should the amount of data being transferred. However, as the I/O size decreases while the I/O rate increases, the amount of data transfer will also decrease. The opposite of this is that as the I/O size increases along with activity, the amount transferred will go up, while the I/O rate will decrease. Thus, when you hear that a resource is discussed as being able to support some number of Mbytes per second transfer rate and some other number of I/O operations per second, people are talking about apples and oranges. This can lead to some surprises, including questions as to why there is such a low bandwidth or transfer rate while the I/O rate is high during OLTP and Web processing, or why the I/O rate is so low during backup.

In addition to activity in terms of I/O transfer rates and bandwidth, latency is another performance indicator. Latency is related to both transfer rates as well as I/O rates; however, rather than being concerned with how much data is being moved, or how many data requests there are, latency is concerned with how quickly the I/O operation is being handled. Latency can also be referred to as response time and transaction delay time. Typically, latency will increase with respect to the activity level, meaning that as things get busy, things slow down as the workload increases. There can be some anomalies to this—for example, with caching storage subsystems, where, as activity increases for certain applications, response time might improve due to high locality of reference of data and I/Os being resolved from cache. In other words, the application is doing many I/Os from cache and thus is able to increase the I/O activity without degrading response time; however, this is an isolated case and not the norm.

Storage access by applications is generally more latency sensitive than typical network access and latency. The reason for this is that storage subsystems today are typically measured with latency of a few milliseconds compared with typical network applications, which could be measured in dozens of milliseconds. While several dozen milliseconds may be tolerable for network access, for storage interfaces this would result in significant delays and bottlenecks. As networks get faster, it might be suggested that performance is not a worry anymore—after all, look at the number of MB/sec that is being pushed over the pipe, lack of droop, and other impressive things. However, the best bandwidth is not good if your latency is increasing beyond what is tolerable, particularly for synchronous applications. As distance increases, the time required for remote acknowledgments to be received increases beyond what is tolerable for

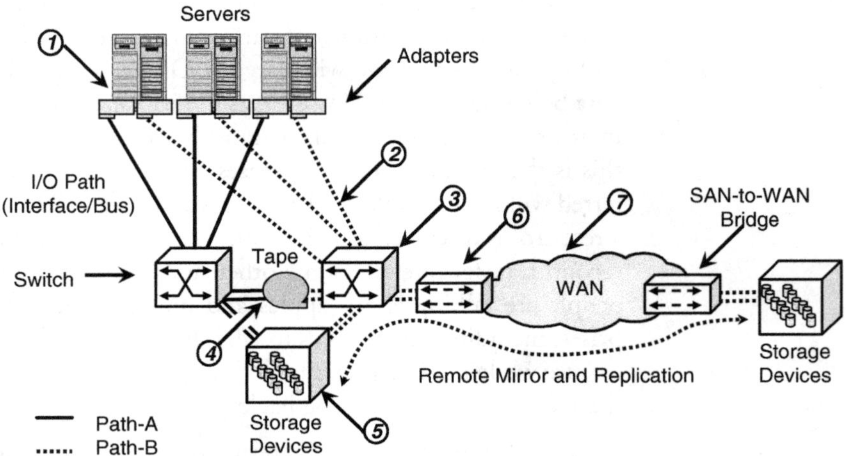

Figure 10.4 *Storage networking performance and capacity planning points of interests.*

acceptable performance. For longer distances, asynchronous mirroring and replication are better suited. The tradeoff is that synchronous provides data integrity while asynchronous supports reasonable performance over distance. For optimum performance and data protection, a combination of host server or storage-based mirroring between two locations and asynchronous to a third could be used.

Figure 10.4 shows various storage networking points of interest from a performance and capacity planning perspective, including (1) servers, (2) I/O path and storage interface, (3) switching and connectivity devices, (4) tape devices including VTS, (5) disk storage subsystems, (6) bridges, gateways, routers, and appliances, and (7) LAN, MAN, WAN interfaces. Each of these components is covered in more depth in the following sections of this chapter.

10.6.1 Server and CPU (processor) topics

Workload and activity arrives at a server via many mechanisms, including from other servers, terminals, workstations, Web, and PDAs. The rate at which the workload arrives at the server, or any resource to be processed, is called the arrival rate. The workload is the amount of work to be processed, sometimes called a transaction. A transaction can be an event or combination of subevents, including creating and sending an e-mail, paying a bill, processing a check, updating an inventory record, or selling something from a Web site. A transaction can result in one or more I/O operations moving some amount of data from memory to storage or storage to storage. Thus, a transaction is variable in size, scope, and complexity. An understanding of your business functions and the high-level transactions being performed to support the business, as well as how those map to application-level transactions and subsequent storage and I/O operations, can provide a common language to communicate with others in the business as well as understanding the resources needed to support the business. By learning to speak and translate the needs of the business from IT terminology (disks, processors, switch ports, MANs, etc.) to business functions (how many business transactions, how much savings per business activity, and so forth) the better your message will be received.

Entire books have been written about server performance, tuning, and capacity planning topics from the perspectives of hardware, operating system, applications, volume managers, and I/O busses. However, while servers are an important part of storage networking, our primary focus will be the portions of servers critical for generating and processing storage I/Os. The primary concern of the server is that there is enough CPU power available to support workload to generate and process I/Os, enough memory to support buffers and storage operation, and enough I/O bus bandwidth to support storage device interface adapters. Some server CPU component items include the speed of the processor, how many processors there are, how utilized the processors are, and how much time the processors are spending processing I/O interrupts. Some server memory component items include how much memory is available, how it is being utilized, and how much paging is occurring, since paging generates disk I/O. A common impact on server performance and the I/O subsystem is an application or utility that is performing too many nonessential I/O or locking operations. For example, an application may improperly take out and hold locks on database items, blocking other activity. Another example would be an application that reads some data, then reads the same data again and again instead of buffering, or pre-fetching the data.

Server I/O component items include how many I/O busses exist, what type they are, and their speed, utilization, contention, and attached devices. With faster storage interfaces available—including 2Gb, 4Gb, and 10Gb Fibre Channel; 10Gb Ethernet; and InfiniBand—many processor busses and adapters are not fast enough to support these interfaces. For example, a slow PCI bus may only be able to support about 1.5Gb/sec; thus, placing a 4Gb adapter on that bus would not utilize the adapter fully. Faster bus interfaces, including 66 MHz PCI, PCI-X, and PCI-X V2, will provide faster busses to support faster devices.

There is another component on the server that is critical to I/O performance and that is the chip technology that sits between the processor and

I/O bus. This technology is sometimes referred to as bridge chips that sit between, for example, an Intel processor and a PCI or PCI-X interface, which, in turn, supports a PCI or PCI-X adapter. Some indications that an I/O bus interface is becoming saturated include excessive CPU interrupt handling associated with I/O activity, queuing of I/Os, elongated response times for devices when there is no other apparent bottleneck, and transfer and I/O rates nearing theoretical limits.

Best Practices: Server performance and capacity planning topics include upgrading servers to support faster I/O busses if more performance and faster devices are to be added. For example, upgrade to servers that support PCI-X or higher if you plan on utilizing 2Gb and faster interfaces. Account for dual and quad path HBA server port needs, including planning for extra switch ports, server backplane bandwidth, path managers, and failover managers. Fibre Channel HBAs and Storage Networking Interface Cards (SNICs) may have multiple channel interfaces attached to a common backplane (e.g., PCI bus). This may lead to the perception that there may be more bandwidth than is really available. From a high-availability standpoint, a server could attach to two separate network (fabric) paths; however, the HBA would be a single point of failure.

How many servers to attach to a storage device or to a given amount of storage is an open question, since it involves different things—for example, how busy the servers are and what types of I/O operations are being performed (lots of small I/Os compared with many large I/Os). You may have some general guidelines or some may be available from your storage vendors based on different workloads. Figure 10.5 shows a simple example of consolidating servers to shared storage devices.

In Figure 10.5 multiple servers attach to a switch, with some servers having dual paths to a second switch. In this example, all servers converge (fan-in) to a common storage subsystem to access their allocated storage. Shown across the top of the figure are some sample performance characteristics for the different servers, including average I/O size in Kbytes, average I/O rate, and average data transfer size. Since these are average usage rates and the time interval is not known, these averages may be for a 24-hour period, including weekends. Consequently, these averages may in fact be much lower than normal workload.

Sometimes you may have to derive an offset or up-lift factor to apply to the averages to be more reflective. An up-lift factor is a value derived by looking at peak workloads and comparing them to averages. An up-lift fac-

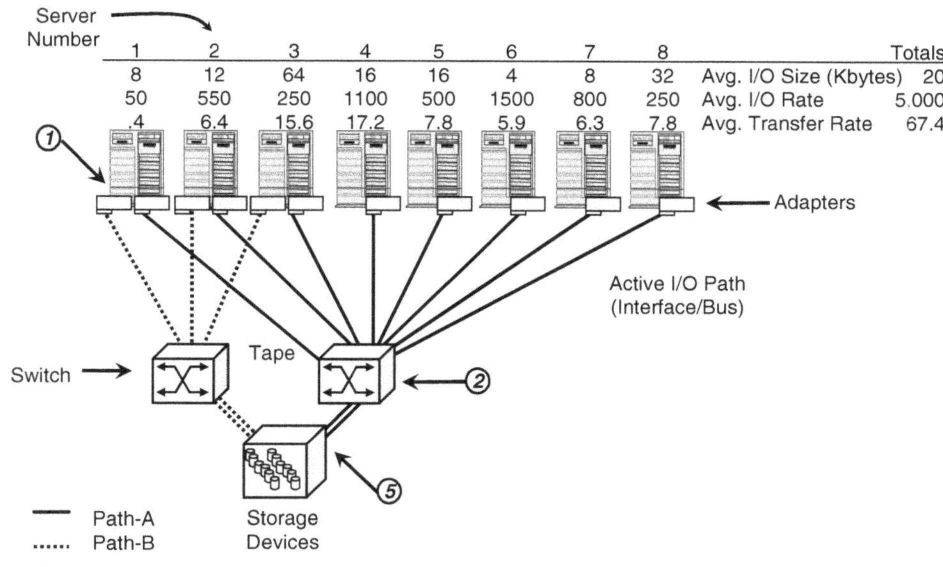

Figure 10.5 *Server and storage activity.*

tor then can be applied to the averages to raise them to a more reflective level. For example, if it is determined that the averages shown in Figure 10.5 are 20 percent lower than needed to more appropriately reflect activity, then increase the averages by 20 percent. Note that in determining your workload you should also apply whatever performance guides you have in place for thresholds. For example, if you determine that I/O activity (either I/Os or transfer rate) will be no more than 80 percent of the interface speed, then you need to factor that in to how much resources you have available and need. For example, in Figure 10.5 the average transfer rate is 67.4MB/sec, so let's assume that an up-lift factor of 10 percent applies (6.7MB/sec), resulting in a reflective server combined workload of 74.1MB/sec. Assuming that you have chosen to use a 70 percent threshold for I/O activity and the I/O interface is 1Gb Fibre Channel (100Mbyte/sec), you would have exceeded your guideline for this interface. Your experience and reported measurement data may indicate that this is fine, or that it is time to spread the server's workload over multiple storage I/O interfaces.

10.6.2 Switching topics

For many storage networking environments switches of some size and type are common components as part of the I/O interface path between servers and storage. In Chapter 8, some performance-related topics were covered, including locality and horizontal and vertical scaling. Building on that and other material in this book, additional performance and capacity concerns include oversubscription, congestion, and overall fabric performance. Some general items to be aware of for performance and capacity planning for switches include:

- Account for any dual or quad HBA servers and their need for switch ports
- Account for storage ports (primary, secondary, and mirroring)
- Account for ISL and trunk ports for local and metropolitan distance needs
- Account for connectivity ports to expand to other switches for growth
- Account for ports for diagnostics, tests, and analyses
- Account for any spare and on-demand ports
- Account for any SAN appliances, including NAS heads and virtualization devices
- Determine where slow devices are located and how they are accessed to avoid head of line blocking

As seen in Chapter 9, there are many permutations of how a storage network can be configured into different topologies along with the number of ISLs. Determining how many ISLs are needed to support different configurations varies based on the number of switches, topology, and required bandwidth. The following text looks at a scenario involving full mesh and an equation to determine how many minimum numbers of ISLs would be needed.

$$\text{NUMBER\_ISL} = \text{L} * \sum_{i=1}^{n} n - 1$$

where n ≤ SWITCH_PORTS and n = number of switches in a full mesh configuration. SWITCH_PORTS is the number of ports on a switch, and L represents the number of ISLs between each switch pair. This is then expanded to look at how many ISLs are needed to support a given workload scenario. For example, a full mesh of four 16-port switches with two ISLs between each switch would be 2 × (3 + 2 + 1) = 12 ISLs at 2Gb each, providing 12 = 24Gb of fabric bandwidth. The number of usable switch ports for servers and storage would then be 64 (4 × 16) ports – 24 (2 × 12), yielding 40 usable ports or 10 per switch. Consequently, 75 percent of the ports would not be local—requiring at least one hop over an ISL to access another port for nonlocalized I/O.

Over-subscription is an indicator of potential performance issues under different workloads, and a design to eliminate oversubscription removes this as a possibility. Congestion is the result of oversubscription, when ports have to wait for access to network interfaces and can be blocked from doing their useful work. A minor example of congestion is when you try to dial someone on the telephone or cell phone and you get a rapid busy signal. An example of complete blockage would be when you pick up the phone and cannot get a dial tone, but you know the power is good and the phone lines have not been cut. Telephone networks, similar to data networks, have some degree of oversubscription built in to help reduce costs. Storage interfaces have traditionally been designed to be nonblocking, nonoversubscribed to eliminate this as a possibility.

Oversubscription results when more ports are present than bandwidth is available to support full-speed communication between the ports. In a single switching device, the core or switching modules should provide adequate bandwidth to be nonblocking or prevent oversubscription by design. This can, however, be overridden on some products that support oversubscribed ports by design to help drive the cost per port down by sharing switching bandwidth. The design premise is that not all servers will operate and need the full bandwidth, so some servers can attach to ports that will be oversubscribed by design. This approach should be used with caution and an understanding of your server I/O workload and profiles to prevent performance challenges from occurring.

For switching devices configured into a fabric, an oversubscribed fabric is one that has more ports than available ISLs and trunks between the devices. For example, if there are four 16-port switches in a full mesh, with two ISLs between each switch, that would yield 12 ISLs to support 40 usable (64 – 24 ports for ISLs) or 10 usable ports per switch. Assuming that 20 of the ports need to talk to the other 20 ports at full bandwidth and there are only 12 ISLs between the ports, there would be an oversubscription of 2:1 and the potential for congestion. Of course, there are the assumptions of full bandwidth being needed and that all ports will talk to nonlocal ports.

Aggregation of multiple ISLs into a trunk ISL can address some performance issues by improving utilization of underutilized ISLs. By grouping multiple ISLs together as a single logical trunk, all the available bandwidth of the ISLs should be usable. Trunking can also lead to performance bottlenecks by giving a false sense of security about available bandwidth when adding workload. In some cases simply aggregating ISLs logically together without traffic prioritization or routing enhancements may not address high-priority traffic. A combination of ISL aggregation, ISL workload grouping by application functions, and routing enhancements is part of a total performance solution.

10.6.3 Network and storage I/O path (interface) topics

The storage I/O interface path between a server and a storage device is an essential component for storage networks for moving data. In a simple storage network with shared storage among servers with dedicated point-to-point connections, the storage network is the cable. For more involved storage networks the network may include hubs, switches, bridges, gateways, routers, and other appliances interconnected with a storage network I/O path. The storage network I/O path interface may be local LAN or SAN, metropolitan MAN or WAN, or a combination. Topologies can have an impact on performance, including placement of devices and level of locality.

Some items that can impact performance over MAN and WAN interfaces include line and link errors and signal degradation. Delays within a carrier-provided WAN can also have impact on performance. For MAN environments, care should be taken in maintaining fiber-optic cabling, connectors, and transceivers (including maintaining adequate bend radius for cable). Fiber-optic connectors and optics should be kept clean to prevent dirt and dust particles with faster speeds (2Gb, 4Gb, and 10Gb). Some other performance topics for storage interfaces, including distance, are:

- Be aware of protocol droop resulting from lack of flow control buffers over distance and when small partial frames are being sent at high speeds.
- Be alert to moving bottlenecks from one location to another—for example, if your previous bottleneck was in switch and interface congestion, moving to faster interfaces and streamlined configurations could move the bottleneck to a storage device or server adapter.
- Account for impact of mixed protocols (FCP, ESCON, FICON, parallel SCSI) on control unit performance and vendor-specific behavior.
- Monitor network for errors, retransmissions, collisions, and loss of signal where network errors cause performance to drop.

- Reduce the number of hops needed to move data from source to destination. Hops are good for beer; however, they add latency to storage I/O processing, which results in increased latency (response time).

10.6.4 Storage device (disk and tape) topics

From a performance and capacity planning perspective, an entire book or series of books could be spent on storage device topics. Storage is a major component for storage networking, with the other being storage networking interfaces. Some general information about storage devices, including disk and tape, from a performance and capacity planning perspective include:

- Proper cache and buffer size for VTS devices, depending on SLAs and requirements to support tape retrieval and tape mount needs
- Adequate buffer configuration for long-distance mirroring from storage devices
- I/O characteristics, including size, reads and writes, random and sequential
- Account for cache impact on storage subsystems with 1Gb, 2Gb, and 10Gb speeds
- Configuration and combinations of hardware and software RAID
- Placement of data on devices and device configuration
- Monitor cache utilization, hits, and effectiveness for reads and writes

For optimum performance, smaller fast disk drives, or LUNs made up of many smaller striped disks, should be used for small random I/O operations. Some techniques that have been used by some subsystem manufacturers are to short stroke a larger disk drive. This means that the drive is configured so as not to use the outer portions of the disk, reducing capacity but improving random, small I/O capacity. With fast 10,000- and 15,000-RPM disk drives, the need to short stroke disks has diminished. Another technique is to place large sequentially accessed data on the outer tracks near the edge of a disk drive. This is done to leverage what is known as Zone Bit Recording (ZBR) on most disk drives today. ZBR leverages the fact that a disk is round, and, like a pie, a slice is narrow at the center and wider on the outside. With ZBR there are more blocks of data on the outside, and the outside is moving faster than the center. This means that on a ZBR the highest sequential throughput is near the edge of a disk, with the portion of the disk near the center having better rapid short I/O response time. Most subsystems can leverage ZBR capabilities as part of their intelligence to optimize performance, so it can be difficult to place data exactly where you want it on a physical disk. To more effectively utilize actual disk capacity, new techniques including thin-provisioning are available. Thin-provisioning enables systems and applications to reserve space ahead of time without actually using it. Then, when they need the storage, it is made available on a dynamic basis. This eliminates the need to add more storage, expand files and volumes, or have excess storage sitting (spinning) waiting to be used.

Table 10.1 shows some various storage media, data protection, and performance options for storing and accessing data, building on what is covered in Chapter 2. While some RAID configurations can improve performance, misconfiguration of software and hardware RAID can lead to unwanted performance problems. For example, a server performing software-based RAID 4 or RAID 5 accessing hardware-based RAID storage could encounter degraded performance. Consult with your storage hardware and software vendors for their specific recommendations and supported configurations. In Chapter 12, additional information on data protection, including RAID, is covered. Another item to watch out for regarding storage performance, is isolating management ports on storage devices. Make sure Ethernet management ports are protected to prevent denial of service attacks on storage device management ports.

10.6.5 Backup and data protection performance topics

Backup and data protection are essential activities supporting the resilient storage networking environment. The following text takes a look at some performance characteristics and concerns regarding backup/recovery, along with mirroring and replication (both hardware and software).

Table 10.2 shows some various components involved with performing backup and recovery, along with attributes and characteristics that can impact performance. In addition to the items shown in Table 10.2, the speed of the target device can have a significant impact on backup performance. Some new backup storage devices have the ability to reduce the amount of actual capacity used by reducing duplicate data and other compression techniques. In the following figures, various backup topologies are shown, along with points of concern for performance and capacity. Compression can have a significant impact on performance and the amount of capacity required to back up data. The more compressible data is, the less data there will be to move over the storage interface or network and a

Table 10.1 *Storage Characteristics and Applications*

Type of Storage	Characteristics	Applications
Cache	Reduces latency by storing frequently accessed data in buffer to offset delay of disk access (read or write). Read cache improves read performance combined with read-ahead, prefetching functions. Write-back cache speeds write processing.	OLTP and I/O-intensive applications that are latency and response time sensitive. For write-intensive applications cache can help to speed up processing and to offset slower disk subsystems.
JBOD	Low cost with performance being determined by the speed of an individual disk drive and its interface.	Low-cost and low-performance applications.
Optical	Long-term, high-capacity data retention with moderate performance.	Archiving and long-term data retention.
RAID 0	Disk striping aggregates multiple drives together to perform I/O in parallel. Disk striping can be tuned for different I/O characteristics.	Applications with data that can be recreated and tolerate downtime should a disk fail.
RAID 0+1	Combines disk striping with mirroring (or mirroring with striping) to provide very good read and write performance and good availability. This requires twice the number of disks.	High-performance databases and files, transaction logs, and journals.
RAID 1	Disk mirroring duplicates I/Os to two or more disk mirror sets for availability. Good read performance by using multiple disks to perform I/O; however, writes can be impacted in order to synchronize the data.	Any application where high availability and good read performance is needed, including database files, journals, transaction logs, and critical files.
RAID 3	Striped disks with dedicated parity that provides good read performance and availability; however, the single parity disk can become a bottleneck.	OLTP and database applications as well as video images. Good for synchronous applications.
RAID 5	Combines good read performance with data protection using rotating parity to spread parity across disks—however, could be sensitive to write due to parity updates. RAID 5 should be combined with mirrored write-back cache for performance and data integrity.	Most any application—however, is sensitive to write-intensive environments when cache is not available. Good for asynchronous and multiuser, multitasking I/O operations where reads out number writes.
SSD	Similar to cache, but SSD functions and emulates a disk device while eliminating seek time and latency delays.	OLTP, transaction logs, journals, indices for databases, I/O, intensive files and data.
Tape	Low-cost, large-capacity medium for backup, interchange, and retention.	Backup, retention, archiving, and data interchange.

Table 10.2 *Backup Performance and Tuning Items*

Backup Component	Impact on Backup
Backup Software	Which backup software or utility is being utilized?
	How is the backup being performed?
	Parallel, multistream, or single-stream backup
	Configuration of backup and backup software
Server	Speed of the processor or processors if multiprocessor
	I/O adapter and bus bandwidth and utilization
	TOEs to offload servers for TCP processing
	Operating system and configuration
Source	Types of files being backed up—for example, database objects
	Type of backup (physical, image, volume, full, file based)
	Compression of data to reduce traffic and needed capacity
	Speed of the interface to the device and contention

smaller amount of capacity required on the backup medium (disk, tape, or optical). TCP offload engines can be used to accelerate IP traffic for general storage access, including NAS and iSCSI, as well as backup. Additional information on snapshot, pointer-based backup, RAID, and other data protection techniques can be found in Chapter 12.

In Figure 10.6 on the left is a traditional network-based backup model combined with dedicated tape drives on some servers. In this example data is moved over the network (1) to a server that has a dedicated tape drive where the data is either temporarily stored on disk (2) or written directly to tape (3). Adequate network bandwidth is needed to support the movement of data between the different servers and the backup server. This may be practical for servers with small amounts of data, and a separate network for backup may be needed as well.

On the right side of Figure 10.6 a LAN-Free backup is shown, where multiple servers can attach to a shared tape library and write data to it without moving data over the LAN. In this example meta or control information (4) is sent from the various servers to a backup server, which is less than what would otherwise be moved over the network. The servers then move the data directly to the tape devices (5), which can be shared or dedicated, to specific servers using various interfaces. Tape library sharing and control software on the backup server controls access to the library. This type of backup can be applied to file servers using NDMP to move data from filers

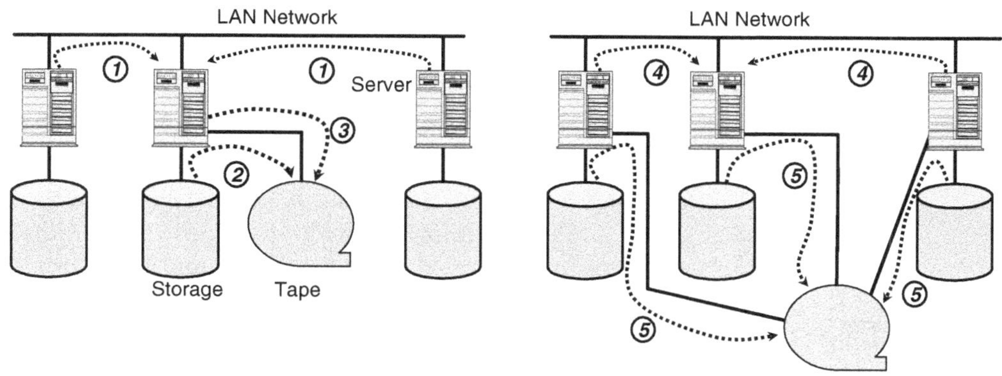

Figure 10.6 *Backup performance components.*

to tape backup devices. This could be done using Fibre Channel, SCSI, or with an Ethernet network and iSCSI. Caution should be exercised when using iSCSI to ensure that you have adequate network bandwidth, or plan for a separate network to support the backup data movement.

Figure 10.7 shows a wide area backup scenario, which could be a single server, a backup server supporting other devices, or other combinations. This example shows how data is written to a remote tape device over a WAN or MAN interface to support off-site backup and electronic data vaulting. This is a relatively new capability for open systems environments, but it has been done in mainframe environments for many years. The tape or backup device (it could also be disk) could be at a remote location—for example, a disaster recovery facility or other location. By using techniques such as tape pipelining and compression, data can be transmitted over long distances while improving the overall throughput. Tape pipelining takes a sequential data stream and groups the data along with compression using a

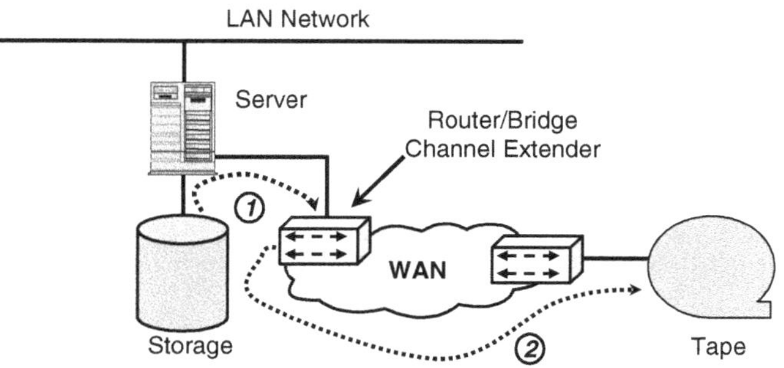

Figure 10.7 *Wide area backup performance.*

bridge device (also known as a channel extender). The bridges help to make the remote backup device appear local to the backup server and the remote server appear local to the backup device. Various vendor implementations and protocols exist for performing this function to help speed up tape data movement over long distances.

Backup can be characterized as data protection to ensure survivability and recovery, while data mirroring and replication assists with enabling continuous access to data due to failure of components or loss of a site. Hardware-based remote mirroring and replication can be done locally within the same computer room, across a campus, across town, across the country, or across the globe. There are, of course, different performance characteristics and concerns depending on the amount of data being mirrored, the sensitivity of the data (how close does it have to be synchronized), bandwidth, and distance.

Hardware mirroring is shown in Figure 10.8, which shows data being written from a server (1) to a storage device and subsequently written to a remote device (2) over a MAN or WAN interface. A channel extender, shown as a SAN-to-WAN bridge, provides interface conversion and mapping to the appropriate network interface and protocol. Performance and capacity concerns include the amount of bandwidth on the network and the protocol being used by the SAN-to-WAN bridge. Another concern is compression efficiency and internal bandwidth of the bridge device, regardless of where it is located. Another not so apparent performance factor is the line quality of the network interface, in that an interface with lots of errors

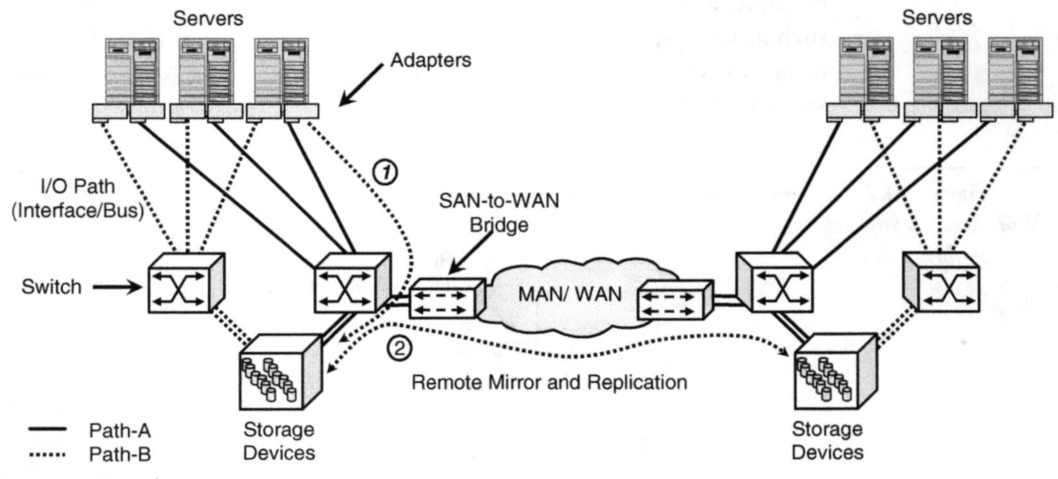

Figure 10.8 *Hardware-based remote mirroring performance.*

will result in lower performance. Similarly, a misconfigured storage device with insufficient buffers and not optimized for distance will not effectively move data over the available bandwidth.

Software (host server)–based remote mirroring and replication are shown in Figure 10.9. The server issues an I/O (1)—for example, a write to the local storage device over one of the storage interface paths. The server also issues an I/O (2) to another server over a network interface, which, in turn, issues an I/O (3) to a storage device it is attached to. Some performance concerns for host server–based mirroring include adequate processing CPU bandwidth and memory for buffers and I/O interfaces to local storage as well as to a network interface. Some additional concerns include the local storage as well as the remote storage, similar to those that would be applicable for other storage functions. One of the more important performance areas of concerns is the network and distance between the two servers that are involved in the mirroring. For server-to-server mirroring, IP-to-IP compression and acceleration in the network can help increase performance in terms of lower response time and higher throughput. Regardless of hardware or software mirroring and replication, synchronous operations will typically be constrained to about 100–150km, depending on the network interface, quality, vendor equipment, and technology being utilized. Asynchronous operations, on the other hand, can be utilized to span dis-

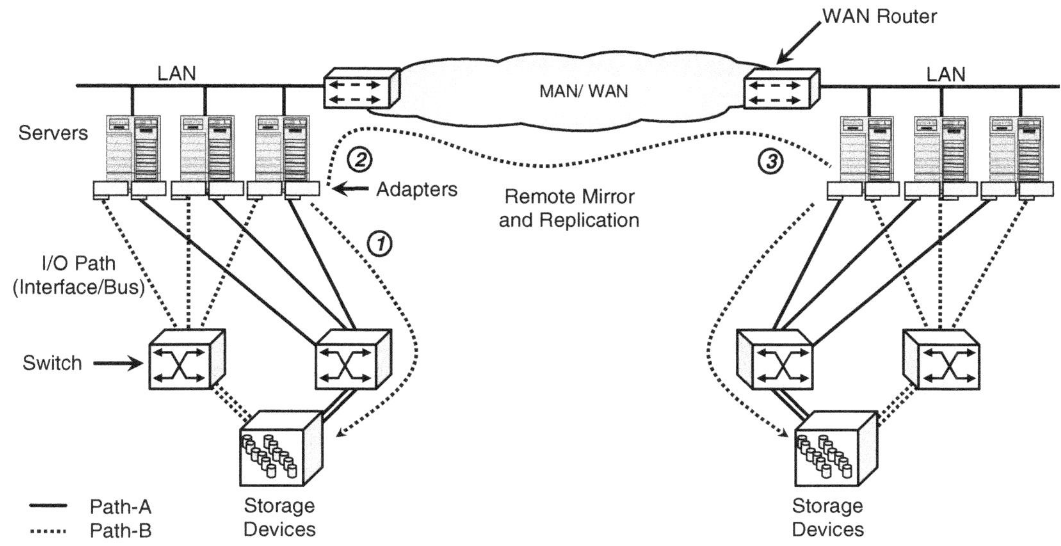

Figure 10.9 *Software-based remote mirroring performance.*

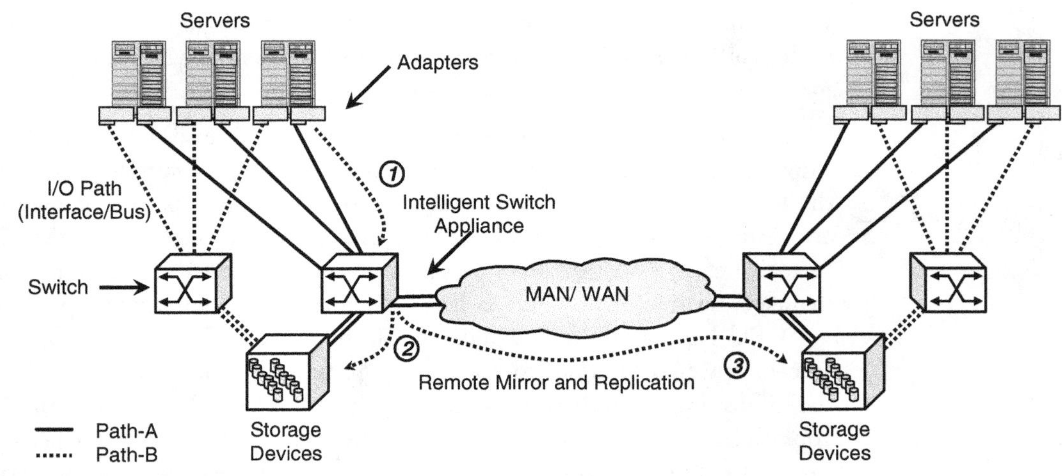

Figure 10.10 *Intelligent switch and appliance-based mirroring and replication.*

tances around the world, as well as being combined with synchronous for multitier protection.

In Figure 10.10 an intelligent switch or storage service (virtualization) appliance is shown performing disk mirroring and replication. In this scenario adequate bandwidth is needed in the network and in the intelligent switch and its associated technology for supporting distance functions.

10.6.6 Availability and reliability topics

Availability can be measured and reported on an individual component basis, as a sum of all components, or a composite of both. A balanced view toward availability would be to look at the big picture in terms of what is your end-to-end, or total, availability. This would be the view that is seen by users of the services supported by the storage network and its applications. Combined with this overall view is that of how the underlying pieces are doing—for example, the applications, servers, switches, networks, and storage devices. In looking at availability, an understanding of what your service requirements and service-level agreement needs are is important. There can also be a cost associated with availability that needs to be understood to determine what your availability objective is. Many vendors utilize terms such as five nines, six nines, or higher to describe their solutions availability; however, it is important to understand that availability is the sum of all components and their configurations. Seconds of downtime per year is calculated as 100% × [(100 – N) / 100], where N is the desired number of nines of availability.

Table 10.3 *Availability and Number of Nines Reliability*

Level of Availability	Number of Nines to Right of Decimal Point	Amount of Downtime per Year
99%	0	3.65 days/year
99.9%	1	8.77 hours/year
99.99%	2	52.6 minutes/year
99.999%	3	5.26 minutes/year
99.9999%	4	31.56 seconds/year
99.99999%	5	3.16 seconds/year
99.999999%	6	1/2 second/year

Table 10.3 shows some availability values in terms of percentage of uptime per year and in minutes. How much availability you need and can afford will be a function of your environment, application and business requirements, and objectives. Availability is the sum of all components combined with design for fault isolation and containment. The following text shows some relationships, including how the availability of an I/O interface is the sum of the availability of switching components and any applicable network and cabling along with subcomponents (GBIC, SFP, XFP, connectors, optics). Some examples for an IO_Interface subcomponent would include switches, network, and cabling. Another example would be storage, including controllers + adapters + cache + medium (disk/tape drives). Server availability would include server = operating system + utility software + processor + memory + I/O bus, and server availability = server + adapter + IO_Interface + storage. There are many more detailed relationships covering the components and subcomponents beyond what is shown here.

In Table 10.4 some terminology pertaining to availability is shown, along with their descriptions. Availability can be described as being as good as the weakest link in a chain or, in the case of storage and storage networking, that of the weakest component, which includes the hardware, software, network, people, and design. Often the focus of availability is put on an individual component, which can be made ultrahigh availability if not fault tolerant but does little to contribute to the overall availability of a system. A good design may not be talked about in terms of how many nines availability it has, but a good design can help eliminate unplanned outages to compensate for individual component failure. A good design removes

Table 10.4 *Some Availability Terminology*

Term or Acronym	Description
Availability	The amount or percentage of time a system or component can be expected to be available for use based on its reliability (usually expressed in hours).
Five nines	Amount of downtime or lack of availability that can be supported in a given time frame (99.99999% uptime).
MTBF	Mean Time Between Failures—Indication that can be measured or estimated on the expected time (usually in hours) of how reliable a system can be expected to be. The higher the MTBF number the better.
MTTR	Mean Time To Repair/Replace—Measurement of estimated or actual time required to repair a system and replace it into service or replace a failed redundant component. This can include the time taken to detect, notify, respond, repair, or replace, as well as perform any restore, reboot, redo of transaction logs, or other recovery.
Reliability	Systems and their components function as expected during specified time frames with some level of confidence.
Outage	Systems and subsystems are not available for use.
Scheduled downtime	Planned downtime for maintenance, replacement, and repair.
Unscheduled	Unplanned downtime for emergency repair and maintenance.

complexity while providing scalability, stability, and ease of management and maintenance, as well as fault containment and isolation.

While high-reliability components certainly help to increase availability, ultimately your design will have as much if not more impact on your environment. Designing in availability can help to support maintenance and upgrades, as well as contain faults and errors when they occur. By assuming that a highly reliable component may fail and designing around it, you can isolate and contain faults from spreading into a chain of events. This is something I feel strongly about, having seen things that were not supposed to fail cause chain reactions that resulted in outages that could have been prevented. Consequently, design in the appropriate level of fault containment and isolation for your application and environment.

Figure 10.11 shows an availability chart with total availability, an availability objective target line, and unplanned and scheduled (planned) out-

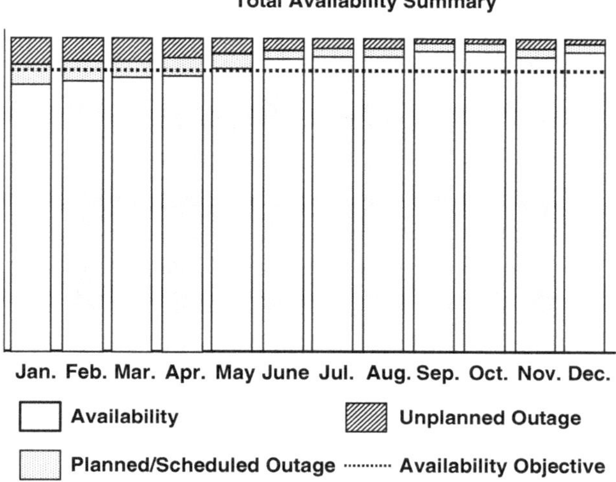

Figure 10.11 *Total availability summary.*

ages. A closing note on availability is to consider the human element in terms of configuration changes, typing errors, change management, and other activities that can result in disruptions to storage and storage networking environments.

10.7 Performance and capacity planning tools and metrics

A challenge with performing capacity planning and performance analysis is knowing what is normal and what is abnormal. Key to creating a baseline and ongoing performance and capacity plan are metrics derived from various tools. These can be simple metrics ranging from how much data is being moved and at what rate to more extensive metrics, involving response times and transaction rates in various forms, such as real time and history roll-up and summaries.

Some commonly available tools that can be used for performance, capacity planning, workload generation, and benchmarking include:

- Third-party performance and planning tools with reporting capabilities
- Vendor-supplied tools on switches, bridges, adapters, storage, and servers
- Standard UNIX tools, including df, dd, sar, timex, nfstat, and iostat

- IOMETER workload generation and performance monitoring tool
- For IBM S/390 and zOS environments: SMF, RMF, SAS, and MICS/MXG
- Various sniffers, analyzers, and probes

In addition to these tools, home-built scripts and tools can take data from these and other utilities to aggregate with other data. Microsoft Excel, as well as other spreadsheets, can be used to track and report on data as well. Vendor-specific utilities and element managers can be used for monitoring and collecting data that can be aggregated with data from other sources.

Storage networking metrics (statistics) have been rudimentary and limited to what's available from a given vendor's switch, HBA, application, or storage device. The collection and flow of statistics have been either intrusive or proprietary formats. New capabilities now exist to collect in a nonintrusive manner complete statistics, including detailed session-level information not available from switches and directors across all platforms and storage devices.

Activity and usage information, including throughput, frames, and packets being sent and received for switches and networks, is needed. This can be to help determine fabric utilization and bandwidth as well as port utilization and signs of contention and congestion. Looking at frame utilization to see how many full and partial frames are being sent can help to determine network efficiency. Utilization can be reported in terms of megabytes or bytes sent and recovered via a port or source destination pair. This information can be displayed using vendor-supplied and integrated tools as well as third-party tools, including those that utilize Fibre Channel generic services (FC-GS3 and FC-GS4), Storage Management Interface Specification (SMI-S), and performance MIBs. The information can be reported at various levels, from physical to Upper-Level Protocol (ULP)—for example, by the port or by protocol. This can come in handy if you have an ISL that is supporting different ULPs across a common ISL—for example, Fibre Channel FCP and FICON traffic. In addition to throughput information, error information is also useful to report and track to gain an understanding of lost resources due to errors and device resets.

Some other metrics include I/O size, number of I/Os, and latency for reads and writes, including minimum, average, maximum, and source, destination, and routing information if applicable. Number of I/Os should be able to be translated from frames and packets per second to a logical, protocol, and interface layer—for example, how many I/O operations of a given size are being initiated by a server, how many frames and packets does that translate into, and subsequent network activity. Ideally this information should be available over different intervals to identify activity for prime-time shifts as well as off-hour periods and different workloads.

10.8 Storage networking benchmarks and testing

Performance testing and benchmarks have different meanings and different areas of focus. There is testing for compatibility and interoperability of components. There is performance testing of individual components, as well as testing of combined solutions. Testing can be very rigorous and thorough, perhaps beyond real-world conditions, or testing can be relatively simple to verify data movement and integrity. What the best test is for your environment depends on what your needs and requirements are. However, with that being said, the best test is one that adequately reflects your environment and the application workload. In addition to reflecting your environment and application workload, a good test is one that can be easily reproduced. Various test tools include Intel iometer (www.iometer.org) and standard UNIX utilities such as dd that can be used to generate and report performance workload and results.

There are various vendor and third-party tests on different components that emphasize speed and performance to leverage specific features and exploit weaknesses of others. While some of the test results can be interesting, if not entertaining, in the game of vendor specmanship and maneuvering, there needs to be an understanding as to whether the tests are pertinent to your application. For example, a test result that shows certain conditions under an extreme workload may not be applicable if your applications do not operate under those conditions. Some testing can be performed using special test equipment to exercise individual components as well as collect data and report on performance. Testing can also be end to end, with workload simulators issuing commands to an application server simulating users, which, in turn, issues I/O requests to exercise the total solution. You can also create scripts using various tools to check on response time from an end-to-end perspective as well as test components to see what's working. For example, create a script that is run under different scenarios and workload to take samples of response time, error counts, and activity to create a baseline. Baseline performance indicators should be established for normal conditions that can be used for comparison during problem periods.

10.9 Computer Measurement Group

The Computer Measurement Group (CMG) is a nonprofit, vendor and technology independent worldwide organization of data processing professionals focused on the measurement and management of computer systems. CMG is the association of systems performance and capacity professionals. CMG members are primarily concerned with performance evaluation, assessment of existing systems to maximize performance (response time, throughput), and with capacity management, where planned enhancements to existing systems or the design of new systems is evaluated to identify the necessary resources required to provide adequate performance at a reasonable cost. CMG activities include an annual international symposium, regional events and conferences throughout the world, conference proceedings and published papers, a journal, and an on-line newsletter. More information about CMG can be found at www.cmg.org.

10.10 Storage Performance Council

The Storage Performance Council (SPC) is an organization that serves as a catalyst to improve performance in storage subsystems. The SPC is a nonprofit corporation founded to define, standardize, and promote storage subsystem benchmarks. The SPC also disseminates objective, verifiable performance data to the computer industry and its customers. The SPC works to foster the free and open exchange of information and ideas to support fair and vigorous competition between vendors to benefit the public. The SPC develops storage-focused benchmarks of components, including disk drives, magnetic tape, optical disks, media-handling robotics, software systems, backup and archive, adapters, controllers, and storage networks to connect storage to servers. Additional information about the SPC can be found at the Web site (www.storageperformance.org).

10.11 Transaction Processing Performance Council

The Transaction Processing Performance Council (TPC) is a nonprofit organization focused on defining transaction processing and database benchmarks and the dissemination of objective performance data. Various transaction-related tests representing different applications and businesses are supported by the TPC. Some examples of transaction tests include the TPC-C, which simulates a complete computing environment centered on order processing. TPC-H is a simulation of an ad hoc decision support environment, with TPC-R representing business reporting. TPC-W represents Web e-commerce transactional activity. For more information about the TPC, its members, and tests see the Web site (www.tpc.org).

10.12 Chapter summary

Having enough resources to support business and application needs is essential to a resilient storage network. Without adequate storage and storage networking resources, availability and performance can be negatively impacted. Poor metrics and information can lead to poor decisions and management. When migrating from 1Gb–2Gb to 4Gb–10Gb or other higher-speed interfaces, assess cache impact on your storage and determine if you will need more cache based on your workload needs and arrival rates. Establish availability, performance, response time, and other objectives to gauge and measure performance of the end-to-end storage and storage networking infrastructure. Be practical, since it is easy to get wrapped around the details and lose sight of the bigger picture and your objectives.

What This Chapter Will Do For You

This chapter looks at various approaches to managing storage networks. Some of the items you will learn about in this chapter include:

- Improper use of storage virtualization and services can increase cost and management time
- Many storage management tools are really monitoring and reporting mechanisms
- Storage is becoming less expensive, however, the cost of manage storage is increasing
- Are you managing your management tools, or is your storage being managed?
- Identifying and improving simple storage management tasks that demonstrate to management the expertise necessary to take on more advanced projects

11

Storage Management

11.1 Overview

There are many storage network technologies looking for problems, and there are many storage network problems looking for solutions. Management of storage and storage networking has increased in complexity with the proliferation of technologies and increasing amounts of storage being deployed. While storage itself has become relatively inexpensive, the cost to manage and protect it continues to increase. This chapter covers storage and storage networking management, including common tasks and associated management tools for supporting storage networking environments.

11.2 Storage networking management

Storage networking management addresses all areas of storage networking, including configuration, provisioning (allocation), diagnostics, resource monitoring, data protection, and security. Storage and information needs continue to grow, as does the value of information, while the relative cost to purchase storage continues to decrease as capacities increase. The dilemma is that while the costs of storage itself continue to decrease, the resources to manage storage remain the same, resulting in a storage management efficiency gap.

As more storage is added, the complexity and cost to determine how it can best be utilized and what data needs to be archived or can be deleted increase. Consequently, in some environments, there is a pattern of simply adding more storage to address the management problem, when, in fact, this is adding to the overall management complexity problem. Management tools, for the most part, still lack the intelligence to leverage and implement policy and automated management; however, emerging technology is improving on this.

Most management is, in fact, monitoring, configuring, and providing a view into what and how storage resources are being consumed passively (waiting for the results) or actively (real-time and predictive). These capabilities are needed to move forward with more intelligent and proactive management tools and frameworks. One of the complexities associated with management tools is the proliferation of various vendor element and device managers, frameworks, and other tools, each with their proprietary interfaces. In Figure 11.1, we see how information and storage needs are growing, while cost and complexity continue to increase. The balance of this chapter looks at what can be done now as well as in the future with some emerging storage networking management technologies.

Figure 11.1 shows the increase in data, with the corresponding cost and complexity to manage it. Even though the relative cost to acquire storage and connectivity is decreasing, while capacity is increasing, the cost to manage storage continues to increase. This has resulted in storage management efficiency gaps that have not kept pace with the information growth.

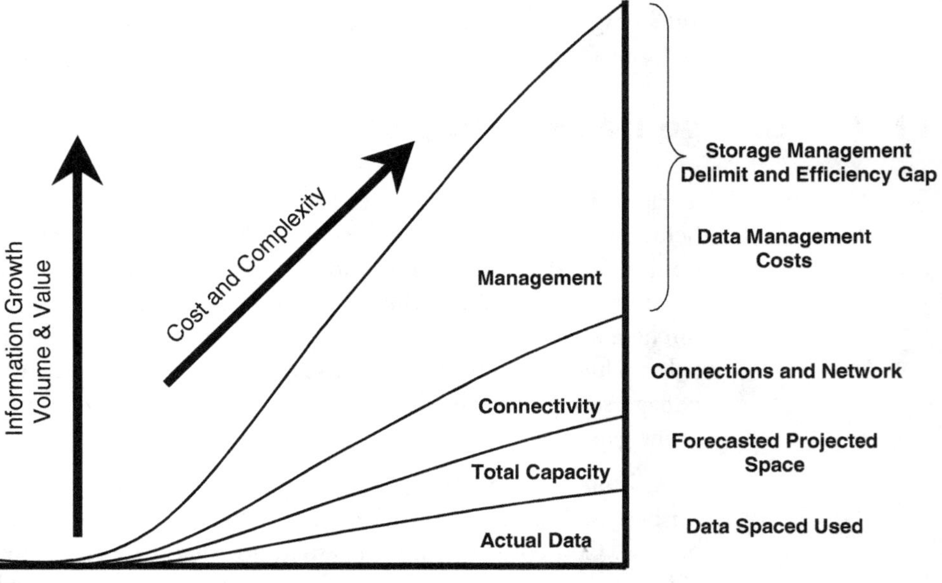

Figure 11.1 *Cost and complexity associated with managing storage.*

An important aspect with regard to your storage network management approach should be a serious consideration of which problems are costing the most in terms of people time, which are recurring activities, and, ultimately, your needs. There are other factors to keep in mind, including your philosophy, your needs for a single integrated tool set and framework from a single vendor, or your desire for a "best of breed" solution set from multiple vendors. Another important question is whether you want to integrate your Network Operation Center (NOC) functions with your Storage Networking Operations Center (SNOC) or have them separate.

11.3 Storage and storage networking management tools

There are various types of storage and storage networking management tools that correspond to different management tasks and functions. These include application-focused tools that can profile data usage and access patterns from a filesystem, e-mail, or database object perspective. Other tools can span multiple areas of focus, such as servers, applications, storage, and networking. Still others are focused on overall storage networking, providing a level of abstraction above vendor-supplied device and element managers. These tools and functions can be broadly categorized as:

- Vendor and device specific—device and element managers
- Domain and resource focused—storage network managers
- Multidomain framework systems—network and enterprise management systems
- High level and application aware—logical data managers

In Figure 11.2 various storage networking management tool categories are shown with some of their characteristics. These tool categories include element and device managers for servers, switches, storage, and other devices.

The sophistication and type of tools needed for your storage network will depend on your management strategy, which tools you already have, which storage and devices you have, and the size and complexity of your environment. Your environment may require multiple tools from different vendors, or you may be able to leverage a common framework for common tasks or a combination.

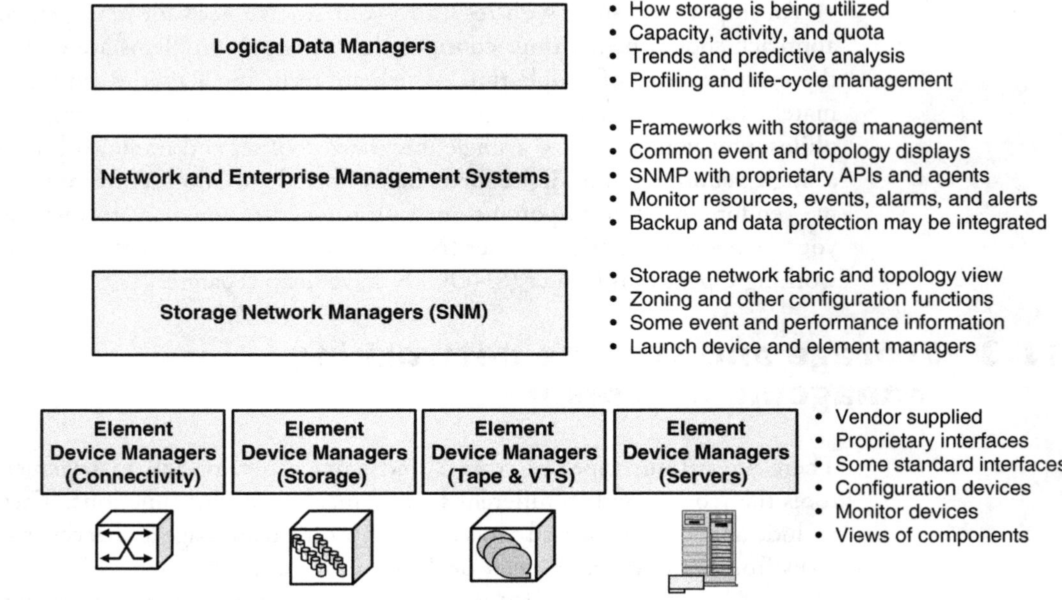

Figure 11.2 *Storage networking management tool categories.*

11.3.1 Logical data managers (storage resource and life-cycle management)

Logical data management tools provide a high-level abstraction and logical view of how storage and data are accessed and utilized to support application and business functions. Some storage life-cycle management functions include resource and capacity usage of storage and bandwidth. Some other functions include monitoring and reporting of individual user and application resource usage quota management. Storage profiling and resource usage tools provide real-time as well as historical reporting, trending, analysis, and indications of resource constraints. More advanced storage resource usage and profiling tools can provide predictive analysis of likely problems due to resource constraints or capacity (space and bandwidth) issues. Storage usage tools can work at the application layer, looking at object-based storage, filesystems, databases, and e-mail among others; they can also look at data usage patterns and create profiles of usage, including what data has recently been accessed and what is infrequently accessed. Utilizing life-cycle management tools can enable you to build data classification models in order to determine which type and class of storage and access methods are best for different applications. Another thing to consider when choosing storage usage tools is to determine which are best suited to your needs. It is also important to understand how much you are willing to invest in resources (people, time, dollars) to research, assess, and test tools for your environment. Data movement and migration is part of a management process that comes into play whenever you replace and refresh technology. Advance planning for future data migration to support technology replacement can help reduce storage costs now and in the future.

11.3.2 Network and enterprise management systems

Network and enterprise management tools can be more encompassing than element and device management tools. Storage networking and enterprise management systems can be part of larger network and system management frameworks or they can be storage specific. These tools provide an integrated approach for managing server, storage, and networking resources, including common event handling and monitoring. These tools provide topology and configuration displays, known as visualization, with various levels of detail of the individual components. The displays can be used for monitoring and reporting activity, events, and alarms across server, storage, and network. Proprietary APIs and plug-in modules are often the interface into management tools, with SNMP being a common integration method. A new management interface is the SNIA Storage Management Initiative Specification (SMIS). Some enterprise management systems have other functions and features integrated, including backup, archiving, data management, data movement, and task and event schedulers, which can be a useful feature for launching different acuities at various times, based on policies and events.

11.3.3 Storage network managers

Storage network managers provide functions that can be part of network and enterprise management systems or that can function as domain managers—focused on servers, storage, or networks. Some functions that storage network managers provide include visualization of storage network topologies and components, zoning, allocation of resources, assessment management, reporting, event notification, launch device managers, and integration with other products and frameworks. These combine to provide a higher level of abstraction and virtualization compared with the device manager function. This approach enables basic functions, including zoning, event notification, and activity monitoring, to be performed from a single window. The ability to launch device managers enables you to "drill down" to perform more detailed management tasks using vendor-specific features.

11.3.4 Device and element managers

Device and element managers are typically designed to leverage the vendor-unique features of a device. Element managers are supplied by vendors for management functions of their products on a device basis. Element managers exist for storage devices, switches, servers, adapters, bridges, routers, gateways, and appliances. Some are able to manage interoperable devices for higher-level functions and interoperate with storage network managers and enterprise management systems. Some functions provided by element managers include monitoring, configuration, and diagnostics of individual devices and components. Visualization capabilities display the configuration of components, including ports, storage, security, environmental, front and rear display, and other resources. Other capabilities can include performance and resource activity information, such as port and device status, thresholds, alarms, and alerts. Device and element managers have had proprietary interfaces, including APIs and agents, with a trend of migrating to open interfaces. Some interfaces being adopted by device and element managers include SNMP, command-line support with secure Telnet, RS-323 command line, menu interfaces, and graphical user interfaces (Java and Web based). Many device and element managers are also adding SMIS provider and client support for interoperability and open interfaces. Some device managers have the ability to launch other applications and utilities.

11.3.5 Storage and networking management interfaces

There are many different ways to interface with management tools, including Command-Line Interfaces (CLI), Graphical User Interfaces (GUI), wizards, APIs, and SNMP MIBs. CLI interfaces can be accessed via RS-232 serial interface ports as well as via Telnet. While CLIs can provide flexible interfaces to perform management functions, they also require knowledge of the command language and underlying system to perform functions. CLIs are expensive in terms of supporting and interfacing to their changing syntax and outputs when using scripting. An advantage of CLIs is that they can support scripting to facilitate automation of common tasks. A downside to CLIs is that they require more knowledge and training to avoid introduction of human error into functions. Some vendors have deployed common CLIs across different products and technologies to help simplify the learning of new products.

Graphical User Interfaces (GUIs) are very common today, with vendor-proprietary and Web-based implementations. GUIs require some knowledge level and can be prone to error, depending on skill set. GUIs can help inexperienced workers perform tasks that might be too complex to perform with a CLI. Wizards and assistants can be a great help to new staff members in becoming familiar with different tasks and in helping to significantly reduce human error. Wizards provide step-by-step help through the process of performing various tasks, including LUN creation, mapping, zoning, and port configuration. Some tools provide learning modes that show you what is being done in addition to guiding you through common tasks.

Two technologies facilitating interoperability and robustness of management tools are industry standard SNMP Management Information Blocks (MIBs), including the Fibre Alliance and IETF MIBs, and the Fibre Channel Generic Services (FC-GS) protocols to pass configuration and status information. In addition to these, vendor-specific APIs are also being exchanged between vendors to enable further interoperability and management from common storage framework tools. APIs require that a library module be supplied, which results in another layer of integration, testing, and compatibility.

Storage network management tools can be accessed out of band using external network interfaces, including Ethernet-based IP networks, and in-band management. In band refers to management and control functions being performed using the data path instead of a separate management path. In-band management can include using Ethernet and IP for SNMP management of storage networking devices. Another use for in-band management is for storage virtualization services command and control using the data path. Out-of-band management utilizes a separate path—for example, Ethernet as an interface and IP as a protocol for command and control functions. For high availability and protection, a separate management network would be a good practice to attach management interfaces and keep them isolated from regular networks. Management tools and interfaces need to be protected with adequate security and virus tools, similar to how your servers should be protected. Storage network management tools can also be accessed in band using the data path to transfer management information. An example of this would be Fibre Channel General Services (FC-GS) and SCSI Enclosure Services (SES).

11.4 Managing storage and storage networks

Sound management and recovery procedures facilitate the disaster recovery process and day-to-day operation of your storage network. Sound and tested practices, procedures, documentation, and policies, combined with good management tools, facilitate effective recovery and resilient storage networking. Utilizing management tools that report on events, their cause, correlation, and root cause analysis are important. New tools are emerging to proactively look at storage networking components (servers, adapters, switches, storage devices, and software configurations) to detect misconfigurations and other potential errors before they can cause a problem.

11.4.1 Configuration and provisionment (allocation of storage resources)

As with many things, allocating storage used to be easier. For small systems the process of adding storage can be rather simple: Attach the device to a free adapter port on a server, verify that the device is automatically recognized, format the device for use, and allocate it for use. For larger environments there can be more involved steps, including:

- Acquiring the storage subsystem or upgrading an existing one
- Installing any new required cabling (copper or optical)
- Upgrading and adding switch ports as needed
- Configuring switch ports for new device and server connections
- Adding new adapters and drivers to servers as needed
- Upgrading tape and backup capabilities to support the new storage
- Formatting storage devices if needed
- Configuring storage for use, including RAID sets, LUNs and spares
- Allocating storage LUNs and LUN masking and mapping
- Configuring switch zoning and other security items
- Updating notification, alert, and monitoring software
- Allocating storage to servers, volume managers, and filesystems
- Updating backup schedules and mirroring schemes for data protection
- Updating disaster recovery plans and assessment management documents

While configuration and provisionment of storage can be done using different vendor-supplied tools, this can be cumbersome, requiring multiple screens and windows. Storage network managers can provide a level of abstraction over the various vendor-supplied element and device managers to perform common tasks across multiple components.

Another aspect of configuration management is change control, which includes keeping track of what is changing and what has changed. Change control involves determining ahead of time what will be changed and how it will be changed, including how and where the changes are staged. This could involve keeping different versions of configuration and changes as well as prestaging changes, called turnovers. Part of the change control process can involve identifying fallback plans and when to invoke them—for example, some number of tasks will be performed during an upgrade and it is determined that two hours will be needed to complete them, including time to restart servers or components. It is further determined in the change control process that, at some point, a decision needs to be made to continue with the changes or fall off (back out) of the changes to ensure that the system backed up when needed. For a switch this could mean that at a certain point in an upgrade, you will have to revert to an old firmware or old configuration such as zone changes. Having redundant paths and components helps for availability, performance, and maintenance to maintain accessibility.

11.4.2 Resource tracking and reporting (SRM and xLM)

Storage resource management and reporting tools help to facilitate life-cycle management of information, data, and storage. The following are questions to consider:

- Are some of your filesystems lacking free capacity?
- Are mailboxes on your e-mail systems filling up?
- Are backups taking longer and having a high failure rate?
- Is there a large amount of storage not accessed in the last year?
- Are some databases running slowly and the bottleneck not known?

The objective of SRM and xLM is to understand which capabilities exist, how they are being used, where they are being used, and who is using which storage resources. These resources include disk space capacity, bandwidth activity, switch ports, and network interfaces. Resource activity includes server views of what is being used from the server in terms of filesystem, files, which applications are using which resources, and related information. Information from storage devices includes which data is being accessed from which servers as well as activity information.

Information that is collected by operating system–supplied and vendor-supplied element and device managers can be combined into spreadsheets or databases to create history and summary views. Vendor-supplied profiling and data collection tools can provide an expanded view into the storage network and how the resources are being consumed. Information should be available in real time as well as from a historical perspective, with composite views across different devices.

SRM tools can be used to indicate where the storage exists, who it is allocated to, what the quotas are if they exist for usage, when the data was last accessed, and what size it is. Additional information includes what the I/O activity is in terms of bandwidth, I/O size, and average response time associated with the files and their associated volumes. Design tools can be used as part of the data collection process in addition to design activities. Design tools that work with various vendor hardware and storage networking components can be used to collect information on available resources in conjunction with other tools. SRM tools can be useful for validating design as well as for collecting information on existing environments.

A composite view allows you to see from a high level "hot spots" at the device level and then focus in on exactly where the hot spot is coming from: which file, which application. Multiple tools can be combined to derive this information or the use of an advanced monitoring piece of software can provide the same functions. These views can be historical, looking at different periods of time for different durations and workloads. If your environment performs resource usage chargeback, then you will need tools, or you can develop your own, to support this activity. Knowing which equipment you have and where it is located is important to support asset management tasks. It is useful to know which equipment is scheduled to come off of lease so that data migration and movement can be planned. Similarly, knowing which equipment is purchased and its depreciation can be useful when negotiating with vendors for storage upgrades.

11.4.3 Data access software (filesystems)

Filesystems and database access systems are not unique to storage networks, since they are part of typical server and storage environments. Storage networking does enable and support additional data access capabilities, including global or distributed filesystems, NAS, and clustered filesystems. Filesystems are available as part of operating systems and as layered third-party software. Filesystems can provide advanced functionality, including high-performance access functions for e-mail and database applications. SAN filesystems support shared access from multiple servers for shared read and write access of data. Clustered filesystems provide access to data for homogeneous servers (all the same type) in a clustered environment for shared read and write access of data. WAN filesystems that utilize caching to enable remote access to appear local use specialized appliances. Filesystem access methods include NFS, CIFs, AFS, and DFS.

Storage can be allocated to filesystems via a volume manager or operating system utilities. Some filesystem utilities include backup and restore, archiving, shelving, and HSM. Additional tools include defragmenters and profiling tools to characterize and perform SRM and life-cycle management functions. Data migration tools can be used to move data from different storage volumes and devices as needed.

11.4.4 Volume managers

Volume managers provide a level of abstraction and virtualization of storage to severed filesystems. Volume managers have traditionally been deployed on servers as part of operating systems or as layered utilities from independent software vendors. Volume managers group physical storage devices and LUNs into logical volume groups and logical volumes that can be allocated to filesystems for use. Volume managers enable multiple storage devices to be joined for data protection and mirrored to remote locations for business continuance. Volume managers enable volumes and filesytems to be expanded, as well as the physical devices to be replaced without impact to the applications. Volume management functions can also be located in appliances and in intelligence switches.

11.4.5 Event monitoring and notification mechanisms

The ability to monitor events and respond to alerts and alarms to determine when storage networking components need attention is a common management necessity. Notification can be done via e-mail, SNMP MIB traps, APIs, phone home, and other mechanisms via device managers and other tools. Timely problem detection, isolation, and determination can help to facilitate replacement and repair to improve availability. These tools help you determine that there is a problem, where there is a problem, the nature of a problem, and, perhaps, provide suggestions as to what to do to correct the problem. More advanced monitoring tools may have event tracking capabilities to issue problem tickets and track incidents through resolution.

The following list shows some common storage networking management tool interfaces and access methods.

- Dial-in, dial-out access for diagnostics
- SNMP alerts (notifications), traps (set values), and gets (reads)
- Predictive monitoring utilities to track errors and incidents
- IETF (formerly Fibre Alliance) SNMP MIB and other MIBs
- Phone and call home, e-mail home, pagers, wireless, and other
- Vendor-specific APIs and mechanisms, including FC-SWAPI
- Protocol-specific, including FICON CUP, FC-GS3, and FC-GS4
- Event and activity logs and third-party manager tools
- Diagnostics and detection equipment to test how things are running
- Monitoring of storage networking components as well as environmental items, including power, cooling, ventilation, and physical security

11.4.6 Server clustering and failover tools

For high availability, servers can be clustered using failover and clustering techniques. These include failover from an active server to a standby server and failover of applications to an active server. Failover can be used to contain a fault and simplify failover operations to a different host adapter, I/O interface path, or storage device. Failover can also involve moving workload and processing from one location to another. Clusters can be on a local basis or wide area basis (also known as stretch and geoclusters). Clusters can be active/passive, where standby servers need to be rebooted or restarted (including applications). Clusters can also be active/active, providing transparent failover of applications and processing. Clusters need some form of heartbeat communication facility to determine the health and status of servers. Distance plays a factor in how effective a wide area cluster can respond to failover between locations while dealing with latency of heartbeat commutations. For metropolitan and wide area clusters pay attention to the heartbeat communication needs of the clustering software being used.

Storage networks enable clustering and high-availability solutions to be supported over longer distances as well as allowing the support of more devices and servers. Some characteristics of clustering tools include:

- Supplied by the operating system vendor or via a third-party provider

- Failover to alternate standby or active server of workload and applications
- Active/active clustering with failover of applications and activity
- Active/passive clustering with standby and restart of applications
- Shared resource clusters with distributed lock management
- Clustered databases and filesystems, including grid computing
- Continuous access systems and fault-tolerant systems
- Path manager failover of devices, including adapters
- Multipath I/O drivers from operating system and server vendors
- Multipath I/O drivers from storage and data management vendors
- Load balancing and alternate pathing in the event of a failure or for maintenance
- Aggregation of pathing to support adapter trunking for performance

11.4.7 Data and storage security

Storage and storage networking security are covered in more depth in Chapter 13; however, some common security functions include:

- Security of servers, applications, filesystems, volumes, and devices
- Authentication, authorization, and access policies
- Encryption and security access devices and appliances
- Zoning and network protection capabilities
- Volume and LUN mapping and masking
- Partitions and logical domains and virtual switches

11.4.8 Data protection and retention (backup, archive, replication)

Some functions tied to data protection include backup, archive, and replication of data to alternate locations. Various tools, including some integrated and some nonintegrated ones, implemented in hardware and software support these activities. Some management activities associated with data protection include:

- Backups to disk, tape, or other medium in order to protect against data loss, corruption, or accidental deletion

- Mirroring and replication to provide and maintain data accessibility
- Backups (full, incremental, snapshots, differential, image, and application based)
- Backup of networked attached storage devices using NDMP
- Disk to tape, disk to disk (D2D), disk to disk to tape (D2D2T) backups, and to other backup mediums
- Long-term data retention and protection for compliance
- Mirroring and replication of data to local and remote locations

Data protection topics, including RAID, backup, and mirroring, are covered in Chapter 12.

11.5 Storage Management Interface Specification (SMI-S)

Part of the cost and complexity associated with management is that layers upon layers of software are being used to manage the management tasks, including APIs, alerts, monitoring, and complex configuration. The proliferation of different vendor APIs and agents has added to the cost and complexity of storage management for vendors and users alike. The different vendor tools have a variety of interfaces for local as well as remote procedure calls, object models, and transports. Instead of developing features, time and resources are spent on developing, testing, and supporting interfaces. This has led to the increase in the size of test matrices, user frustration, more certification work, more updates and patches, delayed interoperability, and delayed features.

While not totally to blame, one of the complexities (and complexity equals cost) with management and interoperability is the proliferation of vendor-specific APIs and management interfaces. Many of the improvements in interoperability have come at the expense of having to support different APIs. This has improved somewhat now that most vendors are willing, or at least beginning, to share their APIs. It can be said that if SMIS and CIM do nothing else for the industry, they will get vendors to share their APIs to enable functionality. In Figure 11.3, on the left, is a traditional API-based model for management, where various independent hardware vendors and independent software vendors share and support each others APIs. On the right is a CIM SMIS model, showing a much more simplified model, where intelligence is in the management model as opposed to having to be written or added to an application.

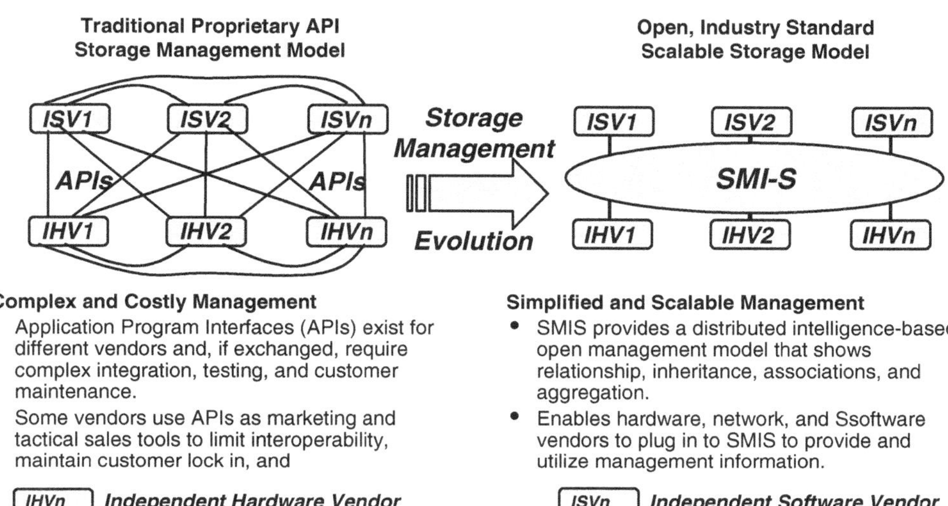
Traditional Proprietary API
Storage Management Model
ISV1
ISV2
ISVn
APIs
APIs
IHV1
IHV2
IHVn
Storage
Management
Evolution
Open, Industry Standard
Scalable Storage Model
ISV1
ISV2
ISVn
SMI-S
IHV1
IHV2
IHVn
Complex and Costly Management
• Application Program Interfaces (APIs) exist for different vendors and, if exchanged, require complex integration, testing, and customer maintenance.
• Some vendors use APIs as marketing and tactical sales tools to limit interoperability, maintain customer lock in, and
IHVn Independent Hardware Vendor
Simplified and Scalable Management
• SMIS provides a distributed intelligence-based open management model that shows relationship, inheritance, associations, and aggregation.
• Enables hardware, network, and Ssoftware vendors to plug in to SMIS to provide and utilize management information.
ISVn Independent Software Vendor

Figure 11.3 *Complexity with traditional API-based management.*

In Figure 11.4, we see the amount of information growing and the impact of increasing storage and storage networking costs. The chart shows the amount of actual storage space being used by applications, along with the total forecasted and available storage. The difference between total storage and used storage may include free space for on-demand provisioning, forecasted growth, and space for performance and housekeeping chores.

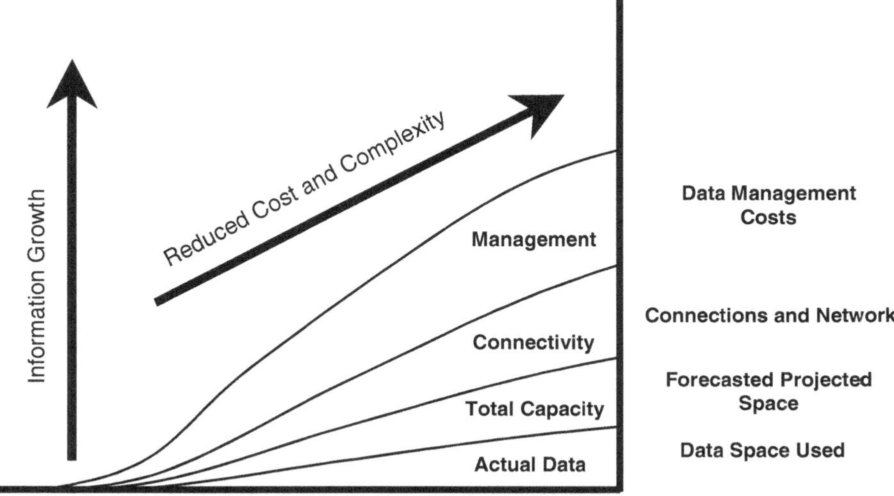
Information Growth
Reduced Cost and Complexity
Management
Connectivity
Total Capacity
Actual Data
Data Management Costs
Connections and Network
Forecasted Projected Space
Data Space Used

Figure 11.4 *Reducing storage networking costs and enhancing scaling.*

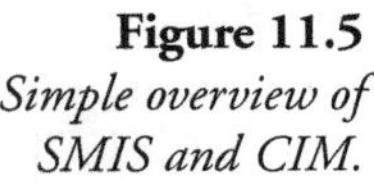

Figure 11.5 *Simple overview of SMIS and CIM.*

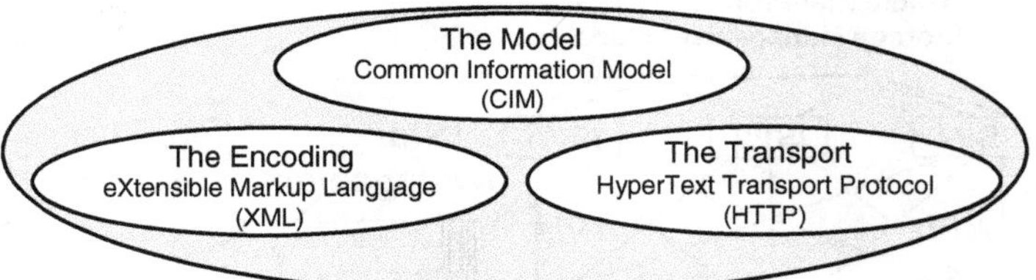

While the overall amount of storage is increasing with greater densities, the cost for storage per megabyte and gigabyte continues to decrease. Similarly, the connectivity costs to attach the storage to a server(s) continue to decrease as more ports become available with more functionality and improvements in distance support.

SMIS addresses the complexity of current management approaches as well as adding intelligence and inheritance to management beyond the APIs and MIBs. SMIS is an enabler for new functionality and supports plug-and-play frameworks and tools.

In Figure 11.5, SMIS leverages common transports, definition languages, and the information model. SMIS is based upon the Common Information Model (CIM) defined by the Data Management Task Force (DMTF). The encoding and definition language used for SMIS is XML, which implements the various schemata that define the storage network objects and components. The transport facility for communicating SMIS information between providers and clients is HTTP, which is also used as an Internet Web transport. SMIS allows for further growth of functionality and for extensions for various devices to be added.

Figure 11.6 shows how various storage networking components and resources can be managed using SMIS with providers (storage devices, switches, and tape devices) and clients (backup and SRM tools). Additional information about SMIS can be found at the SNIA Web site (www.snia.org).

11.6 Virtualization and abstraction

Virtualization, while packaged and applied on different functions and methods, is not new to most computing environments. Yet virtualization, as with other technology trends, has taken on different meanings. A generally accepted virtualization description is any technology that hides useful functions behind an interface that conceals the details of how they are

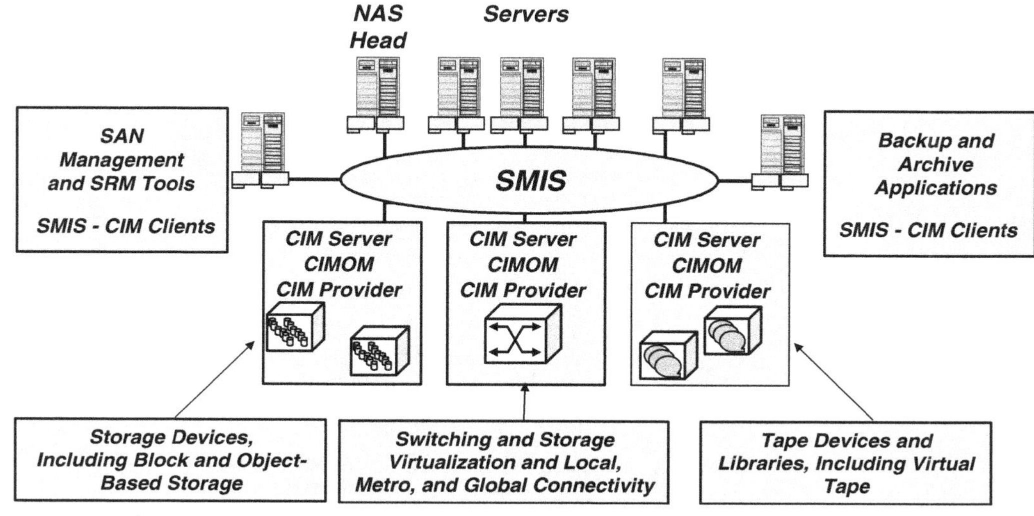

Figure 11.6 *SNIA Storage Management Initiative Specification (SMIS) example.*

implemented. Virtualization can be used to abstract a server's view of storage, including the location of the storage resources.

In Figure 11.7, storage virtualization is shown with physical devices (1), including aggregation of multiple devices (2) by storage subsystems. These are mapped into a virtual storage environment (3), which could be a virtualization appliance or volume manager. Logical or virtual storage is mapped into filesystems (4) that are accessed by different servers. The storage can be backed up as well as mirrored to other volumes for data protection (5), where multiple generations (6) of volumes can be managed. This can be used to support D2D and D2D2T backups, and storage-based recovery appliances.

Some functions that can be addressed with storage virtualization, regardless of where it is located or how it is performed, include:

- Backup and recovery of data and disaster avoidance
- Data migration to support business functions and technology replacements
- Security and pooling of storage resources across different volumes
- LUN and volume mapping and masking
- Resolving interoperability and functionality between vendor products

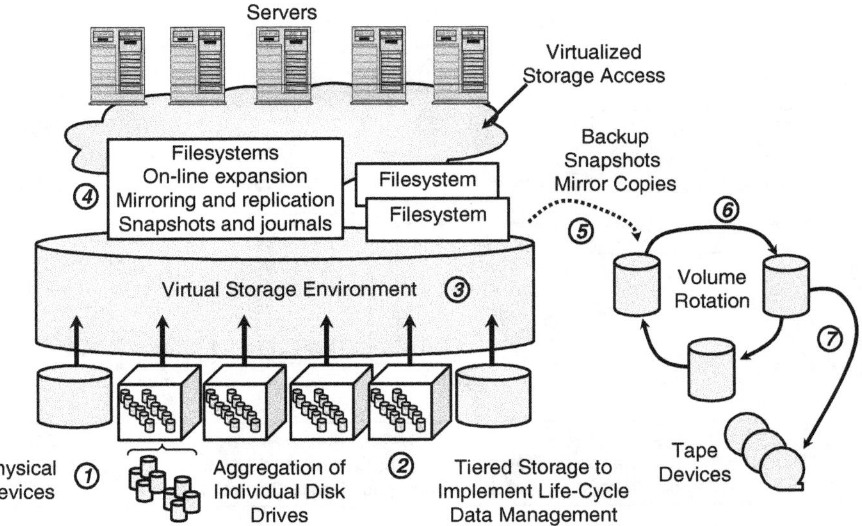

Figure 11.7 *Some virtualization examples.*

- Pooling of storage across multiple technologies to improve utilization
- RAID and mechanisms to maintain data protection and accessibility
- On-line expansion of volumes and filesystems
- Data migration and movement capabilities to support storage replacement and workload movement and consolidation
- Emulation to provide transparent access to applications of different types of hardware and various devices and technology, along with virtual I/O paths

Virtualization can be applied and implemented in different locations to support storage and storage networks, including the following:

Data virtualization

- Database management and access systems
- File and object (application specific, location independent)–based data access and storage (CAS)
- Distributed filesystems (NAS), including NFS, CIFS, AFS, and DFS
- Internet and Web browsers, PDAs, and multifunction telephones
- XML data markup and description facilities

Host server and application virtualization

- Virtual memory to support larger applications on small memory-based systems
- Logical partitions (LPARS), known as virtual domains on processors
- Guest operating systems (Linux on VM and zOS)
- Emulators to enable operating systems to run on various hardware
- Virtual I/O drivers to mask uniqueness devices and capabilities
- Terminal and access program emulator utilities
- Application Programming Interface (API) and middleware
- Virtual device adapters on servers

On the server side, storage virtualization includes volume managers that can aggregate LUNs and physical devices into volume groups and filesystems, perform RAID functions for mirroring and replication, facilitate volume expansion and media replacement, and provide a general layer of abstraction between applications and the underlying storage.

A goal of virtualization storage and storage networking management is to mask the location of where the storage is located as well as how to access it. There are various levels of functionality tied to this, including masking the complexities of different vendor technologies and capabilities. Some activities involving storage and virtual services advancement include the SNIA SMIS as a common mechanism for storage and storage networking management, interchange by vendors, and support for different management frameworks and SNMP MIB interfaces.

FICON can utilize the same E_Port for FICON Cascade over the same ISLs that are used for open systems FCP traffic. Another example is how Linux running on a zSeries can perform I/O using ESCON, FICON, and now FCP (SCSI on Fibre Channel). An example of a mixed storage network supporting mainframe and open systems traffic over local, metropolitan, and wide area interfaces is shown in Figure 11.8.

A common method for deploying storage virtualization is using storage devices providing virtual disks, or volumes, and other storage management functions, including mirroring, parity protection, data migration, and availability. Virtual Tape Systems (VTS) is another example of virtualizing tape functions so that a server and applications think they are accessing tape, when, in fact, they are accessing a virtual tape device. VTS virtualizes tape functions by having a "virtual tape drive" appear to the server and

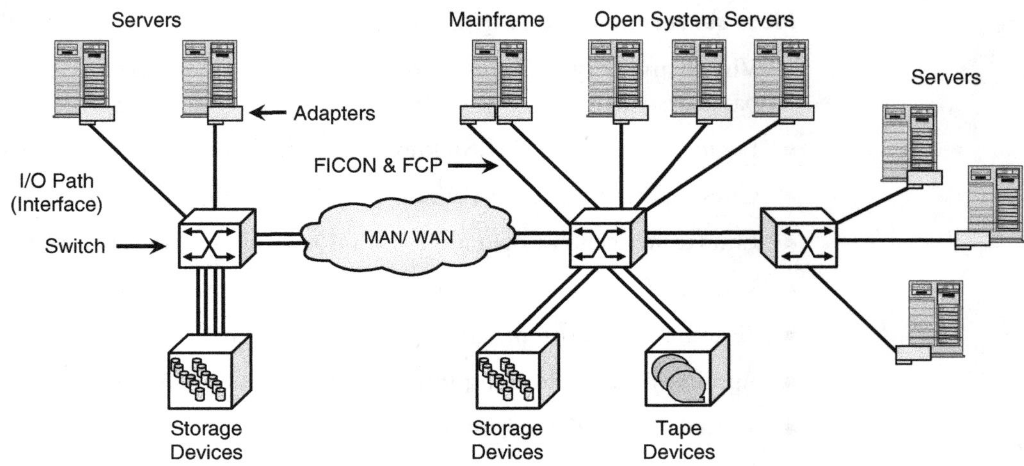

Figure 11.8 *A virtual storage network with mixed open systems and mainframe.*

application while the actual I/O is done to disk and cache memory for subsequent movement to actual tape. New solutions are available that utilize low cost, large capacity ATA/SATA disk drives for backup and recovery appliances.

Storage virtualization can be implemented at the server, in the fabric (switches and directors), using appliances, or in storage devices (disk and tape). This form of storage virtualization utilizes appliances (similar to NAS file sharing) to facilitate storage resource sharing across multiple servers and multiple storage devices. Appliance-based storage virtualization has been available for the open system environments for a few years using either in band (appliance sits in the data path) or out of band (server sits out of the data path as a metadata server).

So how can you tell if virtualization and, in particular, some form of storage virtualization is right for you? Some questions to ask yourself and potential vendor partners regarding virtualization for your environment include:

- Is it disruptive to the rest of your environment or does it integrate seamlessly?
- Does it enhance activities or increase the management and people workload and cost?
- Does it present some form of economical or enabling benefit?
- What are some easy target applications for deployment to gain confidence and learn where virtualization can be used?

- What can be justified with a business case to support the implementation of virtualization and storage services?

11.6.1 Fabric and network based

Virtualization can be implemented in different locations for different functions. There is a technology shift toward moving more intelligence, including virtualization and storage services, into switches and appliances. Storage virtualization can be implemented using out-of-band or in-band techniques. Out of band separates the command and control from the data path using an appliance server and server-based agents. The appliance is used to control access and coordinate functions from the various servers and the storage resources. With in band the command and control exist in the data path. First-generation deployments have utilized both in-band and out-of-band implementations in appliances, with the trend to move the functions into intelligent switches. Fabric-based storage virtualization and service architectures include monolithic processor card (PC on a blade), either tightly integrated with the back-end switching engine core crossbar or simply drawing power from the switching device. These cards can then, in turn, host current-generation storage virtualization applications traditionally hosted on appliance processors. Another architecture is to utilize intelligent processor cards to host current- and next-generation storage virtualization applications to help offload processing and offset the negative effects of traditional in-band virtualization with tighter integration in the fabric. More intelligence is being added at the port for high-volume common functions without being penalized economically and performance-wise on a port basis, while providing high-performance processing and scalability core to perform heavy thinking functions for more advanced functions with open interfaces, virtual switching with logical partitions, and domains to isolate workload.

In Figure 11.9, an out-of-band example is shown with servers having an agent to communicate with an appliance. The agent on the server communicates (1) with the appliance meta and control data and information. The server communicates with the storage device (2) to move data.

An advantage of the out-of-band approach is that control information is not passed in the data stream to enhance scaling. A downside is that a separate interface and component are needed for management and control. Storage virtualization (storage services) can be:

- Block, file, and object-based access and storage
- Server based, appliance based, storage based, and switch fabric based

- Virtual tape and backup recovery systems
- Virtual optical media to support Write Once Read Many (WORM) needs and compliance regulations
- Device virtualization and emulation, including disk, tape, and optical
- Virtual switches (VSANs), partitions, and logical domains
- Virtual lanes and virtual output queues
- Virtual adapters and interfaces for servers

Another approach is in band, shown in Figure 11.10, using two examples. The one on the left shows an in-band appliance between the storage devices and switch. The server accesses the in-band appliance (1) via a switch and then the appliance accesses (2) the storage devices. On the right, a variation is shown where the servers access (3) the in-band appliance using one set of ports, and the storage is accessed (4) via another set of ports. An advantage of in band is the elimination of the need for specialized agents. The downside can be performance scaling, depending on implementation.

Virtualization functions are moving into storage networking switches and appliances using a fast path and control path architecture supported by the Fabric Application Interface Standard (FAIS). In Figure 11.11, an example is shown where data flows from the server (1) to a storage device (2) via a switch port for standard switching functions. For more advanced functions the fast path utilizes the control path to perform specialized functions, including data mirroring, snapshots, and other heavy-thinking functions. A variation of the in-band and out-of-band implementations with appliances is to repackage a card with PC-like functionality (memory, PCI

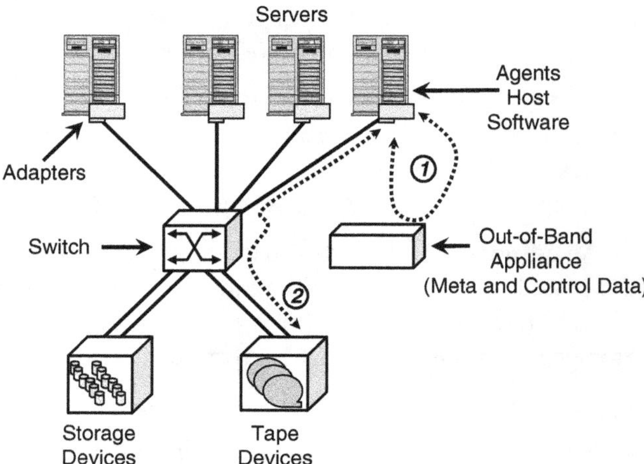

Figure 11.9 *Out-of-band virtualization example.*

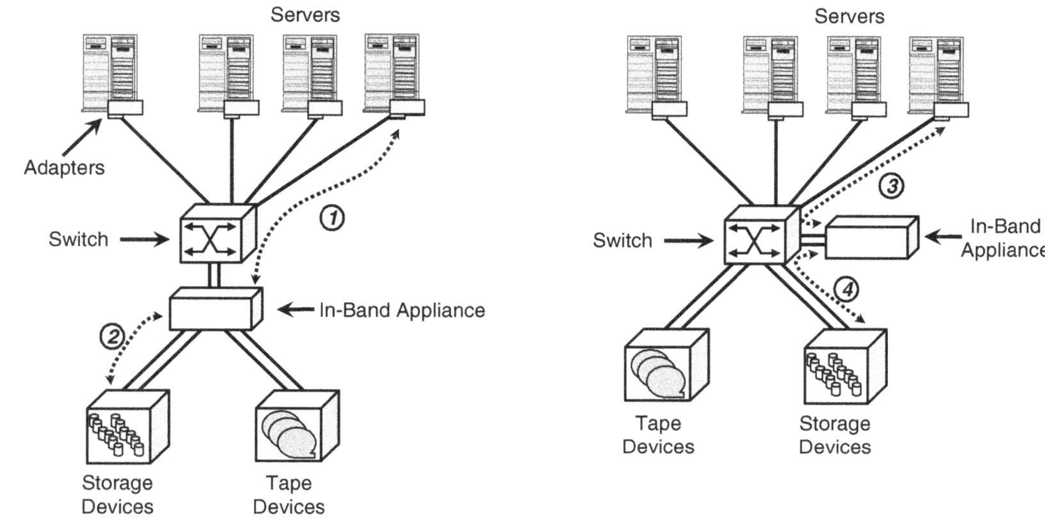

Figure 11.10 *In-band virtualization example.*

interface, Pentium or faster processor) as a blade (computer on a card). This approach is referred to as a monolithic, or cache centric, approach using commercial off-the-shelf technology (COTS). The next-generation products will have specialized processor cards as blades, which, on the surface, may appear as general-purpose monolithic blades; however, they will have specialized processors to support storage-specific functions.

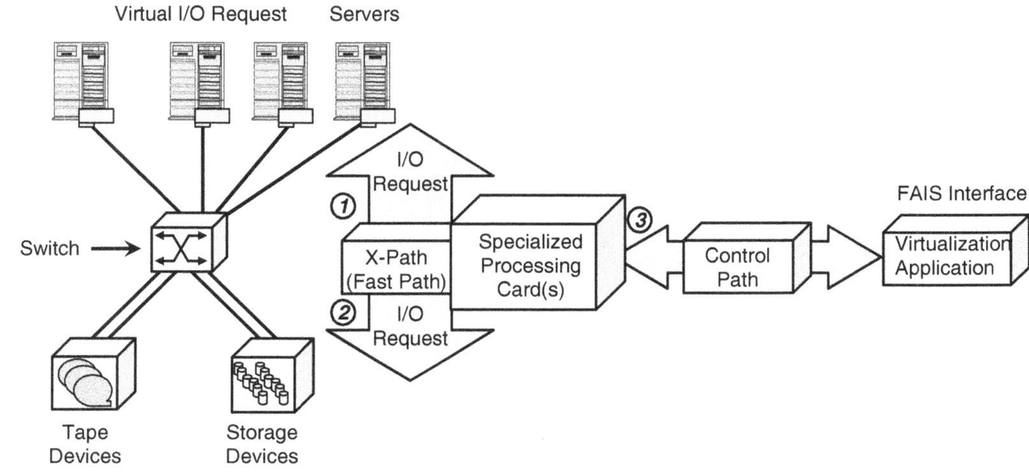

Figure 11.11 *Fast path virtualization example.*

11.6.2 Fabric Application Interface Specification

Building on the momentum of the SMIS initiative, a working group under the ANSI T11 committee is working to expedite the standards process for fabric-based applications. The Fabric Application Interface Specification (FAIS) is being jointly developed as a standard interface by both leading and emerging storage networking vendors. By having a standardized API set, developers will be relieved of the burden of having to do a unique port to each API of specific devices and products. FAIS-enabled products include switches, directors, appliances, routers, gateways, and other storage networking devices. FAIS defines a library of standard functions that can be accessed by storage management applications such as a backup or disk mirroring. The FAIS library translates the application request to perform a function to a device-specific message that is passed to an FAIS services provider in a switch, gateway, or router.

In Figure 11.12, an FAIS topology model is shown with an interface to various applications via the FAIS API. The API accesses a library of routines that can be located and provided in different devices. Many leading industry and new vendors under the ANSI T11 committee to enable development of fabric-based applications are supporting FAIS. Additional information about FAIS and T11 activity can be found at http://www.t11.org/index.htm.

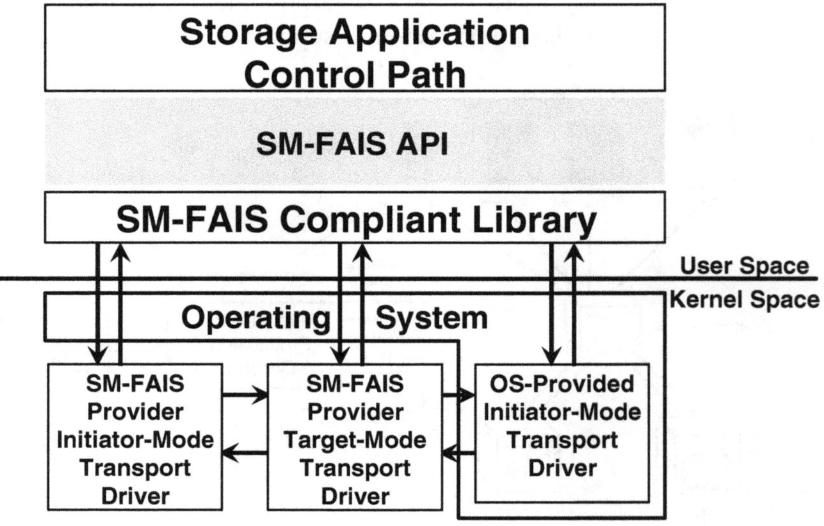

Figure 11.12 *Fabric Application Interface Standard (FAIS) topology.*

11.7 Assessing storage management tools

There are different tools for performing different functions. There can be a trade-off of having a tool that can do several things well as compared with multiple tools that do their single functions very well. A single tool might be very good at reporting, which may appeal to managers and resource planners, while an advanced configuration tool might be a better fit for those having to do those functions. The old saying of using the right tool for the right job applies to storage networking. Tools are not cheap; however, their costs should be compared with a business case to offset the expense of not using a tool. Some functions and features to look at for different categories of storage networking management tools are shown in Table 11.1.

Table 11.1 *Storage and Storage Networking Management Tool Criteria*

Criteria	Vendor A	Vendor B
Storage reporting and utilization		
Bandwidth management and allocation		
LUN creation and management		
Networking provisioning		
Storage provisioning		
Tape and device volume management		
Zoning and security functions		
Archiving and data retention		
Backup and recovery capacity		
Cluster and server failover		
Disk-to-disk backups		
Mirroring and replication		
Path management and failover		
Access control and policy management		
Automated discovery of components		
Design and analysis tools		
Error analysis and reporting		

Table 11.1 *Storage and Storage Networking Management Tool Criteria (continued)*

Criteria	Vendor A	Vendor B
Launch of third-party tools and element managers		
Single point of management for all systems		
Visualization of all components		
Capacity management and tracking tools		
Performance analyzers and probes		
Performance reporting tools		
Storage and file analyzers and profilers		
Abstraction and virtualization		

These items, along with others, could be built into a matrix to help categorize and assess tools for different functions. (For more information about storage management tools refer to the associated Web site for this book (www.storageio.com). While a single tool may not have support for all of these functions, multiple tools from the same vendor, or different tools from different vendors with interoperability, may address your various needs. Assessment of tools may be an evolutionary process to find the correct management tools for new and emerging storage needs and business considerations.

11.8 Some general management topics

The size and complexity of your storage network will have an impact on the management tasks you need to perform. Your storage network may be self-contained, simplifying some of the tasks of routine maintenance, data backup, storage allocation, and other day-to-day tasks. On the other hand, your storage network may be complex, with multiple vendor equipment and software supporting different applications at several locations. You may need multiple management tools to perform the same or similar functions at different locations. Have a clear understanding of what your management needs and priorities are before looking at tools. Have a list of what your current management challenges and objectives are, along with a business case and cost-benefit analysis if possible. Understand your wants and your needs and have business backing and support. Some additional items to consider regarding storage networking management include:

- Management systems have underlying databases that need protection.
- Implement naming standard conventions to help identify resources, devices, their locations, application purposes, and functions.
- Tell your vendors what you want, what you need.
- Find out from your vendors what their road map is and how they will work with you.
- Task schedulers and policy managers can be utilized to perform common tasks, adding a level of automation.
- Look for areas to automate that are common occurrence activities and events first.
- Develop a storage management strategy to coincide with your storage strategy.
- Identify where and how different types of virtualization can help you achieve management goals.

11.9 Chapter summary

As with storage networks, management of storage networks is a diverse topic; it can range from simple tasks to complex activities at multiple locations requiring many people. The level of management and type of management tools needed for your storage network will vary based on its size and complexity as well as your needs. Balance the benefits of an overall storage management tool set to that of individual tools to perform specific tasks. You can always start with a strategy using tools currently available to address specific needs with specific business benefits. Over time you can enlarge your storage management strategy to more advanced tools and frameworks as they evolve and as your business case develops to implement them.

What This Chapter Will Do For You

This chapter looks at essential techniques and technologies for protecting and maintaining access to data. Some items you will learn about in this chapter include:

- All data is not equal in value so why spend the same amount to protect it?
- RAID and mirroring are not replacements for backup to some other medium
- How much downtime and data loss can you afford?
- The importance of compression to reduce storage and networking costs
- Alternative, cost-saving technologies for long-term data protection and retention

12

Protecting Data

12.1 Overview

Data protection, for those not involved with it, may be perceived as an expense item that does not add value to the business. For those who have not experienced loss of data, whether due to accidental deletion, data corruption, theft, or by other means, there may be a tendency to take data protection for granted. This chapter takes a look at some techniques supported and facilitated by storage networks to protect and maintain accessibility to data.

12.2 Protecting data accessibility

Availability is the combination of all components that make up a solution—from the server, application, storage subsystem, network, and storage interfaces. While redundancy and high availability of a single component are important, particularly to contain faults, it is the combination of all components that determines how availability should be looked at.

Some approaches to protecting data include:

- Logical and physical security (refer to Chapter 13)
- Device and component media redundancy
- Data mirroring, replication (local and remote)
- Backup, restore, archiving, and data retention
- Snapshots, journal filesystems, point-in-time copies

Redundant devices and components help to protect data by primarily maintaining accessibility. By having redundant components, accessibility to the data can be maintained and can help isolate faults (fault containment) from spreading into event chains. By using combinations of redundant devices and components, data can be protected by creating copies of the data on different media, utilizing Redundant Arrays of Inexpensive/Independent Disks (RAID), mirroring, and replication. Some examples of device and component redundancy to protect data and accessibility include:

- Server and application failover and clustering
- Redundant I/O paths with automated failover capability
- Mirrored- and RAID-protected server memory with optional battery backup power
- Mirrored read and write cache on storage subsystems, with battery backup power supplies
- Redundant storage I/O controllers operating in active mode (active/active) or one active and others in standby mode (active/passive)
- Hot swappable components (power, cooling, control, devices)
- N+1 architectures for ultrahigh availability environments
- Devices with high-availability features, including ability to load and activate new firmware on-line

Redundant devices and components help to maintain data accessibility and provide stable platforms for supporting storage networking applications. Storage networks offer the ability to span distances, support multiple servers, and provide performance to scale capacity and bandwidth. By leveraging storage networking capabilities, traditional data-protection techniques (including backup, restore, archive, and mirroring) can be leveraged to address distance, scaling, and performance challenges. Protecting data involves both maintaining accessibility to it, with redundant complements and active copies of the data (mirroring), as well as having copies of the data from a specific point in time. Replication and mirroring are not 100 percent safeguards or alternatives to back up by themselves, so you still need to be able to protect against corruption of data, deletion, and other events (such as propagation across mirrors). While RAID protects data primarily from an accessibility standpoint in case of a component failure, including loss of a disk drive, additional protection is still needed. RAID and mirroring by themselves do not protect the data in case of accidental deletion, data corruption, computer virus, or overwriting with a newer version of data or events that impact the data.

To help make a point: If you have data mirrored or replicated between two locations or protected using RAID, then if a file is deleted, it is deleted at both locations; if you have data corruption, you have it at both locations. Hence, while mirroring and RAID protect and maintain accessibility by maintaining copies of the data, they also can mirror data problems. This is where and why mirroring and RAID should be combined with other data-protection techniques, including snapshots, point-in-time backups, file and volume backups, archiving, and off-line copies of mirrored volumes (known by some as business continuance devices and volumes).

Table 12.1 shows some impacts to applications as a result of different data-protection techniques and approaches.

Table 12.1 *Data Protection Impact to Applications*

	Redundant Components and Devices	RAID	Mirroring Replication Remote Copy	Backup Restore	Snapshot Point-in-Time Copy
Availability after component failure	Yes	Yes Redundant paths	Yes Redundant paths	No	No
Availability after data corruption	No	No	Using off-line mirror copies	Requires restore	After rollback of journal
Application remains available after data deletion	No	No	Only if an off-line mirror volume is brought on-line	Once data is restored	Once snapshot or journal rollback is complete
Application remains available after site failure	No Some form of remote redundancy and failover needed	No	Yes Assuming failover and redundant access	Once data is restored	Once data is restored and recovered at remote location
Applications remain available during protection operations	Yes	Yes	Yes	Varies by type of backup	Varies by type of backup
Application and data availability in use during data protection	N/A	N/A	Application-knowledgeable tools required	Application-knowledgeable tools required	Application-knowledgeable tools required
Ability to create off-line copies for other use	N/A	N/A	Mirrors can be frozen and split for other use	Yes	Combined with other types of data protection

Table 12.2 *Various Data-Protection Schemata and Characteristics*

	Redundant Components and Devices	RAID	Mirroring Replication Remote Copy	Backup Restore	Snapshot Point-in-Time Copy
Near real-time recovery from component failure	Yes For failover scenarios	Yes	Yes	No Restore from disk or tape	Rapid restore if disk is still intact
Recovery from data deletion and corruption and specific points in time	N/A	No	Requires off-line copy, snapshot, or some other protection	Yes However, may be time delayed	Yes However, may be time delayed
Recovery of partial information without complete recovery	N/A	No	No Requires off-line copy, snapshot, or some other protection	Yes However, may be time delayed	Yes However, may be time delayed

In Table 12.2, various data-protection schemata and characteristics are shown. Note that while snapshots and journal backups can speed the backup and recovery process, they may need to be combined with other protection techniques. This is similar to RAID and mirroring providing accessibility protection; however, they need to be combined with other protection techniques, including backup, archiving, and snapshots.

To improve resiliency while providing performance with data protection over various distances a combination of synchronous mirroring and asynchronous mirroring and some form of backup may be applicable. For example, locally RAID-protected storage to isolate against local device and component failure may be utilized. Local storage could be mirrored synchronously to another location 100km away using metropolitan and wide area storage networking interfaces for real-time copy protection. By using asynchronous mirroring, a third copy of the data can be made to another site, which could be hundreds to thousands of kilometers away, using slower wide area interfaces. Various combinations of backup and snapshots could be utilized at the primary, secondary, and tertiary sites to provide rapid recovery as needed. The amount and level of sophistication for protecting your data will depend on its importance and value, what you can recreate, and may vary across different applications. Keeping in mind that not all data is equal in value and that different applications have various requirements for accessibility, you may utilize different protection schemes for different data and applications.

12.2.1 Sequential access media

In Chapter 7, various storage networking devices were discussed, including magnetic disk and tape. Traditional data-protection techniques have relied on backing up magnetic disk data to magnetic tape. Another medium that is used for protecting data, particularly for long-term retention and archival purposes, is optical media. Disk-to-disk mirroring and replication is another approach that is used for protecting data accessibility over various distances, from local to wide area.

Data storage media can be categorized and grouped as sequential access and random access. Sequential access media refer to data storage media that are accessed sequentially, compared with random and direct access. An example of sequential media includes magnetic tape utilizing different formats and packaging. An example of random or direct access media includes spinning magnetic disks as well as optical media (including CDs and DVDs). Today, media can be erasable (read and write) as well as WORM based for data preservation and retention purposes. Traditional magnetic disk and tape have been erasable and reusable; however, recent enhancements available with some products enable WORM capabilities for both disk and tape. WORM enables magnetic media to be used for regulatory and compliance purposes combined with specialized applications for managing data retention. Another change to data storage and protection is optical media, which used to be WORM based but can now be rewritten.

There have been numerous tape improvements for capacity, performance, physical packaging, reliability, life span, cost, and interoperability during the past 50+ years of magnetic tape being used as a data storage medium—from 10" reels of ½" nine track tape found on mainframes of years ago to what is available now. Linear Tape Open (LTO) format was jointly developed by IBM, HP, and Seagate; it utilizes linear multichannel serpentine (back and forth) recording on ½" tape medium with hardware compression and error correction. Digital Linear Tape (DLT) is a variation of older reel-to-reel tapes packaged to fit into a cartridge. Advanced Intelligent Tape (AIT), developed by Sony in 1996, utilizes helical scan recording—found in 8mm tape devices utilizing a small-format data cartridge. Mammoth, introduced by Exabyte as a follow-on to 8mm tape, utilizes a multichannel helical scan mechanism.

Table 12.3 *Various Tape Media and Characteristics*

Format	Generation	Native Capacity (GB)	Compress Capacity (GB)	Compression Ratio	Data Transfer Rate (MB/sec)	Compressed Transfer Rate (MB/sec)
AIT	SAIT-1	500	1,300	2.6	30	78
AIT	AIT-3	100	260	2.6	12	30
AIT	AIT-2	50	130	2.6	6	15
AIT	AIT-1	35	90	2.6	4	10
DLT	SDLT320	160	320	2.0	16	32
DLT	SDLT220	110	220	2.0	16	32
DLT	DLT8000	40	80	2.0	6	12
DLT	DLTVS160	80	160	2.0	8	16
DLT	DLTVS80	40	80	2.0	3	6
IBM 3590	3590e	60	180	3:1	14	—
IBM 3592	3593	300	900	3:1	40MB/sec	—
LTO	Ultrium-2	200	400	2.0	35	70
LTO	Ultrium-1	100	200	2.0	20	40
Mammoth	Mammoth-2	60	150	2.5	12	30
Mammoth	Mammoth-1	20	40	2.0	3	6
STK 9940	B Model	200	400-800	2–4:1	30	70

Table 12.3 shows various tape media and some common characteristics. This is by no means an exhaustive list of tape media, as there are many other legacy tape types—nine track reel to reel, IBM 348x tape cartridges, and various 8mm formats to name a few. A common question that comes up is whether tape is dead and has disk finally reached the point where tape is no longer needed. For the foreseeable future there is a place for tape as a data-protection and -retention medium given its low cost and ability to store a large amount of data. However, there are challengers in the form of low-cost, high-capacity disk drives with Write Once Read Many (WORM) capabilities as well as various optical media. The dollar economics of using low-cost, high-capacity disk drives and tape are coming closer to each other. The thing to keep in mind is not whether tape is dead or not, but rather that backup and archiving are still needed; however, there are different techniques and

technologies to accomplish those functions. There will continue be a need to be able to protect and preserve data on alternative media, which can be removed or relocated, combined with rapid recovery capabilities.

12.2.2 Random and direct access media

Random access and direct access media refer to media that do not have to be sequentially processed (read) to access the desired location and data. Some may associate random and direct access media with Direct Access Storage Device (DASD), a term used to describe spinning disk storage on IBM mainframes. The common characteristics of random access and direct access media are that data can be accessed directly by positioning (seek) a read/write head at the desired location and start reading or writing data. Examples of random access media include spinning disk drives, optical devices, and solid-state disk. A term that can be confusing or overlapping involving storage networking is direct attached storage. Direct attached storage refers to storage that is attached directly to a server either internally or externally as opposed to storage network (SAN and NAS) attached shared storage. As magnetic tape capacity and performance have improved over time, so have magnetic disk capabilities.

Some enhancements over the past ten years pertaining to magnetic storage include:

- Improvements to reliability and availability (RAS) and MTBF
- An increase in the amount of data that can be moved
- Reduction in response time (latency) so data can be accessed faster
- Open interfaces, including SCSI, Fibre Channel, ATA/SATA
- Reduction in physical size, heat generated, and power consumed
- An increase in capacity from under 1Gb to over 300Gb
- An increase in the speed of the drives from 3,600RPM to 15,000RPM

Optical media enhancements, including CD and DVD, have improved capacities, utilize open formats, and have the flexibility to be WORM or read/write. For more information on sequential and random access media, refer to the Web site for this book (www.storageio.com).

12.2.3 RAID information

Redundant Array of Independent Disks, more commonly known as RAID, primarily is focused on providing data accessibility protection. RAID is not limited to disk drive—hence, Redundant Array of Independent Devices can be applied instead of disks. RAID techniques for improving availability and performance have been applied to magnetic tape as well as to server memory. A similar marketing term has been used by referring to RAID as Redundant Array of Inexpensive Disks. RAID was originally written in 1988 by a team of researchers (Garth Gibson, Randy Katz, David Patterson) at the University of California Berkeley to address reliability issues of disk drives while leveraging the then emerging low-cost open storage devices, including parallel SCSI. A benefit of some RAID configurations enhanced read performance by performing concurrent I/O operations. RAID maintains accessibility to data; but it does not provide an isolated copy of the data for backup and recovery. A copy or backup is still needed; this could be on tape or on a remote copy that is off-line. There is a myth that if you have RAID storage protection, even with remote mirroring, you no longer need to have a backup/recovery plan.

RAID can be implemented in firmware on hardware devices or via software in operating systems, volume managers, virtualization appliances, and by applications. There are different levels of RAID protection that are numbered to provide various characteristic and protection options. These variations include high availability with good performance at the expense of duplicating the number of disk devices needed for good protection, with good read performance using parity protection to reduce the number of disk drives needed for protection. Using mirroring (RAID level 1) data is written to create identical copies on two or more disk devices or volumes. This provides the highest level of availability as well as providing enhanced read performance by handling concurrent I/O requests from different disk drives. RAID 1 also has the highest cost in terms of the number of devices needed, since everything is duplicated.

Another variation of RAID is to utilize parity information to protect data against loss of a single disk device. Parity information is commonly used in data communications, networking, storage, and server memory to correct bit errors. Bit errors, also known as bit error rates, vary by technologies and media, and parity information is used to correct these errors as well as provide some level of protection against loss of bits. A simple parity example is if you have the value 1 on disk A, 2 on disk B, 3 on disk C, and 4 on disk D, using the sum of the digit parity scheme (note that there are many different parity schemes that can be used) would yield (1 + 2 + 3 + 4) = 10. So a RAID protection scheme with four data disks and a parity disk would have the value 10 on the parity disk (disk = P). Should one of the disks fail—for example, disk C (value of 3)—the data for disk C could be regenerated by taking the sum of the surviving disks (A = 1 + B = 2 + D = 4), yielding 7; subtracting that from what is stored on the parity device (P = 10) would give the value of 3 (P = 10 – 7).

This is a very simplified example, with real-world implementations grouping blocks of data together into horizontal stripes across the disks. Each horizontal stripe of data would then have a corresponding parity value stored on the parity disk. Parity data can be on a dedicated disk drive or on a rotating interleaved basis, for example, RAID level 5 (RAID 5). The benefit of spreading the parity on an interleaving basis is to spread the parity overhead across all of the disks. Parity reduces the number of disks from an n + n basis, where n is the number of disks to be protected, to an n + 1 basis. For example, if there were four primary disks to be mirrored using RAID 1, then a total of four disks would be needed (n + n). Using RAID 5 the number of disks would be 4 + 1 or five disks, reducing the number of devices; however, there is also a performance penalty associated with RAID to perform the disk parity I/O operations as well as parity calculations. Using hot spare disk drives, a failed disk device can be rebuilt using parity information (regeneration) to improve availability and resiliency.

Table 12.4 shows various RAID levels and characteristics along with application benefits and impacts. Various RAID levels may be utilized in your environment for different applications having diverse performance and availability needs. Transaction and high-performance data can be placed on RAID 0+1, while data with high-availability needs and read-intensive characteristics can be placed on RAID 1. Reference and read-intensive data can be placed on RAID 5 and combined with write cache to offset write penalty performance.

12.2.4 Local and remote mirroring and replication

Remote mirroring and replication are similar to RAID in that they provide data protection for accessibility of storage. While RAID is focused on protecting data from component failures within a storage subsystem, remote mirroring and replication provide data accessibility protection across locations. The distance supported by remote mirroring and replication can range from a few feet in a computer room, across a campus or city in a metropolitan setting, to across a country or the world for wide area applications. Similar to RAID, remote mirroring and replication provide protection against loss of access due to failure of a component or of a site location. Remote mirroring and replication by themselves do not protect against damage to data and accidental deletion. So copies of the data need

Table 12.4 *RAID Characteristics*

RAID Level	Characteristics	Applications
RAID 0	Disk spreads data across two or more disk drives to improve I/O performance by performing parallel I/O. 1/nth of the data is on each of the disk drives, where n is the number of disks.	Provides high performance for reads and writes, but there is no data redundancy. RAID 0 by itself should only be used for applications that can tolerate loss of access to data or data that can be reproduced from other sources.
RAID 1	Disk mirroring provides data protection and enhanced read performance. RAID 1 mirrors data across two or more disks so that each disk is identical to each other. RAID 1 utilizes n + n protection, doubling the number of devices needed.	Read-intensive OLTP and other transactional data for high performance and high availability. Other applications that can benefit from RAID 1 include e-mail, operating system, application files, and read- and random-intensive environments.
RAID 0+1	Stripe and mirroring of data to provide high performance (stripe) and availability (mirroring) using n + n number of devices. The loss of a disk drive does not impact performance or availability, as would be the case with RAID 0, while the disk stripe enhances performance.	OLTP and I/O-intensive applications requiring high performance and availability. This includes transaction logs, journal files, and database indices, where the cost measurement is based on dollar per I/O compared with dollar per unit of storage.
RAID 1+0 (10)	Similar to RAID 0 + 1, this mirrors and stripes data to provide high performance (stripe) and availability (mirroring) using n + n number of devices. The difference is striping groups of disks together and then mirroring the stripe groups.	OLTP and I/O-intensive applications requiring high performance and availability. This includes transaction logs, journal files, and database indices, where the cost measurement is based on dollar per I/O compared with dollar per unit of storage.
RAID 3	Stripe with dedicated parity at the byte level and has a single dedicated disk drive that stores parity information using an n + 1 approach in terms of the number of devices needed.	This provides good performance for video imaging, geophysics, life science, and other sequential processing applications. RAID 3 is not well suited for applications requiring concurrent I/O operations from multiple users or I/O streams.
RAID 4	Same as RAID 3 but with block-level parity protection.	Using read and write cache, this is well suited for file serving environments.
RAID 5	Disk striping and rotating parity protection using n + 1 number of components provides good availability with good read performance for multiple concurrent users and I/O streams. Using a hot spare disk drive, data can be reconstructed (drive rebuild) to protect against a second failure once completed.	Reduces the number of components required while providing good availability and good performance for reads, with write performance impact if write cache is not utilized. Good applications for RAID 5 include reference data; read-intensive database tables, general file sharing, and Web applications.

to be kept off-line, or combined with journals for recovery. Think of remote mirrors as an extension of a local mirrored volume, except that there is distance separating the data for survivability.

Asynchronous mirroring and replication, whether implemented in firmware (hardware) or software, can be thought of as store and forward protection to reduce the number of I/Os and wait delays. Asynchronous mirroring and replication can be used to span very long distances using IP, SONET/SDH, and other wide area interfaces to support geographical data distribution, backup, and business continuance. This can be tied into a multitier data protection strategy. By using compression, time-delayed writes, grouped writes, cache, and other technology, communication networking costs can be addressed to more effectively utilize bandwidth. For example, in Figure 12.1 a typical activity chart for a remote mirroring application is shown. The peaks represent bandwidth being utilized to support data movement functions, with valleys showing a drop-off in workload. The peaks could represent a nightly fully synchronized or other large data movement activity, with the valleys showing normal workload.

The expanded 24-hour view in Figure 12.1 shows a large spike during what could be a large data movement time frame, with lower peaks during the normal business processing cycles over a 24-hour period. By using bandwidth compression and aggregation techniques, network bandwidth can more effectively be utilized or even reduced.

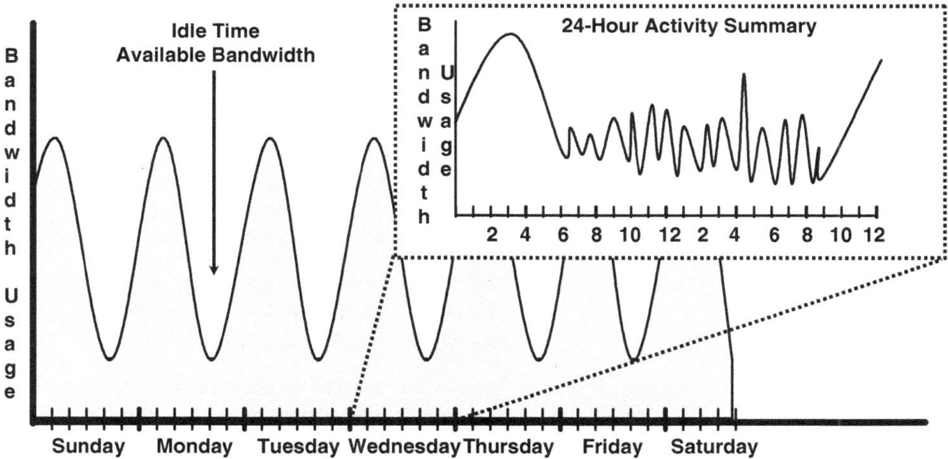

Figure 12.1 *Mirroring and bandwidth usage.*

12.2.5 Backup and restore

Backup is perceived to be overhead and an expense item. Backup with this perspective may be skipped, skimped, or relegated to something that should be done, but to cut corners it's a place to cut costs. Backup is actually an enabler in that you can leverage it to support other functions, including business continuance, disaster avoidance, and meeting regulatory compliance and audits. The cost of doing backup should be balanced and compared with the cost of loss of access to data, or the loss of data. Table 12.5 lists several backup characteristics.

Backup windows are shrinking, since the amount of data to be backed up and protected is growing faster than the technology to protect it. At the same time another force in reducing the backup window is the increased availability required by today's Internet nonstop economies and business environments. Also pressuring backup and recovery is the renewed awareness of data protection and regulatory compliance. Consequently, the traditional sequential approach of running a backup in-between production jobs is not satisfactory today in many environments. Backups need to run uninterrupted in parallel with data availability and processing activities. Similarly, recovery needs to be faster, which can be a trade-off between reducing backup costs by making recoveries take longer—for example, optimizing

Table 12.5 *Backup Characteristics*

Type of Backup	Characteristic
Full	Full backup of all data on a volume is performed; this takes longer but it also contains all of the data to simply restore.
Incremental	Only files that have changed since the last full backup are copied. Assuming that a weekly full backup is performed, each of the daily backups would be subsequently larger.
Differential	Copies the data that has changed since the last differential backup. This shortens the time to back up data, but for restore could take longer to process all of the data.
Snapshot	Point-in-time copy of the data, also known as a pointer-based backup, that copies the pointers and information used to describe the files. This is a very fast backup, since data is not backed up; rather, the metadata and pointers that point to the data blocks are copied. Snapshot backups do not protect against loss of an entire disk; rather, they provide rapid recovery of an individual file or group of files.

tape usage and speeding up recovery by increasing backup costs by using more tape drives in parallel, disk to disk (D2D), and disk to disk to tape (D2D2T).

Leverage applicable technology, including D2D2T, with the primary disk being mirrored, copied, or backed up to lower-cost ATA/SATA technology and later moved to tape located on-site or off. Reduce the amount of human intervention to help reduce cost and improve resiliency. Audit backups and results, including periodic testing of a tape on a different system for restore. After all, in a real disaster you might have to restore your data to a system other than the one it came from.

Some general data-protection and -retention considerations include:

- How quickly data needs to be accessible, including restoration and recovery
- What the data life-cycle policies are toward data migration, removal, and access
- Leveraging data pruning and migration to reduce the amount of data to be backed up
- Utilizing different media for different classes of data to reduce costs
- Backup of state information, including registry data to support a bootable volume
- How data protection is verified and validated (Do you know if you can recover?)
- Type of medium to use for needs, including sequential, random
- Parallel and multistream backup to improve performance and throughput
- On-line copies of data as well as off-line accessible copies of data
- Trade-off of backup cost compared with cost of loss of data or accessibility
- Snapshot backups for rapid recovery of deleted and damaged data

Some backup and recovery considerations include whether or not you are able to perform differential backup to disk where changes are applied to a previous full copy to reduce the backup time and yield an up-to-date recovery. This approach is called synthetic by some, since it shortens the recovery time, but it does not yield a copy in time unless extra copies are maintained. Do you need to overhaul or simply update your backup? For starters you could substitute lower-cost storage as a backup medium, which could be perceived as a cost; however, if it allows you to better utilize your tape devices, you might be able to reduce the number of tape devices in your environment for a cost savings. The cost savings would result from fewer devices—meaning less maintenance dollars being spent on the tape device, interface, and supporting infrastructures. Are you utilizing application-aware software, modules, or plug-in utilities with backups to perform application-level backups while data is being updated? Can you reduce the time required to perform backups by moving less frequently accessible data to media that do not have to be backed up as often?

The Network Data Management Protocol (NDMP) is a higher-level protocol that is used for backup of Network Attached Storage (NAS) filers over an IP-based network. A tape library or server with tape devices attached supporting NDMP (appropriate version) can receive data directly from an NDMP-compliant NAS device under the control of an NDMP backup server that has an NDMP client on it. More detailed information about NDMP can be found at www.ndmp.org, as well as the SNIA Web site (www.snia.org).

12.3 Chapter summary

There are many techniques and approaches to protecting data and access to it that can be combined to support resilient storage networking. RAID and mirroring provide accessibility to data, but other techniques are needed to protect data. These techniques include backup, archiving, snapshot, and point-in-time copies. Storage networks provide distance, bandwidth, and flexible technologies to support data protection over various distances and for diverse needs.

What This Chapter Will Do For You

This chapter looks at various security threats to storage, storage networks, and storage management tools. Some of the items you will learn about in this chapter include:

- Can you afford not to protect your data and storage infrastructure environment?
- What is your threat risk level and how much security do you need?
- Essential storage networking security information to keep your name out of the news!
- Best practices and tips to help secure storage resources without productivity loss

13

Securing Storage and Storage Networks

13.1 Overview

This chapter looks at several ways to secure storage networking components, including switches, directors, and the devices that attach to them. Some techniques to isolate and segment the SAN and device traffic are also covered, an important aspect of securing and protecting the devices and networks locally and over distance. Multisegment storage networks will also be looked at.

13.2 Storage and storage networking security threats

Security of your networks and systems is crucial in normal times and essential during service disruption. Security of the network should extend from the core to the remote access sites, whether home, remote office, or a recovery site. Security is between client and server (or via the Web) and between servers. Securing the home environment includes restricting work computers or PCs, use of Virtual Private Networks (VPNs), virus detection, and, of course, system backup. Security becomes more important the farther away from a secured physical environment you go, particularly in shared environments.

Networking and remote access bring flexibility while exposing information resources and data to security threats. These conflicting results must be balanced between data protection and business productivity. Storage has traditionally been accessed via secure or semisecure interfaces over short distances, as compared with current interfaces, such as Fibre Channel, that can span distances of over 100km and farther, using SAN over MAN, SAN over WAN, or channel extension technology. IP-based storage networks for block (iSCSI), extension (iFCP and FCIP), and file (NAS) can span even longer distances. As storage networking enables storage and information resources to be accessed over longer distances and outside of the safe confines of the data center, more security threats exist and more protection is needed. This is similar to how LAN technology evolved.

Some of the security concerns with storage networking are similar to those found with traditional networking and include:

- Shared access by two or more servers to a common storage device
- Different types of operating systems accessing storage and data
- Storage and data sharing, whether read-only, read/write, or delete
- Shared bandwidth and accessibility to the storage and data
- Shared access to management tools and interfaces

Securing a storage network involves more than managing the security of a switch or fabric, and a better understanding of the various threats is in order. Some threats to a storage network overlap as threats to the storage itself. Simply keeping a storage network confined to a data center is not enough from a security standpoint. Some storage networking threats include:

- Attacks on storage network physical components, including cabling and switches
- Eavesdropping (sniffing) on ISLs and WAN/MAN links
- SNMP traps and alerts, Telnet commands, and so on
- Protecting ports from unwanted access by foreign servers and devices
- Data transmission integrity to prevent eavesdropping and snooping

13.3 Securing the storage network

There are several major areas of focus for securing storage networks. These include securing the fabric and its access, securing the data and where it is stored, securing the components, securing the transports, and securing the management tools and interfaces. Some of the items that need to be addressed with a storage networking security strategy include:

- Securing storage networking ports and devices
- Securing transmission and ISL interfaces
- Securing management interfaces (SNMP, Telnet, IP interfaces)
- Securing storage resources and volumes

13.4 Storage access and allocation security (volume mapping and masking)

Securing a storage network involves making sure that both the SAN itself as well as the storage is protected. LUN mapping works by creating an access table on the storage device that determines which servers, using Worldwide Node Names (WWNN) or Worldwide Port Names (WWPN), shown in Figure 13.1, can have access (read, read/write, etc.) to a specific volume or LUN.

Servers that do not have access to the specific LUN would receive some sort of I/O reject error or may not see the storage at all. Storage-based security is the last line of defense when it comes to controlling access to a storage resource LUN, as shown in Figure 13.2. The storage in a subsystem is partitioned into multiple LUNs allocated to the three servers, with each server only accessing the LUN associated with it. In this example the volumes are symbolically named with letters; however, these could also be shown with the appropriate naming for different operating systems. For example, Server-1 has access to volumes A: and B:, Server-2 has access to volumes C: D: E: F: G: and H:, and Server-3 has access to volume I:.

In Figure 13.2, each of the different servers only has access to the LUNs that are mapped or masked to it using storage-based utilities. The access path to the storage volume, whether from the server, storage, or switch, can block access, or restrict access to read-only mode depending on the specific implementation. This function could also be accomplished using server-based persistent binding and specification of targets, LUNs, and associated WWPN or WWNN. On the left in Figure 13.2, there is a table that shows

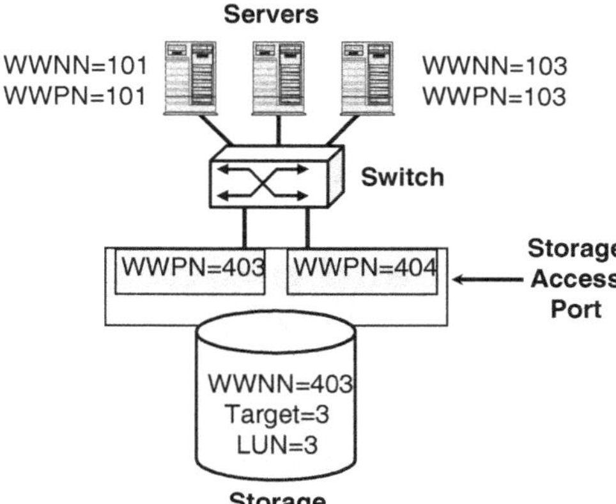

Figure 13.1 *WWNN and WWPN example.*

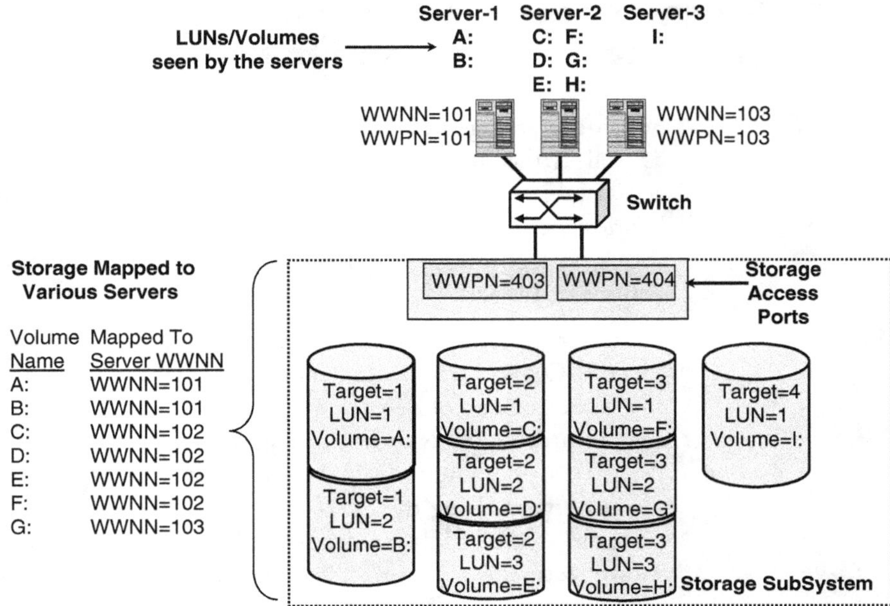

Figure 13.2 *Volume mapping example.*

the various devices that are mapped to the different servers. This is another approach to controlling access to storage resources via a fabric appliance that implements some form of storage-based LUN mapping. The fabric appliance is placed in the data stream or path to control access to the data, potentially at the risk of adding latency. There is still the aspect of securing the appliance, and this can add more complications to the solution that should be simplifying things. LUN and volume mapping in the data path within a switch is still very immature and proprietary, with performance overhead that severely impacts the performance due to the requirement to check and validate frames and their contents. In the future this could become a more practical approach as standards and high-performance, low-latency approaches are developed.

13.5 Access control lists and policies—securing fabrics, switches, and ports

Authentication involves verifying the identity of people and devices attempting to gain authorization to storage network resources. Authentication involves use of a server, such as Remote Access Dial-Up Server

(RADIUS) commonly used in network environments to verify identity credentials. Access control lists implement authorization to determine who and what can have access to storage network resources. When looking at controlling access and isolating traffic within a single switch or director, as well as in a single fabric of two or more switches connected together, the following techniques can be used:

- Fabric, switch, and port binding, with policies and Access Control Lists (ACLs)
- Fabric and device zoning to control access
- Networking segmentation (traffic isolation)
- Fencing and port isolation (port blocks, prohibits, and disablement)
- Partitioning (logical domains, VSAN, LSAN, virtual switches)

Access control policies are implemented using binding to associate which devices, including servers, can attach to which ports as well as which switches and directors can attach to each other. Access Control Lists (ACLs) are created to authorize the connection between SAN components to implement security policies. These ACLs implement device-to-switch access policies (port binding), switch-to-switch access policies (switch binding), and fabric binding. Binding is used to determine which devices can connect to each other, while zoning is used to determine which devices and ports see and communicate with each other.

Best Practices: To minimize disruptions caused by changes to zones and infrastructures, switches and directors should be configured with unique domain IDs and enabled domain ID lockdown. This will prevent switches from having their domain ID changed when merged into larger fabrics, which would disrupt zones based on domain IDs.

13.5.1 Port binding

Port binding can be utilized to determine which devices can attach to a port while restricting access to others. The bound device could be an HBA on a server, tape drive, physical disk, LUN, or storage volume. Port binding utilizes ACLs, which include the Worldwide Port Name (WWPN), device nickname, or alias of the bound device to be allowed access to a switch port. Port binding provides a finer granularity of access control to prevent an unauthorized port from binding (attaching) to a port. Port binding can be used in conjunction with other security mechanisms, including zoning. Port binding can be used to protect against spoofing (presenting a false identity) or changes to WWN that could compromise security.

13.5.2 Switch binding

Less granular than port binding, switch binding determines which switches or directors can connect to each other to create a fabric. The switch security policy implements an ACL, which is made up of 64-bit WWNN, of switches that are authorized to attach to it. If an ACL entry exists, ISLs using industry standard E_Port can be used to create a link between the switches. This binding of switches creates a secure fabric to help protect against rogue (unauthorized, unknown) switches joining a fabric.

13.5.3 Fabric binding

Similar to switch binding but providing more security, fabric binding combines the WWNN and Domain ID of a switch or director. This enables a SAN to be created, which is required to support high-integrity fabrics such as those required for FICON Cascade. Fabric binding is implemented by defining which directors in an Access Control List (ACL) are authorized to create E_Port ISLs for a secure fabric with high integrity. The ports on a switch and director comprise a domain, and each domain has a unique ID called the Domain ID (DID). The DID is used for addressing and zoning in a fabric. The DID is a number in the range of 1 to 239, with different number ranges supported by different vendors. In Figure 13.3, a storage network with bound switches is shown to support a secure fabric, with ACLs defining which switches are authorized to be part of the fabric.

13.5.4 Zoning

While a Fibre Channel–based storage network could, in theory, have approximately 16 million addresses for servers, devices, and switches, the reality is a bit lower. A basic zone to segment a storage network and isolate traffic from other devices is shown in Figure 13.4. Zones can be unique, with devices isolated from each other, or they can overlap, with devices existing in different overlapping zones. For example, a storage device could be part of multiple zones, with each server having a unique zone to a LUN to isolate it from other servers.

Whether your storage network will have a single switching device, 239 in a single fabric, or thousands across multiple fabrics, some level of isola-

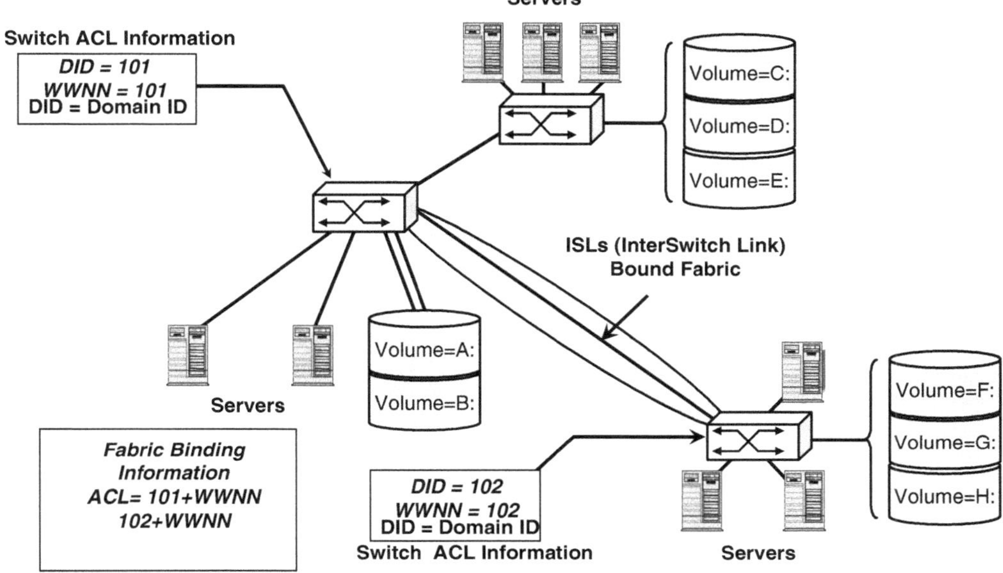

Figure 13.3 *Fabric binding example.*

tion and protection will be needed. This protection could be accomplished with persistent binding; however, for very large environments this becomes a complex management task as more devices are added. Fabric-based zoning is the most common approach currently used to address isolating traffic to specific ports and devices. Zoning enables virtual subnets within a fabric to be created to isolate access and restrict traffic while maintaining common connectivity within a fabric.

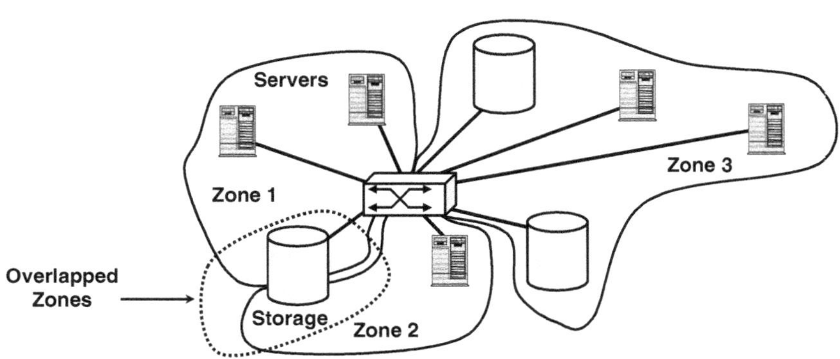

Figure 13.4 *Zoning basics.*

Table 13.1 *Various Zoning Characteristics*

	Name	How Zoned	Standard and Interoperable
Fabric Zoning			
ANSI Type-1	WWN (soft) zoning by device WWPN	By device	Yes By vendor
ANSI Type-2	Physical port (hard) zone	By port	No
ANSI Type-3 (Also known as FC address zoning)	N_Port_ID (port) zone, based on FC_ID of device attached to a port	By port	Yes
Host (server) zoning			
Persistent binding	Host zoning	By device	N/A
IP broadcast zones			
For support of IP over Fibre Channel	IP broadcast zones	By ports	Revised in FC-SW-3
Storage zoning			
LUN mapping	Storage zoning	By WWNN	N/A

Port and fabric security can be accomplished using combinations of zoning, including WWNN soft zoning and WWPN soft zoning as part of the ANSI T11 FC-SW-2 standard (along with hardware-enforced port zoning). Zoning enables ports, servers, adapters, and devices to be grouped together to isolate them from others in the same fabric; this is similar to creating a segment in a network. Table 13.1 shows some different types of zones.

13.5.5 Persistent binding (server-based zoning and isolation)

Most Fibre Channel–based zoning is accomplished using fabric zoning (via switches). Before storage-based LUN and volume mapping became common, and with the arrival of fabric zoning on switches, server-based zoning was more important. Server-based persistent binding is used to supplement fabric-based zoning and complement storage-based LUN masking. Persistent binding enables a server to specify, via its setup and configuration files, how its HBA will view and address SAN devices. These SAN devices (LUNs, physical disk, and tape drives) are usually addressed using a

WWPN of the storage network device. The persistent binding configuration information, including which devices can be accessed and which ones are not seen and how to name them, is done on a server-by-server basis.

Caution: For shared server environments, where trusted servers may be compromised and server-based zoning is required, use a combination of storage-based LUN masking or fabric-based zoning to ensure data integrity.

There are different types of fabric-based zoning currently in use, including those defined in the ANSI T11 interoperability standards. These include zoning by device, commonly called Fabric WWN (soft) zoning, and by switch port, called Fabric N_Port (hard) zoning. There are legacy zoning types, which include physical port zones that are vendor dependent based on addressing and naming conventions, that are not part of the interoperability standard.

13.5.6 Fabric WWN soft zones

Fabric-based WWN soft zoning is a commonly used industry standard, particularly for open heterogeneous environments. WWNN (Figure 13.5) soft zoning performs zoning based upon devices and their WWN. This provides flexibility to move a device from one port to another in a fabric without having to make a zone change. This implies that the zone follows the device, when, in reality, the zone is tied to that device. Should the device be changed—for example, when a tape drive is replaced—the zone would have to be modified to reflect this new device and its WWN.

A LUN could be the physical device name for standalone JBOD or a volume on storage array accessing disk storage. Storage arrays providing RAID and multiple interfaces for storage sharing can have dozens to hundreds of LUNs and would appear as individual volumes (devices) that could be accessed by the SAN.

The zone is the unique 64-bit WWPN (XX:XX:XX:XX:XX:XX:XX:YY) of the server HBA port or storage device to be included in the zone. Soft zoning alone only restricts what the name server presents to a requester. If the HBA already has the WWPN and N_PortID, then access is not denied. A zone member (the devices) can be in multiple zones, as would be the case with a server that is part of a disk zone and tape zone, enabling overlapping zones. Fabric-based WWN zones (Type-1) are allowable in an open interoperable fabric along with N_Port (Type-3) zones under T11 standards.

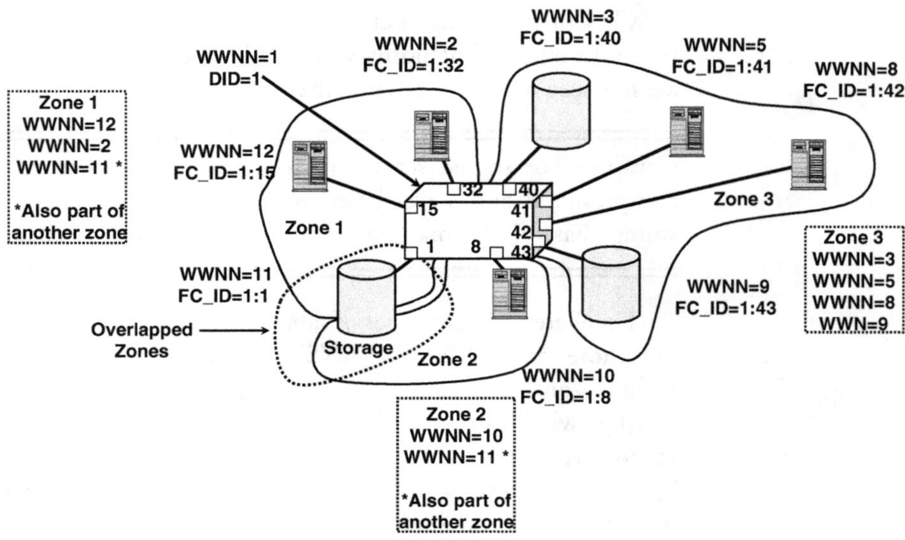

Figure 13.5 *WWN zones example.*

13.5.7 Physical port zones

Prior to the ANSI T11 interoperability standards, different vendors implemented various types of zoning, with one being a physical port-based zone. This type of zoning is sometimes called hard zoning and is based on the Domain ID plus physical address (DD:AA) of a switch port. The effect of physical port zoning is to zone by the port without regard to the WWPN of the device attached to the port. This enables devices to be replaced without having to change the zone information; however, zones do not follow devices as with the WWNN zones. Domain ID lockdown and unique Domain IDs are a best practice to facilitate zone and fabric changes. Where possible and practical, migration to open, industry standard zones should be part of a SAN preventive maintenance program and upgrade. If for some reason physical port-based zoning must be used, Domain ID lockdown should also be used to prevent the DID from changing and disrupting the zoning and fabric. If port zoning type functionality is needed, N_Port zones (see the following section) should be used.

13.5.8 Fabric N_Port zones

Type-3 N_Port_ID zones (Figure 13.6) are similar to Type-3 port zones in that the zone is based on the port and not the device. The differences are

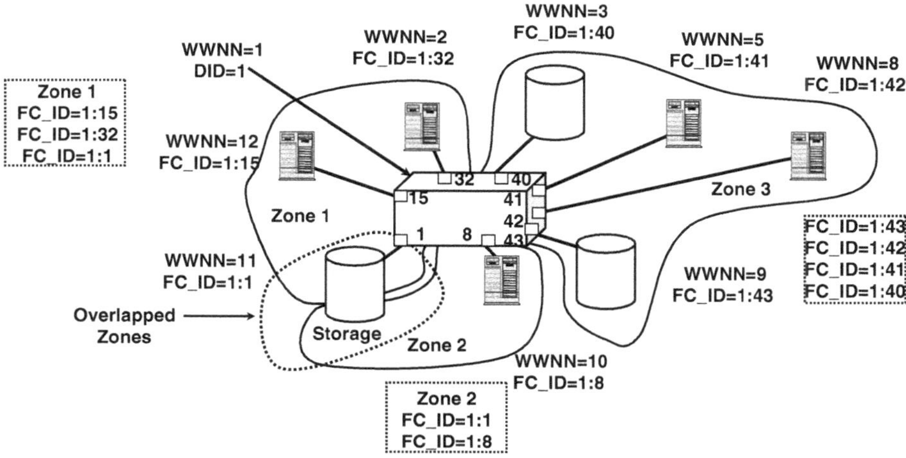

Figure 13.6 *N_Port zone example for tape devices.*

that Type-3 zones include an optional loop address and are supported under T11 FC-MI-2 standards. Following vendor guidelines for configuration, Type-3 and Type-1 zones can be intermixed. N_Port_ID zones are based on the Domain ID (DD), port ID (AA), and loop address (LL), with a format of DD:AA:LL.

The Fibre Channel ID (FC_ID) is a unique identifier assigned to a device when it logs in to and joins a fabric. The FC_ID address is based on the Domain ID (DID) and port ID of the switch port the device is attached to. In Figure 13.6, the UNIX system at the top right would have an FC_ID of 4:49, since the director it is attached to has a DID of 4 and it is attached to port 49. The tape device at the lower left in this same example has several loop tape drives (NL_Port) attached to the same interface, so these would have FC_IDs of 4:10:1 and 4:10:2, assuming loop IDs of 1 and 2. The FC_ID would remain consistent, particularly for N_Port devices, unless moved to a different physical port. This type of zoning provides flexibility in that a device such as a tape drive could be swapped out without impacting zoning information. Multiple zone types can be deployed, but care must be taken to ensure interoperability and functionality. Only Type-1 and Type-3 zones should be mixed in an open fabric, and their implementation should be carefully thought out and deployed.

For those concerned with the potential that a WWN could be altered, this type of zoning alleviates that concern, but it requires that the device being attached is trusted. Note that if a switch has to change its domain ID, it could disrupt the zones—so care should be taken when configuring zones and domain IDs. Domain ID should be used. Type-3 zoning is also the basis for implementing IP broadcast zones in Fibre Channel to enable IP traffic to coexist with FCP (open systems) and FICON (S/390) traffic on Fibre Channel.

13.5.9 Port blocks and port prohibits

Zoning can be used to isolate ports—for example, FICON ports from open systems ports, and traffic. Other capabilities that exist on switches and directors that support ESCON or FICON are port prohibits and port blocks. Port prohibits and port blocks are another approach independent of the upper-layer fabric and name server for protecting ESCON and FICON ports. Unlike fabric zoning, which can span multiple switches and directors in a fabric, port blocks and prohibits are specific to an individual director. Thus, in a fabric environment with two or more switches or directors, a combination of zoning and port prohibits must be used. With the ability of open systems platforms, including Windows NT/2000, to coexist in the same storage network SAN with S/390 and zSeries FICON-based systems, care needs to be given to the setup and configuration.

While on the surface this may sound similar to a form of zoning, port prohibits and blocks are implemented in the firmware of the switch and are independent of the Fibre Channel name server involved with various forms of zoning. Another difference from zoning is that port prohibits are integrated

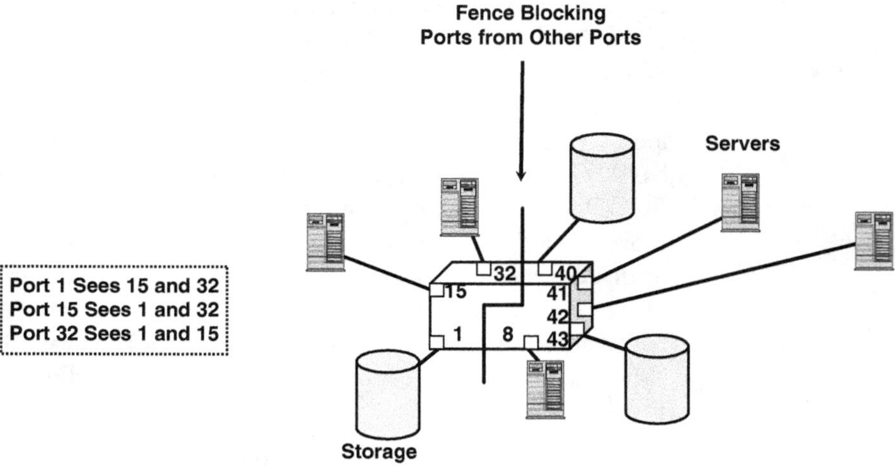

Figure 13.7 *Port prohibit and port block example.*

into the S/390, now more commonly referred to as zSeries environments, more frequently than are zones. In Figure 13.7, specific ports are blocked from use so they don't appear, while others are enabled to each other. These ports can be unblocked for use or grouped together so that groups of ports only see each other.

In the port prohibit example shown in Figure 13.7 only ports 1, 15, and 32 see each other, with an imaginary fence established between these and other blocked ports. Port prohibits can be combined with traditional zoning, as shown in Figure 13.8, which is a best practice suggestion when running in intermix (FICON and open systems) mode.

FICON ports, as seen in Figure 13.8, can be blocked from open systems ports, and tape ports can be blocked from disk storage ports. While this may sound like zoning, the difference is that the associations and prohibits are enforced at a low level, with no knowledge as to the type or identity of the server, storage device, or protocols being used. Port prohibits are local to the domain (switch or director) in that they are defined and are not fabric-wide and also do not apply to E_Ports (ISLs). Thus, it is very important, particularly for open systems environments, that port prohibits only be used in conjunction with traditional zoning.

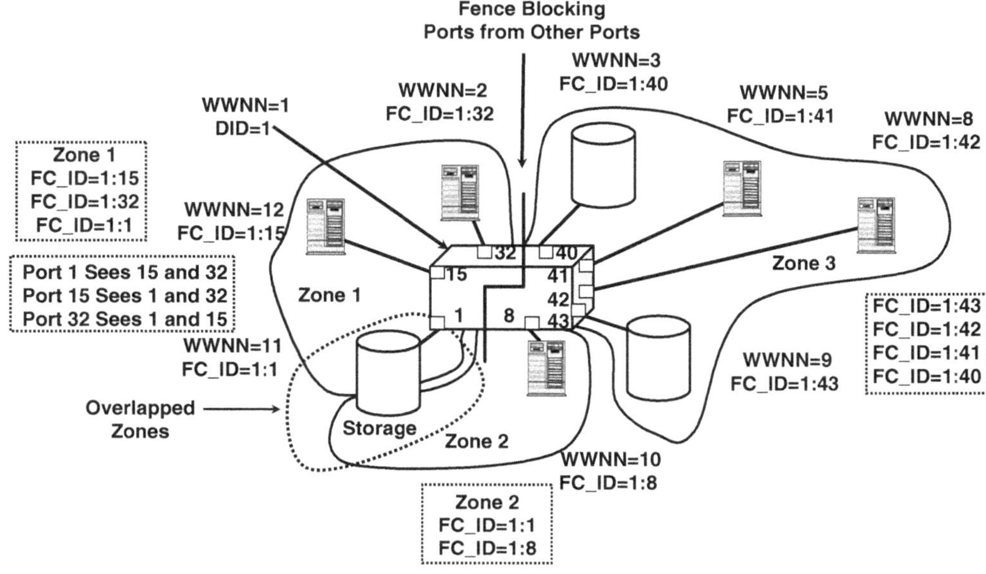

Figure 13.8 *Combining port blocks and zoning.*

Caution: Port blocks and prohibits apply to a single domain (single switch or director) and are not fabric-wide. Port prohibits and blocks should not be used to isolate ISLs and are not applicable to Fibre Channel ports. Port blocks and prohibits are not a replacement for traditional zoning. Zoning should also be used for open systems environments when port prohibits and blocks are used.

13.6 Security for storage over IP, metropolitan, and wide area interfaces

With IP storage interfaces, security for storage networking is more important, particularly as more storage functions extend outside the relative safety of a data center. Security is not just for the data, but also for the management tools and interfaces included in band management.

13.6.1 Securing data transmission and interswitch links

Securing the data during transmissions between locations or sites over ISLs can be accomplished using Fibre Channel–based encryption appliances to secure the data while in flight. While this type of technology has been around for some time in the IP and Ethernet world, it is new to the Fibre Channel storage network world.

As with most new technology, its first or early implementation is accomplished using standalone or integrated appliances, with later migration to the physical port in band—as is the case with Fibre Channel–based encryption that exists today.

The devices (switches, directors, routers, and gateways) need to be kept in a safe and secure environment to prevent unauthorized access to management ports and physical access to ports. Secure your devices, their management, and interface ports (Ethernet and serial) as well as the username passwords of management interfaces and tools. Also consider disabling those management tools that are not needed, or restricting their access. This could include SNMP, Telnet, and others that could be compromised. An important note that may not be obvious is that if you simply connect two separate fabrics, you can create a single fabric. This may be your intention, but keep in mind that in doing so, care should be taken to make sure that devices are uniquely named and addressed to that they work together as expected. You may also want to isolate certain devices via zoning, enabling or disabling of IP broadcasts, and if needed implementation of Resource State Change Notification (RSCN) suppression, state change management, and fabric isolation with autonomous regions.

13.7 Virtual fabrics and storage network subnets

With the convergence of traditional networks and storage interfaces via storage networks, there is also a convergence of networking. At a minimum a basic understanding of relative security mechanisms and their correlations is needed as IP and Ethernet move further into the storage networking realm beyond NAS file sharing (NFS and CIFS) and wide area communications. The counterpart of Fibre Channel zoning in the IP networking realm is VLAN (virtual LAN) tagging, used to segment and isolate LAN traffic. There are a couple of approaches for partitioning a switch or director beyond zoning and binding; these involve either multiple name servers or no name server. Another technique is to implement separate regions, also known as autonomous regions, using border switches and gateways (similar to creating network VLANs).

13.7.1 Logical switches and virtual SANs

An example of partitioning with multiple name servers is to create multiple discrete fabrics, each with a unique name server. Each of these partitions would function as a virtual switch, known as virtual SAN (VSAN), logical SAN (LSAN), logical domain, and other vendor-unique names. With virtual switches ports are isolated from each other and under the control of different name servers—meaning that for one port to communicate with another, a physical ISL "jumper" cable is needed to connect physically adjacent ports. Some switching devices that support virtual switches to isolate traffic also support the concept of a low-cost, low-overhead ISL to move data between partitions with no overhead or latency.

Many current- and next-generation switching devices, which include switches and directors, have the capability to be divided into multiple smaller logical switches. Each of these logical switches shares a common hardware platform, yet they divide some number of ports among themselves, each for their exclusive use. In doing so, a logical switch has its own namespace and generic services (name server), which can function as a standalone switch or part of a fabric with other devices (real or logical). Vendor implementations vary, with different features including scalability, configuration, resiliency of hardware and software, and networking capability.

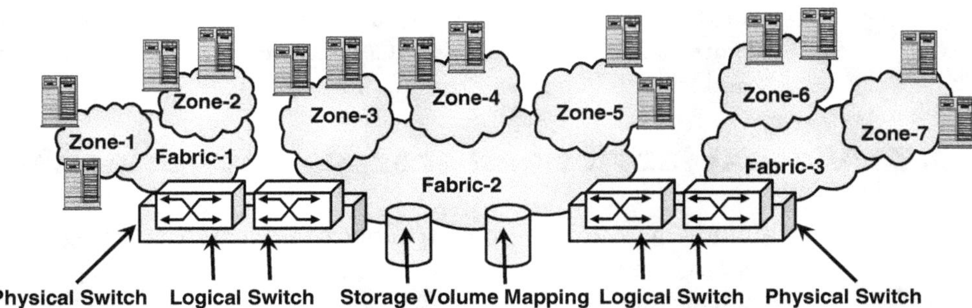

Figure 13.9 *Segmented storage network using zones, fabrics, and logical switches.*

A good use for creating virtual switches is to partition ports to isolate different workloads and applications supplemented with zoning and other security techniques, as shown in Figure 13.9. Switch partitions have another use, which is to support devices with more than 256 physical ports. For example, a 512-port switch may have to be partitioned into two logical 256-port switches to support FICON. The ability to create logical switches should be balanced with other security techniques (for example, zoning and binding) to avoid the temptation to create too many logical switches at a very fine granularity. The idea is to utilize the right security capability for the function at hand to help balance management and the desired level of security and functionality.

13.7.2 Large storage networks, fabrics, segments, and VSANs

Another technique to isolate storage network segments is to create separate regions that may be physically connected yet logically isolated—similar to a network VLAN. Some techniques that can be utilized include using iFCP as a gateway protocol and Autonomous Regions (AR) and device mapping. An iFCP gateway environment can be used to attach Fibre Channel devices to an IP Ethernet-based environment to perform all switching and fabric services to isolate traffic. Autonomous regions can be used to isolate fabrics, but with device mapping can allow certain traffic to be moved between the fabrics.

Similar to a traditional LAN, you could build one large flat fabric, or you could set up separate subnets (segments), known as regions in Fibre Channel storage networking parlance. By using autonomous region technology and border switches, the various switches and directors, regardless of the vendor, could be attached for a true core-edge topology. By using AR the networks are physically interconnected, but separate fabrics are maintained and local traffic is kept local. By using device mapping, devices can be mapped to different regions to enable certain traffic to flow between the regions while filtering unwanted traffic.

Autonomous Regions are implemented using border switches that enforce the FC-SW-2 along FSPF backbone protocol to tie the different segments (regions) together. Various servers and storage devices can communicate across the backbone, while local traffic, including RSCNs and other administrative items, is kept local. By using autonomous regions, along with VSANs, fabrics can be kept logically isolated, restricting local traffic from being sent out over the entire fabric and keeping remote traffic, including management and RSCNs, from showing up on the local fabric. Specific devices and servers can be mapped to access resources in other fabrics, similar to how VLANs and segments function in a LAN.

13.8 Storage networking considerations for servers (processors and hosts)

Securing storage and storage networking resources starts (or ends) at the server. At the server level, basic security starts with proper security of the individual filesystems, directors, files, logical and physical volumes, and access to other storage resources. Access to storage management tools, including volume managers that can be used to provide a layer of abstraction (also known as virtualization), should be restricted to those with the appropriate responsibility and capability to make configuration and provisioning changes. Access tools that can be used to affect the availability of storage resources, whether they be path managers for HBAs, volume managers, filesystems, backup, mirroring, or storage configuration, should be secured and safeguarded.

Some other security concerns from the server standpoint include access to configuration tools of the network and storage interfaces. There are other aspects of security from a server perspective, including application, file, database, and access to other tools, that could be the basis for entire books. Depending on the environment, access to the servers by system administrators, storage analysts, and database analysts may vary. For example, in some environments, storage resources are presented to a specific server via the storage network, with complete control and access to LUNs at the discretion of the individual system administrator. The system administrator may in turn restrict access and allocation to specific volumes and resources to other administrators who are responsible for their specific pieces of storage.

In other environments, a system administrator(s) may have complete end-to-end responsibility and capability to configure the storage network, the storage, and access to it.

13.8.1 Deciphering encryption

Encryption involves protecting data from clear text—that is, readable data—and transforms it into a format that is difficult to understand even by a computer. Various algorithms are used to encrypt data during transmission as well as while it is stored. Encryption, and decryption, the process of transforming data back to an understandable format, is compute intensive. Depending on the level of encryption and type of algorithm being used for encryption, these will have an impact on the amount of processing power needed, which also has an impact on response time. Storage and storage networking security encryption can be done in several locations, and, depending on your environment, you may need a combination of them. Examples of where storage networking encryption can occur include:

- Storage subsystems, including disk and tape of data on the move and at rest
- Storage interfaces at the adapter, switch, or gateway
- At the server in the operating system or using special software
- Security appliances in the network
- Wide area communication equipment, including Fibre Channel over IP devices

Ultra-secure environments may need an additional layer of security, provided by in-place encryption of data while in transit, when stored on a storage device (disk or tape), or both. There are different forms of encryption to provide various levels of protection that can be implemented by native devices or integrated software, either in the data path in communications equipment or via special security appliances. More and advanced encryption and security capabilities are finding their way closer to the actual ports in switches and storage networking devices. Next-generation storage networking switches may have integrated or security coprocessing silicon to help enforce security policies at wire speed. Encryption encodes the information so that even if the information could be read, without the correct key and encryption algorithm it would not be able to decode. Table 13.2 shows some examples of how long it would take to hack various levels of encryption. The right level of encryption is dependent upon your needs and environment.

Table 13.2 *Costs and Time to Break Encryption Keys—SEC1/SNIA Security Group*

Attacker Type	Budget	40-Bit	56-Bit	168-Bit 3DES
Individual	$400	5 hours	38 years	Too long
Dedicated	$10,000	12 minutes	556 days	10^{19} years
Intelligence community	$10 million	0.02 seconds	21 minutes	10^{17} years

Another, often overlooked, part of security is that of physically securing and monitoring, to detect changes and intrusions of physical cabling infrastructure. This can be as basic as ensuring that all switch ports and their associated cabling and infrastructure, including patch panels and cable runs, are physically secured with locking doors and cabinets. More complex examples include enabling intrusion detection as well as enabling probes and other tools to monitor critical links such as wide area ISLs. For example, a monitoring device can track and send out alerts for certain conditions on ISLs for link loss, signal loss, and other errors. This information can be correlated back to other information, including maintenance records, to see if someone was performing work on those interfaces, or if they had been tampered with in some way.

13.8.2 Physical multiplexing as a security tool

Multiplexing is a useful technique for aggregating multiple networks onto a single cable by, for example, using DWDM. A side benefit of multiplexing multiple ISLs or storage interfaces, as well as networking interfaces, over a common multiplexing cable is that snooping and eavesdropping become more complex. While it is not a secure interface by itself, multiplexing does make it more difficult, which may be enough to deter the normal intruder (much like locks on a door).

13.8.3 Disposing of storage networking technology

Finally, care should be taken when disposing of storage resources, including disk and tape, when they are no longer needed. When magnetic tapes are no longer needed, have them properly disposed of, which could entail degaussing or burning. With disk subsystems and storage located in servers, workstations, desktops, and laptops, remove sensitive data and take appropriate steps, including reformatting disks if needed. Simply deleting data can still leave the data recoverable by those interested in doing so. Servers, storage controllers, and switches, if applicable, should also be reset to factory configurations and have their NVRAM cleared. Consult with your manufacturer about its suggested procedure for safeguarding your information and ensuring that disposal of resources does not compromise your business information.

13.9 Storage networking security checklist

The following are some storage and storage networking security checklist items:

- Restrict and limit access to physical components, including cables
- Disable management interfaces and access when not being used
- Secure and rationalize vendor access to equipment
- Evaluate use of SNMP MIBs and agents and how sets and traps are implemented
- Manage maintenance ports, including dial-in/dial-out and e-mail
- Stress ISL security, including fabric binding for FICON Cascade, to ensure data integrity
- Dispose properly of unused and displaced equipment and technology, including erasing media and clearing memory from controllers and other devices
- Perform periodic audits of access to devices and intrusion detection

13.10 Chapter summary

Information about computer-related security is available from the Computer Security Institute (CSI) via the Web sites www.gocsi.com and www.cert.org. Talk with your vendors in order to understand their security capabilities and practices. Ask your vendor how they secure and audit their own systems and storage. There are many techniques that can be used for securing storage and storage networks at different levels. Establishing rings and layers of security with perimeters of defenses using techniques discussed in this chapter can help safeguard your data.

Putting It All Together

What This Chapter Will Do For You

This chapter looks at flexible and scalable storage access infrastructures for SMB, and distributed environments to simplify storage access and management costs. Some of the items you will learn about in this chapter include:

- The value of integrated, turnkey SAN and NAS solutions for data protection
- Essential technologies to support small resilient storage networks
- SMB environments can be at greater risk for lack of data protection than an enterprise
- Is your SMB or SOHO environment at risk, and is your personal data protected?

14

Small Storage Networking Examples

14.1 Overview

Resilient storage networks are not just for large environments; storage networks of any size can benefit from the techniques discussed in this book. Storage networks using different interfaces (Fibre Channel, Ethernet, InfiniBand, USB, SATA) and protocols (FCP, IP, iSCSI, NAS) can be deployed in SOHO and SMB environments. Some examples of where small storage networks can be utilized include:

- Satellite remote, SOHO, and branch offices
- Workgroup and collaborative applications
- Windows, NetWare, Linux, and UNIX Cluster environments
- Small environments with a small mainframe and open systems
- Small and medium businesses and small home offices
- Application-specific environments where isolation is needed
- Web and e-mail systems for various size environments
- Starter storage networks for testing, familiarization, and training

14.2 The small storage network (storage networks for anyone)

Storage networks can be of various sizes, complexity, and utilize different technologies and interfaces, including Fibre Channel (FCP and FICON) and Ethernet iSCSI for block data movement and NAS for file-based access and sharing. Many storage networks (file and block based) have been initially deployed in standalone environments within larger enterprises as well as departmental and small and medium businesses. Smaller storage net-

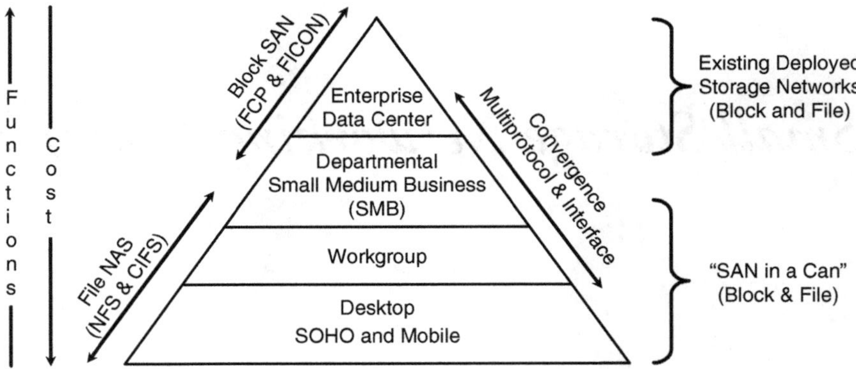

Figure 14.1 *Storage networks (current and future) as of 2004.*

works have been deployed in some applications, as well as function-specific server and storage implementations. In the enterprise data center environments many of these smaller storage networks are being consolidated into larger storage networks.

Figure 14.1 shows various types of storage networks, from enterprise data center to desktop, small office home office (SOHO), and mobile. In-between there are departmental, satellite branch offices, small medium business (SMB), and workgroup environments. As of 2004 the majority of block-based storage networks deployed have been in enterprise data centers, some departmental, and some small and medium business environments. While file-based (NAS) storage networks have been deployed in some enterprise environments, they have been more prevalent in the mid-tier (SMB, workgroup, departmental) environments.

The growth areas for storage networks continue to be in the enterprise, workgroup, and branch office for block-based access and further down into the SMB, SOHO, desktop, and mobile environments for NAS (with variations of this being iSCSI block in the mid to lower tiers as well as file in the upper tiers). However, this is changing as more robust SMB and SOHO solutions are appearing with advanced data protection features. In Figure 14.1, products that scale up into the enterprise environment generally have a higher cost. Products that are better suited (lower cost) for lower-tier environments have less feature function and perhaps lower performance. There is plenty of growth for storage networks, with much of that occurring by new markets and applications, particularly the SMB and workgroups as well as SOHO environments. Today a lot of data movement involving the Internet is upload/download oriented, including file transfers that will evolve by using the Internet for backing up data to alternate locations.

Some characteristics and capabilities of small storage networking environments include:

- NAS gateways for attachment to Fibre Channel (FCP) block storage
- Integrated backup, data protection, and storage sharing devices
- Smaller self-contained storage networking solutions ("SAN in a Can") providing block and file capability and optionally content accessible storage (object)
- Smaller, modular storage subsystems with flexible interfaces that can be changed from parallel SCSI to Fibre Channel (FCP) or Ethernet for iSCSI block access
- Distance support to back up and protect local data to centralized resources, including subscription-based services via the Internet

14.2.1 Small high-availability block (iSCSI) storage network

The following example looks at a small, yet scalable storage network that utilizes Ethernet and iSCSI for block storage access from different servers. This example also includes a secondary site for high availability.

In Figure 14.2, a multisite storage network is shown using Fibre Channel (FCP)–based storage (disk and tape) that is accessed using iSCSI via iSCSI to FCP routers. The various servers, which could include Linux, Novell NetWare, UNIX, and Windows, access the storage using iSCSI drivers over Gb Ethernet for block data access. For higher performance and to

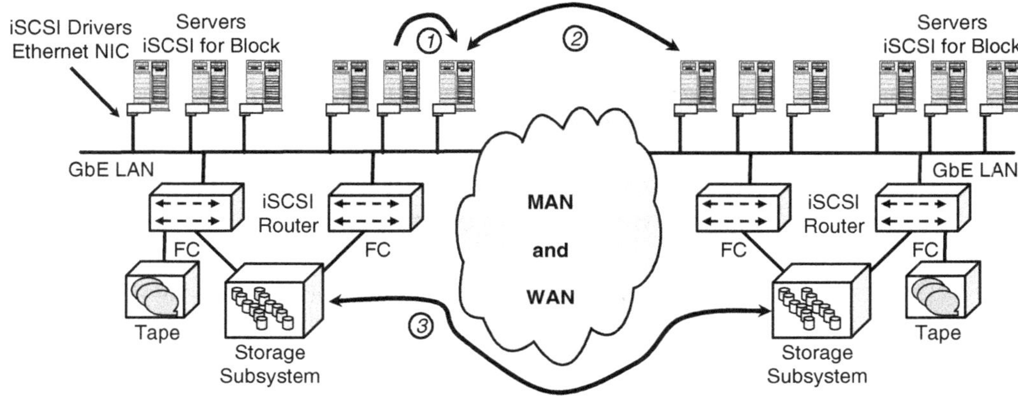

Figure 14.2 *An iSCSI storage networking example.*

offload server CPU processing, TCP Offload Engine (TOE)–equipped adapters could be installed in the servers. Some of the servers (1) could be configured with clustering and failover software for high-availability applications. For high availability, a secondary Ethernet network could be installed to leverage redundant host adapters and access paths via the routers to the storage devices. Also shown is remote mirroring and replication using software-based (2) and storage-based (3) functionality to a secondary site. By using various techniques, including iFCP, FCIP, iSCSI, storage over SONET/SDH (SoS), and DWDM, the MAN and WAN distance can be supported. To improve the performance over the WAN for IP-based implementations, IP-to-IP compression could be implemented to reduce network bandwidth requirements.

Some of the technologies used in the example in Figure 14.2 include:

- IP-to-IP network accelerators for compression and distance support
- Tape library sharing control software and backup status reporting
- Archive and data migration tools for compliance and retention
- Multiple protocol Fibre Channel (FCP and FICON) and IP (iSCSI and NAS)
- Ethernet adapter trunking and aggregation software for performance
- Failover and clustering software for servers for high availability

Some technology and techniques represented in the example in Figure 14.2 include:

- Modular storage with Fibre Channel FCP interfaces
- Fibre Channel switches for open systems with optional iSCSI integrated capability
- NAS gateway to enable NFS and CIFs as well as optional DAFS and iSCSI-based access of Fibre Channel shared storage resources

14.2.2 Small NAS and intermix (open systems and mainframe) storage networks

The following two examples show first a small file-based NAS storage network and a small block-based storage network. The block-based storage network could be for Fibre Channel (FCP) to support open systems, FICON to support a small IBM mainframe environment, or a mix of open systems, with FCP and FICON for smaller environments that have multiple server

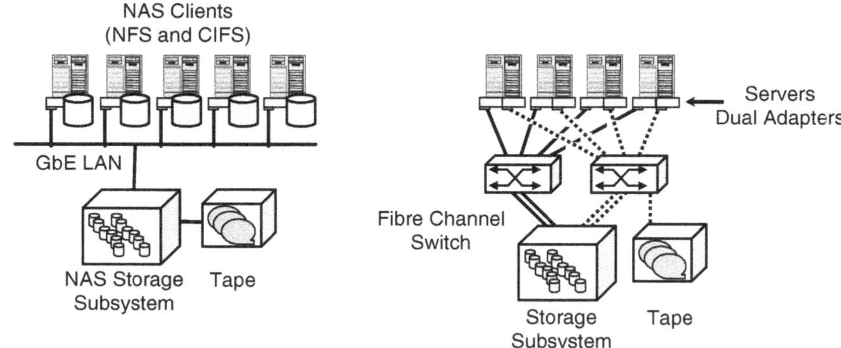

Figure 14.3 *Small NAS and Fibre Channel-based storage networks.*

platforms. For smaller environments with a shrinking IBM mainframe environment, as well as test, development, and quality assurance configurations, being able to share a common infrastructure can help reduce management and implementation costs. The two examples shown in Figure 14.3 can be standalone (SAN islands) or part of a larger storage networking environment, as well as serving as starter systems.

In Figure 14.3 on the left, is a NAS-based storage network using a NAS filer appliance with integrated disk and tape device for backup. The NAS filer provides file and data sharing over an Ethernet (Gb Ethernet in the example) storage networking interface using NFS and CIFS protocols. Newer filers can also support iSCSI for optional block data access for applications such as Microsoft exchange server until it supports NAS-based access. The servers shown in Figure 14.3 on the left also have local attached disk drives, which may contain application, system boot, and other information. These disks can be backed up to the NAS device for data protection.

On the right in Figure 14.3, a small Fibre Channel–based storage network providing block-based storage sharing to multiple servers is shown. These servers can be open systems Linux, UNIX, Windows, IBM AS400, and Novel NetWare, among others, using FCP to access Fibre Channel–based storage. IBM mainframes using FICON could also coexist using intermix mode for FCP and FICON to coexist on the same switches and storage networking infrastructure. The FCP-based servers would access fixed block-based formatted LUNs, while FICON servers would access CKD- and ECKD-based data on storage volumes. For IBM zSeries servers running both zOS and native Linux in separate server partitions, zOS could utilize FICON while native zLinux could use either FICON or FCP to access storage. Note that FICON-accessed storage, regardless of whether it is from zOS or Linux, would be CKD and ECKD format, while FCP-accessed storage would be in standard open systems fixed block-based formats.

Some of the technologies used in the example in Figure 14.3 include:

- Volume managers and file systems (local, distributed, and SAN based)
- Backup and recovery software supporting NDMP, including media management, and disk-based backup
- Tape library sharing control software and backup status reporting
- Element managers for disk, tape, switches, adapters, servers, gateways, and routers
- Multiple protocol Fibre Channel (FCP and FICON) and IP (iSCSI and NAS)
- Ethernet adapter trunking and aggregation software for performance
- Security tools, including RADIUS authentication, authorization, and zoning

14.2.3 Small to medium block and file storage network

The following example shows block-based access using Fibre Channel (FCP or FICON) from servers attached to the Fibre Channel switches. For servers attached to the Ethernet network, iSCSI is used for block data access via gateways. The gateways provide both iSCSI as well as NAS access of Fibre Channel–based storage to improve utilization and sharing of storage resources.

In Figure 14.4, various servers attached to an Ethernet (Gb Ethernet in the example) can access storage via block using iSCSI and via file using NAS (NFS or CIFS). The Ethernet-attached servers could be Windows, Linux, Novell NetWare, UNIX, or Apple among others. Some of these servers have internal- or external-based storage that can be backed up to the Fibre Channel attached storage using iSCSI or NAS—for example, D2D2T backup from a local server to a NAS volume and then migrated to tape. Some servers are direct attached to the Fibre Channel storage (similar to the previous example shown in Figure 14.3). These servers could be open systems or IBM mainframe using either FCP or FICON, respectively, for access.

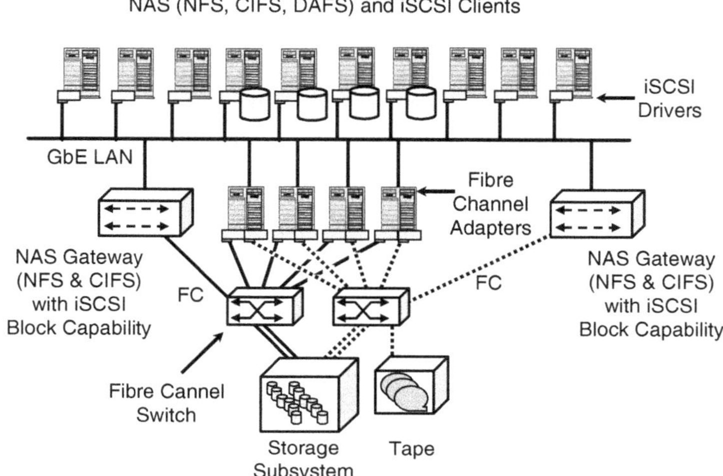

Figure 14.4 *Fibre Channel, iSCSI, and NAS small to medium size storage network.*

Some of the technologies used in the example in Figure 14.4 include:

- LUN mapping, zoning, and FICON port prohibits, blocks
- Volume managers and file systems
- Tape library sharing control software and backup status reporting
- Multiple interfaces, protocols, and access methods
- Storage resource usage and activity (SRM) profilers and reporting
- Security, including RADIUS authentication, authorization, and zoning
- Storage management tools for cross-platform management

Some technology and techniques represented in the example in Figure 14.4 include:

- Fibre Channel switches supporting FCP and FICON for open systems and S/390 mainframe access, respectively, with optional iSCSI integrated capability
- NAS gateway to enable NFS and CIFS as well as optional DAFS and iSCSI-based access of Fibre Channel shared storage resources
- Intermix of 1Gb, 2Gb, and 4Gb Fibre Channel devices with Gb Ethernet

14.3 Chapter summary

Storage networks do not have to be large and complex to qualify as being a SAN; however, they should address some business need or address some problem including providing a flexible, scalable storage access infrastructure. As has been seen with LAN networking, entry-level storage networking hardware, software, and networking equipment will become more popular and readily available for broader deployment. While every home may not have a Fibre Channel or Ethernet switch, more robust and enabling solutions will appear to improve storage access from SOHO environments to the enterprise. For some SMB and SOHO environments, a combination of NAS for file sharing, iSCSI, and shared USB with ATA/SATA storage will be used for creating storage networks.

What This Chapter Will Do For You

This chapter looks at how the flexibility and scalability of resilient storage networks can be used to consolidate storage resources and management across different platforms and interfaces. Some of the items you will learn about in this chapter include:

- How to consolidate storage, servers, and SAN to reduce management time and costs
- What the risks are when intermixing environments and not following best practices
- A phased approach to successfully migrate from dedicated storage to networked storage
- Leveraging multiple technologies as enablers to meet specific data protection needs

15

Consolidation and Intermix Examples

15.1 Overview

This chapter takes a look at various examples involving server, storage, and SAN consolidation. As part of consolidation, examples of intermix of open systems and IBM mainframes using FICON as well as Network Attached Storage (NAS) are shown. Some storage networking consolidation topics covered in this chapter include:

- Server consolidation, including blade servers
- Storage consolidation, including SAN and NAS
- Storage networking (SAN island) consolidation
- Backup/recovery consolidation

15.2 Consolidation of information technology resources

Consolidation of resources is an ongoing topic whether it be for server storage, data center, software, or SAN island to help reduce costs by improving resource usage, elimination of the number of components, and to simplify management. Storage consolidation streamlines backup and other processing as well as device utilization. Server and storage consolidation has been one of the many target applications for building storage networks. Server consolidation can be to support combining and reducing data centers, workloads, and streamlining infrastructures.

A server consolidation example could involve going from a large eight-way processor (Intel or other) to a cluster for database servers to support applications such as PeopleSoft or other large frames and applications. A multitier environment would have the storage connected to the servers via a storage network. Multiple tiers of servers could include database, application, and batch servers. For transaction processing, this could include HP and Sun servers, Dell, Windows 2000 servers, BEA WebLogic/Tuxedo, or IBM WebSphere to name a few. Database systems could be Oracle, SQL Server, or IBM UDB/DB2. A Web tier could be made up of Intel servers running Windows, Linux, or some other operating system with Microsoft IIS, Apache, or another Web server.

15.2.1 Consolidating storage networks to speed recovery

Storage networks can be used to improve and facilitate backup and recovery in many ways, including migrating backup traffic from LANs to free up network capacity. One approach has been to set up separate Ethernet storage networks for handling network backups to move data from clients, to server, and finally to tape. Another approach is to use IP on Fibre Channel to enable LAN-Free backup where backup data moves over the SAN to offload enterprise networks. Storage networks are also being used to provide direct access to shared tape from host systems to reduce backup time and increase performance. SNIA, SSFs and technology demonstrations serve as good models for developing and validating resiliency strategies.

There needs to be a balance between too many SAN islands or subnets and one large SAN. The tradeoffs are that one large, flat SAN is prone to failures and subject to widespread outages and poor fault containment. On the other hand, spreading things out over too many SANs leads to complex management and complex recovery. So the balance is to have at least two SANs or fabrics with dual attachment, so that if something happens to one, the other survives. A common mistake is to create two or more SANs and then interconnect them with ISLs. In the networking world a similar situation arose and was addressed with routers and other devices similar to those being developed for storage networking.

Many first-generation storage networks were vendor specific with many restrictions. As part of server and storage consolidation there is also the need to consolidate SANs into or under a larger storage networking umbrella. History is on our side as we look at how LANs evolved into islands and then were linked together with bridges, routers, gateways, and other technology (hardware, software, services, and support).

15.2.2 From DAS (direct attached storage) to SAN attached storage

Storage consolidation, including migrating from dedicated direct attached storage to servers can improve utilization of storage resources. Many first-generation storage networks utilizing Fibre Channel for block and NAS for file-based storage sharing have been targeted at improving storage resource utilization. An argument can be made that since storage comes with many servers, why not utilize it, since not doing so would be wasting the storage. The flip side to this argument is that the storage needs to be managed across all of the different servers. A simple form of storage consolidation involves multiple servers single- or dual-pathed access to an enterprise storage device with backup on the same, or different, SAN. The example in Figure 15.1, shows, from left to right, the migration from dedicated direct attached storage to shared external storage-to-storage network shared storage.

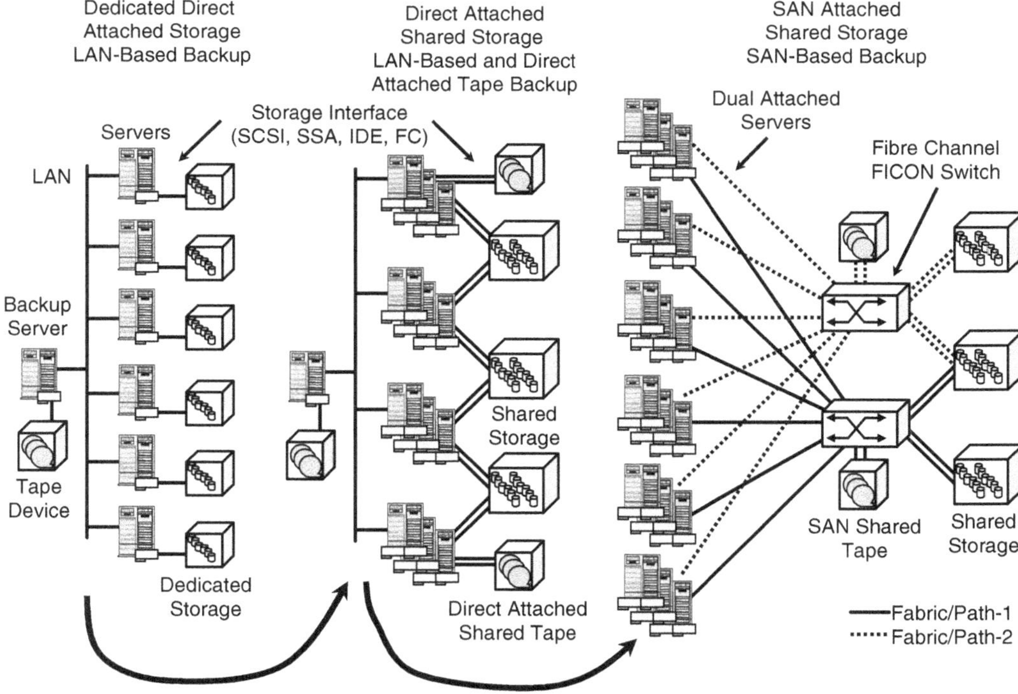

Figure 15.1 *From dedicated to shared to SAN storage.*

In the example in Figure 15.1, an evolution from the dedicated direct attached storage (moving from left to right) model, including LAN-based backup is shown. In the center of Figure 15.1 direct attached shared storage and some direct attached shared tape are shown. The storage can be large enterprise class or modular storage subsystems using parallel SCSI, IDE, SSA, ATA/SATA, Fibre Channel (FCP), ESCON, or FICON-based storage interfaces. Some of the servers in the center of the figure utilize a tape library, with some of the physical tape drives dedicated to different servers while others utilize LAN attached network backup. On the right side of Figure 15.1, SAN attached shared storage and tape using redundant paths are shown. Multiple storage subsystems are shown to support many servers that are dual attached to the storage via redundant interface paths using Fibre Channel FCP for open systems and FICON for S/390 mainframes. For FCP and FICON intermix environments, FICON port blocks and prohibits, along with zoning of open systems ports, should be utilized. Follow IBM FICON intermix recommendations, available via IBM Redbooks and Red pieces (www.redbooks.ibm.com) as well as vendor-specific switch suggestions.

15.2.3 Mixed storage networks

With improvements in technology interoperability and stability, it is becoming more common today to intermix different vendor storage subsystems and tape devices. Of course, where this is being done, best practices are also being implemented, including appropriate level of zoning, device isolation, and configuration. This includes ensuring that devices are properly configured with the right level of firmware and device drivers.

Another consideration involving intermixing devices with storage networking is incorporating existing technology. Some considerations involving existing equipment and software include which technology can be utilized and in which environments. What changes will be needed in terms of firmware, drivers, and operating system patches? What are the compatibilities with other equipment and software that you plan on utilizing? By working with your suppliers and utilizing information from your design assessment, covered in Chapter 8, you can determine compatibility requirements. Your vendors should be able to supply you with interoperability and compatibility matrices to determine what can be integrated, what should be isolated, and perhaps what should be retired. Keep in mind that nothing is free, and this applies to technology as well. For example, you may have an older switch or adapter that is paid for, so why not reuse it or redeploy it. If you can easily have the firmware upgraded on it to enable it to coexist with other devices without incurring extra cost or management activities, that would make sense. On the other hand, the cost to update firmware and continue to support the device might outweigh the perceived advantage of reusing a device. Keep in mind the cost involved with managing and supporting devices, as well as ongoing maintenance costs, instead of simply considering whether a device is paid for or not. Sometimes you can work out deals with suppliers for newer equipment with new warranties in exchange for taking out older equipment and leveraging maintenance dollars. This would also apply to other storage networking components, including storage subsystems and tape. Creativity and flexibility can also help with regard to management tools and software.

While intermixing various storage devices is possible, assess your needs and environment to determine what level of intermixing is needed. Work with your vendors and enlist third parties (consultants and business partners) to act as intermediaries as needed to make sure your needs are met and supported. In addition to intermixing storage, there is also an increase in intermixing open systems and mainframe traffic on a common network. The most common form of intermix traffic is FICON storage access from servers with storage-to-storage remote mirroring traffic utilizing FCP over common Fibre Channel/FICON switches. Whether to intermix traffic or keep it isolated is going to depend on what your management and operating practices are based on. Intermixing of traffic is a technology that is supported by several vendors, including IBM for FICON and open systems, as a capability you can choose to utilize or ignore as a storage networking technology. Whether you are using intermix storage, servers, or different protocol traffic, follow vendor recommendations and implement best practices, including applicable zoning and security.

Figure 15.2 shows a consolidated storage network with some servers being attached via Gb Ethernet for shared storage resources via iSCSI for block and a NAS gateway for file-based access. Some servers have attachments to shared storage resources (block) via Fibre Channel switches using redundant paths. A NAS gateway device attaches to one of the Fibre Channel switches to access shared storage and serve it to other servers via an IP-based network using NFS and CIFS. Using a NAS gateway device supporting DAFS would enable distributed servers to have higher-performance access to shared storage resources. An iSCSI router attached to the Gb Ethernet network and Fibre Channel switch allows iSCSI-enabled servers using iSCSI SNICs and standard NICs with iSCSI drivers to access shared storage. Block-based access would be utilized for those applications that require block access, including Microsoft Exchange (however, this is

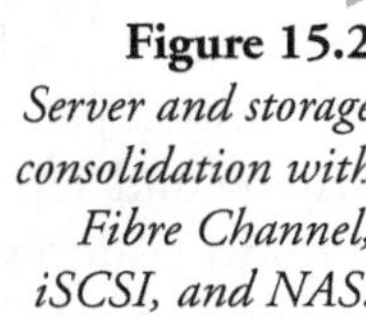

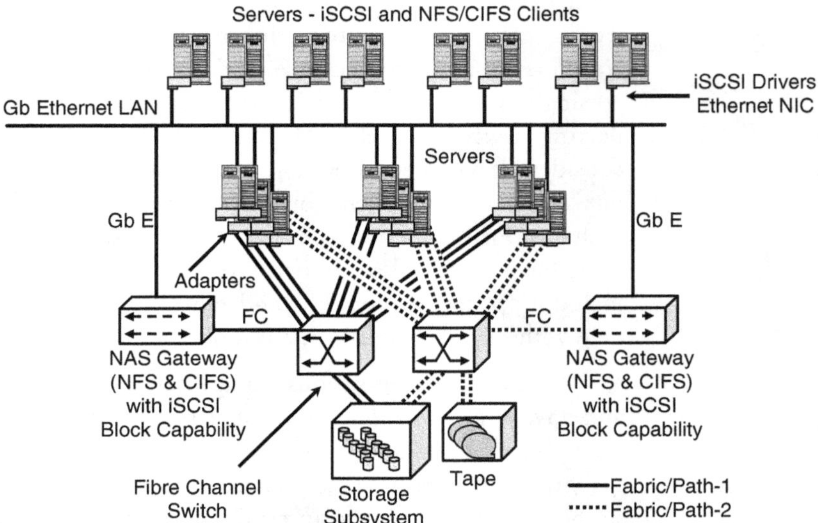

Figure 15.2 *Server and storage consolidation with Fibre Channel, iSCSI, and NAS.*

expected to change). Note that the iSCSI router function could exist as a blade function in the Fibre Channel switch or as a standalone device. To intermix the Fibre Channel switches that support FCP and FICON could provide support for both open systems, storage-to-storage-based remote mirroring, and S/390 mainframe FICON-based access. To support backup, a shared tape library with appropriate library sharing and management software is utilized. This enables servers to back up directly to shared tape devices without having to move data to other servers to perform that function. Smaller servers could still rely upon a backup server to perform functions on its behalf. The NAS gateway device could also be configured to provide D2D2T backup functions for IP-based clients and servers. Storage devices could also be configured to provide WORM functionality to protect data for compliance retention requirements.

Some technology and techniques represented in the example in Figure 15.2 include:

- Fibre Channel switches supporting FCP and FICON for open systems and S/390 mainframe access, respectively, with optional iSCSI integrated capability
- iSCSI routers to enable SCSI block data access between Fibre Channel FCP and Gb Ethernet based IP iSCSI servers
- NAS gateway to enable NFS and CIFs as well as optional DAFS and iSCSI-based access of Fibre Channel shared storage resources

15.2.4 Server consolidation

Server and workload consolidation have been a focus in many environments to help reduce costs, complexity, and simplify management. There are many different approaches to server and workload consolidation, including migrating to larger servers, moving to small 1U rack-mounted servers, and implementing blade servers. Some applications require dedicated resources, including servers, while others have vendor preferences from support standpoints to be on separate servers. The following example shows server consolidation combined with storage consolidation. Physical consolidation of servers can help to simplify management of large numbers of servers, including managing and troubleshooting the software installed on each of the servers.

Blade servers have become a popular tool to facilitate server consolidation, as shown in Figure 15.3. Blade servers enable a large number of servers to be physically packaged in a small footprint and can include internal storage as well as embedded switches (Ethernet, Fibre Channel, and InfiniBand). In Figure 15.3, two blade server cabinets are shown, each with

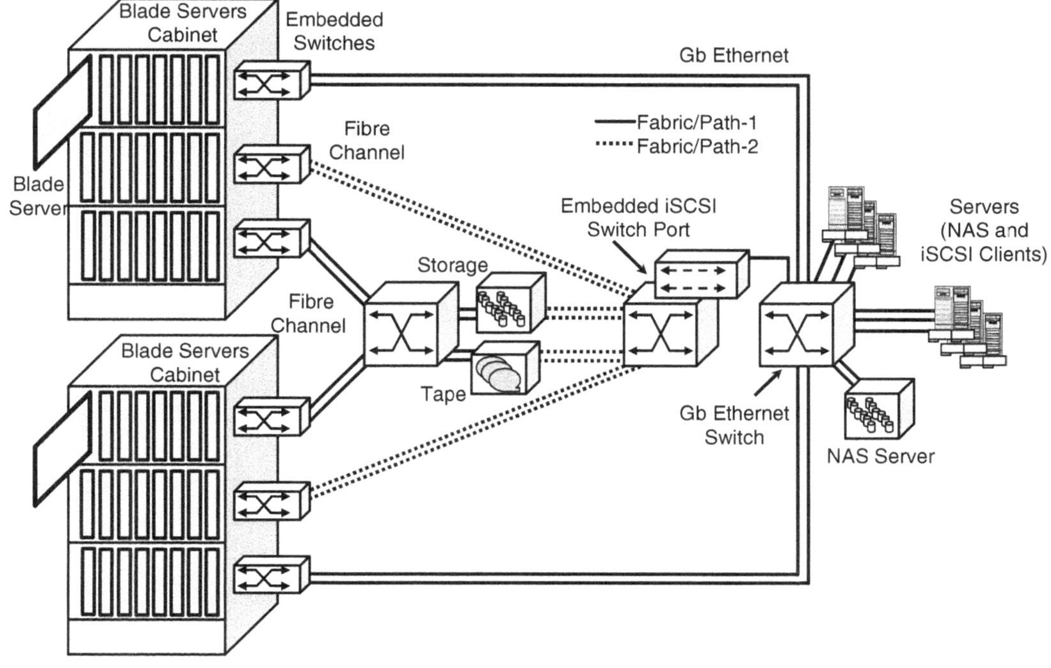

Figure 15.3 *Blade server with embedded switches.*

embedded Fibre Channel and Ethernet switches to access other servers and devices. Using remote and SAN-based boot capabilities, all server storage is located on shared external storage subsystems. The blade servers support a mix of Windows, Linux, Novell NetWare, and UNIX environments running different applications, including ERP, CRM, workgroup, Web, database, and data warehouse. Some of the blade servers could be clustered for high-availability failover and optionally further protected using software- or hardware-based remote mirroring.

A shared tape library enables servers to back up their storage to tape, or to leverage the backup server to make copies of storage on the storage subsystems. One of the Fibre Channel switches has embedded iSCSI capabilities to enable servers attached to the Gb Ethernet using IP to access Fibre Channel shared storage and tape resources. A NAS server with integrated storage attached to the Gb Ethernet provides data (file) and storage (block) sharing using multiple protocols, including NFS, CIFS, and, optionally, DAFS and iSCSI. The NAS device can be configured to be mirrored to another NAS device for high availability as well as data retention using WORM capability. The NAS device can also be accessed from the blade servers via Ethernet to share data and storage resources. Some environments utilize Novell NetWare and NDS to perform network authentication, which is a critical function for accessibility. Placing this function on a server attached to the SAN with shared storage can improve availability and recoverability.

15.2.5 Multiple SAN (SAN island) consolidation

Very large portions of the first-generation storage networks that have been installed have been what are referred to as SAN islands. A SAN island is single or multiple switches, usually not interconnected, that are used to create fan-in from servers to storage and fan-out from storage to servers. The fan-in and fan-out is used to increase the number of servers that can attach to a storage device (disk or tape). In some environments, there may be a few switches that are each a SAN island connected to one or more storage systems and as a separate fabric. In larger environments, there could be racks of individual switches attached to different servers and storage devices, yielding many SAN islands. Combining many SAN islands into a larger fabric of network switches has been one approach to increase connectivity and any-to-any access of storage resources from servers. An example of this is to deploy a core-edge or some other topology to network the switches together. Another example is to move from individual, small, switch-based SAN islands to larger port count switches and directors to create fewer and larger SAN islands or networks.

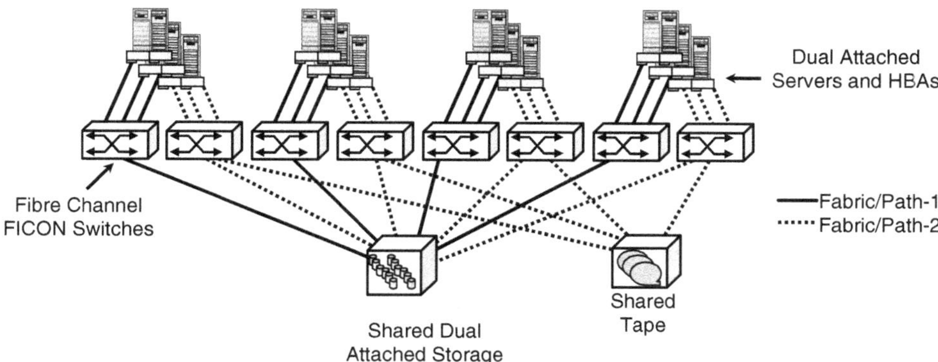

Figure 15.4 *Multiple SAN islands.*

Figure 15.4 shows eight SAN islands (four SAN switch pairs) that enable multiple servers to fan-in to storage devices (disk and tape) with redundant paths. Each switch (fabric) is isolated from other switches, and zoning is used to isolate servers from each other and from different LUNs on the storage device. LUN volume mapping is implemented on the storage subsystem to isolate servers from unauthorized access to storage resources. The SAN islands could be located in the same cabinet in the same room or they could be dispersed around a computer room, in a building, or a campus environment. Protocol intermix could support IBM mainframe FICON activity as well as open systems Fibre Channel FCP traffic.

Figure 15.5 builds on Figure 15.4 by implementing a core-edge topology to increase the number of servers attaching to the storage devices. An alternative design would be to utilize larger port count switches and direc-

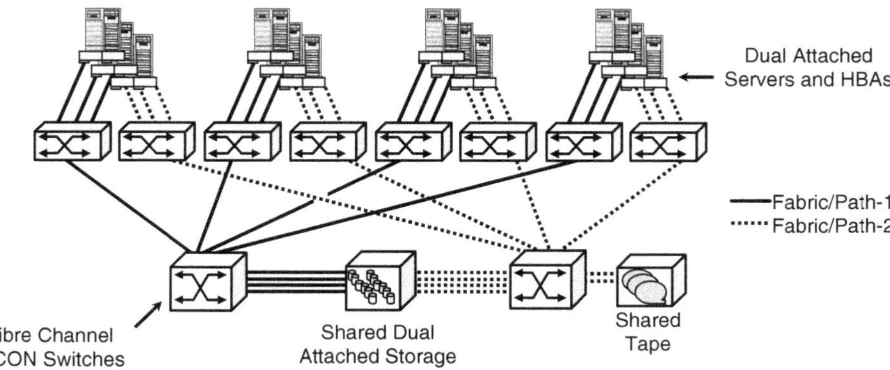

Figure 15.5 *Core-edge consolidation.*

tors to eliminate the need for a core-edge topology. However, for environments with requirements to geographically separate servers and storage, a core-edge topology can be useful. Redundant paths are shown, with two separate fabrics for availability and performance. Server adapter path management software capable of load balancing can utilize both access interfaces for performance. Note that if a common switch were used to attach both ports of the servers and then attached to both of the core switches, this would result in a single fabric being created. For high availability, keeping two separate fabrics isolates against disruptions caused by fabric and switch software and devices. Using the FICON Cascade feature implemented on zSeries IBM mainframes running zOS would enable access to storage across a pair of switches for geographically dispersed environments. Backup can be consolidated by utilizing a shared tape library with management software that enables servers to share the tape drives in the library.

Some management tools that would be applicable to the example in Figure 15.5 include:

- FICON cup and server, along with port prohibits, blocks, swaps, and FICON Cascade
- Security (RADIUS authentication, authorization, and zoning)
- Failover and clustering software for servers for high availability

Some technology and techniques represented in the example in Figure 15.5 include:

- Zoning (WWPN and WWNN), as well as LUN and volume mapping for security
- 10Gb ISLs for switch-to-switch interconnections combined with trunking, if needed
- Remote boot capabilities for servers from the storage network
- Protocol intermix mode (FICON for S/390 mainframe and FCP for open systems)
- FICON for zOS and FCP for zLinux (native) on zSeries mainframe

15.2.6 Virtual switch for consolidation

Most storage networking switches and switching directors support the ability to be partitioned into smaller, logical switches. This partitioning of switch resources is similar to partitioning a server into multiple logical partitions, also known as domains, and LPARs. A virtual switch can enable a large port count switching device to be partitioned into smaller switches, functioning as an independent switch with its own name server (thus, a separate fabric). This enables different workload to be consolidated from many to a few physical switches while enabling logical fabrics to be left as is, including zoning and other specific configuration items. This can be a first step taken before further consolidation from many fabrics to fewer to simplify overall management of multiple fabrics and software configuration. In Figure 15.6, an example is shown that has two physical Fibre Channel switching devices partitioned into four logical switches. Each logical switch, known as a VSAN, LSAN, or logical switch, supports Fibre Channel FCP, FICON, or intermix. In the example logical switches are configured to facilitate physical consolidation from eight separate switching environments to two while maintaining eight separate fabrics.

In Figure 15.6, the physical switch (1) is divided into four partitions, known as logical switches (2). There are eight logical switches (four per physical switch) shown in this example, with different vendor implementations supporting various numbers of partitions. These are shown as logical

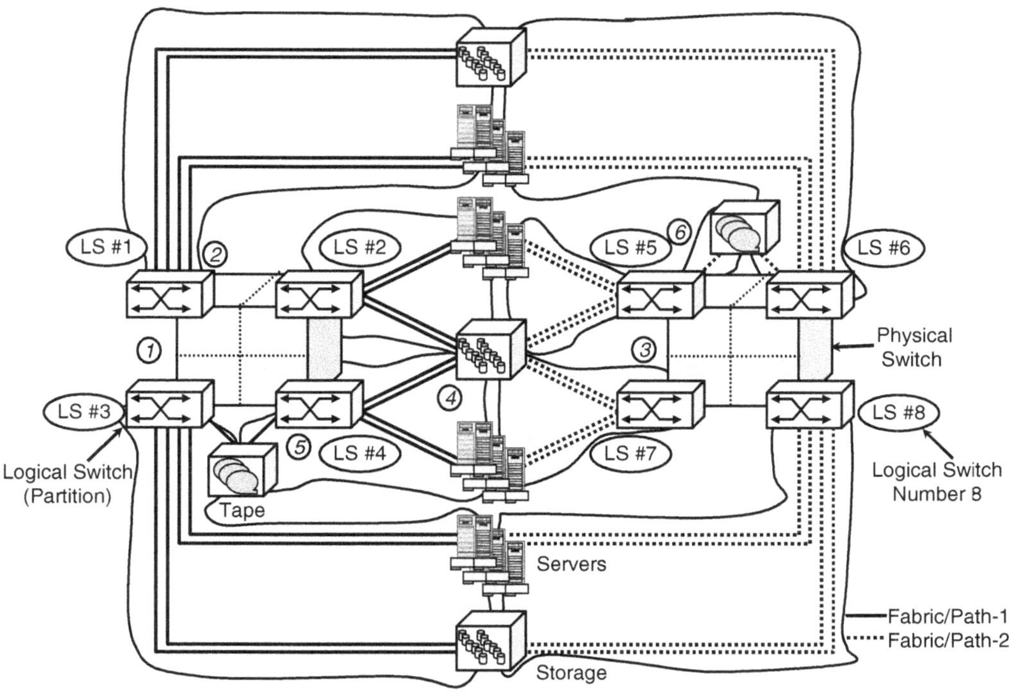

Figure 15.6 *Virtual switch consolidation.*

switch #1 (LS #1) through logical switch #8 (LS #8), each with its own name server and Domain ID. For redundancy two physical switches (1) and (3) are utilized to maintain redundant access. A common mistake is to have a false sense of security by creating multiple logical switches and using them as redundant access paths, but with a common piece of hardware that is a single point of failure. In the example, storage and servers (4) attach to redundant paths, with some devices (5) and (6) being accessible by multiple switches. Note that creating the logical switch partitions, also known as virtual switches and domains, does not reduce the amount of software management involved with managing a storage network. It is a good approach to start consolidation of multiple physical switches as part of an overall consolidation effort.

Some management tools that would be applicable to the example in Figure 15.6 include:

- Content-based storage for WORM access to replace optical storage
- FICON cup and server along with port prohibits, blocks, swaps, and FICON Cascade
- Multiple protocol Fibre Channel (FCP and FICON) and IP (iSCSI and NAS)
- Security (RADIUS authentication, authorization, and zoning)

Some technology and techniques represented in the example in Figure 15.6 include:

- Clustering for high availability and failover using Ethernet, Fibre Channel, or InfiniBand for heartbeat between servers
- Virtual switch logical partitions to isolate storage networking traffic
- Zero-cost ISLs and SAN Sockets to move data between logical fabrics

15.3 Chapter summary

There are production environments with open systems, including Windows, Linux, UNIX, NetWare, AS400s, S/390 mainframes, and others, coexisting and sharing storage resources and common infrastructures. Server and SAN consolidation can increase the number of zones required on each switch. For redundancy, storage networks should be built around redundant switches and directors with dual or quad HBAs. This applies to all storage networking interfaces, including Fibre Channel and Ethernet.

What This Chapter Will Do For You

This chapter looks at metropolitan and wide area storage networking examples to illustrate essential techniques for protecting data. Some of the items you will learn about in this chapter include:

- Leveraging knowledge from previous chapters to enable distance-based SANs
- How to protect critical distributed data at SMB, SOHO, and regional locations
- Deploying the right technology to meet protection requirements and cost constraints
- Without distance, data and applications are at risk

16

Metropolitan and Wide Area Storage Networking Examples

16.1 Overview

Distance is an important attribute for survivability and business continuance. Metropolitan and wide area storage networking enable redundant systems and data to be mirrored over distances. Some applications and storage networking functions that can benefit from variable distances include:

- Data movement to disaster recovery and continuance facilities
- High-availability clusters for campus, metropolitan, and wide area environments
- Remote data protection, including mirroring, replication, backup, and archiving
- Data and storage sharing between various locations and branch offices
- Multitiered, multisite data protection, including D2D2T over various distances
- Regulatory compliance data retention and protection
- Server, storage, storage network, and site consolidation

16.2 Metropolitan and wide area storage networks

Storage networks can span distances of a few kilometers for campus and metropolitan environments to hundreds or thousands of kilometers for regional and global (wide area) applications. For shorter distances, fiber-optic cabling and long-range optics (GBICs, SFPs, and XFPs), covered in Chapter 5, can be utilized, as well as copper. For longer distances, where dark, dedicated fiber-optic cable and lambda services are available,

DWDM, covered in Chapter 6, can be utilized. Where dark fiber is not available, and for longer distances, SONET/SDH optical services can be utilized. For longer distances or where optical services are not available, wide area interfaces, covered in Chapter 6, can be used, including IP services.

Figure 16.1 is an expanded metropolitan core-edge version of a figure from Chapter 15 with redundant paths (separate fabrics). This core-edge example has two separate core-edge fabrics that span two locations to support server-to-storage and storage-to-storage (mirroring) access across the sites. For redundancy there are two separate paths to provide fault containment and isolation at the device, storage interface path, and site level. The distance in Figure 16.1 indicated by the MAN cloud could be a few kilometers, using long-range optics and dedicated fiber, or longer distances, using CWDM, WDM, and DWDM. SONET/SDH and optical carrier (OC-x) optical services could be used where dedicated fiber is not available and for longer distances. For IBM mainframe environments, zSeries processors running zOS could be configured with the FICON Cascade feature to utilize the metropolitan redundancy. Servers at either location can access the local

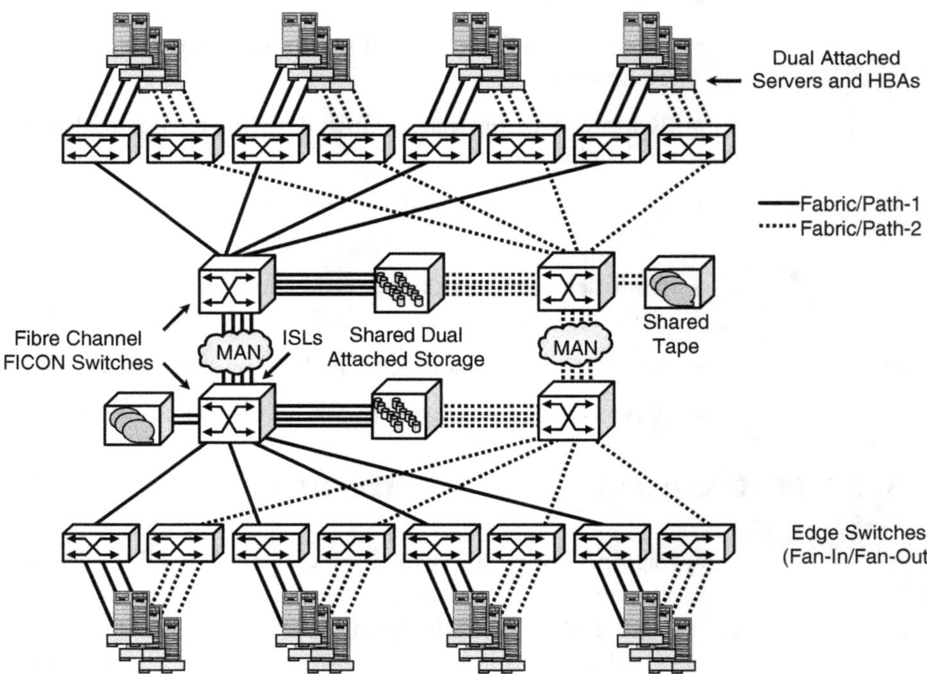

Figure 16.1 *Fibre Channel and FICON core-edge multisite consolidation.*

storage (disk and tape) as well as the remote storage. Clustering and high-availably failover software can be used to implement multisite clusters. For shorter distances, synchronous mirroring could be used and asynchronous mirroring for longer distances. The ISLs between the switches at the two locations (top and bottom) could be 2Gb, 4Gb, or 10Gb and trunked (aggregated together) or left as individual paths. Slower-speed 1Gb and 2Gb interfaces could be used to attach edge switches to the core as well as devices (servers and storage) to core and edge switches.

Some of the software tools used in Figure 16.1 include:

- FICON Cascade for IBM zSeries mainframes, utilizing cascade distance enabling technology
- Storage and data mirroring between locations, using hardware and software-based replication (synchronous or asynchronous)
- LUN mapping, zoning, and security authentication
- Backup and recovery software, including media management and tape sharing with media servers
- Failover and clustering software for servers for high availability
- Appropriate optics and buffer credits to span distances

16.2.1 Multisite network attached storage

Network attached storage is a popular method to share storage by using file sharing, which also facilitates data sharing over standard IP-based network interfaces. To support large distributed environments, as well as enable data movement, sharing, and protection for branch offices, remote NAS devices can be protected to a centralized location. Data at various remote locations can be backed up, as well as replicated, to a central location, where it can be copied to other media, including tape. This is an example of a disk to disk to tape (D2D2T) to support regulatory compliance and other data protection needs.

In Figure 16.2, NAS storage devices of various sizes are shown at remote branch locations. The NAS storage devices are attached via standard IP network interfaces, including 10/100 and Gb Ethernet to servers. The remote locations are attached via an IP network to the primary site, where data can be backed up and mirrored. WORM technology and tape can be used at the primary site for data retention. NAS devices can be backed up to tape using NDMP as well as device-to-device replication. To reduce networking costs and improve network bandwidth utilization, IP-to-IP compression

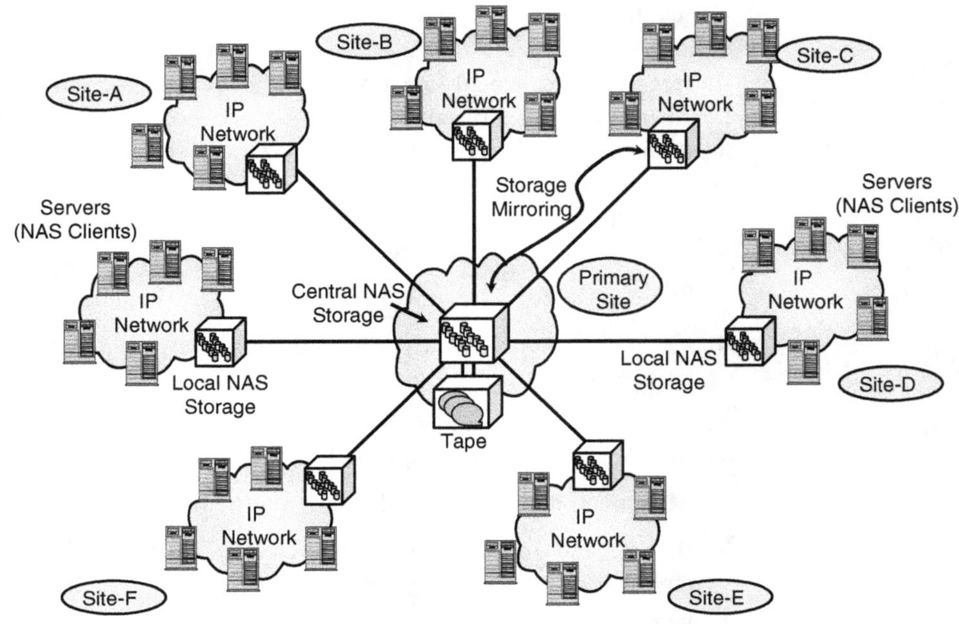

Figure 16.2 *Distributed storage network using NAS.*

and acceleration can be used as part of connecting the various locations together.

Some of the software tools used in Figure 16.2 include:

- Storage mirroring and replication of NAS devices
- IP-to IP-network accelerators for compression and distance support
- Backup and recovery software, including media management and NDMP
- Ethernet adapter trunking and aggregation software for performance
- Security tools, including RADIUS authentication, authorization, and zoning

16.2.2 Combined metropolitan and wide area storage network

A resilient storage network can span various distances and be made up of multiple fabrics and networking subnets using different interfaces and protocols. For metropolitan and campus environments, dedicated fiber optics can be used to support Fibre Channel (FCP and FICON), along with

Ethernet (iSCSI and NAS) for synchronous data processing. For longer distances, SONET/SDH optical networks and other wide area interfaces (IP based) can be used to support asynchronous processing, including data replication and remote tape backup. Various storage interface speeds can range from 10/100 Ethernet for NAS servers and clients to 10Gb Fibre Channel and Ethernet for switch-to-switch ISLs. Remote branch offices using NAS for data and storage sharing can access centralized storage resources, including backup and archiving. iSCSI, along with iFCP, can be used to enable remote open systems servers to access centralized resources. FCIP can be used to enable Fibre Channel FCP and FICON traffic to span distance.

In Figure 16.3, there are two fabrics made up of a collection of switches as edge devices attaching to additional switches to connect to a pair of DWDM devices. DWDM is being used not only to extend the distance between sites, but also to increase bandwidth for Fibre Channel, Ethernet, and other interfaces. An added benefit is that by adding ports or cards to the DWDM equipment, you can achieve self-provisioning to increase bandwidth and obtain new fiber on demand. NAS gateways and

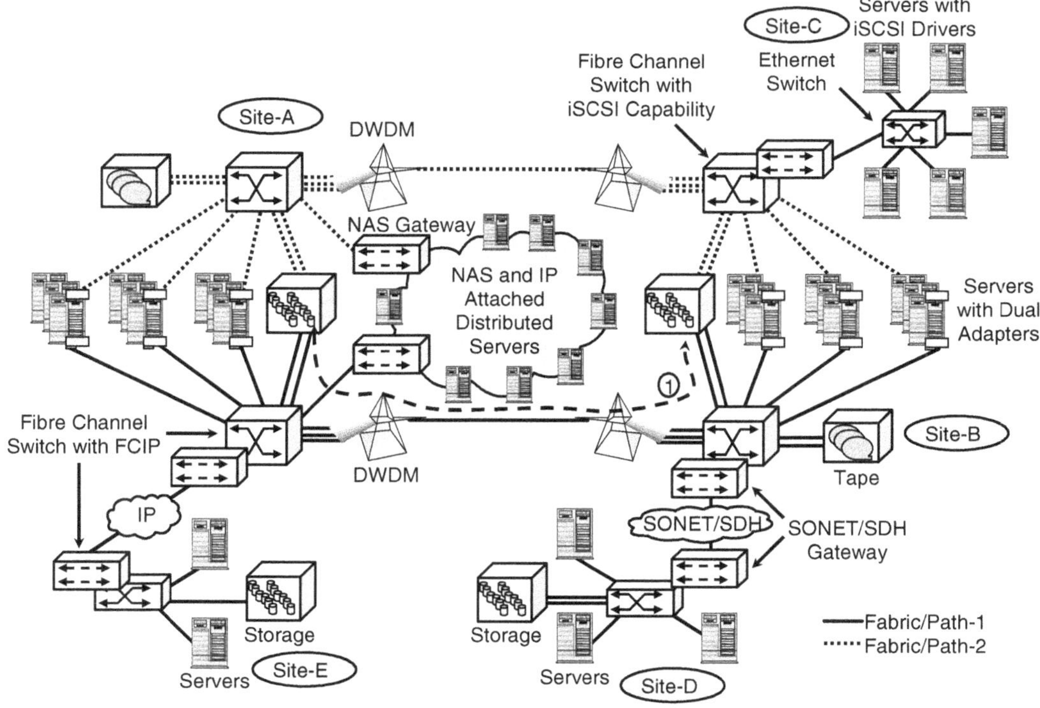

Figure 16.3 *Multisite, multiprotocol redundant storage network.*

servers are shown in the center of Figure 16.3 to provide centralized data and storage sharing while utilizing Fibre Channel storage resources (disk and tape). The NAS devices can be accessed locally as well as from remote locations using standard IP-based networks. Storage is mirrored between two locations over the DWDM devices using dedicated fiber optics and lambda services. An alterative would be to utilize SONET/SDH devices and optical carrier (OC-x) optical services to carry Fibre Channel, Ethernet, and other traffic between the locations. FICON Cascade can be installed on IBM zSeries mainframes running zOS to leverage the multisite storage network for remote data protection and access. High-speed interfaces, including 4Gb and 10Gb Fibre Channel and 10Gb Ethernet, can be used for interconnecting switch devices with lower speed (1Gb and 2Gb) for attaching servers.

Some of the software tools used in Figure 16.3 include:

- Hardware- and software-based mirroring between two locations
- Tape library sharing control software and backup status reporting
- Clustering and high-availability failover software
- Element managers for disk, tape, switches, adapters, servers, gateways, and routers
- Failover and clustering software for servers for high availability

Some technology and techniques represented in Figure 16.3 include:

- DWDM, SONET/SDH, FCIP, iSCSI, and long-range optics
- Multiple protocols supporting distance and business requirements
- Modular and enterprise storage, with Fibre Channel FCP interfaces
- Redundant paths and fabrics, with some servers having dual HBAs

16.2.3 Large multisite storage network

Storage networks can be of different sizes spanning various distances with multiple protocols and interfaces. Storage networks can be made up of multiple separate fabrics, isolated from each other, or connected as a common network. In Figure 16.4, a multisite large storage network is shown, with each site having a redundant configuration.

The various sites shown in Figure 16.4 are connected (1) to the primary site using wide area devices. Wide area gateway devices utilizing FCIP, iFCP, or SONET/SDH are used, with autonomous regions used to

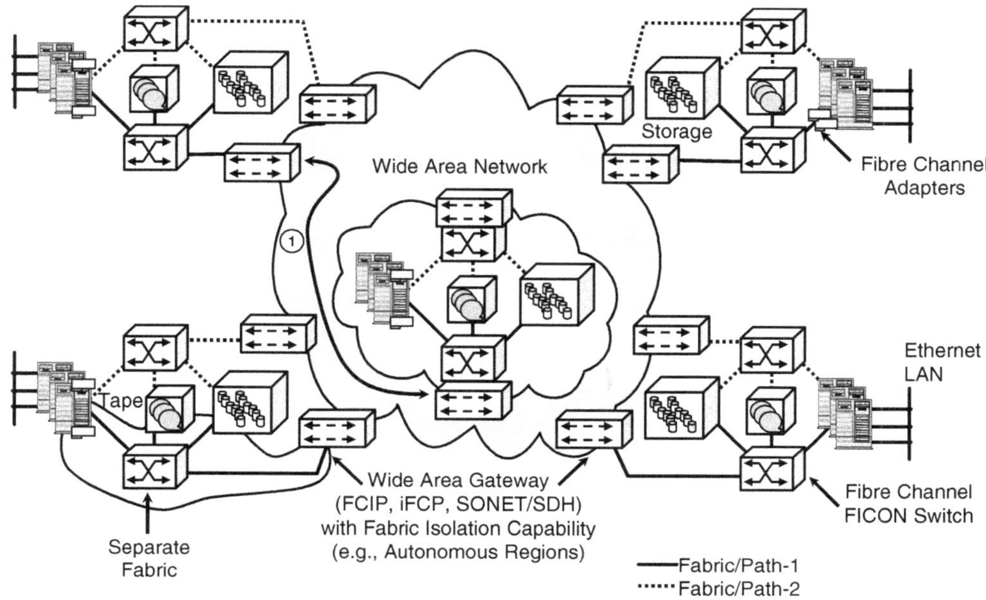

Figure 16.4 *Large multisite storage network.*

isolate the fabrics from each other. One scenario has the individual sites, each with redundant fabrics, function as separate subnets, which, for Fibre Channel, would be separate autonomous regions. If the configuration were using Ethernet, then these would be set up as separate VLAN subnets. In the example, there would be a total of ten separate fabrics (two per location, five locations including the primary site). Another scenario would be to create two fabrics (Path-1 and Path-2), interconnecting the various locations.

Some technology and techniques represented in Figure 16.4 include:

- Wide area gateway devices for interconnecting multiple sites
- Autonomous regions, state change management, and other isolation techniques
- Multiple protocols to support different distance and business requirements
- Redundant paths and separate fabrics, with some servers having dual HBAs

16.3 Chapter summary

Storage networks can span various distances using different technology to meet specific business and application requirements. Distance is essential for survivability, and metropolitan and wide area storage networks enable resilient storage networks.

What This Chapter Will Do For You

This chapter looks at examples, issues, and topics pertaining to large- and high-performance storage networks. Some of the items you will learn about in this chapter include:

- Essentials for successfully implementing large, flexible, and resilient storage networks
- Scaling performance and capacity necessary for large environments
- Making storage, server, and SAN consolidation work for you
- Removing previous myths on how large a storage network can be
- Important design examples to use as templates for what you can build and scale to

17

Large and High-Performance Examples

17.1 Overview

The past few chapters have included examples of small, intermix, and consolidated metropolitan and wide area storage networks. This chapter looks at some large and high-performance storage networks and builds on some of the examples from the previous chapters. Storage networks can be of various sizes, using different storage interfaces to meet diverse needs. Storage networks can be built as one large network or divided up into multiple smaller networks. Large and high-performance storage networks can be used to support many different environments and applications, including:

- Storage- and I/O-intensive processing
- Grid and high-performance computing
- Life sciences, geophysical, forecasting, simulations
- Vertical applications—aerospace, automobile, oil and gas, forecasting
- Video, image serving, and large-scale records retention
- Centralized backup and data protection

17.2 Storage- and I/O-intensive environments

Storage-intensive environments require a large amount of storage to support data mining, data warehousing, imaging, video, archiving, backup, and other applications requiring extensive amounts of data. Storage-intensive environments do not have to have large I/O rates and throughput volumes, particularly if the data is accessed infrequently. I/O-intensive environments can have large, medium, or small amounts of storage, with a large number of I/Os (transactions) processed, large volume (bandwidth), or a combination. An example of an I/O-intensive application would be

OLTP. Applications can be I/O intensive, storage intensive, or a combination. These applications can have a small number of servers or a large number of servers. The servers can be the same type with the same operating system or a mix of different operating systems, including open systems and mainframes. The flexibility of storage networking interfaces and protocols enables different configurations to be implemented to meet various needs. A rather simple approach to scaling is to use vertical scaling, where very large port count switches, each configured as a separate SAN island, are implemented. To increase the available port count, additional large port count switches could be installed, either as standalone islands or networked with others (horizontal scaling).

In Figure 17.1, four SAN islands are shown, each as a separate Fibre Channel switch supporting IBM mainframe FICON, open systems Fibre Channel FCP, or a combination. This example would also be applicable to IBM ESCON mainframe environments or InfiniBand for clustering. Multiple paths from each of the servers connect to each of the switches and in turn to the storage subsystems. This any-to-any configuration provides high performance, a large number of ports, and high availability. For example, by using 128 port switches, 512 usable ports would be available. For an environment migrating from ESCON to FICON, using a conversion ratio (number of ports) of 4:1 (four ESCON to each FICON interface) at 512 usable ports would be the equivalent of 2,048 usable ESCON ports. By

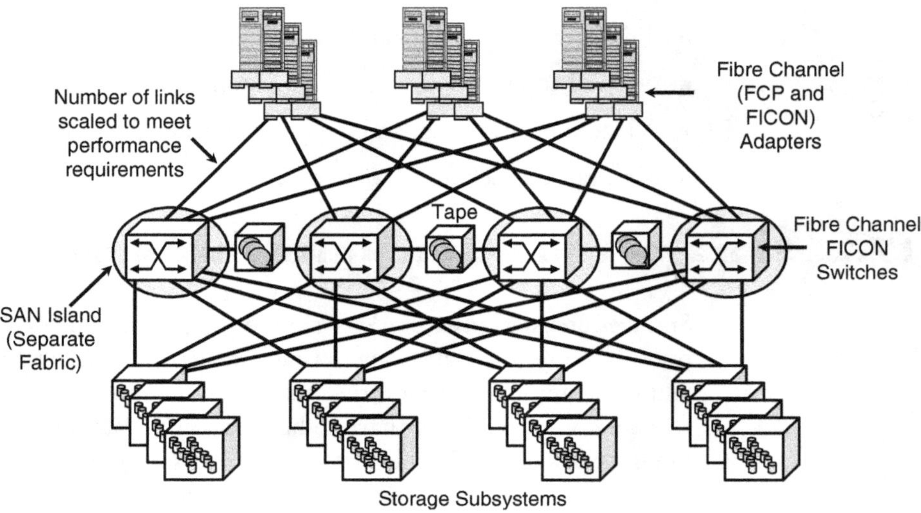

Figure 17.1 *Large high-performance, multipath storage network.*

using 256 port switches this would double to 4,086 ESCON ports and so on. To increase the size of the storage network but maintain separate isolated paths for redundancy, the individual switches in each fabric could be confined into a cascade with another switch. Even larger configurations could be implemented by creating three switch rings (triangle) as well as many other combinations. Caution should be exercised about keeping the configuration relatively simple and avoiding excessive hops between servers and storage devices and switches (hop count). On the lighter side, hops are good in beer; however, they add latency to I/O and data movement, so keep them to a minimum.

The storage subsystems could be a mix of enterprise class systems supporting Fibre Channel FCP for open systems and FICON for mainframe environments. Modular storage devices with ATA and SATA storage could be used for data migration and life-cycle management. Tape subsystems, including Virtual Tape Systems (VTS), are attached to the switches using redundant paths, with media management and tape sharing software installed on the servers. Multiple large cache–centric as well as high-end modular open systems storage can be used as storage devices. High-performance clustered storage subsystems with ultrascalability and virtualization devices can be used to provide large capacity storage.

This configuration could be extended for metropolitan and wide area applications by turning each of the SAN islands into a cascade, with ISLs between the switches. For IBM mainframe environments, FICON Cascade could be used to enable remote storage to be accessed. Storage subsystems could also mirror their data synchronously or asynchronously between locations. Various gateways and routers, including iSCSI, NAS, and wide area devices for iFCP and FCIP, could be used to accessorize this configuration for added functionality and flexibility. SAN management software should be used in addition to element managers, particularly if multiple vendor technologies are being used.

17.2.1 Large core-edge redundant storage networks (2,300 ports)

In Chapter 9, topologies were shown that could be combined with others to create storage networks implemented with various interfaces. The storage network example in Figure 17.2 could be made up of small switches, a combination of small and large switches to scale into the hundreds of ports, or made up of very large port count switches to scale into the thousands of ports. In the previous example chapters, various core-edge topologies have

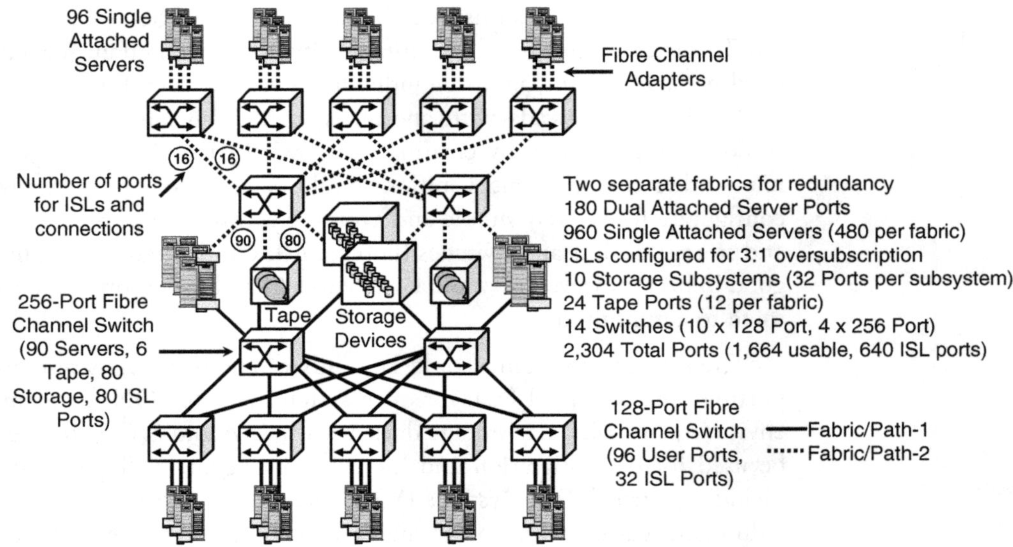

Figure 17.2 *Large, high-performance storage network.*

been shown with servers attaching to separate fabric paths for redundancy. Another variation on this is that some servers may not need to be dual attached if business and availability needs (including maintenance and support) do not require it.

In Figure 17.2, two separate core-edge storage networking topologies are shown, one on the top and one on the bottom. Some servers in the middle, along with storage devices (disk and tape), are dual attached to large port count Fibre Channel (FICON and FCP) switches. Additional servers that do not need full redundancy are attached to edge switches in a fan-in (many servers accessing the storage), fan-out (storage being accessed by many servers) topology. In this example there are four (two per fabric) 256-port switches at the core with ten (five per fabric) 128-port edge switches. In the past the term *edge switch* has been associated with a switch of a particular size in the Fibre Channel world; however, as seen in Figure 17.2, the term *edge switch* refers to a switch performing a certain function (aggregating many services).

The appropriate number of ISLs between the edge and core switches would be implemented to meet the desired performance level. Higher-speed interfaces could be used, including 4Gb and 10Gb as ISLs, as well as multiple 2Gb ISLs trunked together. Some of the servers that are single attached could be attached to a second edge switch in the same fabric to provide some path redundancy for maintenance of switches and adapters. The server, if configured for dual attachment to the same fabric, should be attached to two separate switches, since loss of a switch would result in lost connectivity for that server. However, those servers would not be protected in case an entire fabric were inaccessible, as would be the servers that are attached to two separate fabrics at the core. The decisions to single attach, dual attach to the same fabric, or direct attach to different fabrics, will be a function of your business and storage networking requirements. Plan ahead for adequate ports for expansion and dual, multiple (more than two) attachment of servers and storage devices.

On the right in Figure 17.2 are some speeds and feeds (specifications) for this particular storage networking example; these include 2,304 total ports (two fabrics) with 1,664 usable ports (640 ports being used for ISLs) configured in a 3:1 oversubscription design. A 3:1 oversubscription in this design means that three server ports statistically will share an ISL path to the core. Put another way, this means that the server ports are assumed to be always 33 percent and that they are the same speed as the ISLs (e.g., all 2Gb). The appropriate level of oversubscription needed for your environment will depend on your workload and service requirements.

With cost not a factor, a 1:1 ratio of server ports to ISLs would provide guaranteed bandwidth, but that may not be reality. Another extreme would be to oversubscribe using 7:1 or 15:1 for busy servers to reduce costs without regard to performance. Look at your servers' workloads under normal and peak conditions, plus growth considerations, to determine your workload requirements. Use caution with trunking approaches to funnel all traffic over an aggregated number of ISLs with regard to high-priority traffic. This is analogous to opening up a freeway to more traffic without setting aside a lane or two for high-priority traffic. Use ISL and path isolation techniques, including ISL groups, preferred pathing, and deterministic routing, to fully leverage storage networking bandwidth. Within switches, Virtual Output Queues (VOQ) can be utilized to alleviate bottlenecks associated with head of line blocking of faster devices by slower devices. The software tools and storage networking technology and techniques in Figure 17.2 are similar to those discussed in previous chapters but on a larger scale.

17.2.2 Very large distributed core-edge storage networks

In Chapter 16, a large distributed, multisite storage network example was shown in Figure 16.4 that consisted of ten different fabrics for redundancy.

In that example the various storage network segments or fabrics were isolated from each other using autonomous regions and other segmentation techniques, including iFCP and state change management. Very large storage networks can be implemented using very large port count switches that have 256 to 512 ports, with larger ones on the drawing board. For environments where all of the servers are located in the same room or close proximity, solutions similar to that shown in Figure 17.1 may be applicable. Another approach is needed for environments where dedicated high-speed fiber optics exist between server and storage locations. For example, in Figure 17.3 some servers and storage may be in one part of a computer room with attachment to two different fabrics via switches. These switches connect to other switches in the same room or perhaps different parts of a building or campus in a star configuration.

In Figure 17.3, storage from the group of servers on the top left could be mirrored to the storage device in the center using the redundant paths. For performance the appropriate number of ISLs is configured to meet service requirements. In terms of size, the example in Figure 17.3 could scale from 160 ports per fabric (320 total ports), using 32 port switches, up to 2,560 ports per fabric (5,120 total ports), using 512 port switches. These total port counts would be minus however many ports you need to allocate for ISLs. When determining how many ports are needed or available, besides factoring in ports for ISLs, include ports for spares, expansion for new servers and storage, and ports for attachment of bridges, gateways, and routers (including iSCSI, NAS, iFCP, and FCIP devices).

You may also want to set some ports aside for attachment of monitoring and management devices for data collection and fault isolation. If you are planning on using a cable management system, also known as structured cabling solutions, you may want to plan for diagnostic and test port capability to eliminate disruptions in the future. Nondisruptive diagnostic ports have been slow to find their way into Fibre Channel storage networking switching devices. From a security standpoint, if you have diagnostic ports on switches or cable management systems, be sure to secure these to prevent unauthorized eavesdropping and snooping. The software tools and storage networking technology and techniques used in the previous example build upon those in this and the previous chapters. Regardless of the size of the storage network, pay attention to the number of LUNs that are supported by the storage device you are or will be using. The number of LUNs supported varies, as does the number of servers supported. Different operating systems, volume managers, and filesystems support different sizes of LUNs and volumes. NAS solutions also have

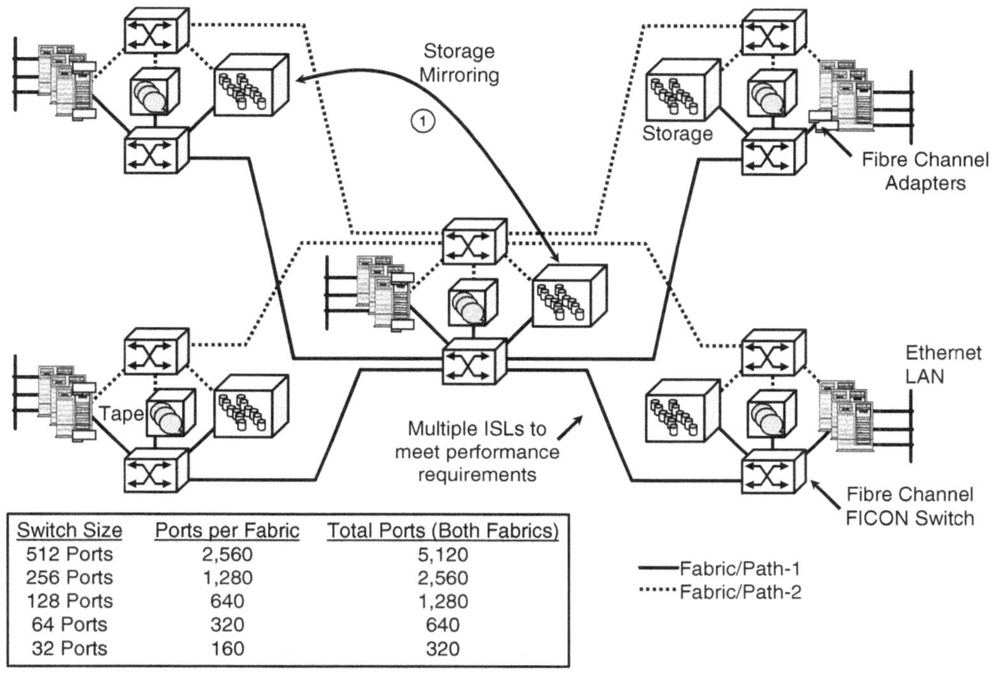

Switch Size	Ports per Fabric	Total Ports (Both Fabrics)
512 Ports	2,560	5,120
256 Ports	1,280	2,560
128 Ports	640	1,280
64 Ports	320	640
32 Ports	160	320

Figure 17.3 *Large storage network.*

limits on the number and sizes of filesystems supported. Check with your storage provider as to how many LUNs or volumes are available as well as what their recommendations for the attachment of servers are, based on different workloads.

Filesystem storage block and cluster size (discussed in Chapter 2) are important as larger storage devices and filesystems are created. Some of the challenges involved with ultralarge storage environments include how to perform backup and recovery and how to handle large filesystems and metadata.

17.3 Chapter summary

Very large storage networks can and have been implemented. Storage networks can have different topologies and configurations, using various interfaces and protocols. What is right for your storage network is what works and meets your needs. Careful design can help improve redundancy and availability for normal operations as well during maintenance and upgrades.

The previous examples have shown various configurations, from large SAN islands to redundant multiswitch configurations. Keep your storage networking design simple yet robust in order to scale, and avoid complexity where possible.

What This Chapter Will Do For You

This chapter provides a wrap-up for the book, tying together and summarizing essential information for implementing and managing resilient storage networks. Some of the items you will learn about in this chapter include:

- Storage networks can be deployed for SMB, SOHO, and enterprise environments
- A storage network is not resilient without a good and flexible design and redundancy
- Understanding design and technology trade-offs to maximize IT spending efficiency
- Without resilient storage networks you are exposed to data availability threats
- Resilient storage networks are the sum of hardware, software, networks, and staff expertise combined with sound procedures, policies, and good design

18

Wrap-up

18.1 Overview

Resilient storage networks can be of different sizes and utilize various technologies, interfaces, and protocols to meet business needs and requirements. This chapter provides closing comments and some tips pertaining to resilient storage networks. You will find additional material in the appendices, including some useful Web sites, check lists, and a glossary of terms.

18.2 Review

To recap, resilient storage networks enable access to data when and where it is needed. Resilient storage networks can be of different sizes and utilize different technologies to meet specific business needs and requirements. Resilient storage networks can be implemented for SOHO and SMB environments as well as ultralarge distributed enterprise environments. The volume of information being generated and stored continues to grow, requiring additional storage capacity and I/O bandwidth to access it. The value of information continues to increase, along with the importance of timely access. Understanding that information has different values can be used to match the appropriate protection, storage access techniques, and type of storage technology to address total cost of ownership. Resilient storage networks provide data protection and maintain accessibility with redundant components, sound design, and good management practices.

Storage networks can be built to support many functions, including file servers, with Network Attached Storage (NAS); block data access, using what is commonly referred to as Storage Area Network (SAN); and object-based Content Addressable Storage (CAS). Storage networks can be implemented to support server-to-server communications for clustering, high-speed data movement, and server data replication. Storage networks can be used to support server to storage (disk and tape) on a local and remote basis, storage to storage for device- and appliance-based mirroring, and to interconnect different networks (SAN to SAN). Interfaces, including Fibre Channel, Ethernet, and InfiniBand, can be used to support storage networking. Storage networking protocols include FCP, FICON, and iSCSI for block data movement; and NFS, CIFS, and DAFS for file-based (NAS) access. FCIP and iFCP can be used for wide area and remote access. Optical networks provide the core for building storage and data networks on a local and wide area basis. For metropolitan and wide area applications, TDM, CWDM, WDM, and DWDM can be used with lambda services and where dedicated dark fiber is available. For longer distance, and where dedicated fiber is not available, SONET/SDH optical carrier (OC-x) services can be utilized to carry ATM, IP, Fibre Channel, and other traffic.

Storage networking devices include servers, adapters, switches (including directors), routers and gateways, and storage devices (disk and tape). Switching devices, sometimes called fabric appliances, and intelligent switches have become more advanced. Switching devices are able to support storage and virtualization services, including data movement, backup, replication, storage pooling, protocol routing, and security functions. Storage networking design should incorporate plans for growth, maintenance, and fault containment. Design your storage network by determining your requirements and then identifying technology and solutions that meet your needs. Avoid designing around a specific technology to prevent future bottlenecks and technology or vendor lock-in. Work with your storage networking technology suppliers to understand what they are currently working on, as well as their road maps for the future. Tell them what you want to do, as well as what you have to do, and get them involved early. Vendors will listen, especially when you characterize things in terms of what you like, what you want, and what you have to have. Keep storage network design relatively simple in order to scale in a stable and predicable manner. Utilize experienced independent analysis and consulting organizations for input, design validation, technology assessment, and industry directions. Keep in mind that a resilient storage network is flexible and scalable, regardless of whether it is supporting block, file-based NAS, or a combination.

Storage network performance and capacity planning are an ongoing process to identify how storage resources are being utilized. Using performance and capacity planning techniques can help reduce surprises by having better information about how your environment is performing under different conditions. Storage management consists of various levels of monitoring, diagnostics, notification, configuration, provisionment, and reporting. When looking at storage management tools, identify which functions you need to perform and prioritize where your time is being spent. Leverage tools to address the functions that you are spending the most time on and build business cases to justify acquisition of tools. Storage networking management software and tools are evolving, and using the philosophy of learning to walk before you run is important. For example, while you may ultimately desire a comprehensive total storage and storage networking management tool set that does everything, look for simple point products that you can use today. Use these management tools to gain experience and to automate some common tasks, such as reporting, provisioning, and other functions. Use this experience to help build your business case for larger, more extensive tool sets.

Storage networking has evolved from research projects and test lab environments to first-generation solutions and production environments. Consequently, a shift from reactionary to tactical to a strategic approach in design and management of storage and storage networking is in order. Do more with less initially so that you can do more in the future; put a good infrastructure and practices in place today to build on for the future. Storage services and virtualization are enabling and emerging, along with other data abstraction techniques and technology. Leverage virtualization and storage services technology where they make sense, and where they can solve real problems. New technologies should not add any more layers of management, resulting in more work. New storage and storage network technology should work for you instead of being yet another technology for you to manage.

Is there interoperability among storage networking components, technology, interfaces, and protocols today? The answer is yes for some components and pieces; for others, there is still plenty of work needed. Interoperability is also a function of your expectations. There are different levels of interoperability, from adapters working with different switches and storage devices (an area that has improved quite a lot), switches working with other switches, software working with other software, and so on. For each of these levels, interoperability varies. Push your vendors, suppliers, and partners to work toward interoperability and adherence toward standards if that is important to you.

Data needs to be protected using a combination of techniques, including RAID, mirroring, replication, backup, and retention using archiving. New data-protection techniques include multilevel backups such as disk to disk to tape (D2D2T), which can involve mirroring data from disk and then to tape. A multilayer, multiring perimeter of defense should be implemented to protect information resources such as data and IT assets. The last line of defense for securing data is at the storage device itself. This includes LUN mapping and controlling physical access to storage devices and interfaces.

Examples of resilient storage networks for workgroup, departmental, SMB, and SOHO environments are small NAS, iSCSI, and Fibre Channel solutions. Storage networks can support servers, storage, and existing SAN consolidation on a local and wide are a basis. By using different technologies, interfaces, and protocols, distances from a few kilometers to thousands of kilometers can be spanned. Storage networks can vary in size from a few devices in an SMB or SOHO environment using NAS to thousands of ports in an enterprise data center to a large, geographically distributed storage network.

18.2.1 Identifying and selecting storage networking solutions

In Chapter 8, we discussed the importance of understanding requirements and assessment. As part of a storage network design or implementation process, you may need to put together a Request For Information (RFI), Request For Proposal (RFP), or Request For Quotation (RFQ). RFIs are useful for gathering information about technologies and capabilities for planning purposes, so be clear to your vendors that you are in a planning process and let them know when or if you plan on doing something. This will help the vendor give you the support you need while allowing it to focus on current business at hand. Get your vendors and business partners involved early on, so that they are not surprised when they receive an RFI, RFP, or RFQ.

When putting together an RFI, RFP, or RFQ, clearly state what it is that you want, and define your criteria and requirements, success factors, and penalties, if any. By keeping your definitions and criteria tight, you reduce the amount of leeway that vendors will have to maneuver around your questions and requirements. Allow vendors to elaborate and present alternatives, but have them respond to your requirements. Also, it is very important to clearly communicate up front the rules by which the process will be performed and how questions and disputes will be handled. State the format for the responses and to whom they should be sent. Identify the points of contact, as well as who should not be contacted. Get management buy-in and endorsement for support as well as for legal purposes. Clearly state what the evaluation process and criteria are, as well as any rating factors and comparison matrices. Identify which information, including questions, is being shared with others and which is confidential. Tell the vendor what you will do and how you will do it. Share with the vendors all the information that you can so everything is out on the table and given the appropriate consideration. An RFP is a legal document, so if you are going to do it, do it right and get the appropriate management and other personnel, including purchasing, involved early. Identify who is responsible for what and how disputes will be resolved. The process should be balanced and work for you and your suppliers and business partners. Allow the right amount of time to perform the process, including preparation, vendor meetings, analysis, evaluations, and follow-up meetings. Keep in mind that these are legal documents and it is important to remain objective and un-biased. The last thing you want to have to read about in the morning paper or on-line Web service is a vendor protesting a bid process in which you were involved.

18.2.2 Emerging trends and directions

Management tools are undergoing significant evolution and development, with large amounts of venture capital funding being invested in new software startups. Life-cycle management is a key approach toward putting data in the right place on storage, with the appropriate level of performance, costs, and protection to match the value of the data. This will help to address current management efficiency gaps. The good news today is that storage, particularly with ATA/SATA disk drives using iSCSI and NAS access, can be used for long-term data retention to help reduce costs. WORM technology is becoming more common on storage subsystems, including NAS, to help with meeting regulatory needs. Meanwhile, software that helps identify, classify, and migrate data to the appropriate medium continues to evolve.

It's a fairly safe assumption that storage network interfaces and protocols will become faster and support more bandwidth with longer distances. Cost, another dynamic component of storage networking, has steadily dropped per megabyte or gigabyte of storage. Two ways of looking at storage network costs are that they can be expected to drop, and, for approximately the same or even slightly less cost, more functionality is obtained. Existing storage networks can be expected to grow or be merged with other standalone storage network islands to create larger networks. New storage networks in the SMB and SOHO space, using NAS and iSCSI, will continue to evolve and grow. A good example of this is to check one of the computer supply magazines; you will find low-end RAID arrays with SAN capabilities along with entry-level NAS devices. For these environments to implement storage networking techniques, they have to be cost effective and easy to use. Servers continue to appear with newer, faster, and more flexible interfaces.

NAS-based file access should continue to be popular for SMB and SOHO environments, with some adopting iSCSI for block access applications. For medium size environments, Gb Ethernet, SATA, and embedded Fibre Channel ports on servers will continue to appear. The middle tier storage network environment, seen in Figure 14.1, is an area where there are and will continue to be many choices. Faster server interfaces, including PCI-X and PCI-Express, should help to support faster interfaces, including 4Gb and 10Gb Fibre Channel and 10Gb Ethernet.

On the upper end of the storage network environment, embedded Fibre Channel and Ethernet switch chips have appeared in blade servers, with InfiniBand positioned as another interconnect. At this level, Fibre Channel for FCP and FICON will continue to dominate until a more suitable interface comes around. You have choices of storage networking interfaces and protocols to meet your specific needs and requirements. You can use the right tool for the right projects, balancing costs, performance, flexibility, and resiliency for your specific business requirements.

18.3 Some comments and tips

Here are some tips and reminders regarding storage networking and disaster recovery that can be used as a cheat sheet or the start of a checklist. These range from planning for growth and maintenance to applying the appropriate level of security to meet your needs.

Have copies of software and firmware available as part of your overall recovery documentation, including manuals, CDs, and other setup information necessary to recover your environment. Also, have copies of any license or software keys needed to restore your environment. Maintain documentation of your storage network, including all HBAs, fabric devices (switches, directors, bridges, and gateways), and storage devices (disk and tape). This information should include which ports devices and servers are attached to, how they are configured, zone information, HBA and other device settings, management software, and SNMP MIB information. Store this information in a safe and secure place and ensure that it is included in your disaster recovery plans and documentation.

Pay attention to your environmental conditions, including power, cooling, fiber cabling, and network access points. Test your configuration and document any differences when at a recovery facility as part of a larger disaster recovery test. Try to arrange some standalone time at the test facility to determine the behavior of your SAN during normal and extreme periods. Also use this time to test procedures and policies and practice maintenance functions, such as applying Nondisruptive Code Loads (NDCL) and Nondisruptive Code Activation (NDCA).

Do you know how long it will take to get new circuits provisioned for your recovery center, or are they ready now? Don't have all your fiber optics located adjacent to each other. Fiber-optic cables are not immune to backhoes and other digging equipment. While it is no different from traditional copper cabling, fiber-optic cabling tends to carry more bandwidth and traffic, so its impact is greater.

Storage networks (SANs) can be implemented with existing storage devices in phases to further simplify management, including backup and recovery. Remove single points of failure by configuring for redundancy, including two or more HBAs per server attached to separate switches, directors, or fabrics. These dual, quad, alternate, or multipathed configurations can be used not only for availability but also for performance and scheduled maintenance, all of which affect the resiliency of the enterprise. Another benefit of creating dual or multipathed configurations is to increase scalability to support growth. Your storage network should be able to support seamless growth in a stable, scalable manner, as well as support new protocols and interfaces for additional functionality.

IP-based storage networks may require special adapters and device drivers, which may have to be isolated and used only for storage networking, as opposed to mixed mode (storage networking and traditional networking such as LANs). While IP-based storage networking may be able to use existing networking infrastructure, unless there is excess bandwidth available, a separate gigabit or IP-based network should be created to avoid bottlenecks and performance issues. Plan for failures and outages (planned and unplanned) to contain faults and increase availability. Utilize redundant power and separate power feeds where available to further isolate and contain faults. Keep in mind that storage networks are I/O channels that require high availability with predictable performance.

Future planning can help maintain and evolve the resilient enterprise by reducing and eliminating disruptions. There is no right or wrong topology for your storage network or a specific fabric or domain; rather, the right topology is the one that fits the needs and requirements for your environment. Use the appropriate technology, topology, and techniques for your specific needs and requirements. With the current flexibility of storage networking technology, the storage network should match the needs of your environment, as opposed to adjusting your business to the technology.

Understand the locality and placement of devices on the storage network relative to their performance needs to contain localized traffic. Use monitoring and performance management tools to understand the workload under normal and abnormal conditions. Do you have adequate bandwidth for normal operations, as well as situations such as increased activity or the need to rapidly recover data from on-line, off-line, or near-line media? While your bandwidth may be sufficient for normal running periods, look at your extremes, including during backups and rebuilds, for an indicator of what your disaster recovery workload might be.

Avoid Domain ID mismatch and other configuration issues that may pop up with interoperability. This can be even more important when going to a recovery site, using floor systems that may not have been preset to your configuration. This could also be true with adding new equipment. A strategy is to wipe devices clean and apply standard templates for your environment, with appropriate changes that you have saved and documented.

To enable Fibre Channel distances of 100km and more, as many buffer credits as possible per port should be deployed. Current switching devices will have 64 or more buffer credits per port. Keep in mind that 2Gb, 4Gb, and 10Gb Fibre Channel will use up buffer credits faster, so you will need more of the buffer credits for distance.

Utilize zoning (WWNN or port) to isolate tape and disk traffic on common fabrics, and from other servers where needed. Some storage technologies, including disk and tape, may require the use of a unique zone for each server to isolate disk and tape activity. This will require the need for more zones as you consolidate and add additional servers and storage devices. Work with your storage disk and tape vendors to identify what they are doing to ensure coexistence of their products, without the need for excessive overzoning and associated management. Use zoning, autonomous regions, virtual SANs, and state change management, including RSCN filtering, where available to isolate unwanted traffic and disruptions to other devices.

18.4 Where to get more information

This book is meant to be technology and vendor neutral, using, where possible, generic examples based on real-world experience. In addition to

Appendix A, which contains some useful storage networking–related URLs and Web sites, additional information can be found at www.storageio.com. If you are a technology vendor, supplier, or service provider not listed in Appendix A or on this book's Web site and you wish to be included, send a note using the contact information found on the Web site.

18.5 Chapter and book summary

Storage networks can be implemented for small environments as well as ultralarge enterprise environments. Distance and redundancy are essential for providing continuous access of information by applications. Resilient storage networks provide access to information on a local, metropolitan, and wide area distance basis. Resilient storage networks have redundancy designed in to support maintenance, growth, and provide fault isolation in the event of a component or site failure. Resilient storage networks are flexible to meet the needs of different environments while protecting data and access to it. Two important elements of storage networking are storage and I/O networks (storage networks). Storage networks can be implemented using various storage, network, and access technologies and techniques. Storage networks enable distance, performance, and flexibility to meet different requirements for various application environments. Finally, protect the people responsible for and involved with storage networks, as they are important for resilient storage networking.

Useful Web Sites

The following is a list of various Web site URLs mentioned in this book. Some additional, useful Web sites for more information about storage networking are also included here. Two companion sites for this book are http://books.elsevier.com/companions/1555583113 and www.storageio.com, which contain additional information on technologies and techniques discussed in this book.

The storage networking industry is constantly changing, with existing vendors merging, being acquired, or exiting the market while new ones appear. Feel free to send a note via the Web site www.storageio.com if there is a missing URL that should be added.

www.10gea.org	10Gb Ethernet industry trade organization
www.1394ta.org	1394 (Firewire) trade association
www.ansi.org	American National Standards Institute
www.asciitable.com	Site containing the ASCII character set table
www.asnp.org	Association of Storage Networking Professionals
www.atmforum.com	ATM Trade Association
www.cert.org	Internet security information
www.cmg.org	Computer Measurement Group
www.datcollaborative.org	Data Collaboration Group and DAPL material

www.dmtf.org	Distributed Management Task Force
www.evaluatorgroup.com	Evaluator Group
www.fibrechannel.org	Fibre Channel Trade Group
www.gocsi.com	Computer Security Institute
www.hgai.com	Storage networking training
www.ietf.org	Internet Engineering Task Force
www.infinibandta.org	InfiniBand Trade Organization
www.infostor.com	Magazine focused on storage and storage networking
www.iometer.org	Iometer performance benchmarking tool
www.ndmp.org	Trade organization for NDMP backup protocol
www.nerc.com	North American Electrical Reliability Council
www.nsic.org	National Storage Industry Consortium
www.redbooks.ibm.com	IBM Redbooks and Red pieces technical articles
www.scsita.org	SCSI Trade Association
www.serialata.org	Serial ATA Trade Association
www.siemon.com	Storage networking infrastructure items
www.snia.org	Storage Networking Industry Association
www.ssswg.org	IEEE Storage Systems Standards Work Group
www.storagemagazine.com	Magazine focused on storage and storage networking
www.storagenetworking.org	Storage Networking Users Groups
www.storageperformance.org	Storage Performance Council information

www.t10.org/scsi-3.htm	ANSI T10 (SCSI-associated information) site
www.t11.org	ANSI T11 page for Fibre Channel information
www.tpc.org	Transaction Processing Performance Council
www.usb.org	USB Trade Association
www.veritas.com/publishing	*The Resilient Enterprise* (a Veritas book)
www.xfpmsa.org	10Gb Multisource Trade Group
www.zjournal.com	Magazine focused on IBM zSeries environments

Some storage networking manufacturers and service providers include:

www.3com.com	Networking equipment
www.3par.com	Storage solutions
www.abovenet.com	Metropolitan and wide area storage networking
www.adaptec.com	Adapters and storage
www.adic.com	Backup and data protection solutions
www.advaoptical.com	Optical networking
www.alacritech.com	Storage networking adapters
www.agilent.com	Host adapters and test equipment
www.alcatel.com	Networking and storage networking equipment
www.americanfibersystems.com	Metropolitan storage networks
www.ancot.com	Storage networking testing equipment
www.apc.com	Power protection
www.appiq.com	SRM software
www.apple.com	Servers and storage

www.bluearc.com	NAS storage
www.bmc.com	Storage management software
www.brocade.com	Switches, WAN gateways, software
www.ca.com	Data management software
www.ciena.com	Optical networking
www.cipheroptics.com	Storage networking security
www.cisco.com	Switches, WAN and optical networking
www.cnt.com	Switches, WAN gateways, software
www.commvault.com	Data management software
www.compellent.com	Storage subsystems and software
www.creekpath.com	Storage management software
www.crossroads.com	Storage networking gateways
www.datacore.com	Storage management software
www.datadirectnetworks.com	Storage subsystems
www.datadomain.com	Backup storage
www.decru.com	Storage networking security
www.dell.com	Storage networking equipment
www.dothill.com	Storage devices
www.emc.com	Storage subsystems software
www.emulex.com	Host bus adapters and embedded switches
www.extremenetworks.com	Networking switches
www.falconstor.com	Storage management software
www.finisar.com	Storage networking optics, test equipment
www.foundrynetworks.com	Networking switches
www.fujitsu.com	Servers and storage

www.hds.com	Storage subsystems and software
www.hp.com	Storage networking hardware and software
www.ibm.com	Storage networking hardware and software
www.incipient.com	Virtualization software
www.infinicon.com	InfiniBand switches
www.infinityio.com	Storage networking training
www.innovationdp.com	Data management software
www.iomega.com	Storage
www.intel.com	Host adapters and chips
www.jdsu.com	Storage networking optics
www.jni.com	Host bus adapters
www.lampertz.com	Data center protection
www.legato.com	Storage management software, part of EMC
www.liebert.com	Airconditioning
www.lsilogicstorage.com	Storage subsystems and adapters
www.maranti.com	Storage switch
www.maxtor.com	Disk drives
www.maxxan.com	Storage switch
www.mcdata.com	Switches, WAN gateways, software
www.methode.com	Storage networking transceivers
www.microsoft.com	NAS software and storage networking drivers
www.neoscale.com	Storage networking security
www.networkappliance.com	Storage subsystems, management software

www.nexsan.com	Storage
www.nortelnetworks.com	Optical networking
www.onaro.com	SAN management
www.onstor.com	NAS storage
www.oracle.com	Data management software
www.panasas.com	Object storage
www.pcisig.com	Site for PCI and PCI-X information
www.procom.com	NAS Storage
www.qlogic.com	Host bus adapters and switches
www.qualstar.com	Tape backup solutions
www.quantum.com	Tape drives and libraries
www.sanrad.com	SAN Router
www.seagate.com	Disk drives
www.sgi.com	Storage networking equipment and software
www.snap.com	Storage
www.softek.com	Storage networking management software
www.solutiontechnology.co.uk	Storage networking training
www.sony.com	Storage devices
www.spirent.com	Storage networking test equipment
www.stonefly.com	SAN Router
www.storability.com	Storage management software
www.storagetekcom	Disk, tape, data management software
www.store-age.com	Storage management software
www.sun.com	Storage networking hardware and software
www.sungard.com	Data protection services

www.tek-tools.com	SRM software
www.tivoli.com	Data management software
www.veritas.com	Data management software
www.xiotech.com	Storage subsystems and software
www.xyratex.com	Storage enclosures, subsystems, test equipment

For a more up-to-date list of storage networking vendors, refer to the Web site www.storageio.com, www.evaluatorgroup.com/charts, or one of the storage networking–related magazine Web sites mentioned above.

B

Resilient Storage Networking Checklist

The following are some useful check list items and reminders for designing, implementing, and managing a resilient storage network.

B.1 Some simple items that are easily forgotten

- Keep It Storage networking Simple (KISS) yet flexible and scalable
- Complexity can increase overall costs and negatively impact availability
- If something can fail, it will and at the worse possible time
- Resources made available will be consumed
- Look for weak links that can cause chains of events
- Protect your equipment, network, software, data, and people

B.2 Designing for survivability and flexibility

- Plan for growth, including technology replacements and upgrades
- Design for data maintenance, including data migration to new storage devices
- Design for maintenance and support including hardware, software, networks
- Design for fault containment using redundant components and access paths
- Utilize redundant adapters on servers to attach to separate networks
- Utilize path management and load balancing software for adapters

- Utilize server failover and cluster software to access resilient storage
- Utilize separate I/O paths and optionally separate providers for wide area interfaces
- Make sure wide area networking paths actually take separate unique paths
- Determine your bandwidth needs to match your requirements and budget
- Avoid treating all data the same, match protection to level of importance
- Align different types of data to appropriate type of storage and access method
- Leverage new disk-based backup storage technologies for secondary storage
- Leverage thin provisioning techniques and technology to reduce storage capacity
- Implement 9-micron SMF fiber optic cabling to support faster interfaces and distance
- Utilize storage management tools to understand data usage patterns
- Deploy new servers that support faster interface and bus adapters
- Migrate less frequently-used data to alternative storage devices to free up space

B.3 Have clear objectives and requirements

- Understand what level of availability you need for your different applications and the appropriate level of data protection to meet your various requirements
- What level of availability is needed—continuous availability, high availability clustering active failover, standby failover, cold failover, or bare metal restoration?
- What is your recovery point objective (RPO) and your recovery time objective (RTO)
- Recovery time involves restoration of data from alternate storage devices plus any database system rollback and server reboot.

B.4 Performance, capacity planning, and design topics

- Identify congestion and bottlenecks in existing environments
- Determine ratios of how many servers to storage ports and network interfaces
- Determine ratios of how many older interfaces can be converted to faster ones
- Improve IP performance and bandwidth using IP–IP acceleration devices
- Accelerate remote tape backup using SAN distance devices and tape pipelining
- Develop a growth plan and resource usage forecast
- Understand differences between theoretical "marketing" and real performance metrics
- Traditional block-based applications including databases can now use NAS
- Have resources (bandwidth, capacity) to support normal and peak workloads
- Implement separate networks for management functions and data movement
- Establish performance base lines under various conditions and track activity
- Shop around for a telecommunications bandwidth providers
- Utilize disk-based backup systems that integrate with media management software
- Thin provisioning can be used to reduce the amount of actual storage capacity
- Thin provisioning can be used to speed up backup and other management tasks
- Regularly backup configuration files for software management tools and devices
- Maintain copies of critical configuration and operation documents in safe place

- The best topology is the one that fits your needs and allows for growth
- Strike a balance between large single networks and many small networks
- A common mistake is to try and create one large physical storage network with any to any access for all devices instead of creating subnetworks.
- Storage networks can scale to thousands of usable ports per fabric using vertical and horizontal scaling with large port switches providing residency and scalability
- When connecting multiple sites together, be careful not to inadvertently create a large single network without isolation and adequate security
- Develop a growth and capacity plan forecast for storage and storage networking resources, including storage, I/O bandwidth, network bandwidth, and ports

B.5 Data protection and security

- Combine RAID and some other form of data protection including backup
- Protect your data with regular backups to tape, disk, or other medium
- Utilize local and remote data mirroring as part of a data protection schema
- Synchronous mirroring should be used for shorter distances under 100km
- Asynchronous mirroring and replication should can be used for long distances
- Utilize off-site storage (on-line, or off-line) for data protection
- Utilize zoning, subnets, autonomous regions to isolate networks and paths
- Implement the appropriate level of zoning without adding complexity
- Change default passwords on storage networking components

- Properly dispose of retired storage media and devices
- Implement rings and zones of protection applicable to given threat level
- Enable authentication (RADIUS) and authorization security technologies
- Disable and restrict access (read and write) to SNMP MIBs and APIs
- Manage external access to management tool interfaces including vendor access
- Monitor backup status and randomly test recoverability of backup
- Hardware products should have N+1 (redundant) hot swap components
- Software and firmware should be nondisruptively loadable
- Look for NEBS- and MIL-STD–certified products for rugged environments
- Optical and tape media can be used for WORM long term retention applications
- Some disk su-systems support WORM functionality for long term retention using block-, file- (NAS), and object-based (CAS) access methods
- Utilize journal- and log-based filesystems with point in time (PIT) copy capabilities
- Employ encryption as part of data transmission over public networks
- Utilize LUN mapping from storage devices as a last line of security defense
- Plan for alternate networking and commutation paths and methods to access systems, applications, and storage networks. What good or value is information that you have saved and recovered if you cannot do anything with it?

B.6 Environmental and general items

- Have backup and redundant electrical power from separate electrical grids and feeds
- Employ electrical power surge suppression in office and equipment rooms

- Perform regular maintenance (check the gas tank) and tests of backup power systems
- Ensure adequate cooling and ventilation for equipment and computer rooms
- Implement physical security, monitoring, and access control systems
- Maintain and test fire detection, isolation, suppression, and control systems
- Utilize meaningful naming conventions for storage networking devices and resources
- Deploy sturdy equipment racks and cabinets that can support cable management
- Use fiber and cable management systems to simplify management and maintenance
- Avoid tight cable bends and kinking in copper and optical cabling
- Utilize good quality cabling (fiber optic and copper) and connectors
- Plan ahead and have extra power outlets and electrical feeds installed
- Utilize testing and diagnostic equipment for cabling and protocol analyzers
- Keep cable connectors and fiber optic transceivers clean and dust free
- Use domain ID lockdown with unique domain ID numbers on Fibre Channel switches
- Stay current with software updates and push your vendors to do the same
- Push vendors for interoperability and adherence to open standards
- Seek out references from other users for technology that you are looking to deploy
- Implement third-party consulting and analysis organizations for storage networking design, education, and technology assessment, and, if you cannot find one, send the author a note via the Web site www.storageio.com.

C

Glossary of Storage Networking Terminology

This glossary contains some terminology used in this book. Additional storage and storage networking–related terminology can be found in the online SNIA dictionary at http://www.snia.org/education/dictionary.

Active-active All redundant components are active.

Active-passive Redundant components in active standby mode of operation (one or more components not active).

ANSI American National Standards Institute is a standards coordinating organization.

ASCII Common computer character set used for open systems.

Authentication Validating the identity of someone or something to verify that he, or she, or it is what they are supposed to be.

Authorization Determining that someone or something is allowed to access a resource or perform an intended operation.

Big-endian Describes how data is stored (the order) for different computer systems. The most significant value in a sequence is stored in the lowest storage address (first). IBM mainframes utilize big-endian ordering.

Cable Wraps Plastic and Velcro straps for organizing cables.

CD Compact disk optical media.

CPU Central processing unit.

DBMS Database management system.

dd UNIX utility for performing data transfers and backup.

Decimal Number system used by people to count, also known as base ten with numbers of 0, 1, 2, 3, 4, 5, 6, 7, 8, 9.

DLT Digital linear tape.

DR Acronym for disaster recovery.

EBCDIC Computer character set used by IBM mainframes.

FC Abbreviation for Fibre Channel.

FC-AL Fibre Channel Arbitrated Loop.

Full duplex Concurrent sends and receives on the same link.

Hexadecimal Number system used by some computer programs to represent data, also known as base 16 with numbers of 0, 1, 2, 3, 4, 5, 6, 7, 8, 9, A, B, C, D, E, F, where A represents the number 10.

HTML Hypertext markup language.

HTTP Hypertext transfer protocol.

IPSec IP security.

ISO International Organization for Standardization.

LED Light-emitting diode used for generating light for short-distance, fiber-optic transmission.

Linux Popular open operating system environment.

Little-endian The least significant value in the sequence is stored first. Open systems typical utilize little-endian, but this can vary by processor manufacturer.

MHz Megahertz.

MIB Management information base for SNMP.

Name server A process that translates between symbolic names and network addresses, including worldwide node names and Fibre Channel addresses.

NCITS National Committee for Information Technology Standards.

Net POP Network point of presence.

OADM Define Optical Add/Drop Multiplexing.

Pentium Popular microprocessor manufactured by Intel.

Private loop device Fibre Channel device that attaches to arbitrated loop that does not support fabric attachment. Also known as PLDA device.

Purging Removing unwanted, no longer needed data from computer system storage.

RAM Random accessible memory.

RAS Reliability, availability, and serviceability.

Resilvering Also known as disk mirroring resynchronization.

Retention period How long data is saved before being deleted.

ROM Read-only memory.

RSCN Resource stage change notification to communicate changes to devices in a Fibre Channel storage network. There are various levels and types of RSCNs.

SAR UNIX performance monitoring and reporting utility.

Sniffer Test and diagnostic device for collecting information about networking usage and activity.

SNMP Simple Network Management Protocol is an IETF protocol for monitoring and managing devices, including servers and components in a network. Devices being monitored organize data in a Management Information Block (MIB) that can be read and written.

UFS UNIX or universal filesystem.

Unix Common open systems operating system.

UTP Unshielded twisted pair.

WiFi Term used to describe wireless data transmission.

Windows Common operating system from Microsoft.

Wintel Industry term used to describe computers based on Intel processors, such as the Pentium and Microsoft Windows operating systems.

WORM Write once read many.

zOS Operating system that runs on zSeries processors to support S/390 applications.

zSeries An IBM mainframe that supports zOS, VM, and Linux.

Index

About the Author

Greg Schulz is a senior analyst at the Evaluator Group, an independent storage analysis firm. Greg has over 25 years experience with UNIX, Windows, IBM mainframe, OpenVMS, PCs and other environments. He started his professional carrier in information technology while in school, working as an operator, loading tapes, key punching (cards and floppy disks), and printing reports. Greg has worked as a programmer (systems and end-user applications), systems administrator, disaster recovery and storage planner, performance and capacity planning analyst, systems engineer, storage consultant, and director of technical marketing. He has worked at various firms and in several industries, including Cooperative Power Electric Utility, DCA Benefits, BNSF Railroad, MTI, INRANGE, and CNT. Greg works with large and small customers from different industries involving storage and storage networking. He has been involved with various storage-related organizations, including the Computer Measurement Group (CMG), Digital Equipment User Society (DECUS), Storage Networking Industry Association (SNIA), RAID Advisory Board (RAB), and vendor-specific user groups. He is the author of numerous published papers and articles on storage, storage networking, I/O, capacity planning, virtualization, security, backup, database, and related topics. Greg has also contributed material to other projects, and he was a coauthor for the Veritas book, *The Resilient Enterprise*. As a well-regarded and popular speaker, he has lectured throughout the world on storage and storage networking topics. Greg has a B.A. in computer science from Concordia College, M.Sc. in software engineering from the University of St. Thomas, and is an aspiring chef.

www.ingramcontent.com/pod-product-compliance
Lightning Source LLC
Chambersburg PA
CBHW080130220326
41598CB00032B/5018

* 9 7 8 1 5 5 5 5 8 3 1 1 8 *